Adaptive Security Management Architecture

Adaptive Security Management Architecture

James S. Tiller

CRC Press
Taylor & Francis Group
Boca Raton London New York

CRC Press is an imprint of the
Taylor & Francis Group, an **informa** business
AN AUERBACH BOOK

First published 2011 by Auerbach Publications

Published 2019 by CRC Press
Taylor & Francis Group
6000 Broken Sound Parkway NW, Suite 300
Boca Raton, FL 33487-2742

© 2011 by Taylor and Francis Group, LLC
CRC Press is an imprint of Taylor & Francis Group, an Informa business

First issued in paperback 2019

No claim to original U.S. Government works

ISBN-13: 978-0-367-45229-2 (pbk)
ISBN-13: 978-0-8493-7052-6 (hbk)

Visit the Taylor & Francis Web site at
http://www.taylorandfrancis.com

and the Auerbach Web site at
http://www.auerbach-publications.com

Rain and Phoenix: everything I do,
the purpose of my being.

Contents

List of Illustrations

List of Tables

Foreword

Over the years security personnel have lost sight of their real purpose within an organization. Security should not be about implementing draconian controls and making it harder for users within an organization to perform their jobs, nor about implementing security for security's sake. However, this is exactly what happens time and time again. In the worst cases, security effectively handcuffs its organization's ability to innovate and change to meet dynamic and fast-changing market demands. At best, security reluctantly applies controls that oftentimes far exceed what is needed and spends inordinate amounts of limited financial resources on a shotgun blast, hoping one of the pellets hits the constantly moving business targets. So the questions begging for answers are, "How did security get here?" and "How does security change its behavior for the betterment of the business?"

In *Adaptive Security Management Architecture* I believe Jim Tiller provides the wherewithal to answer these and other pertinent questions. First and foremost, a critical element missing from many security programs today is gaining a greater appreciation of intent. Understanding what the organization is trying to accomplish from a business perspective is too often missing from security's purview and as such leads to security focusing on tactical remedies that are often not the best fit for the business. But understanding the intent of a business objective is not the only thing missing. Security organizations commonly ignore the intent of the surrounding controls, processes, and business units with which they are working. In the worst cases, security does not even fully understand the actual intent of the very controls it has already implemented. This myopic view is what I believe has significantly contributed to security-constrained cultures within many organizations, which hampers an organization in reaching its fullest potential. Gaining a better understanding of business intent should allow security to stop saying, "You can't do that," and start saying, "Let's talk about how you can do that."

Second, for years security has struggled to determine a proper framework to use in managing their programs. Perhaps inappropriately they often feel compelled to make a choice between one framework versus another, asking themselves whether a risk-based program is better than worrying about capability maturity, or whether a governance-based program offers greater long-term benefit than implementing a proper underlying security management program. Worse yet is when security is not even able to properly differentiate the purpose of these programs in the first place, consequently thinking, for example, that it is trying to address risk and improperly using a governance model to try and achieve it. At the end of the day, security oftentimes ends up getting lost in the nuances of its misunderstanding and misuse of the various frameworks. Arguably, this is yet another example of not understanding intent, in this case of the framework(s) in question; however, I digress. Various framework models actually each have a place within security, and if established and used properly, can greatly enhance security's performance and support of an organization. Readers of this book will hopefully gain a greater appreciation for how to better use several models in conjunction with one another and the proper use for each in order for security to be more agile in its support of business.

Adding to the above missteps, security has placed many constraints on innovation and usability by too often forcing one-size-fits-all security offerings on the various consumers within their organizations. This simplistic approach is by far the most common and inhibiting set of handcuffs security has placed on business. The adaptive security architecture offers a truly compelling alternative to this approach in the form of Security Services Management and expertly positions security services as the backbone of the architecture. By relying on greater interaction within a business and understanding various levels of intent, security services can be structured to better meet demand and the complex needs of an entire organization, and likely with a lower financial impact to the business overall. In other words, businesses will be able to remove the handcuffs that security has placed on them in the past to become the agile and innovative businesses they desire to be.

Throughout this book, Jim does a wonderful job of interweaving common sense topics into a game-changing architecture for security. In fact, you have likely encountered many of the elements described in the architecture and, standing alone, they do not require a great leap of faith to accept. However, the brilliance of the architecture is not in the individual pieces, but rather in how Jim paints a masterpiece made up of common elements, much like Rembrandt did with common paints and canvases, that are woven together like nothing before it. If readers are brave enough to view the pieces as a whole, their organizations will most certainly be appreciative benefactors.

Thanks, Jim, for letting me take the architecture for an early spin and the enlightenment that followed.

Dustin Owens

Dustin Owens is an information security professional who works with global customers in applying advanced risk and security concepts toward strategic business innovation. He has more than 14 years of applied experience in information security and operational risk.

Acknowledgments

I owe a great deal of gratitude to Rich O'Hanley, my mentor and publisher at Auerbach Publications. His patience is unparalleled. This book represents several years of writing and rewriting, missed deadline after missed deadline. Rich unweariedly ushered me through the process with his wisdom, advice, and direction, without which I would have never completed this book. I've had the distinct pleasure of knowing Rich for more than a decade and he has been an enormous influence and a great friend.

Dustin Owens, a close friend and colleague for more than ten years, was an enormous help and a source of encouragement in creating this book. He spent countless hours debating the meaning of security, reviewing material, and providing excellent and thought-provoking insights that challenged my convictions and helped me to push through the edges of my security philosophy.

Last, but of the greatest importance, I owe all to my wife Mary. Despite being someone so completely devoid of security and technical knowledge, and having absolutely no desire to have any, her wisdom defies explanation. Her extraordinary insights, her illuminating perspective, her unwavering support—all found their way into this little book and everything that I am. Even after nearly twenty years of marriage, my respect, admiration, and love for her know no bounds.

About the Author

Jim Tiller started his information security career in 1993 and has since worked with individuals, groups, organizations, and industries around the world collaborating on the development and implementation of business-aligned security strategies. Throughout Jim's career he has worked with and within numerous organizations for the advancement of information security, and through these activities has enabled organizations to achieve their strategic business goals.

Jim has published several books and has been a contributing author to more than seven others, including the *Official (ISC)² Guide to the CBK* and the last six editions of the *Information Security Management Handbook*. His book, *The Ethical Hack: Framework for Business Value Penetration Testing*, is the foundation for classes in universities, such as Norwich University, and is used as the basis of security programs in several companies around the world. His book, *A Technical Guide to IPsec Virtual Private Networks*, remains the standard reference for large-scale IPSec VPN solutions.

For more insights, please visit Jim's blog at http://www.realsecurity.us/
weblog. On his blog, Real Security, Jim provides regular articles about
security from a refreshing perspective that is acutely focused on the future
of security in the business. Information concerning industry involvement
and new writing projects can be found. Readers are encouraged to comment and provide feedback on posts where Jim has provided excerpts and
content from other books that he is currently writing.

1

INTRODUCTION

The information security landscape comprises sophisticated threats, comprehensive regulation, diverse communities, and complex infrastructures that make ensuring the balance between usability and security a constant and demanding challenge. This is most evident in the realm of business. Today's companies are continuously seeking opportunities to build success through entrepreneurial activities, taking on new challenges, driving opportunity, and creating a dynamic environment that demands agility.

Although today's information security practices are comprehensive, they do not readily lend themselves to effective adaptation to the ever-changing needs of the business. Information security can thrive in a consistent and predictable environment, but this is becoming increasingly rare in a highly competitive, fast-moving global market that is employing compelling and disruptive technical solutions. There is a growing divide between business's demand for agility, adaptation, effectiveness, and efficiency and the steadfast, rigid, protective nature of security. Yet security has a rich culture and underlying capabilities that have yet to be fully exploited in achieving greater alignment with business demands.

The adaptive security management architecture (ASMA) is an approach founded on several core principles and the value that can be gained from creating an interconnected security model focused on effectiveness, maturity, and collaboration. The goal is to take much of what exists in the industry today and bind it together in a unique and innovative way so as to produce an adaptive security program. Once the core principles and the important nuances of the interconnectedness between the ASMA's features are realized, the outcome of the security program will be vastly more aligned to the business and as such will be an enabling force in helping the business to achieve its goals and objectives. The ASMA utilizes and reorganizes what you likely already have at your disposal in a manner that promotes meaningful change to enable the business without losing sight of risk and compliance.

In many ways it is less about traditional information security and more about the mechanisms that drive security within a business. The ASMA will change the identity of security in the eyes of a business by focusing on the relationship between security philosophy and business value, which will expose the intent of demands driving how security is applied and realized. Security as we know it today will become simply tools that are governed and applied by a collection of architecture features working together to achieve adaptability.

Importantly, the ASMA harnesses the innate and highly sophisticated security capabilities that are used every day and are well understood, but are not exploited to their true potential. When we thoroughly explore them, we can isolate these deeply rooted processes and reapply them to broader concepts to achieve adaptability. The reapplied intrinsic capabilities in security materialize in the features of the ASMA and how they are interconnected. Empowered with the ASMA, organizations can balance business expectations, such as performance and quality, with security demands, such as risk and compliance, to become a business enabling force.

The ASMA creates an environment that provides visibility into all aspects of security's role in a business while simultaneously providing the means to influence that environment. All too often organizations measure aspects of security that are not actionable and are not much more than measuring the weather. Although this may help in understanding trends, it does not resonate with the business, which expects to have the ability to meaningfully address dynamics. The ASMA provides the means to influence change and does so by promoting measurements that provide specific translation to elements in the program that need modification or improvement. Based on this foundation, many security organizations can achieve the ability to innovate and confidently project the value of their actions to the business, which is at the heart of business enablement.

Security adaptability is about creating a flexible, proactive environment that has the innate ability to address change in a well-defined and effective manner. To achieve this it is important to understand and quantify the intent of change, standards, regulation, and business demands. Although stability in security is important and is needed to create a manageable environment, without clarity of intent the security program will become rigid and inflexible, furthering the divide with the business.

The ASMA brings together different aspects of security that are generally already defined and accepted within the industry. However, it goes a step further and introduces key aspects in the role of these security domains and the activities they are performing. Most importantly, the ASMA creates an environment where each security feature is interlocked with the others in a meaningful way to ensure adaptation is promoted in a controlled fashion. Much of the interconnects within the ASMA are provided herein, but these are not set in stone and will likely change to meet specific differences in each organization. What is important is the objectives of the interconnects and the role of each of the different features of the ASMA. Within this context, the underlying nature of the ASMA is to get you thinking about security from a new perspective. It is an expression of how elements of security can interact in new and comprehensive ways to drive innovative approaches to become far more agile and achieve greater business enablement.

2

SECURITY AND BUSINESS

The adaptive security management architecture seeks to take advantage of existing security practices and build upon them to promote the value of security to a business and to ensure a meaningful security posture. The ASMA is as much about the business and the security organization operating as a business unit as it is about security, risk, and compliance. There are many facets to the ASMA to achieve this, which are founded on capability maturity, applying security through services, and performance, security, and quality measurements that combine to ensure effectiveness and efficiency. Moreover, the characteristics of the ASMA provide clear visibility into operations and security, which ultimately translate to adaptability and enabling the business.

This chapter introduces the high-level reasoning and purpose for an ASMA and goes on to explain changes in the business environment to demonstrate the alignment of the ASMA to the challenges of today and tomorrow.

2.1 Why a New Architecture?

Today, security is predominantly a collection of practices that are applied based on policy and standards to ensure consistency in meeting overall expectations in the management of risk and compliance. These practices are horizontal in nature given that they are usually performed equally across a business and, similarly, across industries. In fact, most security organizations work very hard to ensure consistency throughout the environment to reduce the potential for gaps in compliance and to maintain reasonable uniformity in the environment to effectively manage risk.

However, the focus on consistency has created a rigid model that does not always effectively address shifts in a business. Moreover, the horizontal and standardized application of security practices does not necessarily resonate with a business for two important reasons. First, the business may be forced to apply security in its entirety, which may include elements in which the business simply does not see value, or of which the business does not understand the applicability to its environment or requirement, or that may simply be security's standard approach, which is not tuned to the specific goal.

Second, there is limited understanding of and visibility into the operational integrity of the security group and the application of security practices. For example, how efficiently are the security practices being performed, how effective is the result, what features align to the business's goals, and how do these security practices relate to the overall security program and the mission of the company?

These challenges represent the reasoning for an adaptive architecture that utilizes services as a method for applying security throughout a business. Moreover, and a very important overriding theme throughout this book, today's security is mature, comprehensive, and quite sophisticated, yet how do we unleash that potential and change the very identity of security in the business? Arguably, the consistency fought for within the security industry has merit. Nevertheless, this has also ushered in difficulties in effectively aligning to the dynamics of the business and achieving adaptability.

While security has significantly evolved over the last several decades it has also unwittingly become a limiting factor from a business's perspective. Businesses seek to explore opportunity, increase market share, drive revenue, and differentiate themselves. This means taking on risk and new challenges and always changing. Conversely, security seeks to protect the business and put in controls to ensure compliance, manage risk, reduce the potential for debilitating events, and drive consistency. While this is exceedingly important, balance between enabling the business and protecting the business has not been fully achieved. In fact, one could argue that there is a growing chasm (Figure 2.1) between the directive of security and that of the business. This has become exceedingly evident in the face of massive, global economic turmoil.

The two problems introduced above can be summarized as the application of security and the operational integrity of the security group. The holistic employment of horizontal security practices in their

Figure 2.1   Security and business chasm.

entirety may not meet the business need and may include features that are not applicable, or worse, not include attributes that are critical to the business or the overall security posture. Moving forward, security must acknowledge a business's needs as much as the desire to ensure comprehensive security. Next, of course, is how investments, budgets, and resources in security are employed in providing security and how this is communicated to a business in terms it can readily digest.

The ASMA closes the gap between business needs and security needs and will redefine security in the eyes of a business to be seen as a valuable, enabling force. It does this by doing two simple and fundamental things. First, it exploits the sophistication that exists within most security organizations today, and second, it does not try to fight the consistency battle causing the divide, but rather embraces it in the form of business intelligence and operations.

As security evolved it produced a great number of standards in the application of security practices. As previously discussed, this presents a degree of rigidity and inflexibility. However, beneath this lie extraordinary capabilities to address virtually any scenario. We've all experienced a situation where common approaches fall short and the "go-to-guy" is called in to connect the dots. The resulting activities may be nonstandard and unorthodox, but the ultimate goal is achieved. Essentially, the "go-to-guy" understands all of what is possible and what exists within the realm of security in the organization as ingredients, takes time to understand the need, and composes a solution that utilizes existing nuances to fine-tune security to meet the specific objective. Moreover, this is performed in a manner that not only satisfies the business demand, but also ensures it has value in the larger security posture, such as compliance and risk.

Clearly not all scenarios can be predicted, and therefore they cannot be standardized. As a result, there are many security savvy professionals in the field tuning and adjusting the norm to achieve a goal. This represents monumental value to security and to a business when wielded correctly. Unfortunately, these efforts are rarely indoctrinated because they are seen as one-offs and the value is inexorably tied to the "go-to-guy," who you hope does not quit.

The ASMA, in large part, exploits this organic process by providing an interface between a business and the application of security. Security can have a wide range of depth and breadth in its application and as a result has the potential to be fine-tuned to a specific need or environment. Given the likelihood for complexity and diversity of challenges and environments, traditional security standards cannot be solely relied upon. Moreover, the reliance on individual or group efforts is not scalable and represents single points of failure to the security program, thus challenging sustainability.

Building different security services and spreading horizontal security practices over several vertical—targeted—services can reduce the spectrum of possibilities in the execution of security, which offers the opportunity to predict different scenarios. These options will manifest themselves in the service and ultimately act as governing agents in the application of security.

Although the organization of security into services introduces greater sophistication into the execution of security, this represents only one aspect of the value the ASMA provides. The ASMA focuses energy into the delivery of services, but it also defines mechanisms to ensure compliance, address risk, and ensure that people and processes are interacting effectively, and it introduces specific points of interaction that ensure consistency in the operational integrity of the security organization.

What should become evident is that the ASMA, in part, formalizes and enhances what is already likely occurring in security organizations around the world. It's about embracing all the resources at your disposal and acknowledging the value of organizing security in a manner that truly exploits what is possible, fundamentally converting security into a business enabler. It raises the bar on performance, expectations, and capability, moving beyond common practices to release the true potential of security. Today's challenges, such as addressing multiple regulatory demands and communicating the need for security to executives, will give way to an environment in which these will become by-products. When fully implemented it is likely that security organizations will discover far more intimacy with businesses, have greater clarity on capabilities and expectations, and play a more integral role in the evolution and overall success of businesses.

2.2 The Conflict of Change

Change is the key factor and as such represents the fundamental conflict between security and business (Figure 2.2). It is necessary to acknowledge the opposing forces and find a balance between the heritage of traditional security and the emerging demands of a business.

At the highest level, security is an agent for stability that conflicts with the agent of change within a business. Security seeks to focus on standardization and consistency to ensure a predictable environment, whereas a business is seeking to drive change to increase market share, ensure continued competitive differentiation, or enact progressive products or services.

The key to finding balance is to ensure that change is not simply for the sake of change, but rather for security to have a meaningful role in maintaining posture when change is necessary. Fundamentally, this means having the capacity within security for

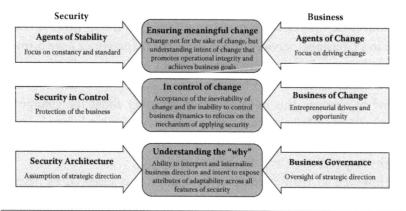

Figure 2.2 Forces driving change.

comprehensive visibility into how the security program is functioning and identifying the options for change as well as the implications of change. Comparatively, today we have change that flows down from the business into security, which is forced to react and ultimately translates to firefighting. Moreover, this has resulted in a security culture of resistance and the formation of policy and standards that create an envelope for the business in how to address change, which has not been enormously successful and will likely not scale with the business over time.

The next level of conflict is the interpretation of control. Today's security has assumed the role of protector as well as enforcer, leading to, in some cases, a police state. This conflicts with the fact that the business is ultimately in control of change to drive business and meet stated goals. It is inevitable that the business will move forward. Of course there are conditions, specifically compliance, under which the business must concede to the needs of security, but this has resulted in a poor identity for security. The balance is for security to accept change, accept the inability to control a business's demand for change, and promote a culture of agility through maintaining control of change. It is necessary to embrace change and everything this implies, and to prepare a security capability that is resilient, proactive, and predictive.

Finally, today's security architecture is the manifestation of standardization and stability, and is reflective of controlling a business. Many security architectures inherently assume that strategic direction within a business conflicts with the formation of such things as business and information technology (IT) governance. IT governance has a connection with business in driving strategy and how this materializes in IT business services. Some security organizations have formed a tight bond and become integrated with IT governance, but for many the conflict remains. The balance is for security to understand the "why" of change. This does not mean learning about the change to dismantle it or fight it, but rather to fully understand the business drivers so that security can plan more efficiently and, more importantly, respond effectively to the change.

However, to truly participate in change it is essential to have a method of operation that is poised for whatever the business is seeking to adjust or accomplish. Therefore, the ASMA is founded on capability, operational integrity, and clear visibility that drives business-aligned security. Today there are security architectures that define security mostly from a security practitioner's perspective and not from a business perspective. It is necessary to reverse this model.

Every organization will experience change. Change may be forced upon a business or be an elective dynamic to move it farther or in a new direction. Regardless of reason or purpose, it is inevitable and as such companies have become astute at managing change. However, change is the least effective part of security, and as a result it has driven a wedge between security and business. Within the security industry there is an overwhelming sense of responsibility and control as a protector. Unfortunately, over time, as the world of business evolves rapidly, change is a constant and security must also evolve to enable change.

2.3 The Four Influencers

The focus on change in security is not academic but rather the result of what is already in motion within the business. The emergence of four major business influencers in recent years will have a dramatic effect on how companies operate into the future and ultimately on the role of security as an industry. These four influencers will intersect in the coming years to represent a shift in business and technology that has the potential to make today's security virtually ineffective in the eyes of business if change is not embraced.

The four influencers are

1. Economy
2. Technology
3. Data centricity
4. Regulation

2.3.1 Economy

Enterprises worldwide are facing increasing economic uncertainty in a time when the spectrum of challenges and threats to businesses seem insurmountable. As companies brace themselves for survival, they are being forced to make difficult decisions that will have far-reaching implications on the sustainability of their business. Many are reassessing their products and services to focus investments toward their core competencies and shedding elements of the business that do not readily align to the mission.

However, there is more happening within the culture of businesses and the perception of value—especially the value of money and returns. At the onset of the economic woes of the early twenty-first century, companies responded as one would have expected—by cutting costs. The first wave of cuts was designed to minimize losses and stabilize the bottom line. Unfortunately, these actions only temporarily stemmed the tide and deeper cuts in spending, employees, and other assets were needed. Remaining employees started being held to various spending restrictions and new policies were enforced to control costs. However, as many companies realized, you can only cut so much if you wish to survive, and the real challenge was to drive new revenue and do so with a weakened infrastructure. As the market started demanding performance, companies began to take a close look at their operating models.

As an example, Dell, after incredible growth for several years, in the fourth quarter of fiscal year 2009 (Q4 FY09) reported a 16% drop in revenue and a 48% drop to its bottom line. Prior to this Dell announced a $3 billion three-year cost-cutting goal and later revised it to $4 billion, to be met by 2011. As a result, a more than $363 million drop in operating expense was realized year over year, but to meet their goal more dramatic reductions were necessary, which seemed impossible and demanded broader action. Therefore, in addition to reducing costs, Dell reorganized into four global, customer-centric business units "to better meet customer and partner requirements through direct relationships, and to innovate without ties to costly, complex legacy technology."

Therefore, Dell was not only seeking to protect profitability but changed the fundamentals of the business. This proves that economic times are not simply about cutting back. Companies are making changes to the operational fabric of their businesses that will have long-lasting effects. Strategic reorganization and dramatic cost cutting alone does not ensure long-term success. Of course, these activities resonate with Wall Street investors and market analysts providing short-term notoriety and positive implications to the bottom line. But the market's memory is far shorter than that of the customer's and the intended long-term stability demanded in the boardroom.

Behind these changes was a radical shift in the interpretation of the valuation of investments and spending within the company. Organizations realized they could be successful if they can ensure effectiveness and efficiency in the operations of the restructured and focused model and do so with a reduced workforce. This may seem to be an obvious Business 101 conclusion, but for large, complex organizations, knowing where to cut, where to invest, how to organize, and how to ensure effectiveness is not always easy or obvious. Nevertheless, the driving factors are effectiveness and efficiency. This was the core lesson learned by companies that cut, cut deeper, reorganized, and are seeing meaningful increases in performance. As such, the culture of spending and what is required to acquire investments has changed dramatically. It has become a "do more with less" environment, and any investment must demonstrate a meaningful role and proven purpose to the business mission and that it will be managed effectively.

The key difference is the depth of the culture change in business. Employees are finding ways to save on everything from office supplies to communication, such as spending more time on the phone and less in an airplane. Savings is omnipresent and with it has come a culture of results-driven measurements throughout the business. It has moved beyond reduction to focus on getting the most from every investment. Although some in the industry have seen this as a barrier to spending within the enterprise space, in fact, many companies are spending vast amounts because there are clear returns or positive impacts in the short and long term for the company.

The long-term implications for the cultural shift in corporate investing can be summarized as operational efficiency and will have enormous effects on security. Security will be judged and valued based on the maturity of operation, and it will be governed through specific business measurements. How security responds and adjusts to changes in the business will define its role. It will go far beyond the comparatively simple act of ensuring security and compliance and move toward incorporating comprehensive demands from the business in business terms. Security groups will have to quantify, justify, deliver, and measure that delivery in security, performance, and quality terms and have the ability to absorb and enact meaningful change based on lessons learned. The business will demand a secure environment, but over time this demand will be surpassed with demonstrable evidence of operational integrity. In other words, achieving security will become one of the many parts of the value equation and business will want to ensure that the security achieved is realized in a financially and operationally efficient and effective manner.

2.3.2 Technology

There are few technological developments in the industry, most notably cloud computing and what is commonly referred to as consumerization a close second, that allow employees to use their personal computing devices for business purposes. The cloud represents a wide range of advantages to businesses and is a natural continuation of IT outsourcing models, but resonates more closely with the agility sought by businesses.

Entertainingly, the cloud is interpreted in three different ways. Some in IT see the cloud as nothing new and reflective of computing models that have existed since the 1960s. Others quantify the cloud as evolutionary. The concept of on-demand services, software as a service, and pay-per-use scenarios have existed for some time in the service provider space and can be seen in such things like Google Apps. Finally, certain groups, specifically businesses, see the cloud as revolutionary. Businesses interpret the cloud as revolutionary because it represents the final abstraction of the business from IT.

Excluding companies that provide IT services, most companies simply use technology to develop and deliver products and services, and as such IT is typically not a core business function. Taking into consideration the economic dynamics, businesses today are acutely focused on core business competencies and shedding non-core business elements. The cloud may virtualize IT, but from the business's perspective cloud computing separates the business from the financial, business, and operational liabilities commonly associated with technology and maintaining a technical infrastructure.

This concept of separation is furthered by consumerization. In short, consumerization is taking advantage of the fact that employees have their own PCs or Macs and mobile devices that can be used for business purposes. The advantages to a company are obvious: a stipend to an employee is far less than actually provisioning a system. Employees are people too and want to use a system of their choice; many business applications can be accessed using just about anything, and more and more employees are working virtually or on the road. This ends up being a win-win. Companies have fewer IT headaches, lower costs, can focus more on their core business, and employees can use their own systems and mobile devices and have them virtually paid for. Combine this with the growing utilization of the Internet and Web-based applications, which may reside in the cloud, and it is very understandable why companies are investigating the value represented by allowing employees to use their personal systems for business purposes. But beyond savings, this represents a deeper realization: greater abstraction and distance of the business in dealing with non-core attributes of the business.

Combined, the cloud and consumerization are fundamentally viewed by the business as a method to facilitate the final separation between business and traditional IT. This is not to imply that IT is not seen as a valuable attribute of the business, but rather the business perceives the cloud and consumerization as a way of promoting focus on core competencies, saving money, and simplifying the relationship between business and IT to promote agility. Just as economic pressures have led many organizations to redefine themselves, technology is forcing companies to take a hard look at who they are. Are they an IT company or a hospital, insurance company, manufacturer, bank, drug, or retail company? Most have come to the conclusion they are not in the business of IT and as such are looking to shed that attribute from their business holistically.

With greater technical and operational abstraction security will be forced to rethink how security is applied. Situational awareness, command and control, security hygiene, and integration with IT providers will become driving forces in security. The business expects security to keep pace with the adoption of revolutionary IT strategies to facilitate overall agility. Of course, this represents a significant departure from traditional IT scenarios and as such will demand changes to how security is realized and measured for success. This will start with creating new relationships with general council in formalizing IT provider relationships to ensure the security posture is supported in the environment. However, this will rapidly migrate to a condition where security will have to orchestrate security capabilities and services that are accurately and effectively applied within the business to ensure that risk and compliance are achieved in a highly diverse environment.

2.3.3 Data Centricity

The initial security focus was predominantly based on a vulnerability-sensitive culture. Security was tasked with reducing and managing vulnerabilities within the technical environment to reduce the likelihood of attack or failure. In fact, in the very early days of security the vulnerability sensitivity culture drove the birth of penetration testing. Before the rigorous compliance we have today, security was justified based on fear, uncertainty, and doubt, and this was facilitated through demonstrating to business owners that vulnerabilities not only existed, but they represented a tangible threat to the business with the hope of promoting security investment.

Although these practices and the concern for vulnerabilities exist today, the security focus has moved to a compliance-driven culture. Justification for security transformed from having to prove the need for security to having it demanded by regulation. Security organizations attached to compliance, allowing compliance to replace the justification through demonstration with external forces requiring security.

Today, security has built upon the compliance wave and is reestablishing a risk management approach with compliance efforts and vulnerability management becoming an underlying element of security along with many other capabilities. However, the ability to effectively measure risk has become more challenging with the continued abstraction of technology and the exponential increase in data. For many, risk became a bottom-up approach that focused on the systems, threats, and impact and sought to roll that information up into risks for the business. In many ways this was due to the lack of visibility into the business and the inability to accurately identify, locate, and quantify information assets.

Difficulties in connecting with the business were exacerbated by dynamics as a result of the economy and technology, and quantification of data assets was, and continues to be, a challenge due to the environmental abstraction, diversity, and the ubiquitous distribution of data. The security industry is working very hard to grasp the data-related challenges, and this can be seen in data loss or data leak protection (DLP) solutions being used for data discovery and the increase in ediscovery technologies and practices.

Nevertheless, as the business expands and contracts, flowing through the cloud, applications, partner ecosystems, and a wide range of providers focus on data—its integrity and confidentiality—connecting that data with the owner in a highly complex and diversified IT environment is going to become paramount. Of the many implications for security moving forward, risk management and assessing risk will begin to change significantly. Corporate data, which is highly distributed, difficult to quantify, and generally unstructured, is used to form information. Information is dynamic, may experience vast changes in value, and is often separate from the processing environment. Of course, information is used in the creation of products and services and as such is mission critical. Last in the data chain is differentiation and the valuation of the overall business brand.

As security attempts to adjust today's practices to deal with the flux that is occurring within a business, a significant lag will appear representing a tangible risk to the business. Therefore, although vulnerabilities and compliance remain, security will move quickly to a data-centric focus in order to address new and challenging IT environments. What this means is that as the stability practices of today give way there is going to be increased focus at the data level and on building a common data model. This will be combined with security services in the application of security to ensure a degree of consistency. In other words, consistency in the security architecture we have today will not scale with the dynamics of the business. Nevertheless, consistency at the information level will be required to maintain a desirable and compliant posture.

As a result the focus on consistency will move away from the infrastructure and toward the data and how security is applied operationally, representing a substantial shift in security practices. Between data and the application of security there must exist a management model that promotes agility. Therefore, as a business moves and changes the concern for security is predominantly based on the data, allowing the more traditional aspects of security to be adjusted in near real-time to compensate. Furthermore, this will also change the way risk is assessed. It will become a more top-down, rapid approach and focus on the combined controls that exist within the new environment.

2.3.4 Compliance

Regulatory compliance has been the foundation of security from a business justification perspective since the mid to late 1990s. If it weren't for regulatory compliance forcing many companies to address information security head-on, it is not likely that security would be what it is today. However, security riding compliance's coattails is a double-edged sword and may become an association security will regret in the future.

In 2009 there were a number of high-profile attacks, specifically regarding millions of credit card records being stolen from several large companies over a six-month period. As a result these companies are not only facing expenses to correct problems and dealing with fines, but they are addressing massive legal liabilities; for one company these are potentially exceeding $150 million. In all the cases the charge is not one of compliance, but rather negligence. Given this type of charge as the basis for the legal actions, questions concerning what is security due diligence are beginning to surface.

Unrelated to the recent legal activities, but that will certainly be influenced over time, is the creation of more prescriptive regulations. The industry has seen this with the Payment Card Industry (PCI) Data Security Standard (DSS) that provides detailed expectations on security controls. This is a different approach from what the industry has seen in the past with such seminal regulations as HIPAA (Health Insurance Portability and Accountability Act) and SOX (Sarbanes-Oxley Act of 2002), which are more directional and open to a degree of interpretation. The prescriptive trend has already begun to materialize in new regulations such as the HITECH Act, part of the American Recovery and Reinvestment Act (ARRA) of 2009, which is an expansion on SB1386/AB700 out of California, and data breach notification laws in Congress (S.495, Personal Data Privacy and Security Act [PDPSA]) and Massachusetts Security Law affecting identity theft and data protection, which is very similar to

Section 114 of the Fair and Accurate Credit Transactions Act of 2003 (FACTA), also known as the Red Flag Rules.

The evolution of regulation, how it is defined and what it is focused on, represents a shift towards data and information and establishing standards of due diligence. For example, NIST (National Institute of Standards and Technology) received $20 million in funding via the ARRA to create the Health Information Technology (HIT) security expectations for protection of personal electronic health records. When one looks more deeply into this and other developments in setting security standards we begin to see greater specifics in data, identity and access management, and capability maturity in defensible security characteristics. For example, 2010 represents a new challenge to those companies in the U.S. utilities industry with North American Electric Reliability Corporation's (NERC) Critical Infrastructure Protection (CIP) security requirements, formerly the cybersecurity standard, which has evolved to define nine security areas founded on critical asset identification and management of access, among other specifications. This will continue to evolve, and more states, like Massachusetts, will set new bars on acceptable security practices. Of course, on the surface this appears to be more of a driving force for security, which on some levels is true. However, there are a few by-products.

The legal ramifications for negligence can result in devastating financial consequences. To avoid such liabilities companies will seek to ensure due diligence in information protection, which inherently is reflective of a minimalistic approach. Moreover, it is generally accepted that compliance does not equal security, and therefore performing due diligence may protect you from legal challengers, but a company may remain insecure. Additionally, over the mid-term until government can ratify federal legislation that supports developments at the state or local government level, there will be a tidal wave of new regulation, each seeking to establish acceptable due diligence practices that substantiate a defensible posture in a court of law, specifically at the state level.

For security and business this development in regulatory compliance will materialize as multiple new external influences, each setting the minimal requirements relative to legal actions and not requirements based on a security platform. As a result, companies will become inundated with demands of compliance, and by association security groups will be perceived as the regulatory police demanding more and more spending as each new law comes into effect. In other words, the negative tone of compliance within business today will be exacerbated in the coming years, and unless information security groups can find a way to provide value to the business and decouple from a compliance-justified identity, security will be relegated to an audit function.

The truth of the matter is that security compliance—any compliance—has always represented the fundamentals of standard security approaches. Although HIPAA, SOX, and others differ on what the focus is, there is undoubtedly a common security theme, and this theme will continue far into the future. Therefore, the logical and most efficient method to address the inevitable flood of regulatory oversight is to create an adaptive model of security that can withstand the dynamics of a business while ensuring that the nature of the regulation is realized. Not only is this possible, but it is required. Emerging compliance is gravitating to a data-centric model, as is business. When security seeks to focus standardization and stability at the data level and apply security in a sophisticated way, and in a manner that aligns to business dynamics and operational integrity demands, there surfaces a natural alignment to regulation, or certainly the ability to address compliance effectively. If an adaptable model does not exist, the organization will have to adjust to each new regulation independently, making for excessive investments and poor investment value, and creating an unmanageable environment. Clearly the objective is for compliance to be inherent to the management and delivery of security and not necessarily an independent feature of the business. This is not to imply that compliance management does not exist in some form, but rather that the role of compliance management will change. Compliance management will become the influencer of decision-making processes and be deeply involved in the delivery of security services.

2.4 Now Is the Time

Security is in a unique position to take a quantum leap forward and become far more ingrained into the success of organizations, and now is the time to prove that potential and realize that goal. There are a number of dynamics occurring within the evolution of business that represent an approaching fork in the road for security. In one direction we have the continued evolution of security with compliance acting as the predominant driver. Security will retain its place in the management of risk and compliance, focusing on addressing gaps to minimize impacts to the business. However, over time these traditional practices will begin to falter as business demands more than what security can address. In the long term, security will become integrated into the fabric of legal, IT, and providers and exist as an auditing mechanism to ensure standards are maintained. In the other direction lies a challenging path, but one that leads to business alignment and security playing a valuable role in the evolution of a business and its success. Risk and compliance will remain and play a pivotal role, but governance, capability maturity, and services will act as the primary connective tissue between the protection of data and enabling the business.

2.4.1 Future Expectations

Within the context of change and the four influencers, businesses are focused on ensuring adaptability, execution, efficiency, and effectiveness in all aspects of the business to ensure long-term stability and growth. To accomplish this executives are not only changing the fundamentals of their businesses, they are changing previously established expectations of performance and capability. Historically, terms such as adaptability, execution, efficiency, and effectiveness were used loosely as general motivators and reiterations of a common understanding. Everyone knows they need to adapt to the environment, rapidly implement, make every action have meaning, and get the job done right the first time. But these were not necessarily absolutes. Conversely, as a result of today's uncertainty and the future intersection of the four influencers, these are becoming the yardstick against which everything will be measured. Adaptability, execution, efficiency, and effectiveness will become the basis of operational maturity.

2.4.1.1 Adaptability The terms adaptability, execution, efficiency, and effectiveness are not entirely mutually exclusive and the leader of the pack is adaptability. This is the defining characteristic of today's business dynamics and will become the guidepost for companies moving into the future. Adaptability is about responding to change effectively and decisively. Historically, adaptation within a company would typically resonate with its products and services leveraging elements that exist within the business to approach a new demand or offer greater differentiation in the market. These changes can range from superficial to deep shifts in focus and investments.

Over the three years, deep shifts in business activities have included a great deal of mergers and acquisitions, and divestitures. Although these activities will certainly continue, there is a groundswell in companies to create a model that promotes adaptability, thus allowing them to take on challenges as well as opportunities more smoothly and with greater predictability in outcome. As a result, there is desired growth in capabilities throughout organizations and at all levels to ensure companies

- Have the ability to identify the change,
- Understand what impacts it may have,
- Rapidly quantify what is under its control to compensate,
- Identify what modifications to the environment are necessary, and
- Make them without hesitation.

Failure in any one of these could have disastrous impacts on the business at worst, and cause it to appear as slow to react at best. Either case is an unacceptable outcome. Organizations demand proactive behaviors because that is what is needed to remain competitive and outlive and outgrow their competition.

2.4.1.2 Execution   Of course, the best plans are useless without execution. Execution is, at its heart, very simple—do it. Don't dilly-dally, don't make excuses about why it can't be done, and don't bring problems without solutions. Fear of failure is the predominant anti-execution de-motivator. However, underlying this is a myriad of cultures, political landscapes, and fiefdoms. Nevertheless, what truly stands out is that execution may require—and almost always does—reaching beyond the norm and pushing the edges of what is traditionally understood as possible. Far too often people respond with, "We've never done it that way before," or, "That's not how it's done," or a favorite, "That's not my job." These are defeatist attitudes and can be the bane of corporate agility.

Execution is about how something can be accomplished, how best to utilize resources, and how to apply those resources in ways that meet the objective. It is the art of bonding institutional knowledge with meeting a demand. Not all processes may be needed or performed according to traditional methods. The important part is balancing the need and existing capabilities, and ensuring the quality of the outcome without adding substantial, undue risk to the business.

For example, in desperate times some companies will make concessions that under normal circumstances would be unheard of, such as accepting excessive legal liability to win a deal. In some cases, this is understood and is reflective of a rapidly changing risk appetite. It also represents the inherent relationship between adaptation and execution. When combined, these provide the means to understand these risks in the light of broader business needs. What needs to be done, and what does that mean to the business—how far is the envelope going to be pushed?

2.4.1.3 *Efficiency*   It should be obvious, especially in rough economic times, that wasteful spending and activities are unacceptable. Not only is this true today, but it will become exceedingly essential to business performance well into the future. Of course, wastefulness has always been frowned upon, but that doesn't mean it's not happening. When the big four car manufacturers were called to Washington, DC, to meet the U.S. Congress in early 2009 to justify their need for billions in taxpayer money, they flew in private jets. At least they could have "jet-pooled." This put the exclamation point on wasteful spending in corporate America. As a result of this and unfortunately thousands of other examples, 2009 ushered in a completely new public distain for waste and an identity that corporations want to desperately avoid.

Efficiency is simply accomplishing what is needed with as little expenditure of resources as possible. This means that as a business identifies a need, such as a project or initiative, it must have the means to accurately

- Define the activities required to accomplish the project,
- Understand what resources are necessary,

- Determine what methods are to be used,
- Establish the duration or expected timeline of accomplishments, and
- Define the outcome or expected results through measurements.

Without the basics in place to define expectations, investments are doomed to not demonstrate returns. Nevertheless, while efficiency is well understood, it still generally eludes companies and manifests itself as bureaucracy that is slowing progress. Much like a bill going through congress, what starts as something relatively straightforward becomes complex, and more and more resources, time, and money are required to accomplish the goal.

Prior to the economic downturn, very few projects ended on time and on budget. According to various industry analysts, as few as 20% of projects met expectations, while other projects seemed to expand endlessly. In a post-recovery world, businesses' tolerance for such inefficient activities will be nil. The weeding out of unnecessary activities within businesses that we're seeing today will be aggressively performed in the future. And it's more than just wasteful spending. Time to market is paramount. As business demands constantly ebb and flow to address shifts in the industry and to accomplish evolving go-to-market strategies, getting projects done quickly and efficiently will be a dominant force.

2.4.1.4 Effectiveness   In many ways, all these elements come down to effectiveness. How effective were you in executing in an efficient manner? Effectiveness is accomplishing something that resulted in the intended purpose. It is important to note that effectiveness, much like the other attributes above, can have degrees of accomplishment and acceptability. For example, there is a significant difference between accomplishing something satisfactorily and doing so exceptionally. Of course, the only way to determine such nuances is to define them relative to what is being performed and to measure them.

Effectiveness is critical to demonstrating value and returns. Companies want to ensure that every bit of energy put into the business is applied effectively to get the most from the effort. This is especially true in today's environment and will set in motion far more granular measurements on business activities.

Measuring effectiveness is nothing new to companies. Whether it is margin, quality, or customer satisfaction, or any other element of the business that helps to quantify performance, it is a long-standing practice. However, moving forward, the degree of importance, breadth of detail, and significance to the business will substantially increase over time.

2.4.2 Security Translation

There is overwhelming evidence that companies are changing the very fabric of their businesses and transforming yesterday's nice-to-haves into must-dos. The primary drivers for business are how businesses must change to align to the market and create a foundation of operational maturity. Underlying these facts is simply achieving resilience and the ability to cope with adversity in a manner that ensures not only survivability, but also progress. All this converges on the fact that companies have to be agile. The environment is extraordinarily dynamic, which demands responsiveness. Even the best-formed plans are meaningless if they apply to a condition that is no longer valid. What this means for information security is that it isn't just threats that are unpredictable, but also the entire business framework that must be made secure. The very foundation of security must be changed to allow for change, something that traditional security lacks the ability to do effectively.

Introduced within the context of business above, the attributes of operational maturity will significantly impact security groups. How security groups address these changes will set in motion the interpretation of value and the role they represent within companies for years to come. Groups that embrace operational maturity wholeheartedly and completely will experience a level of intimacy with businesses that has not been realized in the past.

As an introduction to the overall applicability and breadth of adaptive security management architecture, following are how these attributes, at a high level, will need to resonate.

2.4.2.1 Adaptable Security Businesses as a whole are looking to increase responsiveness and to make tough decisions concerning operational structure, processes, and long-standing practices and assumptions to accomplish this. Business changes of this nature are going to place greater and greater demands on security and the ability to address challenges quickly.

Adaptable security is one of the more difficult emerging attributes being demanded from security groups. Security is founded on the consistent application of controls defined by standards, required by regulations, and representative of best practices in protecting business assets. However, as organizations seek to gain ground on competition and aggressively approach new revenue opportunities, security is put in a position where traditional methods may simply not be applicable. Moreover, the usual approach may conflict with core initiatives and hinder development. Of course, this is contrary to building a closer relationship with the business and creating an identity of business enablement.

A significant underpinning of the adaptive security management model is building a risk-reward model with business. Additionally, it is up to the security group within the organization to take the initiative in working with various groups to find common ground so there is clear value in the group's involvement. For security it's about coming to the table with solutions that satisfy traditional security demands and facilitates the business in achieving its objective.

The risk-reward model prioritizes activities based on risk as well as where the greatest opportunities are for the business. By becoming intimate with business goals and mapping against elements of risk, what begins to surface is a common thread that demonstrates a point where the business and security goals become more closely aligned. A good place to start is within the project management arena, in which risks to the initiative or its life cycle will become apparent, in addition to helping identify critical paths and what is most important to the business unit or group. Using information of this nature, combined with institutional knowledge possessed by security groups, one can begin to interpret demands and risks in business initiatives and quickly find areas of common ground.

The pivotal characteristic that ensures adaptability in security is the amalgamation of security services delivery, which is influenced by risk, compliance, and governance and is built on a platform of capability maturity. Each action of security not only has a specific reason and purpose relative to the mission of the business, it will also produce performance, security, and quality measurements that can be related to other areas of the security service delivery capability. When combined, security can take a holistic look at the program, its ability to deliver, expected outcomes, how risk and compliance will be managed, and how key performance objectives are quantified against emerging requirements.

2.4.2.2 Executing on Security As demands from the business begin to permeate throughout the organization and security groups are pushed to provide greater flexibility and adaptability, issues in execution will likely surface. These issues stem from the fact that well-established practices in security are going to be faced with tough questions concerning their viability and role within the mission of the company. Without a model that fundamentally supports adaptability, promotes management oversight, establishes a governance model that ensures performance is communicated outwardly and reflected internally for improvement, and creates a foundation for meaningful measurement, the result from business pressures can lead to chaos as well as a reduction in security posture.

For example, a business needs to accomplish an objective and the security group applies a standard approach that does not intersect effectively with the business. As a result the security group attempts to accommodate the need—temporarily giving way for an urgent initiative. Assuming this is successful from the business's perspective, the security group is forced to operate outside of normal expectations. This may result in anything from disgruntled employees to poor execution of requirements that are not well defined. On a tactical level, standards and processes may not exist to support the effort, or the activities required conflict with existing processes and policies. Also, not all in the security group may be aware of the reason for breaking with the normal approach, making it appear disjointed and illogical. Lastly, once the business realizes it can get what it needs, special concessions rapidly convert to standard expectations of the security group. Of course, the worst-case scenario is when the accommodations the security group makes are not successful, undermining the entire group and exacerbating the negative perception of security by the business.

The above is a common occurrence in some organizations and results in an extraordinarily rigid security program, because security groups don't necessarily want to be put in a position of failure or provide one-off solutions they must live with. This typically evolves into a risk-acceptance model. In other words, the business must apply all the security the way the security group defines it or "sign here" on the dotted line to accept the risk. Conversely, if the program doesn't become more unyielding it may dissolve into a reactive, fire-fighting set of activities that attempts to maintain some normalcy and compliance in the midst of seemingly alien requests coming from the business.

It's a catch-22. Security needs to be consistent to ensure a meaningful posture, but it also needs to be responsive to certain business needs. Too much focus on either end of the spectrum can spell disaster. On one end you have an "all or nothing" rigid approach to security to ensure consistency, which results in a lack of meaningful alignment and in some cases reduces security to a process of managing risk acceptance. On the other end of the scale you have an overly reactive security model that attempts to satisfy the business at the cost of meaningful security, which results in fire fighting and a reactive posture at best.

The lesson to be learned is that without a security model that promotes alignment with business demands in some form and helps to translate them into common security practices to support adaptability, execution scenarios will work against evolving the security program. The key is to be helpful, supportive, and meaningful to the company while ensuring security is reflective of risk appetite and compliance requirements. However, if you're flexible without the means to consistently support that flexibility, security will be ineffective. If you cannot perform security that flows with the business, security will not be a part of the business's success.

Many have tried to ride the balance through relationships, gives and takes, and creating islands of one-offs to accommodate needs while minimizing divergence from common practices. Although this is effective in some environments, this is not a long-term solution. Adherence to common practices only works when the practices are applicable. However, in today's environment, the life cycle of applicability fluctuates.

2.4.2.3 Security Efficiency   Within the context of security, efficiency can range from increasing automation to addressing multiple threats and risks through a single control. It is the ability to identify activities that are related to the objective and security requirements, accurately apply resources using the correct methods and technologies, and have clarity on the end state of what security is providing. The ability to identify security activities that clearly map to the traditional role of security is easy. Compliance is a good example of defining information security expectations in which there is very little, if any, concern for the business within the context of compliance. However, to evolve and become more integral to long-term business success there must exist a repeatable process that promotes the accurate identification of objectives that interface with security and business objectives.

The probability of efficiency for a project is significantly increased when the correct resources are applied and, more importantly, the most applicable methods are used. Given the diversity of security—ranging from technical expertise to comprehensive analysis of risk—the breadth of security skills required for a project may be considerable. Additionally, the methods used throughout the project will play a role in how well actions are executed against objectives. For many, the allocation of resources is not the problem. A great number of companies have strong security capabilities and have developed capable teams over the years or have formed strong relationships with vendors. However, what stands out is the application of methods. Methods are a combination of best practices, prescriptive processes, and intellectual capital captured over time, which help ensure efficiency through consistency and lessons learned.

Over the years, many sets of methods have been created for use within the security team to promote standard approaches to issues that best reflect its environment and capabilities. Nevertheless, for some this has become a point of friction for business alignment and agility. As a result, even good resources must be strained to maintain efficiency when using poorly aligned methods, and success is typically based on individual skills, experience, and institutional knowledge. As companies become far more dynamic it must be accepted that not all methods are applicable to every situation for which they were designed. This is not to imply that the existing methods are no longer useful, but rather that the best use of them must be made relative to the unique demand, which is the basis of adaptive security.

Efficiency is best realized when the end state can be visualized and understood, which is achieved by simply ensuring that everyone is clear on the objective. Within information security practices, especially those founded mostly on compliance, the end state is simply adherence to the security requirements. It can be an application, server, network connection, or database when completely reduced to the most salient point; security is typically less concerned about the deliverable as it is about the risk and security posture. This is completely understandable and is the core to maintaining consistency in the security program, and ensuring compliance and manageability. However, by aligning more closely with the end product and its purpose in business terms, security can move closer to demonstrating enablement while allowing standard security requirements to feed into the process as opposed to governing it. The result is a greater balance between the business and security basics and thus increasing overall efficiency, especially in the eyes of the business.

2.4.2.4 Effective Security   Effective security has traditionally represented a conundrum: when security is doing its job, you don't hear about it. This concept is the bane for many security professionals and manifests itself in having to continually prove to executives that there are real reasons to invest in security. Historically, this has failed miserably. As a result, governments became more involved by placing regulatory demands on companies and forcing them to address security through compliance. Over time, risk management has become a predominant force within businesses to ensure controls are in place in order to minimize exposure. However, all of these approaches still lack the ability to connect with businesses because they are essentially based on threatening. If you are not compliant, you'll be fined. If you do not do this, you will be hacked. All stick, no carrot. One could argue that through years of this approach the security industry has trained businesses to accept this as the only reality of security—a hole into which the businesses throw money because they have to, or else.

Demonstrating effectiveness in security is the biggest opportunity facing the security industry today and the underlying value of an adaptive security management capability. Again, the challenge lies in the fact that when security is doing its job, you don't see or hear about it. There are many security organizations that pride themselves on not being front and center and work at being the quiet protector of the business, while others are very vocal about the need for security to thwart hackers and maintain compliance. In the eyes of businesses the former has obvious implications and the latter can become abrasive and threatening.

The opportunity lies in demonstrating effectiveness in ways beyond simply security. Of course, this is not new, but exploiting this approach to its maximum potential is. Historically, security has tried to present its value as achieving compliance or reducing risk. However, these approaches have some deeply rooted issues.

Compliance does not necessarily mean a company is secure. Many organizations that were compliant with industry and government regulations have suffered from debilitating attacks. This has left many executives trying to make sense of their investments when compliance was presented—or potentially implied—as security. Of course, using risk to articulate the need for security controls is commonplace; its ability to clearly articulate effectiveness is undermined by the dynamics of threats. For example, risk may show a control is needed to address a threat that exceeds the level of risk the organization is willing to accept. But that does not mean that the company will not be impacted by that threat or a different threat. Business executives live in the world of risk every day. But they do so with expectations of predictability and a desire for outcome. Security placing its sole interpretation of value on a process that is arguably fraught with unpredictability and not even a hint of absolutes is fundamentally a weak platform in the eyes of business.

Risk and compliance are core to security and are proven methods to managing security, and as such play a critical role in the adaptive model. But, when viewed from the boardroom there are gaps, unpredictability, and in some cases expectations of failure. The answer lies in communicating security activities in a manner that respects both the value of security and the demands of the business with regard to operational maturity.

Within the context of the management model the objective for demonstrating the effectiveness of security is to embrace business metrics in combination with security risk and compliance. This isn't simply security metrics, but rather a combination of performance data that helps executives interpret the value of their investments. There has been a great deal written within the security industry about returns on security investments. As a result it is generally accepted that security does not directly produce returns in a traditional business sense. Nevertheless, security can and does produce returns in the form of doing more with less or more efficiently, or utilizing existing investments to increase the security posture. However, these are more in alignment with value statements and not material returns. It can be argued that the use of "returns" by security organizations introduces a greater tendency for confusion among business owners who are already having difficultly seeing the effectiveness of security in the light of business goals.

As a result, adaptive security seeks to demonstrate value to businesses by creating a framework that ensures services are performed, tracked, and monitored in a manner that is effective relative to the business's goals. The basis for achieving this is an acute focus on how security activities are initialized, applied, and managed not only from a traditional security best practices perspective, but also from a financial and resource utilization perspective. In other words, it's simply not enough to say that the investments resulted in greater security or compliance. Security organizations have to demonstrate that the investments and resources were applied efficiently and effectively, and that the most is being realized from the effort.

2.5 Adaptive Security Management Architecture Overview

The adaptive security management architecture is a method of organizing security—how it is applied, managed, supported, and incorporated into a business—to provide better business alignment, demonstrate value to the business, and be an enabler of success. Ultimately, with these capabilities in place, the objective is to create an operating environment that allows security to adapt to changes in the business and security more efficiently and effectively.

The ASMA is, in part, founded on the fact there is a great deal of untapped expertise and capabilities that exist in most information security groups and in the industry. Although these can be very powerful, there is a wide range of definitions of what security should be in the industry and in business, which results in varying forms of how security is performed. The science of security is still maturing when compared to other disciplines, which leaves room for interpretation in security and how it is mapped to an organization's needs and goals.

The key is gaining access to inherent sophistication, but doing so in a manner that promotes and supports flexibility in how security is applied to a business. In many ways, the unique and powerful capabilities that exist in virtually every security program are hindered by current security management practices, the overreliance on standardization of practice without purpose, and, most importantly, resistance to change. Therefore, at the heart of every security program are all the unexploited ingredients for changing how security participates in the success of a business. Unfortunately, not all security programs are structured to promote and leverage these inherent properties, and in many ways this is the root of the disconnect between security and business.

These inherent sophisticated characteristics of security can be summarized as follows:

- Compensating Control—In security circles this is understood as applying security alternatives in a manner that achieves the intended purpose of a specified control that is not possible or feasible, usually defined by compliance or policy. Although mostly associated with technical controls and typically seen as a simple fixture in security that is performed every day, the underlying logic, approach, and processes represent meaningful sophistication that can be codified into how security is applied and managed, greatly enhancing security's effectiveness and agility. These underlying concepts are defined as Optional Measures.
- Security Depth and Granularity—Security can be applied in a number of ways with varying degrees of complexity and intensity. Typically, the more comprehensive the methods applied the higher the level of confidence and accuracy in the final result. Today there are some existing practice areas of security that employ ranges of application and are quite common across a wide range of organizations, but this is not reflected in the majority of security strategies. There is a tendency for an "all or nothing" approach in security citing standards, policy, and regulation as the driving forces creating a

dichotomy for business: apply the standard or accept the risk. In reality, the process of discerning the level of depth and granularity of security that should be applied is extraordinarily compelling. When incorporated into the fabric of how all security is applied to a business a far greater level of value may be realized.

- Commonality of Security—Regardless of how security is organized or compartmentalized, there is a fundamental set of basic security features that are common to all forms of security. These common aspects of security act as ingredients that are combined to formulate an overall approach. Any resulting approach will have inherent relationships between seemingly separate aspects of security that can be exploited to achieve new levels of balancing security to become the core enabler of adaptation.

The ASMA is a method for tapping this potential in security that may not be entirely explored in today's approach to security management. The ASMA is comprehensive and not only introduces standardized concepts that may have not fully resonated with the security industry in the past, but also looks to explore broader possibilities with established security practices. Again, many elements that exist within security today represent an enormous foundation, but they are currently not always leveraged in a manner that reflects all possibilities. Therefore, the ASMA is about pushing the envelope of what is possible in security and its relationship with business based on the fact that these capabilities exist and a framework can be provided to take advantage of them.

Adaptation is the end result of three major development phases that represent the basic framework of this book:

1. Organization of security activities into services that can be applied to the business in a manner that promotes business alignment
2. The formation of a management architecture that bonds risk, compliance, and governance with services management, all of which are founded on a capability maturity model to drive effectiveness, efficiency, quality, and performance working together to evolve business alignment to business value

3. Last is adaptation, the process of utilizing all the features from the previous development phases to exploit the business's value to enable the business through comprehensive and sophisticated management of security and business dynamics.

The term value is used throughout this book to express a business's interpretation of security with regard to its ability to assist the business in achieving its mission and goals. Moreover, value is also used to express the attributes of a security program that work together in facilitating a meaningful security posture relative to business demands. Each of the major development phases is intended to provide value and as such reflect a more basic evolution of the value of security in the eyes of the business. As previously introduced, and a constant theme throughout, businesses simply do not see a great deal of value in security because there are few, if any, indicators that demonstrate security helps the business to achieve its goals. Security is perceived as a must-do cost of doing business and as such is rarely welcomed with open arms.

Therefore, there are specific steps in changing a business's perception of security. Clearly, doing so cannot happen overnight and requires a degree of tenacity on the part of the security organization. The steps are elementary to the overall objective and resonate throughout the major development phases, and they are core to achieving a meaningful relationship with the business and eventually adaptability. The steps are progressive, building from one to the next, and as such each step is reliant on the stability of its predecessor. They are as follows:

1. Make it more palatable—Given that the business does not see a great deal of value in security relative to its mission and goals, and that security is generally perceived as a cost of doing business, security must accept that businesses have difficulty with security being forced upon them by policy and compliance as a must-do. This is further exacerbated when there is no association of security to the needs of the business. However, there are methods to creating a model, starting with services, that helps the business accept security by lending it characteristics that are more readily digested by the business. These characteristics represent features and capabilities that are already

typically practiced in security, but need to be organized and presented to the business in a manner in which it is used to dealing.

2. Make it more manageable—As security is applied to the business or business units over time there are opportunities for the security organization to become more ingrained with them. The more security is aware of the business's operating principles, people, processes, goals, mission, and expectations the more accurately and effectively security can be applied. Moreover, it allows the business to learn more about how security is being applied and managed within its organization. It is essentially about rhythm and embracing the unique characteristics that exist within the business in order for it to not only easily see how security is manifesting itself as part of its organization, but to promote its participation in the management of security.

3. Make it more informative—There is a tendency in the delivery of security to simply perform the task and move on. Moreover, this is also reflected by the axiom, "When security is doing its job you don't know it's there." This is the antithesis of how security needs to operate in the formation of business value. As security is applied to the business a great deal of data is usually produced, and over time valuable information can be generated from the data that can help the business in critical decision-making processes. Security groups need to accept that the framework used in their valuation of information may be very different from that of the business, and therefore they must seek every opportunity to provide information and visibility to the business.

4. Make it more strategic—The ultimate objective is to demonstrate that security plays a role in helping other groups meet their business goals. However, prior to achieving this security must demonstrate how its involvement with the business unit has helped in meeting security goals for the unit and the organization as a whole. By articulating the outcome of security activities in terms that express how the business unit has met a security objective, such as compliance with a policy or regulation, and how the results fit within the larger aspect

of the corporate security posture, the business unit can better understand its role locally and generally in security terms. It involves helping the business unit to understand it is supporting a more comprehensive strategy while also meeting security needs specific to the unit.

5. Make it more goals oriented—In demonstrating value to a business there are two dominating groups of goals that will drive all aspects of the security program: business goals and security goals. Unfortunately, goals from these two groups do not always align well and in some cases may represent conflicting principles. It is important that goals in security be tied from top to bottom so that each layer of security operates in a manner that feeds up to strategic security goals. Driving security goals at the top are business goals and the goals of business units and groups, which must also be acknowledged in each layer of security and how it is applied. Additionally, goals alignment is omnipresent and includes actionable supporting features and attributes such as measurements and metrics concerning performance against both business and security goals.

6. Make it more tangible—Security organizations are themselves a business unit tasked with a mission, goals, objectives, and fiscal responsibility, and as such they play a role in the success of a company. How well security performs as a business unit will be heavily weighed by other business units driving the perception of value. This is based on the development of mutual respect, which is formed when business units share many of the same business-related pressures. When a security group can demonstrate fiscally sound operating principles and promote effectiveness, efficiency, and quality while doing so, it creates an identity of security as a business unit that others can understand.

These steps set the evolutionary foundation of how security can be developed and applied within a business context and are at the heart of the ASMA. As each step materializes and creates a foundation for the next in each of the three primary phases, the perception of value will become more concrete and will eventually become an integral part of enabling the business.

Throughout this book the term "applied," as in the application of security or applying security, is used to help convert the traditional delivery of security as the system or strategy of security to a system whose results are security. In many security organizations the foundation of the group is typically only about security, which of course is completely logical. However, systems of this nature are defined and identified by the security that is realized. In other words, the security group is not and will never be more or less than the perception of security in the business. Given that the business has difficultly seeing the value of security, this by very definition inhibits the formation of value in the security organization. The intent is to create a system that results in security, but is not necessarily defined only by this one characteristic. How is the group managed, what level of performance in the operation of the security business unit is being realized, how is quality being managed and maintained, what is the performance against stated business goals? The list can be quite long and have nothing to do with traditional definitions of security. Therefore, the ASMA presented herein is based on the aforementioned development phases and elementary steps to creating value and directed at creating a new system with a wider vision of role, responsibility, and identity.

For many organizations, information security is one of their most valuable assets, but it is often the most difficult to fully understand or align to business goals and objectives. Successful organizations have recognized the benefits of information security and have found methods to effectively communicate these to the business. This has typically occurred through the orchestration of security activities to not only address risk and compliance, but to also express impact on business goals, effectiveness in operations, and efficiency in the application and management of security controls.

Traditionally, security is based on holistic risk and compliance management, which are fundamentally the measurement and management of security controls and their ability to address identified risk or alignment with regulatory demands. Usually, the justification of security in this model is based on risk—the impact of the lack of controls on the business from threats or implications of noncompliance. Unfortunately, these are difficult to align to business goals and there is limited focus, if any, on the operational effectiveness in security and the maturity of security practices.

There is a need assure the business that not only is security addressing risk and compliance, but it is aligned with the business and demonstrates value. Value in business terms is effectiveness, efficiency, and the ability to adapt to changes in the environment. Security organizations need to satisfy the demands for quality, fiduciary responsibility, and security requirements relative to risk and compliance. Today, understandably, many security groups are focused on risk and compliance but lack the ability to demonstrate business value. Although the employment of security metrics is a tool used to express security capability, few are easily connected to business goals and will typically lack performance metrics that translate to quality and operational integrity. For security to be successful in delivering against business requirements in today's environment, management must establish a model that links business goals to information security, provides visibility into performance and security metrics, ensures the maturity of program operations, has the ability to measure achievements, and creates a meaningful connection with the business owners.

The focus for adaptive security management architecture is on creating compensating security features with supportive processes that define areas of responsibilities across planning, management, delivery, monitoring, measurement, and improvement of comprehensive security capabilities. The ASMA and supporting processes allow security to bridge the gap with respect to risk, compliance, process and technical controls, the application of security, and communication of value to business stakeholders.

Every organization is increasingly concerned with how well security is being managed. This encompasses capabilities concerning risk treatments, maintaining compliance, and assuring a meaningful security posture. However, it also includes broader elements, such as alignment with industry best practices, adequacy in execution, and relevance to industry peers. Moreover, are security activities functioning as expected, can waste be reduced, or are controls managed effectively? These characteristics are essential for businesses to find a cost-benefit balance, understand current conditions,

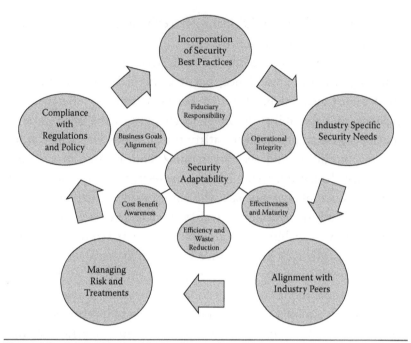

Figure 2.3   Relationship of architecture focus and security focus.

and appreciate the requirements, advantages, and positive impacts of improvements.

As demonstrated in Figure 2.3, today's security practices are mostly focused on risk, compliance, industry and security best practices, and what others in the industry are doing. These are important characteristics in developing and supporting a comprehensive security strategy. The adaptive security management architecture acts as an underlying business management framework that introduces focus on the integrity of the security program and supports the existing security strategy. The objective is to create a foundation of business alignment targeted at demonstrating value in how security is applied and managed. The premise is based on the fact that the outer layer in the figure is understandably security focused. However, what is typically lacking is the ability to bond security philosophies with the business in a method that resonates.

The goal of the ASMA is to create a supporting capability that helps to answer "why," "what does this mean to the business," and "how well is security performing as a part of the business" questions. By creating a supporting capability that is focused on addressing the business side of security and ensuring alignment, the ability to effectively adapt to changes in the business and the environment is realized.

Security organizations, although well defined, have limited visibility into the maturity of processes, management, and resources. How well information security is managed can be directly correlated to the ability to manage risk, ensure compliance, and demonstrate value. Understanding how well processes are defined, managed, and employed, along with how well resources understand them, use them, and manage the results, can have a dramatic and positive effect on the security posture of the organization and a business's perspective of value of the program. The more mature a program, the more effective and efficient it is in meeting business goals and objectives. It helps to ensure agility and acts as the foundation for business cases concerning investments and strategy.

Capability maturity is core to the ASMA due to the process-rich nature of security and the need to demonstrate value. As a feature of the ASMA, it works to absorb information, compare against expectations, and influence improvements where necessary to achieve business goals, which is an essential foundation for promoting adaptability within the security program. The importance of maturity within any security program is considerable. This is represented by the fact that capability maturity is deeply integrated into the ASMA, not only as a supporting feature, but in how processes in all the features are defined. In other words, by the very definition of the ASMA, there is an innate high level of maturity. For example, the existence of the services management feature and all the responsibilities contained within it are represented as the process for the management of services and reporting on performance and security. Services management would be ineffective without characteristics that are reflective of what is required to achieve meaningful levels of maturity. Based on this, one could argue that adaptive security management architecture is as much a maturity model as it is a security program architecture.

Within the adaptive security management architecture all the features work in collaboration with one another and focus the demands of the business and the needs of security into the security services. Security services act as the "tip of the spear" in how security manifests itself within the business and across business units. Risk and compliance management influence service delivery processes to ensure that strategic, traditional security purposes are met. However, service management, governance, and capability maturity management provide compensating capabilities to ensure business goals are met, the integrity of operations, and close alignment with the business. The ASMA is based on processes and process improvement with a focus on end-to-end control. The topic of adaptive security management architecture is inherently complex and the intertwining of traditional security approaches with business alignment requires adjustments in existing strategies. For these reasons—and others—the importance of maturity in processes and interactions between the features cannot be overstated.

2.5.1 Features and Characteristics

The adaptive security management architecture is a mechanism that converts current security activities into business services and provides several features that have specific roles in promoting business value. It is helpful to note that the features of the ASMA are not mutually exclusive, and they play a specific part in the program's overall success. Although there are several features of the ASMA that are not new to security, the way they interact and interconnect with each other is the basis of the ASMA to exploit opportunities that demonstrate value. Therefore, it provides the ability to expose opportunities as well as create capabilities to ensure long-term success.

Organizing many of security's activities into services to govern how security is applied within the organization is one of the predominant characteristics of the ASMA. Nevertheless, each feature exists to ensure that security is applied to meet compliance and manage risk, and information concerning how it is performing as a business unit is carried through the system for ensuring effectiveness, efficiency, and ultimately adaptability. Through the incorporation of a services-based strategy as part of the ASMA, a number of characteristics begin to emerge that can act as program enablers to help address security and even non-security challenges that face every security organization.

2.5.1.1 Features   Several core features within the adaptive security management architecture make up the foundation of the ASMA and establish the operational nature of the program. As previously introduced, these features have specific roles but would be virtually ineffective without all the others working to support and interact with one another (See Figure 2.4).

The features are as follows:

- Services Management—In some ways this is analogous to project management and all it implies. However, projects are typically comprised of a wide range of resources, tasks, and objectives to accomplish a common goal. Moreover, projects tend to be finite, highly targeted, and don't necessarily lend themselves to repetitive scenarios. Services management provides the ability to quantify security so that it can be applied, managed, tracked, improved consistently, and made repeatable. Moreover, through clear definition and the repetitive nature of services, nuances in delivery can be leveraged to tune services to best meet the needs of the business. Of course, services management takes into consideration resources, tools, quality control, performance measurements, and budgeting, which all combine to demonstrate effectiveness and efficiency in the delivery of security.

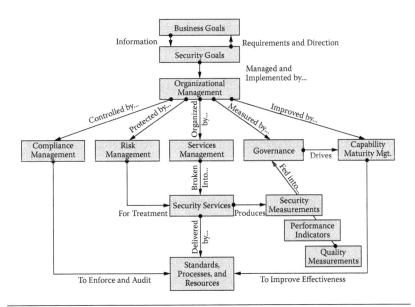

Figure 2.4 Management architecture overview.

- Risk Management—Within the adaptive security management architecture, risk management is enhanced to ensure
  that when services are employed they not only address specific business needs but also ensure that the overall security
  posture is maintained to the desired level. From the purely
  traditional role of risk management very little is changed.
  In fact, the ASMA relies heavily on existing risk management capabilities, models, and methodologies to act as
  a guide to how security is implemented. Although existing risk management approaches are compatible with the
  ASMA, some changes and additions are needed to achieve
  the goals of the ASMA. These relate to how risk management is used for business communications and the ability to
  rapidly determine risk in a highly focused way, again based
  on existing, proven methods but oriented to meet a specific
  need. The importance of risk management cannot be overstated. Once the ASMA is implemented, risk management
  is one of the key features that ensures overall alignment of
  the security posture as the program adapts to changes in the
  environment.
- Compliance Management—Compliance management within
  the ASMA has two primary roles that are intimately intertwined to achieve fully integrated compliance in the program.
  First, it ensures compliance with external and internal forces,
  such as regulations and policies. These manifest themselves as
  attributes in service definition, delivery methods and activities,
  and in reporting. As services are executed the resulting information from the activity and management of the service is used
  to determine adherence to compliance requirements. Second,
  compliance also ensures that the overall security program architecture itself adheres to established expectations. Compliance
  monitors the entire management architecture for compliance
  against the processes by which it is defined. The adaptive security management architecture is, for the most part, a collection
  of processes. Some are directly responsible for risk, compliance,
  and security, whereas others are focused on capability maturity,
  process improvement, management, performance, security, and
  quality tracking. As such, compliance management is important

to ensure the program is operating in a manner that is reflective of the intent and established processes.

- Governance—One of the key goals of the adaptive security management architecture is to grow closer to the business and provide value through efficient use of resources, effective application of security, and driving adaptability. Governance provides two important services to the program and the business. First, it acts as the interface between the business and the security group, a role typically belonging to risk management in traditional programs. Governance collects and converts information flowing from services, risk, and compliance management into key business-oriented indicators to demonstrate the status of security and the integrity of the security program as an organization. Second, governance provides the platform for constant improvement. Acting as the interface, governance also gains insights to the effectiveness and efficiency of the program from the business's perspective. In collaboration with compliance, services, and capability maturity management, improvements and adjustments to the program can be facilitated. Ultimately, governance acts as a source of information to the business and a feedback mechanism from the business back into the program to enact change. In short, governance is the connective force between security and the business.

- Capability Maturity Management—Services management is the oversight of execution of services; risk management exists to ensure that what is being performed meets the needs concerning overall risk; compliance management ensures that regulations and policies are addressed and the program is performing as defined; and governance focuses on business communications and process changes for greater alignment. Capability maturity management exists as an underlying force to ensure all processes related to the entire program are operating at optimal performance. Capability maturity management is a huge benefactor of governance due to the exposure of potential gaps and areas for improvement. It is not simply enough to have a process, method, or collection of tools used to deliver and manage security activities. It is necessary to understand and manage how well these are being performed to reduce waste and increase effectiveness. Moreover, capability maturity management is intently focused on corrections and improvements within the program. Maturity is a foundational characteristic of the ASMA, and capability maturity management is tasked with assessing, maintaining, correcting, and improving processes that translate directly to effectiveness, efficiency, and the ability to rapidly adapt to change.

- Organizational Management—Of course, all these features have to roll up to the senior executive staff responsible for security. Typically this is composed of a chief security officer (CSO) and may include a senior management team representing each feature. Organizational management deals with the entire program's operation, interfaces with the business and business units, and is a key fixture in the establishment of security committees. Each of these features interface within one another and use independent and shared processes to ensure the organization is meeting expectations concerning risk and compliance in a manner that is efficient and constantly improving performance. Organizational management is important to provide key oversight, address challenges, and orchestrate the entire program. Finally, there are security functions that are strategic in nature, such as policy, that are not managed by other features and are instead covered by organizational management. These features are focused on ensuring that the application of security activities within the business is meeting business and security goals by combining to make certain that security of the organization is managed, controlled, protected, organized, measured, and improved.

An important note on the features, which will be reintroduced throughout the book, is that they are used as an organization method for the ASMA and should not be directly associated with the physical organization of the security group. To elaborate, although not the most optimal scenario, it is feasible for one person to enact this entire architecture. Of course, security groups come in various sizes and geographical distributions, and each will have to determine how the ASMA and its features are formally organized to best meet the needs of the group. Finally, and a large part of resource management in services management, is the incorporation and utilization of resources beyond the security group, such as those in other business units or third parties, which can act as extensions to the program allowing different features or portions of features to be provided by others, thus reducing the load on the security group. The important point is the ASMA is a process model and as such can exist in the smallest to the largest environments.

2.5.1.2 Characteristics   A vast number of benefits can be realized from using an adaptive security management architecture. Some of these are core to the overall business value of management architecture and arguably are better defined as features. However, these are exploitable results of the program's foundation and can be used in different ways to increase the overall effectiveness of the program in the eyes of the business. Characteristics are not only outcomes from the program, but are common to all the features in meeting the demands of the business. While features provide the opportunity to quantify different parts of the ASMA, characteristics exist as common themes that resonate throughout the program, manifest as meaningful and tangible results from the program, and act as attributes that define the identity of the security organization.

- Business Measurements—When all the features of the program operate as expected they produce detailed information concerning the efficient use of resources, such as people, money, partners, tools, technology, and processes. Moreover, information may be garnered that demonstrates the effectiveness of security in meeting stated goals and objectives as an organization. This enables security organizations to report on operational elements in business terms, not security terms. These can include reports on quality, customer satisfaction, achieving key performance indicators, resource management, and budget and expense management. Although not new to security organizations, the ASMA does provide the means of generating detailed evidence and other material in support of demonstrating operational integrity. Being that demonstrating returns on security investments—in the form of hard dollars—is exceedingly difficult and virtually impossible to do consistently with any degree of predictability, security must be able to demonstrate value. This can come as savings, enhancements, doing more with less, streamlining activities, or exploiting existing investments, among other things.

- Security Measurements—On the other side of the business measurements coin, it is necessary to perform traditional security measurements in order to provide a comprehensive view of the program. These can include such things as understanding the state of compliance, vulnerability status, risk posture, threats, and technical aspects, such as anti-virus, event monitoring, and network controls. Measurements of this nature reflect business measurements, but with greater focus on security activities. For example, these measurements concern the effectiveness of incident response, how well tools discover vulnerabilities, or security's involvement in code review, change management, and business continuity. Security measurements are used by many organizations today to gain visibility and understanding of tactical security activities.

- Adaptability—Of course, a primary goal of the ASMA is to ensure adaptability. Adaptation is not extraordinarily common in information security due to the focus on standardization that is needed to ensure a degree of stability and predictability. However, inherent to security are compensating controls, the ability to indirectly address a security need through the use of other methods when a more direct route is not feasible or possible. Through the use the ASMA and the capabilities realized from the features in the oversight of security and alignment with business, organizations can gain extraordinary visibility into the overall security posture and relate that posture to budgets, resources, activities, and management across the business. Based on this visibility, security can be adjusted, enhanced, and prioritized in order to rapidly optimize the program to address business dynamics. It is possible to expose relationships between different services and features that help organizations predict and exploit interdependencies in the program that can be used to rapidly compensate for changes in the environment. Within the context of this book, adaptability is the highest level of achievement for a security program, and the path leading there results in greater effectiveness and efficiency for a business and in meeting security demands.

• Quality—All the features combine and intersect to promote quality control, and therefore it is more of a benefit than a core element of the program. Of course, governance and compliance management operate as quality control mechanisms, with governance interfacing with the business and promoting change and compliance ensuring alignment to established expectations on execution. Quality is an attribute with which anyone can resonate, especially when quality is lacking. It is the root of value and acts as a guiding principle in the execution of security and operating effectively as a business unit. Quality is usually associated with the outcome of a process. While this is applicable within the definition of the ASMA, it also includes how the process is executed. Results are not always indicative of process quality. Although the outcome may be of high quality, the process may have been an overly expensive one, fraught with errors, or difficult to repeat. Within the ASMA quality is holistic and is a focal point of how processes are executed as much as the results. Alignment between action and result is essential for demonstrating value and key to maintaining a business-aligned security posture.

In many ways, these characteristics are points of justification for the ASMA and what organizations can expect as far as visibility into the program. As the program matures, these will provide management the primary indicators of success and areas where improvements can be made. Moreover, the business will naturally gravitate to these characteristics and will directly relate them to how the security organization is perceived in meeting the strategic goals of the business.

The characteristics of business and security measurements are quite comprehensive and require further explanation with regard to the ASMA. As demonstrated in Figure 2.5, each feature maintains involvement and responsibility with stated goals in processes for service delivery, the services themselves and shared customer goals, how

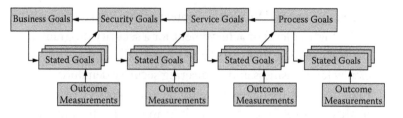

Figure 2.5   Goal alignment and evolution.

these resonate within the overall security strategy goals, and ultimately the alignment with business goals.

Throughout the execution of activities, which are driven from stated goals, measurements are taken that ultimately act as visibility into the outcome of the activities performed. Goals start with the business and move through the ASMA to ensure they are driving downstream goals and activities. As high-level goals are mapped, stated goals drive those farther downstream, eventually setting specific goals for processes. As measurements are generated they are compared to the stated goals and ultimately to strategic goals, which are compared to the next level of goals and how well measurements align. The objective is to ensure continuity in goals from the business all the way through specific activities within the security architecture. Moreover, it is critical to ensure that measurements are taken not only to ensure alignment with the stated goals of a specific level, but also to relate to measurements and goals defined in upstream goals feeding back into the business. By connecting goals between different focus groups of security and measurements occurring in each, the overall program has specific visibility into local achievements or gaps as well as how these successes or failures impact upstream demands. In many ways, this defines governance and the flow of information back into the business as well as ensuring that each layer in the ASMA meets expectations and incorporates information from the business. However, although governance is responsible for bi-directional communication and awareness, every feature in the ASMA is responsible for managing goals at each level, from business to process, given that these exist not only across the program, but within each feature as well.

In Figure 2.5, goals flow from the business through security into services and eventually to processes, each related to activities that are measured and then compared to upstream goals and measurements.

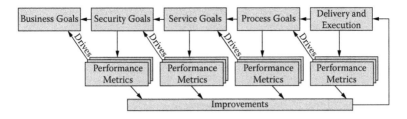

Figure 2.6 Metrics, goals, and improvements.

Although information is provided and analysis occurs at each point and flows back to the business goals, these do not necessarily drive goal attainment, but rather ensure that goals from the business and at each level resonate with strategic, remedial, and technical activities. It is necessary to also have performance indicators that define measurements to convey how well the security group, services, and specific processes perform in reaching the stated goals. Basically, although goals may be clearly communicated and activities measured, this does not necessarily provide a clear perspective on progress against goals, but only that goals have been incorporated into the program's functions.

As demonstrated in Figure 2.6, performance metrics, as a result of measurements over time, offer leading indicators about whether the goals will likely be reached. Based on this interaction of goals, activities, measurements, and metrics at each level within the ASMA, performance metrics can be improved to close gaps or accelerate goal attainment, and eventually begin to drive higher-level goals.

These interactions and natural points of management and improvement exist at every level, all of which are founded on capability maturity and provide a continual improvement-support cycle based on attaining goals in processes, services, security, and the business. The structure allows for continual improvement throughout the ASMA directed at meeting operational, security, and business goals. Moreover, as improvements are realized, goals can be reset in order to promote growth and development. The relationship established through the management of goals, measurements, and metrics at all levels is the center of the ASMA and the basis for adaptability.

For example (see Figure 2.7), by having a closed loop between goals and improvement with processes and activities being managed and measured, any changes in the business can be rapidly addressed. Of

Figure 2.7   Between goals and improvements.

course, this places a great deal of focus on the quality of processes and how well their execution is managed, which is the basis and purpose of capability maturity management in the ASMA. Each feature has a responsibility concerning process execution and management relative to its role within the ASMA. Organizational management seeks to manage all the features and governance is intimately intertwined at all goal and measurement levels to effectively monitor and communicate with the business.

2.6 The Interconnects

At the heart of the ASMA is the "connective tissue" that binds it together. While each feature has a specific mission in ensuring security is applied in an effective manner, the features also must interact like characters in a play. Only by working together in a comprehensive manner will security be a compelling business-enabling force. As each feature performs its assigned role it must interface with all the other features. These interconnects ensure balance to avoid overcompensation or to ensure that the needs of the business and security are effectively realized. The structure of the features is purposefully defined to not only promote a reinforcing framework of security, but to ensure representation of the different aspects of business and security as decisions are made.

The interconnects between the features act as compensating measures to ensure that a single point of view or perspective does not dominate how security is applied. Conversely, they also ensure that every characteristic of security is interwoven to drive meaningful security through intense collaboration that not only ensures the needs of the business are being met, but allows for the investigation of every opportunity for improvement and innovation within the security program. In short, the interconnects exist to ensure that there are checks and balances in how security is managed and applied. Moreover, the objective is to constantly seek improvement, pushing what is possible and in doing so to drive greater business alignment. Finally, underneath the interconnects and the features that comprise the ASMA is intent. The intent of the business, regulation, and even threats all resonate within the architecture and in how the features of the architecture interact.

Within the context of intent, the interconnects provided herein are a guide to demonstrate the overall objective and role of the ASMA's interconnects. The examples are a starting point to express the intent of the interconnects, and as organizations begin to develop their own unique approaches new and different interconnects will be formed that best reflect the culture and operating principles of the company.

When one looks at the ASMA's overall role within the business there surfaces five major areas of focus:

1. Risk Posture Management—The interactions between all the features that ensure the overall management of risk are realized and specifically targeted at maintaining the desired risk posture. Although the risk management feature of the ASMA is acutely focused on risk, it is the interactions with the other features that ensure the posture is understood and maintained.

2. Compliance Posture Management—Each of the features are interested in ensuring compliance: compliance with established policies and standards and applicable regulations, and compliance with stated expectations within the security program and architecture. The features must work together in compelling ways to ensure compliance is achieved, but do so in a manner that promotes business agility.

3. Performance Improvement and Management—Performance management and the focus on improving security are essential to the role of the ASMA. All the features play a role in

ensuring that the security organization meets performance objectives and goals, and looks to continuously improve the inner workings of the security program.

4. Policy and Standards Management—As expected, at the core of a security program are policies and standards. In many ways, adaptability is achieved through comprehensive oversight and management of policies and standards and how these relate to business and industry dynamics. Given that each feature is focused on the sound and business-aligned application of security, it is a communal effort to oversee and manage all aspects of these security attributes.

5. Service Management and Orchestration—Within the ASMA security is ultimately realized through the execution of security services and the responsibility of the service management feature. However, how services are defined, measured, managed, communicated, monitored, and applied is the responsibility of all the features. The ability to adapt will quickly surface in how well the features work together in the overall management of services.

Using the above as an initial expression of overall program focus, each of the features can be mapped against these primary objectives to highlight the primary, initial interlock with another feature, the intent of the activity, the necessary inputs to the process, other features that will need to be intimately involved, the target of the activities, the output, and the other features and beneficiaries of the interactions. As each feature is introduced, interconnects within this framework will be provided to help express the expectations of how they function as a combined management capability.

2.7 About the Book

There is a plethora of materials in the industry that explains a number of different security architectures, control frameworks, and models. Everything from International Organization for Standardization (ISO)-27000 series, NIST's Special Publications 800 series, and CoBIT to Information Technology Infrastructure Library/ Information Technology Services Management (ITIL/ITSM),

Information Assurance Capability Maturity Model (IA-CMM), and ISO-21827:2008 (formally Systems Security Engineering [SSE]-CMM) models, all of which provide information on controls, measurements, metrics, and implementation concepts. Many of these are founded on an assess, plan, do, and manage cycle that supports a protect, detect, and react model. These also include base-lining, assessment, and management functions. The information provided by these and other industry publications is very valuable and is referenced throughout this book. When using this book it is recommended that you review these other materials to enhance the overall concepts provided herein to make for a well-defined, comprehensive management capability.

Moreover, the basic concepts of the adaptive model presented herein are similar to the direction provided by the Software Engineering Institute's (SEI's) Capability Maturity Model Integration (CMMI). CMMI is "a process improvement approach that provides organizations with the essential elements of effective processes that ultimately improve their performance. CMMI can be used to guide process improvement across a project, a division, or an entire organization. It helps integrate traditionally separate organizational functions, set process improvement goals and priorities, provide guidance for quality processes, and provide a point of reference for appraising current processes." CMMI defines three areas of interest: product and service development; service establishment, management, and delivery; and product and service acquisition. Each area provides the basis for the improvement plan and layers specifically defined practices areas on a foundation of capability and maturity. Arguably, the adaptive security management architecture is in some ways synonymous with an area of interest and defines the primary practices areas as core features. For those familiar with CMMI and other CMM-based models, CoBIT and ITIL/ITSM, to name a few, will quickly resonate with the fundamental intent of the ASMA.

Many other materials of this nature in the security industry do not always effectively address how they relate to business. The ability to relate to business means that security must embrace what it means to be a business unit and have the wherewithal to demonstrate not only effectiveness in information security practices, but also in running as a business. As such, security organizations need to be able to articulate operational and security performance against strategic goals, financial goals, quality goals, and operational goals. Additionally, as discussed above, the adaptive security management architecture is founded on capability maturity and ensures that measurements and metrics used to track security are actionable. The ability to accurately influence change in the system to ensure metrics are moving in a desirable direction is somewhat rare in the industry.

Most of the models that exist are typically focused on one area, such as a standards framework, security measurements and metrics, service delivery, risk and compliance management, and security controls. These typically fall into one of three groupings: capability maturity, security architecture, and security controls, but rarely cross these lines and connect with the business. CoBIT, CMMI, and ITIL/ITSM are some of the few that bond maturity with a controls framework that is directed at business goals. Unfortunately, there are few, if any, security models focused on demonstrating security value, and addressing business more directly and security organizations operating as a business unit.

Adaptive security management architecture acts as unified theory between security and the business by blending these three major attributes and aligning them within an information security program. The features identified as part of the model exist in many organizations today and ways in which these can interact are provided to promote adaptability on the foundation of effectiveness, efficiency, and business value. The organization of this book is primarily based on the features, and the chapters continually refer back to the three main areas and the characteristics. The objective is to provide information in a manner that exposes the evolutionary nature of the ASMA to create an atmosphere of excellence. To achieve adaptability, which means reaching a level of sophistication in which dynamics are addressed in near real time and have innate value to the business, requires a solid foundation. In creating the foundation there are milestone benefits that surface to help maintain momentum and ensure the development of the program progresses. For example, given that compliance and risk management exist in nearly every security program today, the introduction of services and services management is typically the starting point for implementation. Once realized, there are significant benefits that can be had from this early stage. These not only help as points of justification, but they provide a preliminary view into what will materialize over time from the program as it forms.

Obtaining incremental results over the evolution of the program's development is an important aspect. All too often projects designed to enhance capability over a period of time typically fall victim to lack of results. This typically translates to dissatisfaction and only realizes 20% of the original plan. For a project of this nature to survive ebbs and flows in focus from the security group and the business, every opportunity must be made to capture successes at key milestones, which are supported within the ASMA. As introduced, each feature plays a role in the overall program and works with the other features to formulate the final structure. However, each has its own purpose and can offer some value independently from the others as they are developed. This is especially true with capability maturity management, which can be formalized quite readily and have an immediate impact on existing areas of the security program.

In addition to providing tangible benefits over the development life cycle of the ASMA, as each feature and capability is introduced there is an exponential increase in the value the program develops. This appears not only in work products, but metrics used to track the performance and quality of the program begin to increase. In other words, as the program develops, it—as one would expect—increases in effectiveness and efficiency. The intent is to present the information so that not only can the ASMA be communicated, but it can also be made actionable.

3

ACHIEVING ADAPTABILITY

In many ways, this chapter is beginning at the end. Before the ASMA can be detailed it is helpful to provide a perspective of what security adaptability is and the applicability of the ASMA's features. Adaptability is the product of a great deal of organization, management, and attention to detail. It is acknowledging that there are very fundamental and long-standing characteristics of security that offer enormous value when exploited effectively and accepting that there are some that hinder security's potential. Introduced in the Adaptive Security Management Architecture Overview section of the previous chapter, adaptation is the end product of a comprehensive security management system that is comprised of a collection of features that collaborate to create an environment of excellence. This chapter discusses this end result, and the details underlying what is presented are covered in following chapters. Albeit a slightly unorthodox approach, in this case it is more effective to present the end state and then provide the finer points in how it can be accomplished.

3.1 Security Adaptation

Adaptability is not inherent to information security. In fact, changing security to the prevailing winds can result in a very poor security posture and fire fighting, which can introduce unnecessary risk and noncompliance. In short, it can be a disaster. However, through the employment of an adaptable architecture and the exploitation of well-defined and commonly used practices that are deeply inherent to security, adaptability can be realized and even become commonplace.

The objective is to create an environment of excellence and maturity that resonates with the business in meeting its goals. By implementing the features of the ASMA, security can obtain an enhanced relationship with the business, incorporate compliance demands more efficiently, and be applied effectively within the business. With capability maturity as a foundational element to the program, security groups will experience a mode of operation that instills a high degree of confidence in actions and outcome. Ultimately, there is clarity in mission and purpose.

With the combination of all the discrete information and processes used to ensure the meaningful delivery and management of security, and how this is presented to the business and organized to improve performance, security organizations have the ability to view the overall security program in ways that have not been entirely possible in the past. More than ensuring optimal operations, performance, security, and quality, it becomes the foundation for managing change, and as introduced, this is the final frontier for security. Having the ability to address change and do so in an efficient manner and, more importantly, do so with a high degree of confidence in the outcome of change is enormously valuable.

Throughout discussions concerning adaptability, change has been predominantly articulated as something passed to the security organization as a result of shifts in the business. Although this represents the most common occurrence, it does not fully express the ability for security organizations to initiate, predict, or even promote change to provide the business with more options to achieve stated goals. The ASMA provides much, if not all, of the information needed to predict the implications of change that allow security organizations to experiment with new ideas and innovative techniques to enhance its role in enabling the business. In short, this is about taking the initiative and promoting what is possible by having a higher level of certainty in the outcome of the proposed change.

Of course, the opposite is true. Predictability of outcome can provide meaningful insight to increased risk, which allows the security organization to approach the business with well-defined and well-supported evidence that a change may have undesirable implications that need to be weighed during the decision-making process. The act of demonstrating security issues with change goes beyond today's typical risk-warning approach and ties it directly to performance, capability, quality, and business performance indicators. It's about moving away from managing risk acceptance and playing a key role in helping the business make informed decisions concerning security and the role of security in the change. Of course, with predicting the outcome of a potential change or predicting the implications of a change, the ability to formulate meaningful solutions that resonate with the business and risk and compliance are realized, which is a key feature of adaptability.

There is an innate fear of change and it is partially rooted in the unpredictability change represents. Today's security has worked to create an environment of stability and consistency to ensure a degree of predictability. However, this form of predictability is based on an established envelope of expectations, and anything outside of the envelope is a special case or nonstandard. Of course this approach has merit in security but lacks integration of business attributes, which translates as business dynamics being addressed as nonstandard. In many ways this is the result of overly focusing on security itself as opposed the operational characteristic to ensure security. Once that focus is turned inward towards how security groups apply security, a deeply rooted and dramatic shift occurs. Security moves from being the system to becoming the result of the system, and that system provides new perspectives on how the result can be manipulated, adjusted, and managed within the context of business and security. Based on the existence of the ASMA, specifically the ability to fine-tune the delivery of services, maturity in processes, and the comprehensive collection of meaningful performance, security, and quality measurements, organizations will have all the ingredients to not only address change, but to have greater confidence in predicting the outcome of change, ultimately driving innovation.

Ultimately, the ASMA provides the basic framework to formalize a system that focuses on the operational aspects of security as a business organization. Based on this approach, information concerning the operational integrity of the security group in meeting business expectations as well as information concerning the security posture is combined to promote effectiveness and efficiency. More importantly, the existence of an organized model that increases visibility into business and security performance also provides the necessary elements for adaptation.

In this chapter we review how adaptability can be achieved, which sets the foundation for articulating the ASMA's details. Throughout the chapter several examples and concepts will be offered to express different aspects of managing change. However, not all of these will be entirely applicable to each unique business environment and security culture. Nevertheless, the objective is to express theories that can be used as a guide to finding methods of achieving the same results within your specific environment.

3.2 Compensating Controls Theory

The concept of compensating controls within information security is a well-understood practice that is used quite frequently. In short, a compensating control is where one or more security controls are implemented to achieve the intent of a specific control that is not possible or feasible in the current environment. For example, a regulation may specify a security control of a certain type and logical location within the environment to ensure the desired security posture, i.e., the intent. However, there may be conditions unique to the environment that make implementing the required control impossible, thus requiring a different set of controls that achieve the same intent. Another aspect is when a control is specified but other existing controls within the environment achieve or exceed the intended security. In both cases compensating controls are essentially alternatives that meet or exceed the intent of a required control.

The concept is loosely tied to defense-in-depth strategies where layering of controls helps to delay or prevent various attack vectors. The combination of access controls, filtering communications, data encryption, malware detection and removal, and monitoring are common practices that reflect the integration of controls as layers that work in unison to reduce exposure. The principle is based on the idea that if one control fails or is circumvented, other controls will act as barriers to the attacker. Moreover, it is also assumed that the diversity of controls means that the same tactics cannot be used from one control to the next, thus disrupting the attack vector and methods. All this assumes that as each control is successfully attacked the next control will delay or stop it, and so on. Additionally, the layering may slow the attack, and thus increase the opportunity for detection and buy more time for an effective response. Finally, defense-in-depth more than implies that combining different security capabilities complement one another and make for a posture that is greater than the sum of its parts. Through the combination of filtering, access control, and monitoring, different areas of security that are focused on a specific area of the environment, a far greater awareness and control is obtained. In this example, the controls do not try to stop an attack in different ways, but complement each other.

Within the context of compensating controls, defense-in-depth acts as the overarching principle in the formation of security controls that impact architecture design, implementation, and management as methods for realizing the intended level of security. The thought process of defense-in-depth strategies is at the root of forming meaningful compensating controls. The goal is to interpret the meaning of a required control in order to determine what alternatives can be implemented to achieve the same objective. Therefore, compensating control theory is founded on not only understanding the intent of a demand, but on the further requirement of understanding the intent of the control.

There are endless scenarios in which compensating controls surface. Usually, they materialize as increasing the level of controls in other areas. For example, a standard username and password combination is used for a given application, but in the face of other limitations due to the inability to implement a specifically defined control, the identification and authentication process may be enhanced to incorporate two-factor authentication. It may also materialize as the employment of new technology, such as hard drive or data encryption, to increase data confidentiality. Or, these methods may be combined, such as the use of public key infrastructure (PKI) and certificates for encryption and authorization. The list of combinations is virtually limitless and reflects security strategy, infrastructure, technology, investments, capabilities, risk, and culture. Nevertheless, the point is that compensating controls may result in increasing an existing control's capability, adding one or more additional controls, or a combination of both to reduce the exposure realized from the absence of a standardized control which is simply not possible due to unique conditions.

Not only is this an exceedingly common practice in security, but security professionals are very astute at exposing gaps of this nature and architecting meaningful solutions to close them when obvious controls are not feasible. It is the result of attention to risk and the attributes that impact the level of risk realized. Security professionals are faced with these types of challenges regularly, and this capability is core to ensuring a sound security posture and compliance. Over the years security professionals have developed an innate sense of the intent of security as opposed to being locked into a specific control capability. Although there is a great deal of tactical focus and discussion concerning which technology or collection of technical point solutions will provide the desired state, behind this is a culture focused on overall risk. It becomes less about a control and more about what is needed. For example, organizations facing Payment Card Industry (PCI) compliance have a prescriptive set of controls that are necessary to achieve compliance. However, these are not always possible to achieve as specifically defined in the Data Security Standard (DSS), which demands that the security architect determine the intent of the specification, interpret it from a position of risk, and translate it into a new structure of controls that ultimately drives modifications to new or existing technology and processes to meet the requirement. Security professionals perform this naturally. In many ways this capability has come from years of having to achieve security without a great deal of executive or financial support. In other words, security professionals are typically resourceful and find ways of addressing the need for security in innovative ways. Today the industry generally ignores this powerful facet of security capability and undervalues the concept of compensating control and the inherent complexities that exist under the cover of simplicity. Granted, some are better than others in visualizing and creating compensating controls, but as an industry it is a core attribute that is not fully exploited.

When a security professional is faced with a situation that demands a compensating control the professional's mind is thrown into a vast array of internal decision-making processes: What is the intent of the standard? Why have they specified this control? What is the intent of the control? How does this control relate to others? What is the risk that is being addressed? What information do I have about my infrastructure, and does it truly represent a barrier to this control or do I have an opportunity to address this challenge through other means? Unique things occur in the mind of a person going through this challenge. The person not only questions the intent of the demand and control the standard or regulation has stipulated or alternatives that come to the surface, but even the framework of the person's decision criteria. In short, the person—even if only very briefly—explores all possibilities and potential devoid of barriers. It is commonplace to hear security professionals working through a problem like this to say, "Well, if we could do this it would not only address the requirement, but would greatly improve this other area." However, at some point the reality of possibilities sinks in and they quickly surmise that it is simply not possible: "But, we can't do that because they would never agree." The processes that occurred just before this point, when security professionals were interpreting intent, controls, and risk and forming concepts that take into account things they normally would not have considered, are the basis—the root—for compensating controls theory. The goal is to exploit this and apply it to a larger framework that promotes exploration of security and operational elements.

So far the interpretation of compensating controls has been within the technical space. However, once the sophistication of processing the information to come to a meaningful conclusion is recognized, we see that it can be applied to a wide range of security-related challenges and more. If we accept that alternative scenarios can be formalized to achieve a desired posture, we must also accept that this process can be applied to everything security can offer. Moreover, when empowered with information concerning the operational integrity of security and performance against stated security and business goals, we can then use the same theories in developing complex combinations that address business and security dynamics. To put this into perspective, the thought processes behind creating compensating technical controls involves understanding the intent of the control, what is driving it, the conditions within the current environment that make it not possible, and the intimate knowledge of alternative measures that can achieve the determined intent. Clearly, information supporting the thought process is critical, such as threats, risk, control capabilities, infrastructure, and compliance requirements. Arguably, the amount and comprehensiveness of the information made available to the decision-making process can be directly tied to the effectiveness and accuracy of the resulting solution. Therefore, if we can incorporate information from all aspects of security and business operations concerning performance against goals and metrics, we can rightly assume that the end result will be far more tuned to the environment and to the betterment of security and the business.

In many ways this holistic view of developing meaningful controls occurs in many security organizations. However, some organizations lack all the information needed to fully understand the implications to the business. Moreover, not all security organizations promote activities of this nature to ensure standardization. The reason these and frankly many other hidden capabilities within security have not been completely taken advantage of is simply the lack of an operating environment that promotes inventive thinking and therefore does not provide meaningful insight or confidence in the outcome. Of course, compensating controls happen within the technical space every day with mixed results and acceptance, and must be proven and interrogated to reduce fear. Even in cases where compensating controls have an obvious advantage, there is little evidence produced that can be directly tied back to the value that the control or controls offered. Some of this is the result of a focus on security as opposed to a focus on the system of applying security. Compensating controls represent a departure from the standard and as such are seen in a negative light, and through association the interpretation of its value becomes marginalized. The simple fact is the core of adaptability (the ability to change) that is lacking in today's security environment actually already exists within the security program and represents untapped potential. In fact, the potential for realizing change is so great that without a security architecture designed specifically for managing change it would become overwhelming and fail catastrophically. Therefore, the ability to truly change the identity of security and become an enabling force within the business exists within many security groups today. The barriers have been obtaining clear visibility into all the operational characteristics of security and business, understanding how to effectively apply the security capability, and do so within a framework that exploits the positive features and outcomes.

Adaptability and compensating controls are virtually interchangeable terms in this context. In fact, a distinction must be made between the common term of compensating control and that of the intricate underlying logic, approach, and processes, the root of which we're seeking to unearth with the adaptive security management architecture. Therefore, the meaning of compensating controls within the ASMA is best articulated as "Optional Measures" given that the goal is to provide meaningful security options to the business through a comprehensive analysis of capability, risk, compliance, objective, and intent.

Armed with an adaptive security architecture as the foundation for applying strategic security intelligence and combining this with key business acumen, security organizations will gain the ability to address a wide range of complex scenarios. The operational information (i.e., goals, performance, quality, and other information from across security and business) generated from the security architecture in the application of security services will provide the basis for adjusting how security is applied relative to the dynamics that may occur within the business or as initiatives stemming from the security group.

3.2.1 Basic Areas of Optional Measures

Optional measures are the result of processing information about the desired condition against the basic areas of security that act as guiding principles and the business drivers that together represent decision-making input. In this case, the process is the inherent strength that is found in virtually all security groups and professionals that commonly surfaces as compensating controls. From this we can extrapolate that the process can be applied to all things in security up to and including the operational aspects of security. Information from security operations and the basic areas of security are used as inputs from which to draw meaningful options using this process. Partnering the security-related information with that from the business, such as drivers, goals, objectives, and mission, provides a full picture of intent that encompasses security, operations of security, and the business. With a far more comprehensive collection of criteria to work with the process that is born from the balancing of compensating security controls and defense-in-depth strategies can now be fully exploited.

As previously introduced, security services are the definition of how security is applied, and therefore services are interconnected and act as the basis for compensating for security demands. By applying the ASMA there is a sound foundation for formulating security relationships due to the ability to manage them based on meeting security goals, quality, and performance. Therefore, security services represent a method to not only to address more traditional aspects of specific compensating controls, such as technical controls, but also provide the means to understand the operational aspects of security.

Additionally, business goals, performance, and strategic interactions through governance management provides the much needed incorporation of business alignment, which acts as yet another basis for input into the overall process in formulating optional measures and ensuring adaptability. Adaptability means having the facility to mange change effectively with a keen grasp on the risks to business and security represented by the change. Therefore, change can come as business shifts and dynamics that need to be responded to, or demands from external and internal forces that require direct and indirect adjustments. Within the realm of business adaptability is the making of myriad changes to compensate for various forces, such as the economy, competition, legalities, fiscal performance, and many other dynamics that companies face every day. Basically, these are fundamentally the same, although the instigator of change and the approach in assessing risk and formulating a solution may be different. The key to the ASMA is creating a model that promotes business and security visibility and allows these two seemingly different philosophies to combine in order to drive comprehensive security in a manner that enables the business. Moreover, it creates a method to digest business demands into security activities and allowing security to respond to, and in some cases predict, what can be done to ensure the security posture and do so while being conscious of business impacts.

In short, there is much to gain in combining business and security goals when contemplating change and determining what is within the realm of possibility in effectively adapting to the change. There is an element of art in adapting business and security to address various dynamics. In some cases, one may provide more concrete direction than the other, thereby reducing the number of potential options to a more workable collection and thus streamlining the decision-making process. Additionally, the existence of the ASMA provides the much-needed visibility into the characteristics of security, such as risk and compliance, as well as the business performance characteristics. The act of generating, collecting, and processing the wide array of business and security information offers greater confidence in predicting the outcome of the adjustments because business and security complement one another.

Before we delve deeper into the nuances of adaptation, we first need to look at some of the basic areas of security that act as guiding principles and the business drivers that influence the decision-making criteria used in the processes that produce optional measures.

3.2.1.1 Primary Security Input Areas   When creating security-compensating controls there is understandably a great deal of focus on security, specifically risk, compliance, and overall posture. The role of risk and compliance management is to ensure that changes in when, how, and to what depth security is applied facilitates the respective need. Of course, these are not always in alignment with what business may expect or demand, creating much of the friction experienced today. Nevertheless, the basics of security are sound and can be summarized as follows:

- Technology Related—The most prevalent compensating control activity within security is in the technology domain. It is the process of determining what technical controls can be improved, changed, or added to indirectly address a specific need.
  - Determining what additional capabilities are necessary in existing technology solutions that can be employed to compensate for the lack of a standardized control. This form of compensation seeks to exploit unused available capabilities in existing technologies.
  - Determining what new technical solutions are necessary and feasible in the specific environment to compensate for the lack of a standardized control. In conditions where existing technologies do not have unused resources or do not have the ability to address the desired level of security, additions to the environment are usually necessary.
  - What combination of existing technology enhancements and new technical solutions is possible to compensate for the lack of a standardized control. In scenarios where existing options do not facilitate the desired level of control they are supported by the addition of new controls.
- Process, Procedure, Standards and Policy Related—The intent of improving, changing, or adding to standards, policies, and the like is to change operational behavior. In many cases, this

is tied to technology, such as changing password complexity requirements in a policy, and will be substantiated (enforced) via modifications to technical controls. Nevertheless, changing the organization's standard on how something should be performed can have measurable results in security.

- Determining if enhancements to one or more or any combination of processes, procedures, standards, and policies can be employed to compensate for any identified and undesirable gaps in security controls. Simply stated, this involves investigating existing processes, standards, etc., to determine if changes can be made and, more importantly, enforced to close gaps in security with a focus on how security is performed.
- Determining if there is a lack in one or more of these areas that can be facilitated to compensate for the security control. In some cases, compensating controls can be realized with the addition of processes and/or standards that seek to modify actions taken or be managed to achieve the desired level of security.

- Risk Related—Risk is one of the drivers for determining compensating controls. It seeks to understand the intent of what is to be accomplished and finds a balance with other forms of controls, such as technical and procedural, to compensate. The primary factors are threats and the valuation or risk attributes related to the assets that are potentially affected.

  - Determining the combination of controls that reduces the identified exposure as represented by the lack of a standardized control. Risk is responsible for interpreting the collection of technology and process areas to determine if an available combination meets the intent of the desired security control.
  - Understanding the taxonomy of the threat(s) that the standardized control addressed and what combination of new controls and enhanced controls addresses the same threat. Risk is the balance of threats and controls relative to assets and their valuation. In order to ultimately conclude that a compensating control or compensating

control combination is effective requires accurate association to the threat that the original and unobtainable control attempted to address relative to the asset(s).

- Compliance Related—As with risk management, compliance seeks to determine the intent and formulate an acceptable technical and procedural control that facilitates the regulation. The primary difference between risk and compliance is that risk is most concerned with the threat and its impact potential to the organization, whereas compliance is focused on meeting a specification in a regulation or standard, which may have very little to do with traditional risk. Of course, lack of compliance is a form of risk, but the primary driver for compliance is to address required specifications.

  - Determine the intent of the regulation or specification relative to the required control in the formation of a compensating control that will satisfy the regulation. Each regulation will express and define a security control. In some cases the definition may be general or specific. In either case, or when the desired control is not feasible, the intent of the regulation must be interpreted in order to identify one or more compensating control features that will satisfy the regulation.

  - Determine the risk to the organization, beyond compliance, concerning the compensating controls. In other words, do the compensating controls identified for compliance represent any conflict with other controls or activities that may introduce additional risks that may be unique to the organization? Of course, collaborating with risk management in this determination is essential.

These represent the major areas of decision criteria, and there are a number of other aspects to compensating security that fall within them, for example, physical security, business continuity and disaster recovery, legal and liability, audit, vendor and partner management, and hardware-related controls and management. Nevertheless, decision criteria will still roll up to technology, processes and procedures, risk, and compliance in some form and will typically differ depending on how security is interpreted and quantified and how controls are designed.

3.2.1.2 Primary Business Input Areas

How security decision-making processes and activities relate to business and how compensating controls take into account business expectations are equally important in meeting business demands. Risk and compliance work to consolidate security and business features to present findings, options, and recommendations for improvement. In most cases, cost is the overwhelming business attribute that is incorporated by security in managing security decisions. Although other business characteristics surface in the justification of security, these are typically value-add commentaries with little or no evidence to substantiate tangible returns, such as increased effectiveness, efficiency, quality, savings, and capability within the context of meeting business goals.

High-level business criteria can shed light on many of the features that need to be incorporated into adaptation activities to make security truly effective. These fall within the context of "means of production" as some of the basic elements of a business to function and produce goods and services.

- Resources—The collection of capabilities used in the production of goods and services. It is critical to the business that it maintains operationally and fiscally sound resources that provide the means of production of products and services for customers. How resources are managed, changed, reallocated, and applied is the result of addressing business dynamics and the desire to ensure profitability and growth while offering a foundation for innovation and development.
  - Infrastructure—A broad term representing the business assets, such as technology, facilities, tools, machinery, and equipment. Businesses are keenly focused on ensuring that assets are maintained, demonstrate returns, and are aligned to the goals of the organization. Moreover, businesses want to ensure the balance of resources relative to production and optimize capacity. Too few or too many unused elements of infrastructure can represent an imbalance that results in excessive costs and inefficiencies. From a security perspective, how well the infrastructure used

in the delivery and management of security is managed, especially in times of change that impact efficiency, will be of great interest to the business.

- Personnel—Regardless of the level of automation, human resources are needed in the overall management and delivery of products. Managing human resources can be difficult and as with infrastructure, managing and understanding capacity is essential to operations. There is far more unpredictability with human resources when compared to other forms of resources, specifically capability and stability. Businesses spend a great deal on resources and want to ensure that the correct number and type of resources are being deployed in a manner to optimize effectiveness. This relates to security in the application of resources to areas of security that are clearly identified as having a need, and the ability to adjust resource allocation based on visibility into demands the business places on the security organization. Moreover, it requires understanding the relationship between people and their skills, capabilities, and experience in incorporating change into the environment. For example, the introduction of new processes, standards, or technologies may include human resource demands that are not entirely achievable with existing resources, which forces the organization to look for outside support, additional resources, or training, all of which introduces direct costs. Indirectly, this may reduce the overall effectiveness of existing teams, representing a less tangible loss in previous human resource investments. Also, when there is a misalignment between the modifications and the capabilities of the people responsible for that environment costs may come in the form of training and education that is needed to fully realize the potential of the change and the existing investments in people.
- Knowledge—Business knowledge can manifest in a number of ways, such as information and processes, but also in proprietary production methods, capability, heritage, and culture. Businesses are focused on several keys areas of knowledge: development, sharing, management, and

protection. Organizations spend a great deal of money and time in the development of knowledge, and they want to ensure that those investments in people and process are effectively exploited without introducing risks or liabilities. How security is managed and delivered will play an important role in the valuation and, more specifically, the protection of knowledge that is valuable to the company, such as information assets and proprietary information. Knowledge relates to people's understanding of the environment, which for security is important in developing optional measures.

- Relationships—Business relationships represent an operational ecosystem comprising customers, partners, vendors, and suppliers all working together to achieve an objective and realize a goal. It is important for security to operate in a manner that helps the company rapidly embrace and exploit business relationships with minimal introduction of risk or threats and ensuring that relationships do not result in the exposure of sensitive information.

  - Customers—Although the term customer defines the consumer of goods and services, who the term represents may be very different depending on perspective, mission and charter, and, of course, the products being supplied. For many organizations the customer is obvious, such as patrons of a restaurant. However, for internal groups or partners the customer may also relate to the consumer. It should be of no surprise that businesses are focused on the consumer of their products and as such work to ensure that the needs of the customer are being met, which requires a mix of quality and adaptability. Moreover, this drives interpretations of capability and the capacity of existing or proposed capabilities. Putting aside the definition of customer for a security organization, the implications of business responses to customers act as one of the driving principles of change and adaptation. Of course, there are tactical attributes for security, such as compliance, the protection of customer information, and the integrity of customer-facing resources.

However, moving forward, security organizations will be increasingly exposed to the end-customer and must have the means to interpret pressures being placed on the business by customers and adapt.

- Suppliers—Most companies require some form of external input to business capabilities. Whether in the form of products or services, companies usually need resources from other companies to facilitate their own production. Businesses are very focused on optimizing the cost and liabilities that may be related to providers. Focusing on the cost of supplier goods or services is obvious because of the impacts to the bottom line and earning potential of the business. Equally important are any liabilities represented by the supplier, which can range from being forced into long-term commitments to get good pricing and thus reducing downstream options, or legal ramifications concerning product or service quality, or lack thereof, being passed through the business to the end-customer. There are obvious areas for security, such as ensuring sound policies and information security in the sharing of resources with suppliers. In fact, this security aspect alone will become an area of focus as organizations begin to adopt cloud computing. Nevertheless, many businesses see security as a form of supplier and as such security organizations must be prepared to demonstrate value and differentiation in assisting the company in meeting its goals.

- Identity—Also understood as brand recognition, identity is how people, other companies, competitors, and even governments perceive the organization. For example, when asked what company the color brown reminds people of, the large majority will say UPS. Many organizations will promote their brand through many avenues, including marketing, philanthropic activities, community involvement, and sponsorship, representing enormous investments and a great deal of overall valuation of the company. Security organizations can quickly resonate with their responsibilities relative to brand valuation. During the twenty-first century alone, a number of companies have become synonymous with a debilitating security event, virtually negating any previous brand development investments. Although this responsibility of security remains, it must also include the perspective of enabling the brand, not simply protecting it.

- Social Responsibility—A broad and encompassing term, it can include such things as using green energy, waste management, community involvement, and philanthropy, and it can be extended to such things as ethics, legality, and political activities. For security groups this can resonate as directives and demands coming from the business that are not typically associated with normal day-to-day business activities, which represents another opportunity to help the organization realize its goals.

- Contribution and Role—An organization's ability to contribute to the industry can develop in many ways, but mostly in the form of innovative offers or solutions that further differentiate the company, offset competition, and produce new revenue streams. Nevertheless, these can also appear as methods to create new standards and approaches that set a new bar of consumer expectation that others in the industry begin to replicate. An example is the Apple iPhone, which dramatically changed consumer buying patterns and the way others produced products.

- Strategy—Every organization has a strategy, which is likely to change over time due to changes in leadership, industry shifts, and economic conditions. Strategy is not necessarily the mission, but rather the mechanisms to achieve the mission. Business strategy can encompass a wide range of topics and actions, such as international expansion, increasing customer satisfaction, and expanding operations. A security organization's view into a business's strategy will become one of the foundational elements for adaptation and offers the ability to demonstrate value and enable the business. Understanding the decision-making process relative to strategy, including the aforementioned business input areas, security groups can adjust more readily and have a view into potential outcomes and pitfalls of those adjustments. In many ways, it's helpful to look at some of the drivers that influence strategy.

- Sustainability—Given the economic challenges of the last few years, sustainability has been a pervasive term. The business-level perspective of sustainability can range from concerns around the delivery of products and services, such as logistics, materials management, production facilities, and processing, to tactical elements, such as network uptime, system availability, information backup and retention, which is generally understood as business continuity and disaster recovery (BCDR) in the IT and security space. Within the context of optional measures and how these resonate for security sustainability will have deep and broad implications for the security strategy. Security experts quickly connect with the concept of sustainability from the perspective of availability. However, sustainability—and ultimately adaptability—is about resiliency, which is a fundamental shift in the security approach. Security organizations will have to learn how to adjust relative to sustainability and resilience as opposed to the concept of simply locking something down. This will resurface in many areas of the adaptable architecture, especially in services and the application of what is needed for the business as opposed what security may interpret as being required.

- Innovation—A key element to virtually every business is determining what can be introduced into the business that is new and different to support the vision and mission of the company. In most circles, innovation is understood as driving opportunity and exploiting untapped resources. This can exist as changes, such as reorganization, or new developments in process, technology, and people. When approaching innovation from a security perspective the first step is to understand how the company innovates and how critical it is to their success. Some organizations thrive on innovation, such as Google and Apple, whereas others on the opposite end of the spectrum may base their value on well-established, long-standing practices, for example, breweries in Great Britain, Germany, and

Australia. Of course, innovation can materialize within the business strategy as growth through mergers and acquisitions or more organic processes that leverage existing assets to approach new markets directly. The reason for innovation and the fundamental approach a company has for innovating will echo in the extent of security's role and how an identity of enablement will form. For security to effectively formulate optional measures that demonstrate value to the business beyond simply security, innovation—how important it is and how it is measured—will need to be digested thoroughly. Again, optional measures are an amalgamation of different points of value and importance compared against the intent of a demand. The more information that can be fed into the process and interpreted, the far more effective and aligned the end result will be.

- Cost/Investment Management—Managing costs and determining what investments gain the most attention is something security organizations are familiar with, and the role of cost in adaptation will be elaborated on below. Within the context of business strategy and understanding the influencers for that strategy, combined with the capacity to ensure they influence how security is applied and managed, cost and investment management needs to be viewed from a different perspective. The extent to which a company makes decisions can ultimately be tied to the associated costs. In fact, one could rightly argue that it is actually less about the cost and more about the returns. This is not to insinuate that companies don't want the best deal, but rather they want the best deal on something that will show dividends for the business. This may seem painfully obvious, and frankly it is. Therefore, the true purpose of this type of awareness is to better understand the criteria associated with investing and what success metrics dominate the business. For security to effectively gauge optional measures, the perspective of investment strategies will be as important as cost itself. There is always a detailed history of investments in projects and initiatives within an organization, and with a post-investment perspective security can accurately quantify measures of success and failure, which can be incorporated into the process. Again, this is not simply a cost analysis, but an investment and returns analysis that takes into account tangible, intangible, and cultural forms of valuation.

3.2.1.3 The Role of Cost in Adaptation   Perspective concerning the justification of investments and the associated valuation of cost can vary greatly between business and security. Given that cost is such a significant consideration in business decision-making processes, it is worthwhile to highlight the role of cost valuation within the context of security adaptation.

As stated above, cost—especially in today's climate—is a significant driving force in business decision-making processes. Although many things play into costs there are initial considerations for direct and indirect costs, such as evaluating the costs related to an identified new technology and/or those associated with enhancing existing technology. New technologies represent a direct and tangible cost as well as ongoing costs. Additionally, as more and more technology is introduced, the complexity of the environment is increased, which represents potential downstream costs to the business. Conversely, the exploitation of capabilities within existing investments can be viewed as a return. However, there may still be costs that need to be evaluated. For example, effectively turning on a feature in a router, firewall, or other technical element within an established system may include overhead in the management, support, and licensing of the feature. Nevertheless, in most cases, the costs and other cost-related impacts will likely be less than a completely new solution being introduced.

From a security perspective cost is typically put in the light of its relation to loss, whereas business perceives cost as a form of generating return in the form of hard dollars, strategic valuation, or building equity or potential. It is generally accepted within the realm of business owners that security does not provide direct returns on investment like traditional investments. However, this does not preclude the business's intent on getting something for its money. Security tends to base the value of an investment on the percentage of what could be lost. For example, a security control that costs 10% of the potential loss that would be experienced without the control would appear to be more acceptable than one that costs 50%. Nevertheless, even a small percentage is still a cost to the business, and as such the business will want more information concerning the implications of the investment beyond security.

In short, the business seeks financially related benefits for its monetary support of, in this case, security. Conversely, security usually takes the position of spending to protect existing investments. Both have merit, but they are opposing forces; one expects something in return, while the other assumes costs are inherent to the existence of assets. Given that security justification processes are inverse to traditional business approaches to investment and security has had a long-standing challenge in clearly articulating its potential, the opposing perspectives of investment become the foundation for debate, and hence the omnipresence of risk management and analysis in today's security approach.

The financial benefits sought by businesses are trailing indicators of the success of strategic or tactical activities. The inability to identify this nuance has represented challenges for various security managers seeking budgetary support focused on presenting a protective, risk-based argument. Businesses will always spend when there is confidence that the investment will translate to quantifiable benefits, but security has historically placed emphasis on risk and far less, if any, on benefits. It is within the area of demonstrating benefits and their relationship to achieving goals that is achieved by the ASMA and the evidence the ASMA produces. Executives will use the lack of financial benefits to displace initiatives that are not compelling to the mission of the business, and very rarely is security financially compelling. Adding to the challenge is the fact that benefits must not only exist, but they must have strategic merit. Theoretical or "out of left field" benefits may not gain attention because there are other higher priority strategies in play that do not gain from the proposed benefit.

The justification of security based on risk without reward and doing so with only tenuous association with strategic goals, which may not be a priority, will gain little attention. Additionally, this tactical approach translates as a commodity to the executive community and therefore is not necessarily compelling. It is for this reason that some security executives find themselves presenting an internally generated security initiative that is converted to an outsource scenario because it did not differentiate itself or was not compelling.

To successfully drive a security initiative that requires investments from the business it needs to be compelling, provide convincing benefits that relate to high priority goals and objectives, and be founded on quantified, defendable evidence that can be readily absorbed by the business. And the type of evidence businesses respond to is operational characteristics, such as performance, capability, capacity, and quality, and not necessarily risk and compliance. This relates to adaptation in the use of information and supporting evidence to support proactive behavior in security, and the ability to garner executive confidence in the projected outcome of proposed changes to address a need. Moreover, when this information includes specific details concerning performance and quality, among others, the business will see more benefit from the process than what it has traditionally experienced.

3.3 The Depth and Granularity of Security

Everything in security can be performed with varying degrees of depth and granularity. How comprehensively security is applied is governed by a number of conditions present in the business, such as security posture, culture, policy, risk, and compliance. It always comes down to how much is enough to satisfy the desired balance of all the applicable conditions. As mentioned above, much in the way defining optional measures (i.e., compensating controls) represents a fundamental and valuable characteristic of security capability, understanding what level and to what detail of security is needed for a particular situation is equally compelling. Again, this is something that security professionals perform regularly, and few within the business community successfully grasp how this manifests within the context of security despite employing a similar form of logic.

It is important to acknowledge that the methods employed in security are controlled by a combination of security- and non-security-related business influences that drive how much and to what depth security is applied. While it may seem obvious that security and business would collaborate to find a balance, in reality differences in opinion have acted as the catalyst for friction. In one hand you have the culture of security, which is driven by a set of formal and informal practices used to thwart an ever-changing set of threats and demands and strives for perfection when it is clearly understood that perfection is impossible. In the other is a business culture, which is driven by the growth of operationally and fiscally sound resources that provide the means of production for customers and strives for efficiency and simplicity. Business is about seeking opportunities and having a firm grasp on expending energy, doing so only when there is a return that ensures the growth and expansion cycle. However, security must defend against poorly understood adversaries and use continuously evolving tactics against a sea of vulnerabilities to create a defensive posture that attempts to compensate for virtually all conditions. In short, these are opposite cultures.

The challenge for security today is the lack of meaningful information that can be used to not only fine-tune the controlled environment relative to threats and demands, but that can act as clear evidence for the justification for security investments. The inability to truly quantify the exact control structure, whether technical or operational, has left many to rely only on standards that must be applied in their entirety. This is not an oversimplification of the existence of balance that is sought through risk analysis and management and the natural properties of negotiating security needs. However, one cannot deny the lack of specific information and how this becomes the basis for debate in qualifying investments. With the addition of compliance driving security in many organizations, it is no surprise that standardization relative to auditing is a strong force. Within this context, standardization has impeded the potential for security flexibility by defining what is required, and when faced with change security attempts to rationalize it relative to the standard. As alluded to above, this is not a survivable basis for security in the long run because standardization that is too rigid and lacks a clear understanding of "intent" hinders agility and adaptability.

Everyone in security understands the importance and relevance of "give and take" between business pressures and security drivers. Unfortunately, when these conditions surface it only contributes to the existing friction experienced with the business. One of the more difficult challenges security organizations will face moving forward is coming to grips with the fact that not every condition can be addressed by applying everything security demands. This is going beyond today's negotiation of security solutions where varying options are debated relative to cost, value, and effectiveness in trying to find the balance. It is about acknowledging this well ahead of time and creating a method to interpret demands and compare them to capabilities in order to accurately facilitate the level of security that achieves balance between the business and security.

It is extraordinarily common for a security group to be tasked with performing a security function but have restrictions in scope, time, or budget that eventually impact the level of security realized. Ultimately, this represents the age-old battle for many security organizations of garnering support from the business to ensure a meaningful security posture. However, just as the business has difficulty seeing the value of security and how it may relate to meeting its goals, which is at the heart of the disconnect between security and business, security has not necessarily taken advantage of its ability to quantify depth and granularity in relation to the business and security.

An excellent example of the depth and granularity phenomenon is found in vulnerability testing. Vulnerability testing, or more accurately the value of the results of vulnerability testing to security, is highly sensitive to scope, type, and depth. Let's look at each of these independently within a testing scenario targeted at identifying vulnerabilities in the demilitarized zone (DMZ) environment. When it comes to scope, assume that there are 50 unique IP addresses, one for each system residing in the DMZ, but the business only wants 20 systems targeted for the test. These systems perform certain services that are different from the remaining systems in the environment, hence the focused scope. While clearly reasonable from a business perspective, from a platform of security it is far better to test all the systems given that a vulnerability in one system can be used to initiate an attack against another in the same environment. This perspective of security is quite sound but is potentially difficult for the business to fully accept, and even if it does there are interpretations of risk that follow that lead back to the lack of solid evidence.

Next is the type of test. Given that the systems in scope are very similar in configuration and type, the business wants the test to focus on operating system vulnerabilities. However, the services that are being provided by the systems are based primarily at application level. From a security perspective it is best practice to also perform an application test given that this element of the systems is most exposed to the Internet, and other security controls such as firewalls limit access to lower system functions. In short, performing a test against the operating system and the application will provide the best visibility into the true state of vulnerabilities that exist in the systems and environment. However, the business may not fully understand these differences and not see value in performing both, especially considering the additional costs. Moreover, there may be budget limitations, time restrictions, or political drivers that influence the type of test.

Next is the depth of the test and why vulnerability testing is a good example to express the nuance of applying security. In testing for vulnerabilities, regardless of scope and type, there are typically levels of intensity, each of which provide more information on the viability, criticality, and type of threat characteristics related to the vulnerability. In simple terms this can be expressed as vulnerability scanning, vulnerability analysis, and penetration testing. Vulnerability scanning is exactly what the name implies. A scanning tool of some form (i.e., Nessus, etc.) is directed at the environment and performs an automated scan, and based on the existence of open ports and responses from the system a list of vulnerabilities is provided. From a security perspective this is a minimalistic approach but does offer some value. However, it lacks detail, validation, and is prone to false positives and false negatives. In short, it's a quick, cursory check. Nevertheless, this may be more than enough to satisfy the business, which may be required to perform a scan quarterly through policy or regulation.

As an extension to scanning, vulnerability analysis takes the testing beyond the tool and begins to validate and confirm identified vulnerabilities and seeks to expose any relationships between vulnerabilities that when combined represent a larger risk. Vulnerability analysis is a more in-depth review of the systems to better discern the criticality of a vulnerability relative to unique environmental characteristics. From a security perspective this provides substantially more value than simply scanning and offers a more concrete perspective that can be used to drive meaningful remediation activities. This process is more comprehensive, and so is the resulting information, and therefore the test is more valuable in implementing meaningful security.

Last is penetration testing, the final layer, if you will, to testing vulnerabilities. Until this point, interrogating the system and basing conclusions, such as criticality, on how the system responded and the interpretation of vulnerability combinations identified vulnerabilities.

In penetration testing the identified vulnerabilities are exploited to expose the true potential they represent to a threat agent and the impact this may represent to the organization. From a security perspective this can be very valuable. You can determine the criticality of the vulnerability relative to impact, the type and sophistication of threat agent needed to exploit the vulnerability, and the vulnerability's role in an attack vector. From this, highly tuned corrective actions can be articulated and supported with clear evidence proving the need. Given the depth of the test the results can be used to drive new standards, implementation practices, and future design requirements to reduce the likelihood of such a condition in the future. Moreover, the higher quality of the information concerning the true criticality of the vulnerability increases the effectiveness of remediation activities, thus representing greater efficiency.

However, in this example the business has elected to perform a vulnerability scan because that is what a requirement states, e.g., compliance, or that is what is understood as needed. Although greater depth may offer more visibility, who is to say that the same remediation performed from just scanning would not reflect actions taken with a more comprehensive test? Therefore, what is the value to the business in performing a more aggressive test to a broader scope that includes the application layer and penetration testing? Basically, the decision of the business concerning depth and granularity may have very little to do with security, if at all. The business is typically concerned with minimizing cost and doing only what is necessary, mostly due to the fact that rarely is business value tied to what security represents.

As a result two important points are raised. First, how does security interface more effectively with the business to demonstrate the value of approach relative to its goals? And second, given that security professionals can quickly understand the implications of more or less depth and granularity in the application of security, how can security be organized so that a balance is achieved between these two conceivably conflicting drivers?

The answer begins with organizing a security service so there are multiple methods of application that are reflective of the different levels of depth and granularity that are possible, thus allowing it to be tuned to the business demands. These service levels act as options to the business in having security applied in a manner that best meets its needs at that point in time. However, as implied, the business may elect to perform only what is required, a minimalistic approach, which may not benefit the overall security posture. Again, this is ultimately driven from the fact that security does not typically demonstrate business value, but rather is seen as a cost of doing business. Nevertheless, before security can start proving its value it must create a method to prove there is the potential for value and do so by leveraging the innate capabilities in balancing depth and granularity. In other words, security groups must fully embrace their existing capabilities in understanding the nuance of how security can be applied, codify it into the service, and express it in service delivery models that resonate more effectively with the business. From this platform a new relationship will begin to form with each party gaining more understanding of the role each plays in the success of the business. Ultimately, the business will see more of security's value to their mission and security will gain more appreciation of the demands being placed on the business.

3.4 The Commonality of Security

If we accept that the identification, definition, and management of optional measures are inherent and foundational to every security program, then we also accept that these philosophies are applicable to the execution of services, or more accurately, the execution of service combinations. The best way to understand this is to view security services in a compensating control model where they lend themselves to layering and offsetting one another to achieve an objective. This is possible due to the commonality that exists within security.

Although different organizations and different industries approach security in different ways and there is a wide range of security regulatory oversight, the fundamental elements of information security are extraordinarily similar. Nevertheless, how security materializes within an organization—how it comes to be and is managed over time—is influenced by a number of characteristics that are unique to each company. These include such things as culture, skills and experience, capability, technology, investment decision-making processes, interpretation of risk, legal liability, size and geography, and a number of other scenarios that add color to security in each organization, but all having a common theme. In other words, although each organization may feel it has a unique security approach, it is very likely that the fundamentals of its security program are shared with every other organization in the world. It typically comes down to depth, granularity, and, ultimately, focus that differentiates one program from another.

It is very important to recognize that regardless of how security is organized, there are inherent and unavoidable relationships that exist. By building an understanding of these relationships security adaptability can be achieved. This is not unlike compensating controls in the technical domain. The practice of compensating controls works because there is an underlying theme—an intent—that can be achieved by finding a combination of controls that not only meets the need, but does so effectively for that specific environment. Within the ASMA, security services involve the application of security in an organized manner, and given that security services are the manifestation of security, on some level they are inherently related to one another. The other features of the ASMA, such as risk, compliance, governance, and capability maturity management, work to ensure that services are applied effectively and are in alignment with business and security goals. In doing so the program produces information about security, security services, and business alignment. From this information the inherent and fundamental relationships of security that naturally exist between the security services can be exploited to address change.

For example, you may have a service for patch management and a service for vulnerability management, two different services that have inherent similarities in the mission—to reduce vulnerabilities. In fact, this scenario will exist with all the security services created simply because they have the same fundamental goals; it is generally their execution and focus that varies. This conclusion is based on the fact that security services are the commoditization and packaging of core security principles and capabilities in a manner that helps security be applied to and digested by the business.

Everyone in the security profession acknowledges that information security is very broad and omnipresent, and as such it is difficult to fully quantify in its entirety. As a result the security industry has compartmentalized security to express all its facets in a manner that promotes organization; ISO-27002 is a good example of compartmentalization of security. Although compartmentalization of security is quite common, few approaches look to take advantage of the relationships between them to optimize security. The ASMA not only seeks to accomplish this, but it introduces business-specific information to add to the layers of data to make informed decisions and increase the confidence in addressing change.

The adaptive security architecture uses security services to organize and apply security, not unlike many security standards organize security into groups that can be managed. However, it takes several steps to ensure that the different areas of security—security services—are interlinked within the program and reflect the natural security relationships that already exist between them. Without this interconnectedness in the program and between services, stovepipes in security materialize. It is common for a security organization to have several groups focused on different aspects of security, which results in the loss of the ability to capture and act on the intrinsic relationships that have become blurred.

Typically, is it only the CSO sitting atop the entire security program who can clearly see all the discrete elements of the program coming together to make for a meaningful security posture. However, the ability to make valuable decisions within the separate stovepipes is greatly encumbered. Information must flow from each to the CSO, be processed, and then be passed back down. Clearly, a more effective and efficient model is for each of the areas to be aware of its role as it relates to others. For example, how does one group that is responsible for vulnerability testing adjust its methods, scope, and processes to compensate for activities occurring in a different and distant security group focused on perimeter security? The answer is it doesn't always happen and when it does happen, it's typically based on relationships, organic communications, or sound management that identifies the relationship and takes action. The critical point to be made is that each individual group works towards specific goals and objectives that relate to its mission and charter as well as an overall security vision. However, what does not necessarily happen is those tactical targets taking into consideration the activities of others in different security groups with different specific goals and objectives. Albeit, each of these stovepipes are typically pointed in the same strategic direction, but the ability to adapt and do so quickly and effectively requires an additional dimension of operational awareness into other groups, or specifically, other services. The concept of interconnectedness within the program and between security services involves mirroring what is already a reality in security: That regardless of how security is organized and compartmentalized, there will always be tangible relationships between them affecting how security is realized and managed.

Covered in more detail in following chapters, security services are a method for packaging security activities so that they are more easily aligned to the business, produce information for the betterment of security and the business, and ensure that the security program has operational integrity. The overarching management structure in risk, governance, and compliance management helps ensure that the program functions as a whole. Nevertheless, it is the services that ultimately connect the security group to the business and are used to maintain the security posture and compliance. As such, the security services can be tuned and adjusted in how they are applied relative to not only their specific goals and performance, but to each other to achieve an optimal balance between business and security.

In this light, services are analogous to technical security controls and interact in much the same way being combined to achieve a greater level of security. To continue with the patch management and vulnerability management services example, each gains value from the other and one is not necessarily a predecessor or overly reliant on the other to facilitate the objective. Patches may be applied to specifically address an identified vulnerability or be used to ensure system stability. Vulnerability testing may expose a weakness that can be addressed through the application of a patch or modifications to other controls. Nevertheless, there is an inherent relationship between these two services that can be exploited to address business dynamics and ultimately facilitate adaptability. Interestingly, relationships of this nature will exist between all the services in some fashion. However, to truly take advantage of these relationships and not become unmanageable, it is necessary to identify key factors that not only exist between two or more services but do so in a manner that promotes adaptation. In other words, while there may be numerous connections and valuable interactions between services, some are far more valuable to the mission of the security group and business than others; nevertheless, all are applicable.

3.5 Adaptability and Services

At this point we've acknowledged the value of optional measures and the reality that although security services are unique a tight relationship exists that connects all of them to each other based on the fundamentals of security. The "connective tissue" that binds the security services together is predominately based on the innate core principles of security, meaning a change in one service—how it is defined, applied, and managed—will inevitably have implications, small and large, to all the other services and, of course, the security posture. Although some of these natural interactions may be unnoticeable, they occur on some level. Comparatively, changes to one or more services can show very visibly how other services are performing relative to the security mission. The key is having the ability to identify, predict, and exploit these interactions for the betterment of security and the business.

However, given the definition of security services and all that is implied in the adaptive security architecture, there are other relationships between services that go well beyond security. The discussion so far has been focused mostly on the interactions as they relate to security. The example of the relationship that exists between vulnerability and patch management was provided as an introductory illustration to make a point from a security perspective. Nevertheless, we understand the ASMA as a comprehensive model that is ultimately concerned with the application of security in the form of security services that are aligned with the business. Security services and the supporting features comprise an array of processes that seek to expose many operational aspects of security, such as performance, management, quality, business alignment and value, costs, resources, and methods. In fact, it can be argued that the act of traditional security in the definition of a security services is minute compared to the other business characteristics that define a service. In their entirety, these other non-security-related characteristics of a service and all the mechanisms within the supporting features of the ASMA can be defined as the business side of the security program. All of the features defined are directed at connecting with the business, driving effectiveness and efficiency in the application of security, promoting improvement, and most importantly gaining visibility into the operational effectiveness of the security program as a business unit.

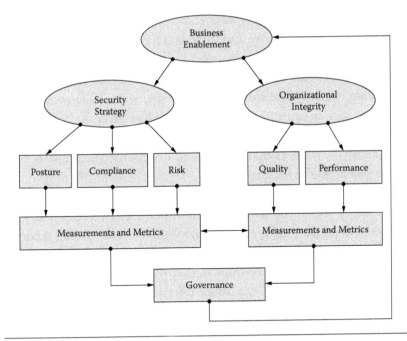

Figure 3.1   Two forces.

Within the security architecture there are two forces at work. As demonstrated in Figure 3.1, on one side is the focus on security and the resulting measurements and metrics that define the level of success of ensuring compliance, managing risk, and ultimately effectively balancing threats, controls, and assets.

On the other side is organizational integrity, which ensures efficient and effective business operations and the focus on performance and quality measurements and metrics. Both produce information that is used in providing value to the business. When combined they provide compelling properties that promote adaptability.

3.5.1 Implications of Change

The business-related information adds granularity to the possibilities of adaptation of security activities, including the traditional application of security as well as the operational characteristics of security. Performance, quality, posture, compliance, and risk combine to give a holistic view of security that will allow security to adjust to a more informed perspective. To illustrate, assume that you have a service that is, from a security perspective, clearly associated with another. You can accurately identify and understand how changes in one may affect the other in how security is applied and realized. Based on this relationship you also identify operational characteristics, such as cost, budgeting, quality, resourcing requirements, service life cycle management, service utilization, success and failure rates in contributing to business performance indicators, and a plethora of other information across the services that can be used to enhance the decision processes when faced with change.

Within this context, change must take into account both business and security attributes. Changes in how one area of security may be applied will affect other areas of security and even the overall security posture due to the inherent relationships in security. The objective is to understand these relationships so that when changes are necessary the security organization can adapt effectively to meet revised business and security needs without introducing unnecessary risk. The same can be said for the business expectations and how operational elements of security are performing. The objective is to not only find a balance in the application of security that meets both business and security goals, but to have the means to maintain that balance (adaptation) in the face of changes that may stem from new security needs or business dynamics.

Nevertheless, any form of change can have direct and indirect implications for security, the business, or both. Regardless of how change is introduced into the environment, whether proactive or reactive, it results in a collection of actions and adjustments. How these adjustments materialize represents the difference between compensating and adapting, with the former being more tactical and focused on the specifics of the change, whereas the latter takes into account more diverse information to determine a broader spectrum of impacts, both positive and negative.

To elaborate, assume for the moment that the cost for delivering a service exceeds expectations, creating additional gaps in quality and effectiveness. The gaps can be related to the introduction of new tools that were not planned for; more time and material than expected that was consumed in the delivery of the service; the allocation of additional, unplanned resources; or as inefficiencies related to wasteful acts. However, the service is meeting security-related objectives and the metrics demonstrating the effectiveness of security are optimal. Without the perspective of business performance incorporated into the model, this scenario would appear successful because it is meeting security goals. Unfortunately, this is common in the industry because most security organizations are, understandably, acutely focused on meeting security expectations and not necessarily specific business measurements. This is not to imply that security organizations are not concerned with or measured against costs and business goals. However, business goals are typically high-level and encompass all of security or its major elements. As such, they may not be integrated in the application of specific security activities, so when gaps in operational effectiveness surface they are typically rolled up with other areas of security that are performing well, thus presenting a better picture of overall performance.

Of course, the opposite can be true, in which costs are optimized and are meeting business expectations, but the security portion of the equation is not successful in managing compliance or risk, which can be related to poor planning or overly optimistic projections. It can also be the result of a minimalistic investment strategy in security by the business, which is usually rooted in the inability to effectively justify the true costs of security. Basically, there is the potential for the performance of the organization from a business and security perspective to not be in sync. In either case, there is a requirement for more information in order to make an informed decision on how to make corrections to get the service in line with security and business expectations.

In either case adjustments have to be made to the service, but how to do so without reducing the security posture, introducing risk, affecting compliance efforts, or affecting business expectations is the root of the challenge. In traditional scenarios in which a division or group within the security organization fails to meet security and/or business goals, changes are made directly to that group. For example, a group within the security organization is responsible for all vulnerability testing. This group not only has resources dedicated to testing networks, systems, and applications, but it supports a partner model to incorporate testing from vendors to supplement the program. Based on a performance review of the group, management finds that spending is too high and it begins to make changes to reduce costs to an acceptable level. As a result, management decides to cut or reallocate 35% of the staff within the vulnerability-testing group and focus on one partner that provided testing for the best overall price when compared to the others. The basis of the shift is to minimize cost and shift more of the activity to a third party in order to reduce overhead and HR-related costs.

Although vulnerability testing continued, there were unintended consequences directly associated with the changes in the group. For example, not all the testing required for certain business units could be performed by the selected vendor without additional costs, the level of quality expected by the business waned due to a gap between internal processes and those of the provider, there was an increased occurrence of false positives, and more systems were directly impacted by testing than before causing an increase in downtime. Additionally, there were consequences related to security in other groups. For example, information about application vulnerabilities was no longer effectively incorporated with the code review team, which affected their ability to address issues in development, testing of vulnerabilities became out of sync with patch management activities resulting in more management in both groups, and alerts increased in the security monitoring group causing more tickets that needed to be processed.

This is a common approach to addressing cost issues in a business unit, especially in difficult economic times, and the question becomes, what will be the impacts to the security posture, other areas or groups within the security organization, and in meeting strategic security and business objectives by implementing such changes? Few can answer that question because the information simply does not exist, which does not allow the business an opportunity to consider those attributes or other areas of security in the decision-making process. Management is typically intently focused on correcting the problem that was identified and supported by direct evidence as opposed to attempting to quantify less tangible qualities of the program. It's a natural process in business: inspect what you expect and make corrections swiftly and with focus. Frankly, this applies to virtually all things in business. However, as discussed above, security has very deeply rooted relationships where any change in one area of security will have an impact on other areas of security and will affect the overall posture.

In this example, the differentiating factor is the indisputable evidence of business performance inexorably setting the scope of information for decision-making purposes, making less tangible, indirect implications for security pale in comparison. Therefore, it is important for security organizations to develop the means to express inherent security relationships in a manner that produces evidence of equal importance to expand the scope of information influencing the decision.

Although a simple example, not only is this very common, but there are many levels to the depth of implications that can resonate far and wide, affecting the security posture and the effectiveness of security-related activities. This brings us back to defense-in-depth and compensating controls. It's the understanding that security is a balance of interconnected people, process, and technology that is working together to ensure a meaningful security posture. Once this perspective is fully embraced, those empowered with detailed information on all aspects of security and business can better adjust the operational characteristics of security with a great deal of clarity and foresight into the implications that may impact the security posture or the ability to achieve business objectives.

3.5.2 Services as Optional Measures

Up to this point several compelling and related assertions have been made that are worth summarizing prior to exploring the role of security services in adaptation.

- Compensating control: The untapped sophistication that exists within every security organization to identify and employ alternative measures to achieve the desired security posture. The processes used in the formation of optional measures are at the heart of adaptation.
- Depth and granularity: The reality that security can be applied in varying degrees in order to achieve the desired balance between threat and asset according to the business demands and risk. As opposed to an "all or nothing" approach, the application of security can be tuned to the environment based on a combination of business need, security requirement, risk, compliance, and time.

- Security commonality: The intrinsic relationship that exists between all elements of security regardless of how they may be organized or standardized. Although there may be differences in how security is employed, managed, or measured, virtually all security programs have the same underlying ingredients. It is important to facilitate a model that reflects these relationships in security and leverage them to manage change more effectively.

- Implications of change: Understanding that any change in one area of security, how it is performed, managed, or applied, will have implications to other areas of security affecting the security posture. Changes in process, capability, technology, method, utilization, application, or depth will inevitably resonate in some form throughout the program and within the business. Having the ability to identify and ultimately predict implications of change based on comprehensive information will substantially increase the confidence in the outcome.

- Business and security information: Based on the two primary forces at work within the ASMA, information concerning the security performance and the business attributes of a service, when combined, offer substantial value in addressing change. By incorporating information about business and security performance into the decision-making process a greater balance between the security posture and the demands of the business can be achieved.

Each of these philosophies builds on one another to create the foundation of adaptation. When combined they express the core attributes that are needed to effectively address business and security dynamics. Of course, while some are inherent to security today, others need to be created, specifically the information that is the result of combining business and security performance. As introduced, services, along with the other features, provide this information. As one of the essential parts of the ASMA, the way services are defined plays a critical role in the ability to adapt. As an introduction, services are not simply an alternative to the organization of security, but rather a comprehensive collection of operational, delivery, and management attributes that are packaged in a manner to address nuances in the business. Each service represents a particular area of security, such as patch management, incident management, or security monitoring, and within each are degrees of applicability that define how that service will be applied for a given condition. Detailed in the following chapters, these degrees are referred to as metals (i.e., gold, silver, bronze, etc., or whatever model ultimately suits your organization) that express service options in how the service will be applied. Determining which metal is appropriate is based on the collaboration between the various features of the ASMA, such as risk and compliance, and the business unit's (or customer's) needs. Based on the different delivery methods that exist within each service combined with the above list of assertions, adaptation is not only supported by visibility into security and business performance, but is enabled by how services are defined and applied.

Through analysis of the services it is found that there are dynamics between them. For example, one service is meeting business expectations and not security, one is overutilized compared to the others, or there are ample, unused resources in one versus another service that has limited capabilities. Given the amount of information concerning the delivery and management of security services, there can be a wide range of variance. Of course, some of this may be by design, whereas in other cases it may express areas for improvement.

In addition to the direct business and security performance measurements and the like from services, there is an identified relationship between a given failing service and others that may be less utilized, which can be combined to present a compensating blend to achieve the intent of the failing service indirectly, all the while not introducing more cost or risk. Of course, there are several important considerations. First of all there are always implications of change to a service in the realm of security. Therefore, while the compensating services appear to offset the failings of the primary service, other areas of security may exist that could be impacted by the change. Secondarily, the adjustment must take into consideration the achievement of business and security goals that were being met by the failing service. As the adjustments are made it is necessary to review the business and security performance of the service and the compensating services to ensure there is alignment. In virtually all cases, there will be a gap. The gap is the result of the fact that each service has its own set of goals and objectives, and if this were not the case the service would simply not exist—it would be redundant. The question becomes more of how large the gap is as opposed to if one exists. As a result, when changes are made directly to services or how they are applied in combination to address a dynamic that is occurring in the business or as a means to correct deficiencies or increase effectiveness, perfection is difficult to achieve. However, minimizing the gap between corrections and results is far more possible due to the available information driving adjustments, from the results of adjustments, and the existence of capability maturity management and governance to fine-tune underlying capabilities.

Additionally, it goes beyond adjustments in the application of multiple services to achieve optimal overall performance and include the modification of the service options, thereby simply making changes to the service in question. For example, the options (e.g., metals) in the service may be radically changed to hone the service to the point where a balance can be realized. Of course, as discussed, every change will have an effect on each of the other services in some way. The key is to understand the dynamics between the services from a security and business perspective. The point to be made is there is far more information that can be collected about services and their security and business performance. Moreover, there are deeply rooted relationships that naturally occur between security services that can be used to address a number of challenges, in addition to the variances that can be made directly to the service.

In managing adaptation in the security program it is essential that the relationships between the services from a security perspective be identified. The more comprehensive the matrices of these interactions, the more effectively and efficiently change will be managed. Much of this information will stem from the development of services. The act of defining services and the various levels, options, and capabilities required to deliver them will provide direction in formulating a perspective on how they relate to one another. Moreover, risk management will play an important role. Risk management will have a more comprehensive view of the security posture and as such will have a unique perspective on the implications of dynamics that may be occurring between services, and especially how they are being delivered and at what level of granularity. Determining interactions is a top-down approach and begins with the formation of the security strategy, which ultimately manifests itself in the formation of security services. Services will be mapped to different aspects of the strategy to make for a complete picture of the mission of the security program and what is in its remit. Like pieces to a puzzle, services will interconnect to fill the gap that makes up the envelope of security.

3.5.3 Defining Service Relationships

There are a number of approaches to defining service relationships. As shared, security has a strong foundation of consistency, and although different organizations will have a wide range of approaches, the fundamentals are similar. Of course there is a tangible connective force between the structure and type of services and the ability to exploit service relationships. To get to a point where relationships can be identified and exploited for adaptation, the evolution of security and how it manifests in the company needs to be reviewed.

There is a collection of core security ingredients that act as the basis for any security program. These pass through influencers that are distinctive to an organization and form the unique approach that a company will have to security. The result will drive how security services are organized and defined, and to what granularity. Therefore, the objective is to isolate the core ingredients and evaluate basic associations so that once the services are defined a common set of themes can surface that can be used in adaptation.

3.5.3.1 Core Security Ingredients   As with all things related to security, there is much room for interpretation and opinion; therefore, obtaining agreement on the core ingredients for security can become elusive. The goal is to attempt to quantify security in a manner that can be applied in general to any environment as a whole or in part. One approach is to leverage established standards, such as ISO-27002, among others, to touch on the major areas of security. However, it is helpful to think of the very foundation of security … the existence of controls to protect assets from threats—simple. Threats are undesirable elements that can cause harm, steal or destroy information and assets, or inappropriately use resources. Simply put, controls are methods for reducing opportunity for threats to come to fruition, and vulnerabilities are basically gaps in controls and offer opportunity to threats. Technically speaking, everything else is a method of organization. For example, compliance is an established set of expectations to quantify assets and define controls, and risk is a method to evaluate what challenges these combinations represent. Both are vehicles for expressing the fundamentals of security in a manner that help us to quantify and qualify security. Once defined, relationships can be loosely created to draw out how one may influence another. An important aspect of this initial exercise is to avoid too much detail or complexity and keep the points of reference at a high level. Table 3.1 provides one example for demonstration purposes.

3.5.3.1.1 Security Associations Associations can be projected from the collection of basic security ingredients. Clearly, how these are formed has a great deal to do with what ingredients were identified and their interpretation. Basic security associations are used as a reference during the development of security services, but most importantly when implementing changes to adapt to various conditions. Security associations can be very strong, meaning there is little room for interpretation between their roles and heavy reliance on one to another, or light or distant associations in which they are not intimately intertwined, but each gains advantages over the other. Moreover, associations are typically bidirectional with some acting as more dominant in the relationship. For example, there is a relationship between network security and remote access security, but it is likely that network security features, such as policies, standards, and practices, will act as the foundation to many of the design and implementation practices of a remote access solution.

The objective is to establish associations based on a set of criteria that when combined exposes interdependencies with different levels of potential interaction representing the strength or importance of the association that will act as the foundation for adaptability. As demonstrated in the Figure 3.2, security ingredients A, B, C, and D have one or more relationships with the others based on certain characteristics represented as lines labeled 1, 2, and 3. Therefore, A, B, and C have an association based on characteristic "1," A has a characteristic of "2" with B and C, and B has an association with D based on characteristic "3." Each characteristic (line) may represent different forms of relationships that define the strength of the bond. However,

Table 3.1 Security Mappings

SECURITY AREA	CORE INGREDIENT	SUPPORTING FEATURE(S)	DESCRIPTION/RELEVANCE
• Setting expectations	• Security policy	• Guidance • Procedures • Alignment to controls	Defines the overall expectations of security that ultimately influence how security is realized and managed within the organization. Policy will organize corporate expectations of security behavior into statements that are typically supported by guidance and direction. For organizations using policy management tools, procedures, standards, and controls are linked to the policy as well as interlinks with regulation. It is not uncommon for today's security policy to be a comprehensive collection of information and security influencers tied together to stated corporate requirements.
	• Security standards	• Industry standards • Regulatory-based standards • Internal standards	Standards help to organize and specify the underlying workings of security expectations set by policy or regulation. They can be quite comprehensive and represent different levels of focus. Some standards set overall frameworks, such as ISO-27002; others provide for specific activities and methods, such as NIST's Special Publications 800 series; and others may state specific and detailed requirements, such as PCI's Data Security Standard. A policy or regulation may make a statement and provide guidance, but it is typically the standard that establishes the structure and details addressing what is necessary and prescribed to meet that expectation.

(Continued)

Table 3.1 Security Mappings (Continued)

SECURITY AREA	CORE INGREDIENT	SUPPORTING FEATURE(S)	DESCRIPTION/RELEVANCE
• Threat domain	• Vulnerability management	• Testing and verification • Patching/updating • Configuration management	A very fundamental aspect to security, for obvious reasons, is having the ability to understand and manage vulnerabilities. Of course, there is a relationship between vulnerabilities and threats, and security's basic responsibility is to accurately understand the state of each of these environments, how they may interact over time relative to changing conditions, and the ability to leverage this knowledge to effectively apply controls. One could argue that virtually all the work that is performed by security is either identifying and fixing a vulnerability, or implementing a security control to address a gap (aka vulnerability) between a threat (hackers to compliance) and an asset.
	• Threat analysis/ management	• IDS/IPS • Monitoring • Anti-malware	Threats come in many forms and can be seen as hackers and malware to employees and compliance. Threat analysis is a fundamental attribute of security in the identification and classification of threats to ensure that security is addressing a plausible condition. Secondarily, from these activities, security must apply controls that are primarily (not entirely) directed at mitigating identified threats to reduce risk. Anti-virus software and technologies such as IDS, as the name implies, is to fundamentally stop identified threats.

| • Incident management | • Identification
• Classification
• Response | The relationship between threats, vulnerabilities, and controls, and all that is implied, represents a basic proactive nature. Learn about threats, discover and repair vulnerabilities, monitor the environment, and implement controls that deal directly with the threat or controls that are meant to reduce the spectrum of threat. Nevertheless, at some point an event will be realized. It is necessary to have the means to identify that an event is occurring or has occurred, and the ability to classify the event that will ultimately determine the response. As with many basics in security, incident management—how it materializes in an organization—can encompass a wide range of other security features and activities. But when viewed strictly from a fundamental view, incident management is a response mechanism for when there is a gap between controls and assets. |
| • Control domain | • Identity management | • Identification of users, processes, systems, and applications
• Access requirements | Identification of those resources that may need or require access to systems and services. Although usually associated with just a username and rarely separate from passwords and access controls, this focuses on the attributes that define the resource in order to ensure that all downstream security controls are effectively applied. With the ability to accurately identify a resource, the assets that are needed can be precisely quantified, which results in the more effective and efficient application of security controls. For obvious reasons, identity is rarely distinguished from access controls. But, from a basic perspective of security, identity management is the quantification and qualification of those elements that are or are going to be permitted to utilize resources and assets. It is the antithesis of threat analysis, and defining the characteristics of a person or system needing or wanting access is a critical and fundamental aspect of security. |

(Continued)

Table 3.1   Security Mappings (Continued)

SECURITY AREA	CORE INGREDIENT	SUPPORTING FEATURE(S)	DESCRIPTION/RELEVANCE
	• Access and authorization control	• User access management • Network access control • System access control • Application access control	Building on the basic principle of security in identifying resources that require access to assets, security is fundamentally about ensuring those resources have been authorized to use stated assets in order to effectively control access. Feeding this process is visibility into information value and classification and the methods of access that provide the perspective of threat. Access and authorization represent a tipping point in security as a balance of who, what, how, and why related to the basic interaction between communities (which includes threats); assets, such as information, systems, networks and application; and controls. Ultimately, this deeply rooted characteristic of security results in changes in the control environment. Therefore, identity management and threat analysis offer a view into the spectrum of wanted and unwanted features approaching the controlled environment. In many, if not most, cases there are overlaps. How access controls are implemented, what type of control it may be, and how it may be bonded (layered) with other controls is inexorably tied to the spectrum of communities.
	• Continuity	• Change management • Fault and error management • Audit	Continuity, in this context, means continuity in posture. Much like regulatory compliance, business continuity represents a feature as a result. The term gives the impression of business continuity and disaster recovery plans, systems, technology, and strategy, which is natural. However, fundamentally, continuity is the root driving all these elements. Even in the security triad of CIA, the "A" is an expression of continuity and as such is fundamental.

| • Operations | • Methodologies
• Third-party management
• Roles and Responsibilities
• Planning
• Maintenance | Regardless of the dynamics that may be occurring, at some point or within different areas of the environment there is some form of security stability. A basic element of security is maintaining that environment. Although there are adjustments needed for changes in the threat and vulnerability environment, it is virtually impossible for a system to be implemented and left alone. Environments must be maintained, and therefore methods and the people that perform various management functions have to be defined. Frankly, one could argue that operations is not a fundamental element of security, and that it is yet another vehicle for security and indicative of many other elements of security coming together. Yet contrary to this, operations can be seen as a mechanism to apply security. |
| • Asset domain

  • Data and information
    management | • Backup and recovery
• Cryptography
• Information classification | Clearly, information security is focused on information assets. In its purest form, everything about security is based on assets, because without assets there is no need for security. There is an inherent demand by security to know what information is important (or not); its relevance to the mission of the company; the impact if it were lost, stolen, destroyed, or changed; and where it is located. Of course, this is exceedingly difficult to determine in today's businesses, hence the focus on threats, vulnerabilities, and controls. Nevertheless, some of the controls are encryption, which is in high demand, such as hard drive encryption and backup and recovery solutions. Moreover, security is finding a role in data management and data warehousing. |

(Continued)

Table 3.1 Security Mappings (Continued)

SECURITY AREA	CORE INGREDIENT	SUPPORTING FEATURE(S)	DESCRIPTION/RELEVANCE
	• People	• Training and education • Human resources	People are a critical asset and security is involved with people in a number of ways. Security is tasked with ensuring people are trained and educated about security. Without a general understanding and awareness of threats and security expectations (i.e., policy) people can inadvertently introduce threats, cause harm, or introduce—or act as—a vulnerability. Moreover, security is concerned with providing a safe and sanitary (i.e., malware-free) work environment. However, people can also represent threats, such as disgruntled employees; employees who do not conform to policy, which represents potential legal liability; employees reacting to workforce reductions; employees collaborating with external threats (i.e., espionage); and a number of other conditions can represent a challenge to the security posture. Ultimately, security is concerned with the safety of people. Mostly associated with physical security and disaster recovery, it can be said that many of security's focal points are to ensure people are protected and empowered.

- Physical
  - Secured areas
  - Equipment security
  - Facility security

There is some argument concerning the role of traditional security related to guns, guards, and gates. Many organizations separate information security and physical security while others combine them. There is no wrong or right answer. Nevertheless, security—fundamentally—includes physical attributes, whether very comprehensive or concerned only with specific areas relative to information, such as the physical security of backup media, and security will have some role concerning the nature of controls in the physical domain. Arguably, this feature can be easily placed in the physical control domain as opposed to the asset domain. Nevertheless, physical assets have a unique way of directly correlating to controls. In other words, it is typically more about the physical asset that needs to be quantified, which drives how physical controls materialize. Regardless, this is one of those basic elements of security, like operations, that can be moved or removed.

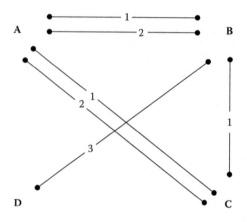

Figure 3.2 Basic associations.

more importantly is the number of shared characteristics that may exist between two or more ingredients, which demonstrates an even greater bond. Therefore, we're looking for the type and quantity of characteristics that can be found between core security ingredients to help evaluate potential optional measures in the resulting services.

In forming initial perspectives of security associations, the following is a set of characteristics that can be used: security intent, security domain, operational interactions, and business indicators.

3.5.3.1.2 Security Intent Security intent is related to the general approach and purpose of the ingredient relative to others. For example, identity and access management is a foundational element to any security program and its intent is to ensure that people and processes are identified, authenticated, and provided the assigned authority prior to accessing or using company resources. This intent, or role in the security environment, has very close ties to data management, such as data classification, data encryption, and data backup and recovery, to name a few. Identity and access management has relationships with network security, operations security, compliance, and application security, and distant relationships with physical security and human resource security. In short, security intent is simply understanding security interdependencies that may exist based solely on the security definition and not taking into account business attributes or other considerations.

Defining the intent and matching it with other elements of security can be far more challenging than one may assume. In simple terms, there is a great deal of interpretation and opinion that can affect how security intent associations are formed. In an attempt to avoid over-complication, one approach is to define the basic role and security attributes for each of the ingredients and start by matching the attributes. For example, the security ingredient forensics has the simple attributes of investigative, evidence, responsive, and you find shared attributes with monitoring and incident management. The challenge becomes ensuring focus and weeding out weak links because, as discussed, security has very deep, inherent relationships regardless of organization, and this will become exceedingly clear during this entire exercise. Therefore, it can be rightly argued that forensics (and every other security ingredient) has an association with virtually every other part of security, but not all of them are truly meaningful. It is important to acknowledge that this is only one of several characteristics that will be used to form relationships, and overly interpreted associations will quickly become unmanageable.

3.5.3.1.3 Security Domain Security domains are basic areas of security that can act as methods to establish relationships that can be used later. If you break security down using the fundamental philosophy of applying controls to protect assets from threats, you find that security can be articulated in simple terms. For example, one form of simplification can be managing vulnerabilities, establishing and enforcing policy, controlling access, monitoring activities, and responding to events. Of course, there are others, such as "protect, detect, and respond," "confidentiality, integrity, and availability," and "threat, vulnerability, and impact," for which there are a number of other variations. Generally, these can be anything that resonates most deeply with the security organization. However, they need to be few in number and represent the very basic feature of information security and not overly high level. For example, "compliance" would not be a good area because compliance is simply another vehicle used to collect security into a set of expectations, which in turn can be further reduced. It is likely many will see every security ingredient having a role in each of the basic security domains, which is not helpful. However, focusing on the dominating trait of the security ingredient is essential in order to assign it to the best domain. To offer an example, two basic ingredients may be network security and system security. Network security could be more aligned with controlling access as opposed to managing vulnerabilities for system security. As this simple example demonstrates, the value of the exercise greatly depends on how the security ingredient is defined, which will be the primary factor in determining which of the basic security domains best represents it.

The objective is to determine the very basic role of a security ingredient relative to the fundamental nature of security. For example, the ingredient configuration management may play a role in vulnerability management, policy, controlling access, monitoring, and response, but based on how configuration management is focused in your organization you may determine that the most relevant associations are with vulnerability management and policy. Another way to view associations based on security domain is identifying the top two to three activities that would be employed in the event of a change. For example, a new vulnerability is published resulting in a number of actions that may begin with a vulnerability test and move to applying patches and making configuration changes. These may be followed by changes in policy, standard system builds, adjustments to application development and a broad collection of downstream activities. In this case, the basis for the relationships is relative to how security activities are prioritized in the organization, which helps place the focus on the associations that best reflect the security strategy.

3.5.3.1.4 Operational Interactions Operational interaction starts to move away from a strictly security perspective and introduce attributes that demonstrate relationships concerning how security is applied and delivered. Understandably, this particular characteristic may be challenging for some organizations, especially for very small security groups. Operational interactions seek to define relationships between security ingredients based on capabilities across people, process, and technology. In all cases each ingredient will, by definition, include a set of processes that people must perform in order to realize that area of security, and may include specific technology ranging from tools to security systems. In many cases, organizations will find shared resources as well as specialized resources for different parts of security. For example, the security ingredient called application security may share tools and resources that are also used in performing vulnerability tests on applications. It is not uncommon to find the same people who test applications to be intimately involved in the development life cycle of applications. The same group responsible for data encryption (cryptographic controls) may be deeply involved in identity and access management. Technology used in monitoring and log management may be essential to performing forensics and incident response. In fact, it may be found that the person who is responsible for incident management is also a resource used in forensic investigations.

The goal of establishing relationships of this nature is to expose areas of delivery capacity, process management, and technical requirements. It does not require a detailed analysis of existing processes, capabilities, and utilities. Any gap in one of these areas to address the high-level associations should be readily identifiable, as well as shared features that may exist. Associations derived from operational aspects of security are quite valuable in the light of adaptation, acting as part of the foundation for decision-making processes relative to capacity and resource management. As challenges in meeting business and security expectations are identified it may be the result of poor resource allocation, which can be exacerbated by making changes that on the surface appear reasonable but fail to take into account the impacts on other areas of security. Moreover, establishing security ingredient relationships that take into account people, process, and technology will help identify areas for increasing efficiency and effective employment of resources.

Within this context are a few results that show how the operational interaction relationships are defined. In some cases there will be what amounts to gaps in overall capacity, such as overutilization of human resources, meaning that one person, or a few, have the roles and responsibilities of many, are lacking in processes, or do not have the necessary tools or all the tools necessary. Conversely, there may be areas of overcompensation, in which there are collections of specifically skilled resources and purpose-built technical solutions that are not only underutilized, but cannot be effectively applied to other areas of security. By investigating operational interactions in the early phases of quantifying security ingredients within the organization, the ability to develop services that are initially aligned to established delivery models for security is streamlined. More importantly, it provides visibility into how services and other supporting features can evolve to achieve greater alignment.

3.5.3.1.5 Business Indicators   Business indicators cover a broad set business features, such as goals, objectives, and financial requirements, that can help to relate one security ingredient to others. In theory this is similar to basing relationships on security intent, but as opposed to doing so strictly from an information security perspective, the goal is to objectively review the intent of an ingredient from the business's perspective. By performing this exercise security associations can be formed based on a shared responsibility in meeting business goals and objectives, which can include strategic security goals, assuming these are also aligned with business expectations. Arguably, this can be very difficult and some may find that differentiating one security ingredient from another relative to goals is challenging due to the broad nature of business goals. It is recommended to start with IT goals and objectives and any existing security goals in an effort to offer some granularity that can help associate security ingredients. Assume for the moment that a business goal expresses the importance of the relationships with business partners and suppliers. This further resonates in the IT objectives as enabling technology, processes, management, and infrastructure to facilitate partner data services. How these materialize will have implications for security, such as network security, perimeter security, access control, and monitoring, for example.

Another aspect of business indicators deals with the fiscal attributes of security that encompass all costs implied by the security ingredient's life cycle. As with goals and objectives relating to security intent, the same analogy can be made between fiscal associations and operational interactions due to the obvious connection between resources and cost. While operational interactions are more focused on the delivery of resources, capacity, and capability, fiscal associations are based on the cost a security ingredient represents to the business. It is at this point where external resources are incorporated. For example, one or more third parties may provide forensics and monitoring, and one is transactional whereas the other is long-term, respectively. This represents not only different costs, but also different cost structures. Additionally, associations based on fiscal attributes may expose areas of security that are fundamentally more expensive than others. Of course, a number of combinations may result from the process, but usually these will fall into one of the following categories:

- One-time costs versus long-term operational expenditures. For example, small projects versus strategic, long-lasting initiatives.
- High initial costs with low long-term maintenance. For example, acquiring new technology solutions that require meaningful up-front investment, but move quickly into maintenance costs.
- Low initial investment with predictable long-term costs. For example, hiring new resources and taking into account payroll, benefits, and other costs associated with them.

The benefits of forming associations of this type are to gain a better perspective of which ingredients of security represent, as a group, the financial liabilities for the organization and what form they are taking. This information will become enormously helpful in the structuring of security services and will play a critical role in evaluating the business impacts of adapting security activities relative to change.

3.5.3.1.6 Example of Ingredient Relationships   Once there is a general structure to the associations based on the characteristics defined above, we can evaluate the strength and importance of the relationships. As demonstrated in Figure 3.3, the strength of the association between A and B, and A and C is pronounced by the existence of associations based on all the characteristics. To a lesser extent there is

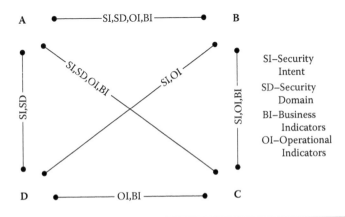

Figure 3.3   Detailed associations.

a bond between B and C. There are distant relationships between the remaining ingredients, A-D, C-D, and B-D.

Furthermore, these can be organized based on prioritization helping to isolate strong ties relative to actionable relations and distant relationships. String relationships are those that are going to play a significant role in the adaptation of security. The depth and breadth of the associations spanning security, operations, and business—at least at a high-level—will govern many decisions concerning not only what adjustments are possible, but determining their implications.

Actionable relationships are those that will also play heavily into the adaptation of services and approaches, but will be less complicated in realizing and testing. It is noteworthy to add that actionable relationships differ from strong relationships in one important way in that they represent opportunity. Strong relations exist because of the breadth of shared attributes and characteristics. As such, the tight relationship can reduce flexibility in options. For example, if several security ingredients have a shared, tight bond, a change to any one of them will have broad effects on each of the others. This represents a degree of complexity when evaluating options due to the potential for unintended consequences. In some cases this can be an advantage, such as killing two birds with one stone, but more often than not it represents a significant challenge and most organizations will seek to establish a steady state. Conversely, actionable relationships, although also broad and deep, do not necessarily introduce unmanageable complexity. In fact, the ratio of complexity to potential weighs heavily on the side of potential for positive change. It is the actionable relationships where a great deal of focus will naturally gravitate because meaningful changes can be realized with a high degree of confidence in their outcome (Table 3.2).

Distant relationships will act predominantly as trailing indicators of adaptation success or failure. Moreover, in some cases distant relationships will influence decision-making activities concerning other areas of security supporting "what if" scenarios. Therefore, as the security program adapts to a business or security dynamic the high-priority relationships will govern the process while distant relationships will provide value-add in helping to discern one dominating approach from another. For example, when considering a significant change

Table 3.2 Association Summary

PRIORITY	RELATIONSHIP	DOMINATING CHARACTERISTIC(S)	TYPE
1	A–B	All characteristics with multiple associations in SI and SD	Strong
2	A–C	All characteristics with some additional associations in OI	Strong
3	B–C	Some SI commonalities, but several in OI and BI	Actionable
4	A–D	Primarily based on close security relationships in SI and SD	Actionable
5	B–D	Shared SI and supported by several OI features	Actionable
6	C–D	No security relationships, but identified OI and BI ties	Distant

in approach and planning modifications to services and delivery, it is likely that several potential solutions will surface. Distant relationships can assist in reducing the spectrum of unintended consequences and act as markers contributing to one solution over another. Finally, as time passes distant relationships can provide information used in evaluating the overall effectiveness of the changes implemented. It is typically the smaller, less obvious interactions that can expose deeply rooted issues or positive outcomes.

3.5.3.2 Basic Security Influencers Building on the core ingredients and relationships example, we can begin to introduce influencers that will ultimately transform the basics of security into how they materialize in the organization and ultimately into security services. In earlier sections the four major influencers (economy, technology, data centricity, and compliance) were offered as high-level contributors to the future of security. Additional influencers were added in the context of primary business input areas, especially concerning those driving strategy. Expanding on these we can review others that affect how the organization approaches and prioritizes security, which can be expressed in two major categories:

1. Horizontal—Represents a set of characteristics that directly influence security architecture, decision making, and the overall management and role of security within an organization. This is mostly associated with culture and focus of

security. For example, an organization may rely heavily on risk management as the platform of their security program or be technology rich and base the security posture on the capabilities of the technology.

2. Vertical—As the term implies, this represents the influence on security of the market industry of which the organization is part. As an industry vertical, it represents a collection of influencers, such as regulation, legal, and business attributes in the production of goods and services that sets the security priorities.

3.5.3.2.1 Horizontal To elaborate on the various themes of security and how these can be used in exposing security relationships we can start with common features. There are typically three fundamental components:

1. Vulnerability Sensitive—An organization that is predominantly concerned with managing and reducing vulnerabilities in the environment. Although risk management may exist, the foundation of the risk program will likely be reducing vulnerabilities. Organizations that typically have this culture such as manufacturing will have few, if any, regulatory requirements affecting information security. Without considerable external force, the security strategy is typically focused on minimizing exposure to ensure sound business operations through the implementation of industry best practices.

2. Risk Averse—An organization that is acutely focused on managing risk. Managing vulnerabilities and even compliance is secondary and considered part of a risk management–based security program. Organizations of this type can be characterized as "having something to lose." Financial and pharmaceutical industries and government entities will typically fall into this security culture. In short, they usually have a clear understanding of the valuation of information assets, and the controls they are willing to implement usually exceed that required by regulation or implied by best practice.

3. Compliance Driven—An organization that has clear and significant regulatory oversight affecting information security

practices. Organizations of this nature will usually have information security regulation targeted at information assets that are core to their business, or noncompliance represents a significant risk to the company's stability. For example, in the United States, HIPAA and HITECH (Health Information Technology for Economic and Clinical Health) are major influences in the healthcare space mostly because they directly govern the management of patient information, which is core to their business and therefore quite important. The same can be said for the retail industry and PCI. However, regulations like SOX, which affect organizations from a wide range of industries, are mostly a threat to public trading, again core to the company, but security is implied and indirect. An underlying characteristic to compliance-driven organizations is that without a regulation driving security it is very likely that security would not be as prevalent and they would probably have a vulnerability-sensitive culture at best.

Granted, these can mix and change in priority and don't represent the entire spectrum of horizontal influencers, but they are a meaningful starting point. For example, other horizontal attributes can be technology, which is reflective of organizations that base security on technical capabilities, or a standards-based security organization. Many security groups will base their approach to security, and all that this implies, on standards such as ISO-27000 series or CoBIT. Horizontal is simply a prioritization of security that is based on characteristics that are common to any company, regardless of industry or business type.

What is fascinating is that some executives will say these are all equally important, whereas different middle and lower management in security will typically place more emphasis on one or another. Regardless, at some point in the development life cycle of the ASMA one of these cultures will surface as a dominant driver.

These different cultures represent focus and may even conflict with the existing security strategy, which is not uncommon. Nevertheless, determining such influencers, like culture, helps to orchestrate the discussion of security and the priority of how the ingredients are addressed and to what degree, and helps determine which ones are of no interest.

3.5.3.2.2 Vertical As previously introduced, vertical characteristics represent areas of focus that are reflective of the industry. Again, security may materialize across industries differently, or, better stated, be "realized differently with ranging degrees of scope and depth"—yet, albeit fundamentally, be the same security foundation. The same holds true for organizations in the same industry, but differences are typically fewer than what is seen with cross-industry comparisons. Verticals that could be of interest are as follows (in no specific order):

- Financial—Regulated, risk averse, leverage technology and the Internet extensively, and represent a high value target to threat agents (aka hackers).
- Healthcare—Highly regulated and manage vast amounts of private information. Growing dependence on technology.
- Energy/Utilities—Emerging regulations (i.e., NERC CIPs) and technical advances, such as SmartGrid, represents a shifting focus on security.
- Life Sciences—Sophisticated environments focused on information protection and integrity in the face of increased demands for collaboration. In some cases this industry attracts specific threats.
- Government—Security is essential and fundamental to mission success, especially in an increasingly technology-rich environment on the battlefield.
- Transportation—Use of technology in planning and logistics are critical to the business's success. A great deal concerning the physical assets of the business and asset support systems.
- Retail—Growing in regulatory focus and security in e-commerce. Major drivers are around product and facility management, logistics, customer management, and processing.
- Manufacturing—Focused on efficiency and quality. Process-rich environment, highly competitive, and typically a low-margin/high-volume model.

Within each vertical there are trends and consistencies in how security may materialize that are due to a number of things, such as

- Compliance—Compliance affecting an industry will usher in common approaches to security across a number of different entities. For example, it is not uncommon to see different healthcare organizations approach (e.g., prioritize security) similarly due to the influence of HIPAA. It's worth adding that healthcare security strategy (specifically in the United States) is predominately driven by HIPAA. Conversely, the retail industry is affected by PCI, but this alone may not be the driving force of security strategy. When interpreting the use of a vertical approach in the organization of services it is important to weigh the influence of compliance and the scope of that compliance relative to the industry.
- Community—Many organizations from the same or similar industry will typically collaborate on approaches to security practices. This organic activity is based on the basic desire to not do (e.g., spend) more or less than others with similar environments. Adding to this basic driver is sharing ideas and concepts between organizations in the same industry to understand what works and what does not given that many are dealing with the same demands, drivers, and external forces.
- Competition—Typically a significant driver that stands as the basis for strategic decisions and investments, companies will act on and respond rapidly to shifts in their respective industry to maintain or enhance their competitive edge. For some verticals this will influence security, such as with research and development, media and entertainment, telecommunications, and pharmaceutical organizations.
- Industry Expectations and Characteristics—Organizations within an industry may have their security program prioritized based on the features that are unique to that industry. Many of these resonate as risk. For example, the aeronautical industry (i.e., commercial airlines) shares common risks and threats that may not apply to manufacturing. Pharmaceutical companies face a different set of risks than companies found in the financial industry. Beyond risk are expectations of the industry. For example, one industry may be greatly influenced

by environmental protection concerns and requirements (i.e., fisheries, power production, waste management, etc.), whereas another industry may not have the same pressures. Risk (and threats) and expectations related to the industry can resonate significantly with the security strategy and how it is prioritized.

3.5.3.3 Mapping to the Organization Eventually, security ingredients, along with their associations and prioritization, are passed through the influencers unique to an organization that is creating a security approach. As discussed, the objective is to codify that approach into security services so that security can be applied effectively and to create a focal point for improvement, governance, and overall security posture management relative to business demands. Although the initial security ingredients may or may not be fully reflected in the security services, the relationships identified will be carried through and materialize in how services are managed and delivered (Figure 3.4).

The development of security services and ultimately the identification of relationships that will be used in the adaptation of the security program move through an evolutionary process. Starting with the fundamentals

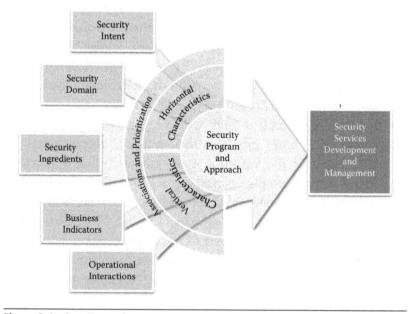

Figure 3.4 Security mapping.

of security, devoid of organizational and business influence, this evolves to include security- and business-related information as characteristics to expose initial associations in the basic security ingredients. It is at this point where what is important to the organization and security culture begins to influence how the collection of associations are formed and prioritized. As this information is compared to the influences an organization faces, the security ingredients and tuned associations and prioritizations take on far more definition to relate more closely to the business and the business environment. In its entirety, the results become the basis for service definition and act as the foundation for adaptability in security employment. Although the end result—security services and means of adaptation—may not obviously reflect the security ingredients, the prioritized associations will have long-lasting effects in how the security organization adapts to change, how it is measured, and how resulting improvements are performed.

3.5.4 Balancing Services

As gaps in the strategy materialize due to a number of changes that may occur, the matrix of security interactions will guide management in determining what other service or services can be used to compensate to maintain the security posture by filling in the gaps left in the strategy by a different service.

Once the security service adjustments can be articulated, the business demands and expectations concerning the performance of the services can be incorporated into the adaptation model. Business attributes will have specific performance expectations for each individual service, and therefore will be measured independently for meeting targets, indicators, and goals. Through measurements the business of security can identify over- and underachieving services. Similarly, the business performance of all the services can provide a perspective of the overall performance of the security program. This is nothing more than rolling up performance measurements to ensure the program is within budget and that key goals and quality expectations are being met. Of course, there are several other business-related attributes, from resourcing, planning, and management to technology, training, and tools. All of these and more can be represented as business expectations.

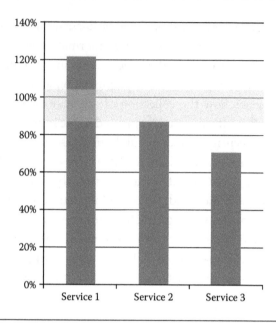

Figure 3.5 Service cost performance.

For demonstration purposes, I'll start by focusing on costs associated with delivering services. The following is overly simplified in an effort to express the fundamentals of the relationship between the two forces (business and security) and between security services, and how the business may view service and overall program performance.

In Figure 3.5, we see that the majority of services are operating below projected costs with one exceeding cost expectations. Overall, the net of cost performance is positive. Nevertheless, one particular service is consuming far more than projected, whereas another is consuming far less. Again, the overall performance of the program is positive, but substantial divergence from projections—good and bad—raise questions concerning accuracy, management, and performance. Businesses desire accuracy in forecasting, and failure to meet forecasts greatly reduces confidence in the team, which translates to the inability to accept predictions.

The change in cost versus expectations may be the result of a number of situations. For example, one service may be utilized far more than planned and the other service may simply be more efficient in completing its mission. From this perspective it is necessary to introduce other metrics relating the business's valuation of the

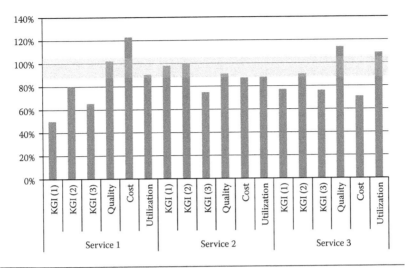

Figure 3.6   Business metrics performance.

services. For example, in Figure 3.6 we see that the business has three key goal indicators for each service and quality, cost, and utilization expectations. In the simple graph, the bars represent percentage of attainment. For example, the quality goals for service 1 may be 8.2 on a scale from 1 to 10 and the measured quality was an 8.3, representing just over a 100% achievement. Conversely, the quality goal for service 2 may be 7.2 with a measured result of 6.8, which is slightly under expectations. Nevertheless, in both cases these results fall within the margin of what is acceptable. Therefore, each service can have different goals, but the acceptable percentage of attainment of goals across all services is normalized. Moreover, the KGIs (key goal indicators) may be different for each service, which may be rolled up into a summary of goals, demonstrating that this is a service-level view.

A few perspectives can be garnered from the figure. For example, service 1 is not meeting business goals and has exceeded projected costs, but the quality and utilization are optimal. In short, customers may be satisfied with the overall process and work products, and the service is being employed as expected, but it is fundamentally failing to meet business expectations and consuming valuable resources in the process. Conversely, service 2 is generally meeting expectations except for meeting one of the KGIs. Service 3 has room for improvement against KGIs; however, the returns for cost are seen as being very high quality despite being overutilized. In other words, service 3 is cost-efficient but not necessarily effective at meeting key business goals.

Although this provides a business performance perspective, there may be security-specific information for each service that adds granularity to determine how all this is related to the security posture. In Figure 3.7, two additional security goal attainment data points were added to each of the services. In this example, we see that the worst business performing service (service 1) is playing a key role in ensuring that security objectives are being met. Conversely, the best business performer, service 3, is not meeting established security goals.

This information can lead to a number of conclusions resulting in different actions. First, we must make a few assumptions, such as all measurements are accurate and established levels of achievement are realistic. We must also acknowledge that this is a point in time of performance and does not specifically express that a business dynamic is occurring that must be adapted to. We're simply looking at the potential relationships between the two primary forces: business and security. As such, it is necessary to examine options for finding a more manageable balance within the program.

Stated earlier, security has inherent relationships between services. Although business attributes exist within each service and can be rolled up into a collective view, the business implications of one service relative to another are not as deeply rooted as we find in security.

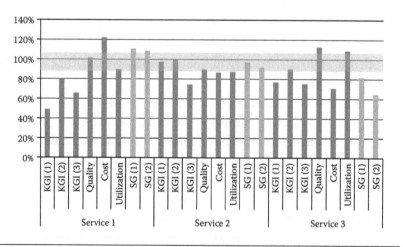

Figure 3.7 Business and security metrics performance.

From a business perspective, interactions can occur in how the services are delivered. For example, services 1 and 3 may share several human resources and use many of the same systems and tools, representing certain economies. However, for demonstration purposes, assume that these were calculated into the cost metric. Viewing the mixed information we see that service 2, when compared to the others, is the most balanced in business and security performance and has room to grow. Assume that we have identified a strong security relationship between services 1 and 2, and to a lesser extent between 1 and 3, and 2 and 3. Based on the information, we find that we must reduce costs in service 1 and do so while finding a better method for increasing our business goal attainment. Moreover, increasing utilization may not be an option and quality needs to be maintained. Finally, there is an association between cost and meeting security goals. For example, the security goal may be correcting all identified critical application vulnerabilities in 30 business days, and through the use of multiple resources and additional tools the service corrects vulnerabilities in 20 days or less. Therefore, reduction in cost will almost certainly increase the time of remediation affecting the security goal attainment.

Based on the strong security bond between services 1 and 2 combined with the fact that there is room for increased utilization, we find that service 2 can be used to offset some of the inevitable decline in security goals in service 1. Of course, with increased utilization may come increased cost, which may impact the ability of service 2 to maintain performance against its own security goals. For example, service 2 may be security code review or security quality assurance (QA) processes within the application group. By placing greater emphasis on the code review/QA security service there may be fewer critical application vulnerabilities that need to be identified and corrected by service 1.

Given the fact that services 1 and 3 are sharing certain resources, it is likely that the cost of service 3 will be impacted, which may also affect utilization rate. As this shift is put into action the priorities of the security group, and to some degree the business, begin to change. Service 2 becomes a higher priority in delivery while service 1 becomes more secondary. Over time, the priority of service 3 may increase to offset the other services and to increase its security goal attainment rate.

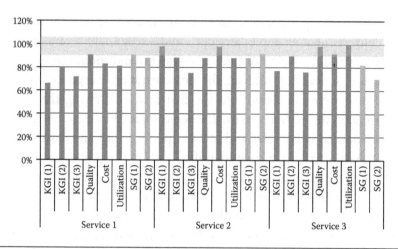

Figure 3.8 Changes in business and security performance.

In Figure 3.8, we see the initial results of this fictitious exercise. Cost, utilization, and security goals have dropped for service 1, and we see minor increases in meeting key goals, assuming cost has an influence on business goals. Service 2 experienced a drop in security goals, a decline in quality, and a measurable increase in cost, but all are generally within acceptable ranges. Finally, service 3 has jumped in cost and declined in utilization, making up for the reductions occurring in service 1 and the pressures that are being placed on service 2 to compensate from a security perspective, and as a result, we see a minor increase in security goal attainment.

The above example is, again, oversimplified, makes a number of assumptions, and offers perfect results. However, the fundamentals of what is being expressed are very real. Arguably, the example is crude because it does not offer perspectives on how mature the program is, at what point in time these measurements were taken or the amount of time between measurements, or what the services are, and, more importantly, it does not express how long the program has been formalized. These conditions and more will have an influence on how examples herein and real-world results will be interpreted. Nevertheless, it is important that we acknowledge the existence of all the features and functions of the ASMA provided in subsequent chapters, especially capability maturity, when viewing the above example. When these features exist and are operating in a meaningful manner, having the ability to understand what needs adjustments and predicting the outcome of those actions is well within reason. This is possible because each characteristic of the model, from the processes within a service all the way to how governance is executed, have specific goals that align with its subordinate features and up to what it is supporting. This creates a trail of how minor goals facilitate higher goals, and so on. Therefore, regardless of business or security goals, there is a path that can be followed leading you to the core areas needing improvement.

Multiple influences and interactions are occurring, specifically between security services and how these achieve business expectations. Utilizing the adaptive security management architecture the program is primarily focused on the operational aspects of applying security and, frankly, less on the mechanics of security itself. Performing in this manner is founded on the lack of business intimacy and operational integrity in many of today's security organizations, but who have an acute capability in ensuring security. Additionally, the incorporation of business and security goals and performance allows for the security leaders to extract meaningful information in order to explore potential changes that help in the achievement of business expectations, but also gives them a clear perspective of the implications—positive and negative—to the desired security posture.

In this section I discussed the basics of the interactions that occur from a static state in order to express the relationship between the two major forces—security and organizational integrity. With this as a foundation we can better understand how to address dynamics that occur in a business that force security to react, or in best-case scenarios, take the initiative and enable the business.

3.6 Exploiting Adaptability

A number of topics covered in this chapter introduced such things as a compensating control theory, commonality of security, and depth and granularity and how security ingredients can be associated and prioritized based on security and business characteristics. Included were basic examples of how one can balance services in how they are performing against security and business expectations. This section seeks to tie these together more closely and introduce a wider set of considerations that addresses the strategy of adaptation.

This section jumps ahead to a condition in which many of the services are defined and the other features of the program are developing. As described in the first chapter, the remaining chapters in this book provide the underpinning details of the various features of the program to make adaptation a reality. While some are more comprehensive than others, as part of the ASMA they provide services in the program that feed into the exploitation of adaptability.

3.6.1 Creating a Strategic View

Adaptability is based on several fundamental principles, many of which were highlighted in this chapter. However, there are additional mechanisms that drive the strategic nature of adaptation that will help to ensure a business enabling capability. First of these is creating a strategic view of adaptation to ensure there is a consistent framework for the decision-making processes. In creating this view, there are several steps:

- Adaptation analysis
- Business drivers analysis
- Exploration of technical and operational possibilities
- Creation of initial view
- Value exploration
- Current state and gap analysis
- Determination of strategic adaptation plan

The purpose for creating a strategic view of adaptation has many facets. First, the exercise provides a platform to ensure consistency in what adaptation means and the methods for realizing it. Second, it helps to identify areas such as gaps and existing program features that may not have been previously addressed. This is especially important in the early development phases of the ASMA in managing heritage and legacy security practices. Third, it provides a vision for the program that creates an evolutionary path. A roadmap is typically the result of the activity. Finally, and important to the success of the program, is the physiological effect the ASMA can have. Introduced in the first chapter, a dominating characteristic is to help unleash the potential that exists in virtually every security program. Every possibility covered and beyond is well within the reach of any organization. However, not all security groups have a platform that promotes innovation and excellence. This is most evident in compensating controls—the inherent sophistication in balancing security. The hope is that the ASMA will create a vehicle to realize the potential for security to become far more aligned to the business.

The development of the strategic view of adaptation does not have to be exhaustive. In fact, if the process takes too long it is very likely that the process will become derailed at some point. The strategic view is just that—strategic. It is a method to ensure alignment and create a plan for the evolution of the program. Finally, it is highly recommended that an analysis of this nature is performed at least annually. Doing so ensures that the security organization is continually evolving and is validating its position at a strategic level. Therefore, each step in the analysis provides value to the security organization regardless of the current state of the security program or architecture.

3.6.1.1 Adaptation Analysis Prior to performing an analysis it is necessary to perform general preparation in quantifying the business, especially how the business is seen from the outside in. This is to help in understanding how the business presents itself to customers and shareholders, which ultimately conveys what is important to the success of the company. Moreover, a perspective of competition and differentiating factors is helpful in evaluating the position of the company relative to the market, again, shedding light on where the company places value—what is important at the highest level.

Once there is a basic understanding, the goal of the initial analysis is to establish overall business situational awareness and characterization in terms of external and internal forces. It is at this point when you quantify the competitive landscape and interrogate what may be occurring in the realm of security. For example, are competitors relating to security in some form in their message or ability to approach new business opportunities? From here one can review the company's suppliers and partners and their relevance in supporting the business's mission. Of course, understanding the customer is paramount as well as determining what characteristics comprise the customer base.

From this it may be possible to determine the importance of security to customers. In some cases this may be obvious, such as with banks, or less so with food and beverage organizations. Next is to understand regulatory pressures and the role of technology in the business. These will shed light on the security implications that are deeply rooted in the organization.

Again, this activity does not have to be overly comprehensive. The intent is to determine in some way what enterprise-level demands are being placed on the company and how these may materialize as dynamics in how the business may approach opportunities and challenges that affect specific areas of security and may need the most attention for adaptation.

3.6.1.2 Business Drivers Analysis From the initial overview analysis several business drivers will surface. Various business drivers were touched upon above, and this is an opportunity to identify the drivers that are specific to the organization and build on those identified in the adaptation analysis. The first step is to define the business drivers or certainly extract them from documentation, interviews, and other sources of information. Once there is reasonable assurance that the primary business drivers have been identified, it is helpful to characterize them. Different areas—or qualifications—of drivers can be expressed according to what they represent to the company, such as their significance or the implications of the drivers as positive or negative influences on the business. What type of evidence can be collected to express where the business has been successful in addressing major drivers, or what is not working?

The objective is to get a sense of what is compelling the business, how the business is responding, and how well that response has been going. From this information the security group can better identify opportunities to reduce risk, improve operational aspects, and even determine if there are opportunities to enable the business in addressing drivers. The outcome is a better picture of where the business may be more dynamic in addressing change. It will also shed some light on the culture of change. Are responses to drivers conservative or dramatic? This can help mold the adaptation strategy and set levels of acceptable change as opposed to proposed changes that may not be well received by the business.

3.6.1.3 Exploration of Technical and Operational Possibilities A lot has been covered concerning creating relationships in security services and other features. However, this is an opportunity to build on that foundation and use the previous analysis to identify areas where improvements and relationships in the security program can be further exploited. In very simple terms this is informed brainstorming and is not extraordinarily different from developing a list of security ingredients and establishing relationships. Exploring what is possible for adaptation using established architecture features is a method for exposing opportunities.

The ASMA is a method to promote adaptability when the demand surfaces, but it cannot identify areas of possibility. Exploring possibilities is a critical step in exploiting adaptation. The existence of the tool alone does not translate to adapting to business needs. Having all the features available and understanding the operational technical capabilities of the organization will promote forward-looking discussions concerning what can potentially be accomplished. One can argue that this is the "lighter" side of adaptation. Much of what has been covered and what will be detailed in following chapters is predominantly mechanical and prescribed. Conversely, this is an opportunity to investigate potential outcomes once empowered with the ability to not only address change but also to influence directions in the security group that enable the business to achieve its goals.

This is the opportunity to ask: Where can security help the business? In other words, move beyond the protective culture of security and put out ideas and solutions that unlock the value security can offer.

3.6.1.4 Creation of Initial View Based on exploring opportunities an initial view of the strategy will begin to take form. This will likely materialize as a collection of high-level solutions and objectives that are targeted at an objective. It will be necessary to begin to define the various solutions that map the overall vision. Solutions can comprise a wide range of activities and scenarios. However, with the model and adaptability, what will typically surface are solutions concerning organization, improvement, delivery methods, and service definition. In fact, many solutions will ultimately surface in service structure and in building stronger connective forces between services and the features.

A significant activity during this phase is the formation of security- and business-related measurements for security services, compliance, and risk management. By using the business drivers and results from the exploration of possibilities, approaches to security are compared to how performance is determined. This exercise seeks to establish the strategic nature of the model within the business. Creating an initial view will encompass refinement of service delivery and service management, service depth and breadth (e.g., metals), and measurements concerning performance and how adaptation will materialize.

At this point the overall business and driver analysis creates a platform to explore potential uses of adaptation capabilities to promote business alignment. From this it is necessary to create a view of how adaptation will be applied and how different features can be tuned to the specific business environment.

3.6.1.5 Value Exploration Now that a high-level analysis has been performed, options have been explored, and an initial vision of the role and details of adaptability has been created, it is necessary to review what has been accomplished and compare it to interpretations of business value. This introduces two major activities: comparison of the solution to business and security goals and drivers, and interrogation of the vision in business terms.

Although the vision of the adaptation model within the business stemmed from business goals and drivers, there is the potential for the strategic view to become misaligned during its formation. There are a number of reasons that can contribute to misalignment, such as time consumed in creating the initial view, number of people involved, and misplaced interpretation of goals. Regardless, it is a simple process to review the major features of the strategic view and compare them to the identified business and security goals and business drivers. If the business is aggressively pointed towards international expansion and the adaptation strategy does not clearly reflect the challenges of such a mission for information security, there is misalignment. Take each goal and ask: Does the strategic view of adaptability help enable the company to achieve that goal? And if the answer is yes, then ask "how" the vetting of interpretations will be ensured.

The next major activity is an extension of the first but interrogates the strategic view from a results perspective. In the first step the strategy was compared to goals to ensure that the approach demonstrated alignment with the business objectives. Once confirmed, it is necessary to demonstrate that the actions and methods contributing to the goal produce the necessary measurements. To elaborate, in the previous phase part of creating an initial view was creating measurements across the program concerning business and security performance. Now that we have confirmed goal alignment, it is necessary to confirm the measurements and how these translate back to the business. Of course, governance is a critical feature in this exercise and has the ability to interpret the meaningfulness of results.

Take, for example, the fact that specific business goals and drivers have resulted in a strategic view that emphasizes capability maturity management and greatly increases the delivery options in services by changing service definition and management activities to best suit the interpreted business need. From this a collection of measurements are determined that are believed to help quantify performance against security and business goals. In exploring the value of the resulting vision the original goals and drivers are compared and confirmed. However, when it comes to interrogating the measurements concerning service and capability maturity management it is critical to review all forms of performance, such as quality, fiscal performance, effectiveness, efficiency, security, and all the other points of business interest that may or may not have been part of the formation of the strategy. Simply stated, you are what you measure, and in developing a strategy concerning measurements all aspects, positive and negative, have to be incorporated.

3.6.1.6 Current State and Gap Analysis   With the initial strategic vision of adaptation in hand, it is necessary to compare the forward-looking concept to existing features of the security program and identify any gaps. The difficulty of this task is directly related to the current state of the ASMA development and implementation and the degree of departure the strategy represents. Many in the early stages of ratifying the ASMA will find that the identified gaps are simply development tasks that have not been completed. In other cases, the process will expose additional areas of development not fully considered and will assist in prioritizing next steps.

Organizations that have progressed well into the implementation of the ASMA will find that the identified gaps help to refine ongoing implementation practices and enhance existing processes. Moreover, it is an opportunity to verify assumptions of capabilities within the program and create a plan to correct them. Finally, for those organizations that have fully implemented the ASMA and have been operating for some time, this process is critical to avoid stagnation. Although features exist within the ASMA to maintain business alignment, there is always a risk of becoming decoupled from the broader role of security and the business relationship.

3.6.1.7 Determination of Strategic Adaptation Plan Having examined the current state of the program and compared it to the strategic view to identify gaps and prerequisites for change, it is necessary to quantify the strategy into a formal plan that ushers the program from current state to future state. The plan should provide high-level objectives across a spectrum of people, processes, and technology against 1-, 3-, and 5-year timelines. Each time this overall analysis is performed, it is an opportunity to introduce the previous plan and gauge performance against execution. Over time, the plan will evolve to not only present strategic direction, but also to act as a method for tracking performance against past projections, thus helping to refine future analysis and plan development.

3.6.2 Program State and Condition

In all cases of addressing adaptation there are two basic characteristics of the security program that should be considered with respect to the effectiveness of adaptation: state and condition. There are three basic states of a security program and they are typically cyclic. Beginning with steady state, this represents a security program that is functioning consistently and experiencing minimal change. Nevertheless, nothing can remain static, and once a steady state is achieved for a meaningful period of time there is a groundswell of innovation. People begin to seek out improvements, expand capabilities, and find new methods for streamlining activities. It can be argued this is the most valuable state in a program or organization, assuming it does not result in wasteful activities or excessive spending without results.

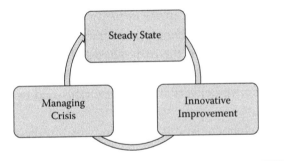

Figure 3.9 Security program states.

To the latter point, innovative activities are typically not well managed given their organic nature, and as a result the predictability of the program as realized in steady state begins to falter. Inevitably, the program experiences a gap that quickly widens into a crisis. The program finds itself drawn into fire-fighting challenges and is forced to place half-implemented innovations on the back burner in order to regain stability, and the cycle repeats (Figure 3.9).

This means that the security program itself may be in a state of change, which may reflect innovative scenarios such as developing capabilities, growth in scope, management, and responsibilities, or addressing a crisis, such as a decline in resources, funding, or management. Significant changes that occur within the program arguably complicate the process of reaching adaptability due to the instability of the environment. Of course, there are degrees of change that will directly translate to the effectiveness of adaptation: the more dramatic the change that is occurring in the security program, the more important is the ability to adapt.

Secondarily, the longevity of the security program and its practices concerning measuring and documenting risk, compliance, security controls, management, goals, performance, and quality, to name a few, will also have a direct impact on the ability to adapt effectively. None of these characteristics completely inhibits adaptability; security organizations today adjust to various demands from the business regularly. However, these conditions do affect the existence of sound information and ultimately the confidence in the predictability of the outcome. In short, a security program must continually strive to mature in order to reach a point in which controlled adaptation essentially replaces both innovation and crisis management. Depending on what state is dominant in the security program, some organizations may experience challenges in extracting as much value from the ASMA as possible in the early phases of program implementation. Therefore, the ability to adjust and exploit optional measures in services and service delivery will be inexorably tied to the evolution of the ASMA.

The second characteristic is condition, which represents phases of security activities that may occur in one of the three states. As demonstrated in Figure 3.10, the conditions are as follows:

- Quantify—The orchestration of a solution or an approach to an identified need.
- Justify—The validation and vetting of the solution or approach in business and security terms in order to proceed.
- Develop—The detailed planning and design of the solution to express specific details concerning implementation.
- Execute—Perform the necessary activities to implement and integrate the developed solution.
- Measure—Monitor the solution's business and security performance attributes to determine alignment to original goals and expectations.
- Improve—Refine the elements of the solution to address identified gaps through measurements or increase effectiveness and efficiencies based on lessons learned.

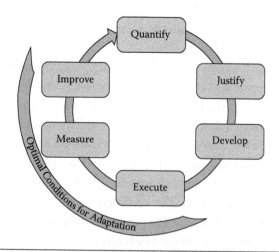

Figure 3.10 Security program conditions.

One of the major goals of the ASMA is to reduce the demands being placed on senior security staff concerning justification. With clear visibility into the security program combined with the ability to accurately demonstrate value, justification will become less of a burden. At a distant second is the simplification of quantification and development activities. Quantification of a solution or an approach to a challenge can be time-consuming and littered with unanswered questions, which leads to making assumptions that may resonate poorly over time. The existence of the ASMA drives increased awareness of possibilities and the ability to understand their positive and negative features. Moreover, as discussed, there is greater confidence in the outcome if it is founded on a more comprehensive view of the solution, thus significantly streamlining development of the solution.

However, it can be rightly argued that these advantages stem from the ASMA as opposed to products. The ASMA enhances processes that directly relate to execution, such as services, and the ability to accurately measure security and business attributes, and provides a method to facilitate improvement. Many security organizations are understandably focused on the quantify and justify cycle and move quickly to develop and execute it, given that many are in a state of crisis. There are also many security organizations that have found a steady state and use their time to flush out standards and find areas for innovative activities. Although state, combined with the longevity of the program development, will have an influence on the results of the ASMA in realizing adaptability, many will quickly find movement away from crisis management and into a steady state with increasing focus on execution, measurement, and improvement. In a short time this will compress into two states: steady state, and the innovate and improvement state.

It is important to take into account the state and condition of the security program with respect to the degree of implementation of the ASMA so as to not lose focus on what is possible at any given point in time and to have clear visibility into what remains to be accomplished. Businesses demand results, and long-term projects, such as implementing a new security management architecture, can push the limits of acceptable thresholds of executive management. Therefore, it is necessary to identify opportunities to demonstrate value throughout the life cycle of implementation. However, doing so requires an accurate assessment of the state and condition of the environment in order to plan effectively and prepare for business-level interrogation.

3.6.3 Influencers, Audience, and Priority

Numerous features and characteristics exist throughout the underlying framework of the ASMA to promote and enable adaptation within the security program. Nevertheless, these eventually have to take into consideration the larger aspects of what influences change, who are the beneficiaries or those most interested in the effects of change, and how changes are identified and prioritized.

As discussed in previous sections, influencers can take on many forms and are usually related to the targeted environment. For example, there are strategic influencers, such as the four influencers covered in the previous chapter, and mid-level influencers, such as those described in concert with how security ingredients are molded into a program unique to an organization. Within the scope of this section influencers are broader and directly relate to what drives adaptation. For example, threats, dominating features that contribute to changes in the security environment, are a dynamic that will influence how adaptation is initiated and in some ways executed. Threats encompass all forms of potential challenges to the security posture and will be driven from risk management to oversee change. Additionally, there are business influencers that undoubtedly represent the bulk of adaptation within the program. Much of this will be fed into the program from governance as requirements from the business that will initiate changes in the program to meet business expectations. Finally, compliance is a meaningful influencer to any organization. As implied, compliance management is responsible for identifying changes in compliance requirements from external forces or internal audits and initiating the appropriate changes to reduce liability and overall risk to the organization. In total, these influencers and the features within the ASMA that manage them will, in combination, contribute to how the need for adaptation is identified and the characteristics that comprise the projected actions that need to be employed. Finally, it is the responsibility of risk, compliance, and governance management to ensure that changes in one area affect others according to an established plan. Again, it is not about determining whether or not there will be effects, but rather to what extent.

The audience includes those entities that are most impacted by the adaptation of the security program. As with all changes, they will be involved in the entire program and all elements of the business in some fashion. However, based on the influences for adaptation, one audience will surface as the primary beneficiary. It is important to acknowledge and accurately identify the audience due to the downstream measurements concerning quality, satisfaction, and effectiveness of the changes. The target environment is a major source of trailing indicators of success or failure. Shared above, there is typically an alignment between influencer and audience. This is not a rule, but rather a common eventuality. For example, the basic definition of threats will typically be associated with an audience focused on infrastructure and technology. Internet-borne threats or those that surface from within are usually addressed by the implementation of technical controls and/or modifications to the infrastructure design and management to mitigate or reduce the potential for impact. Influences from the business, such as business units and groups, address an audience comprising not only the business units driving the change, but organization and management that exists within the security program and overall corporate management. In other words, when business drives change managed by governance in the program, the audience includes the business (e.g., customer) and overarching executive management. The principal audience for compliance is the executive team and in many cases the board. Moreover, depending on how executive teams are formed in the organization and the existence of executive committees, it is likely that these groups are part of the audience as well.

Prioritization is a multifaceted method for addressing the complex interactions between influencers, audience, and the process of decision making in adaptation. These interactions are necessary to avoid fire fighting when possible and to avoid initiating rash changes to the program that can be addressed more directly and in a tactical manner. Within this context influencers instigate the need for adaptation in the program to satisfy the intended audience. Of course, with only these two characteristics taken into consideration adaptation will be reduced to nothing more than an endless stream of changes ultimately destabilizing the security program. Therefore, prioritization has to take into consideration several additional inputs to

1. Ensure that adaptation is required as opposed to a relatively simple change in service delivery, technology, or the like.
2. Validate the intended outcome of the proposed adaptation of the program relative to addressing the influencer and audience expectations (not all influencers require adaptation and not all audiences accept that there are implications to their demands).
3. Accurately quantify the changes necessary to realize adaptation of the program relative to the state and condition of the other areas of business and security.

The first step in ensuring that adaptation is required is necessary to not only protect the security program from the business (as in demanding deep changes when not necessary), but to also protect the business from unneeded costs and confusion. Performing this step is very common in every aspect of business and IT, and is simply needed to ensure the scope of what needs to be addressed to satisfy the business or customer. In short, not all demands from the business constitute making adjustments to the program, but rather making modifications to execution, which are two very different approaches. Therefore, each demand has to be evaluated against potential needs and whether these are necessarily program modifications or execution modifications. It is noteworthy to add that changes to the program versus execution do not imply one is more costly, time consuming, or complicated than the other. Security groups may find that modifications to execution, such as tools, technology, skills, and methodologies to compensate for a condition, is far more exhaustive than making more deeply rooted modifications to the program. Of course, the opposite is true. However, the most significant difference is adaptation of the program will have resonating impacts across the program and will take longer to realize than simply making adjustments in execution. This aspect alone will become a governing factor to help determine which approach is best.

The most challenging aspect of determining the type of change needed is deciding if the demand is something strategic and may resurface in other areas of the business driving a decision of adaptation, or if the need is a one-off scenario that does not offer long-term benefits to the security program or demonstrate value. Although on the surface this may appear to be an easy decision, it is far from it. For example, some very large demands, such as those related to projects or significant shifts in the business, may lead some to believe adaptation is required, but in reality the size is not relative to the fact that it is short-lived and not strategic. Therefore, by the time adaptation is implemented and changes begin to surface in the program and appear more pronounced in the application of security, the project or initiative may have ended or evolved. To state the obvious, the opposite can be true. Security groups may decide that only cursory changes are needed in the application of security only to find out that they have fallen short by not meeting expectations, and thus find similar challenges surfacing in other areas.

The importance of this initial step cannot be overstated. In truly disastrous conditions of poor analysis an organization may find that the program is locked in a continual flow of adaptation that generates duplicate and overlapping efforts that will overcomplicate the ASMA and seal its ultimate failure. On the other hand, excessive adjustments in specific practices to address tactical needs will create an overly complex interface with the business and make the underlying architecture virtually meaningless. The rule of thumb is to always view any demand from a business and security goal perspective. Every demand represents an opportunity for improvement and to evaluate potential adaptation exercises from a strategic perspective: Does it make sense in the long run? Again, this is change with a purpose, not change for the sake of change. If addressing demand is not deemed as strategic, approach tactical changes carefully. Basically, there is slightly greater risk in one-off corrections than with managing adaptation. Moreover, creating point solutions to problems creates a foundation that will be continually exploited.

Assuming that a strategic adaptation is justified, the proposed set of actions needs to be objectively reviewed to ensure the intended outcome is a reality. In short, this is a proactive approach to change to determine the scope of the change and outcomes. The important aspect here is that the proposed modifications are limited to the identified need stemming from the influencer and audience. The objective is to maintain the focus of the proposed adjustments to ensure that they translate directly to the demand. The difficulty of performing this validation directly corresponds to the depth of change in the program to adapt to the environment. For example, adaptation may require slight modifications to one or more service definitions to ensure standards and methods are incorporated into the application of security. Conversely, governance, compliance management, risk management, or capability maturity management may need to make deeply rooted modifications to processes to modify a wide and diverse set of activities. The more deeply rooted the change in the program the broader the implications of the change, which may be an advantage but requires more analysis to confidently predict that the outcome will accurately meet the specific need. Basically, this is a process of identifying the proposed changes and running them through various planning scenarios to ensure they meet expectations.

Once the projected changes of adaptation are validated against the specific demand, it is necessary to determine the collateral effects. It is this activity in which risk, compliance, and service management and working with capability maturity management and governance play a critical role in evaluating the overall business and security posture based on the implications of the proposed adaptation. This is typically the most difficult and final step of the prioritization process. Of course, the level of difficulty is related to the state and condition of the security program and the maturity—or completeness—of implantation. The more mature the ASMA the more refined the underlying processes, and hence this last step is made easier. However, organizations attempting to address adaptation for the first time will experience challenges, but this also represents an excellent learning and improvement opportunity.

The first activity in evaluating the implications of adaptation beyond the specific scope of the demand is involving risk management. Risk management is responsible for maintaining the security posture of the organization and will have the best perspective in evaluating whether modifications to the program and the way services are to be delivered will affect the organization's posture. Take a simple example where a business demands reduction in costs and has identified that a reduction is needed in patch management. Assume the business feels that the costs associated with acquiring, testing, and distributing system patches are too great. In the second step changes to the program are identified that are designed to meet the business requirement. However, risk management may determine that reductions of this nature will have far-reaching implications to the overall security posture. Moreover, compliance management will play an equal role with risk management to ensure the demands of the business do not introduce undesirable gaps in compliance. Building on the example, patch management may be needed as part of a regulatory requirement.

It is at this point that risk and compliance management seek out other modifications to the program to compensate for the demands of the business. Starting at this point ensures the security organization simply doesn't respond to the business with "we can't do that" or "please sign this risk acceptance form," both of which are detrimental to the value security can provide and security's identity in the eyes of the business. As a result, risk and compliance management evaluate the prioritization of compensating service scenarios to expose optional measures in using one or more other services, or even modifications to the service in question, to minimize impacts to the security posture or state of compliance. As with all modifications to the program, governance and capability maturity management are involved to negotiate options. Governance works directly with the business to better understand the ultimate goal (i.e., reduce expenditure) and determine the methods that highlighted the service in question, in this case patch management. Capability maturity management feeds into risk and compliance management potential options where standards, processes, and technology may be improved and modified to offer alternatives to the business—via governance—in meeting the overall intent of the demand. Of course, information of this nature is provided to risk and compliance management.

To further the example, compliance management, in concert with governance and capability maturity management, may determine that regulatory requirements demand patch management, but not necessarily to the extent it is currently being practiced. Therefore, changes to the service can be made to reduce costs, but the minimum requirements for compliance can be maintained, demonstrating an option to the business. Risk management may take the position that the priority of patch management is high within the context of overall security posture and change could introduce unnecessary risk. However, risk management may have identified that other services, potentially ones less utilized, can be used to achieve the same objective, but through alternative methods of security delivery. To add yet another level of interaction, compliance and risk management have combined approaches and worked with governance to demonstrate that similar savings may be realized by dramatically decreasing the priority of patch management and only increasing the demands on other services that have not reached full capacity to compensate, so there are no or minimal cost increases in the other services.

Finally, in addressing prioritization an organization has to interpret the environmental complexity. This is simply comparing the full scope of proposed changes to a service comprising processes, procedures, methods, and technology. To express the meaning of this consider a service in which a wide variety of options are defined and a change is needed, or additional options must be added to compensate for adapting to a demand. The complexity of the target environment and that of the service will influence the importance and depth of changes needed. For example, the service in question is generally simple in execution, does not require vast skills or technology, and is mostly defined by different delivery structures. Given the relative low complexity, changes can be made to have a positive impact and create less of a burden. Moreover, a situation like this can help exploit the optimization of processes and delivery models and actually decrease the overall business load the service represents. Naturally, the opposite condition may exist, forcing the priority of the service and resulting modifications to be increased to compensate for other services in meeting the business's expectations.

As a result, the prioritization of security services is relative to the specific demand, overall implications of the changes, and other services within the spectrum of security delivery to manage risk and compliance. Of course, this is an oversimplified example, one dealing with one service and a business demand that concerns strictly cost, and does not lead to many other aspects, such as meeting security goals, performance objectives, and quality metrics, to name a few, all playing a part in the prioritization of adaptation.

This high-level set of complex interactions is demonstrated, and somewhat simplified, in Figure 3.11.

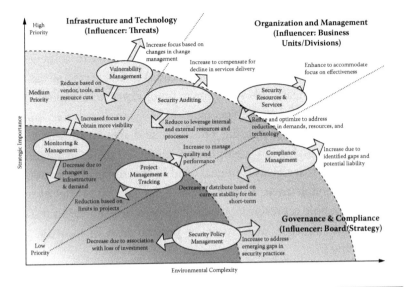

Figure 3.11 Balancing services.

First, it is necessary to provide an overview of what is being expressed. Moving from the bottom left out to the top right is level of priority—or shown on the *y*-axis as strategic importance. This is the foundation of what security services—in this example, represented by the bubbles—more or less take precedence over in importance relative to the overall posture and each other. It's also noteworthy that the spectrum of priority is influenced by environmental complexity as shown on the *x*-axis. The graphic is further divided into three sections representing a mix of influencers and audience, threats with infrastructure and technology, business units and groups with executive management and executive committees, and compliance with senior executives and the board.

Within this are services, again shown as bubbles, which generally fit into one or more of the major sections. As a side note, these are simply examples and can be whatever services an organization may define, and their placement on this graphic is for illustration purposes only. Each service has arrows pointing towards lower priority and the higher priority directions, which demonstrates that services can move up and down the prioritization stack at any time. In very simple terms this is the basis of adaptation: The ability to adjust multiple characteristics of services, which ultimately changes their priority relative to the other services, and meeting business and security expectations.

Of course, as will be demonstrated in subsequent chapters, a vast array of underlying mechanisms is needed to permit this to happen. This is where optional measures surface as a method to achieve balance. Taking the different elements of the ASMA, services—as they are applied and measured—may move up or down to compensate for reasons spanning the entire spectrum of program attributes, such as security goals, cost, increasing efficiency and effectiveness, managing customer satisfaction, compliance, quality control, utilization of resources, and other measurements used in the application of security for business enablement. In fact, it has been suggested that even the size of the bubble representing the service can be used to express core features, such as cost, utilization, or performance in meeting goals and objectives.

Next to each arrow are basic, high-level examples of conditions and interrelationships between services that can influence a service's movement up or down the importance stack. Again, these are merely examples, but what is being conveyed is that building an adaptable architecture allows organizations to formulate a level of predictability that helps to not only promote efficiency and achieve the desired security posture, but gets you closer to business alignment.

4

DEFINING SECURITY SERVICES

Security services are the proverbial tip of the spear in the application of security within a business, and the entire adaptive security management architecture is designed to ensure this is accomplished effectively. As such, although security services are not one of the core features, it is necessary to define security services before detailing the activities and roles of the core features.

Services are the backbone of the program and will be the primary interface between the security group and other areas of the business. Although there is a prescribed structure and intent of a security service, organizations can create services of any type to best meet their needs. Granted, there are conditions under which too many or too few services can cause issues in management, organization, and delivery, but in virtually all cases what the security group is performing today can be organized into a custom collection of services. There is a tendency to model and organize services based solely on current security practices, security best practices, or security standards. However, the intent of the ASMA is not only to enhance how security is applied to the business, but also to create a tighter bond with the business. Therefore, the formation of security services must take into account the business mission and goals, how security is to be applied, and how services are going to managed and balanced. Finally, and most importantly, we must take a hard look at the nuances of how security is typically performed and create a method to exploit that capability. As discussed in the previous chapters, compensating controls theory sets the foundation for achieving balance between security posture and business dynamics. The same is true in defining security services. There is an inherent sophistication in how security is performed today that few seek to take advantage of in a systematic way.

In this chapter not only do I explore all the security and business attributes that must be taken into account in the development of services, but I also look at the current, untapped sophistication in how security is naturally being performed today in order to encode it into the fabric of security services.

4.1 Service Characteristics

Defining begins with understanding business goals, organization, and corporate policies and procedures. It is necessary to understand these business characteristics to address all the elements of the service structure. These can be categorized into the following groups and will be discussed in detail throughout this section:

- Tenets of Value—The core characteristics of services that need to be used as the overarching principles in service definition.
- Customers—The demands and expectations of business units and groups based on individual characteristics, such as role, mission, goals, objectives, geography, laws and regulations, established practices, culture, project management, and leadership.
- Economics—The cost management, budgeting, or cost recovery model that is employed, the characteristics of investment within the organization and business group, and how this is managed and tracked.
- Resources—The process of acquiring, managing, and leveraging resources within the security group and outside of the security organization. It is necessary to address procurement, training and education, infrastructure, life cycle management, project management, and budget management.
- Ecosystem—The collaboration between the security groups and other business units, and collaboration between business units concerning the execution of services. This includes addressing shared resources, leveraging extended resources, and using third parties in the delivery of services.
- Security—The collection and orchestration of security activities that are to be provided, managed, and delivered in a manner that reflects the security strategy.

4.1.1 Tenets of Value

There is an overriding principle that must be considered in the defining of security services. Services exist as collections of activities that provide value to the business unit or group (e.g., customer) in light of corporate demands and business goals. Therefore, a service—as a primary goal—has to be something of value to the customer, has to have a purpose that is relative to the customer, and has to help the customer address pressures from internal and external forces. Of course, the execution of the service can have positive by-products for other elements of the business and for the mission of the security group. However, these by-products should not be the basis of the service. This can become exceedingly complicated with information security and ties back to business enablement. In most cases, security is a requirement and not an elective for the business. Therefore, the key is to provide value and help the customer while addressing security needs that are commonly perceived as having no value to the customer.

For example, one of the services that will likely exist in every security services collection program is vulnerability management or vulnerability testing. Testing for vulnerabilities as a service to a business unit is valuable to the customer and the entire organization in minimizing risks associated with vulnerabilities. Many companies, especially those within the financial industry, have groups empowered with skilled employees, tools, and processes to test systems, networks, and applications and provide results and recommendations for remediation and improvements to the targeted business unit.

From the security group's perspective, they are providing a service that ensures the overall integrity of the corporate environment, reducing risk and achieving compliance. The targeting and execution of the service—vulnerability testing—is typically governed by policy and audit, which is usually perceived by the customer as a "have to do," and as such does not offer value to the customer's specific mission. When executed properly the customer's perspective can change from something it has to do to something that helps it achieve its goals. Accomplishing this is about how the service is executed and how the results from the service help the customer. In virtually all cases it is how the service is initiated and planned, driving specific delivery features that will define value in the customer's eyes. When defining a service begin to ask questions that will help guide the development of the service from the customer's perspective and interpretation of value.

There are five primary areas that can be highlighted in determining the tenets of value from the customer's perspective:

1. Tuning—Does the service lend itself to different methods and degrees of execution?
2. Output Value—Will the output from the service help the customer in other areas?
3. Value-add—Does the service provide additional value when employed regularly?
4. Delivery Model—Does the service provide for various delivery models?
5. Cost Model—Does the service provide for different cost models?

4.1.1.1 Tuning Tuning a service to the particular need of the customer is of significant value to the customer. Tuning provides options that affect the depth and breadth of the execution of the service. For example, vulnerability testing can be highly tuned to meet a specific need. This helps address costs to the customer as well as ensuring that the service is being performed in a manner that reflects the need of the customer. Tuning of the service is the foundation for providing value and helps to ensure the service is simply not the security group's defined way of doing things and provides the customer the option to influence the service's execution.

Of course, there are considerations. What is the potential negative impact to the overall security program and risk to the company if the service is not performed in a given way? Additionally, when considering tuning options, these have to be clearly translated to differences in service results and deliverables. The service depth may be shallow and as a result the deliverable will be shorter and potentially less valuable to the customer. It is important to always link inputs and execution structure to the output of the service so that customers clearly understand the implications of their decisions.

Finally, tuning options are just that—options. As options, there may be cases where a particular delivery option is not available due to larger needs and constraints. This is of particular importance when defining and publishing services. Case in point: if a service is usually performed monthly there are likely more options concerning the depth and breadth of the service. However, the options governing depth may not be available at the end of the year (i.e., for annual testing) or if a particular business unit has not had the service performed within a specified time frame.

4.1.1.2 Output Value   A question that can be asked is, is patch management helpful to the customer in meeting its goals? From the perspective of security, there is obvious value in patch management—the reduction of vulnerabilities and the promotion of greater system stability. However, from the customer's business-driven perspective, making the connection between patches and business is far from obvious. Understanding how the output from the service can be leveraged in meeting other business objectives can make the difference between a successful service and one that fails miserably in being seen as valuable to the customer. Output value can be articulated in a few ways:

- Business Goal—Each business unit or customer of the security program will have business goals established. These either come in the form of mission and charter statements or exist within the culture of the group. Articulating impacts to their ability to achieve stated goals and the role of the service in reducing the likelihood of impacts is one approach. Typically, this is directly related to risk management and is a large part of the reasoning behind rapid risk assessments (detailed below). Nevertheless, goals can be converted to certain operational attributes, such as the security standard triad: confidentiality, integrity, and availability, or other, more detailed attributes such as up-time, continuity, resilience, response time, time to market, intellectual property protection, and the list goes on.
- Education and Enablement—This can materialize as providing information that helps customers reduce the need for the security service in the future by empowering them. For instance, the results from an incident response service can educate the customer on how to better identify potential events and respond more effectively. Some services provide output that is very valuable, such as forensics services. For

example, a business unit may be concerned about an employee or situation that is impacting or may impact business operations and larger goals—such as competitive differentiation. Through forensics services they are provided information that enables them to make key decisions in addressing the risk. This can range from information to support the termination of an employee, defend an employee, or take legal action against a person or group. Another example is code review. Not only can it help customers identify weaknesses in applications, but also the results from the service can be used to educate application developers on methods to reduce the vulnerability in future projects.

- Metrics, Measurements, and Audit—There are a number of internal and external pressures on the business and even within business units. When the results of a security service can help customers in meeting expectations—security and non-security related—it can be very valuable to them. The obvious one is audit. When a group is audited there is usually the need for providing evidence for having performed certain activities. Security services that can be tailored to support these types of pressures represent an inherent and cost value. Other scenarios may include business metrics and measurements that assist executive management in determining the health of a division or group. Finding methods for attaching the role of a given service to assist the customer in meeting business metrics, albeit difficult, can make decisions concerning the employment of the services obvious.

4.1.1.3 Value-add It is one thing to provide value in the service itself but another to provide added value from the employment of a service over time. This is not related to the reporting on the performance of the service, efficiency, or necessarily the effectiveness of the service. That is typically the role of governance management and is rolled up to executives, committees, and the board. In this case, value-add comes from the employment of the service over time by providing greater visibility of the results in a manner that helps the customer gain insights that may help it in the future.

In the execution of a service a great deal of information is usually collected and created. Using this information to offer insights can be enormously valuable to the customer. For example, using vulnerability testing again, a quarterly report can be provided showing the volume and classification of findings for systems, applications, and other targeted elements over time. Based on this information, the security group providing the service can find consistencies and trends—good and bad—and highlight these to the customer as a trusted advisor. By doing so, the customer can change certain operational activities to reduce the cost of performing vulnerability testing in the future or meet other objectives. Value-add elements of a service offer the best ratio of value to effort and are highly recommended as key components in the development of all services. They are not overly complicated to perform, they provide excellent information that is useful to the security group, and there are a number of uses for the information to the customer.

From the customer's perspective it is employing a security service to perform a function. If visibility into that service is limited to points in time there is a great deal of uncertainty in the overall interpretation of value in using the service. As a service is employed over time there will be broader impacts—both positive and negative. This falls within the law of unintended consequences, which states that any purposeful action will result in unforeseen results. Although the terms unintended and unforeseen usually carry a negative tone, there is a great deal of opportunity to demonstrate value by monitoring, measuring, and reporting on the impacts of the service over time.

Therefore, when defining a security service and reviewing the actions and general output of the service, seek out conditions under which the program can demonstrate positive results in the employment of the service. How does the use of the service save money over time? Where did the service have a positive impact on business metrics and measurements? Is there a reduction in help desk calls from the group as a result of the service over time? Has employee retention increased? Have skills and capabilities within the customer increased? Other questions concerning the role of the business unit in the overall measurement of risk can be used as well: Has the risk profile of the company been reduced? Has compliance been addressed and managed effectively as a result? Have down time and system faults been reduced?

Frankly, there are a limitless number of questions and these will surface as you interrogate the goals, mission, and charter of the customer and the organization as a whole. Nevertheless, the point is to provide additional information to the business that helps it gain a better understanding of the path it is on in using the service.

4.1.1.4 Delivery Model   A service model combines several features in security, predominantly depth and granularity, with business requirements that drive security activities and the delivery scenarios that relate these to one another. Using the aforementioned vulnerability testing example, we have vulnerability scanning, vulnerability analysis, and penetration testing as representative of security depth; from a business requirements perspective we have regulation driving the expectations concerning scope, type, and depth and the cost of having the test performed as major contributors. When we look at this scenario specifically from the perspective of security at a high level and consider the delivery scenarios that may be possible that work to security's advantage and help satisfy how the business may perceive security, we can draw a few very basic conclusions within the context of vulnerabilities, for example:

- Time—Time can play an essential role in the vulnerability condition of an environment. For example, an environment tested on Monday with no critical vulnerabilities found may have very different results if the exact same test is performed the following Monday. Basically, new vulnerabilities can surface regularly and typically with little warning.
- Change—Changes to the environment can have a direct impact on the posture of the environment from a vulnerability perspective. Changes in configurations, additions to system services or features, or changes in the infrastructure can represent the addition of new vulnerabilities or expose existing ones to new threats. It can be loosely assumed that the extent of change can be correlated to the amount of influence on the presence of vulnerabilities. For example, a small configuration change may represent a small security concern, whereas the introduction of several new systems into the environment may represent the introduction of a wide range of new vulnerabilities.

Of course, these can be linked to represent the potential for change over time, resulting in more or less concern for the type and criticality of vulnerabilities that may exist in the environment. Granted, this is very basic, but the intent is to demonstrate the fundamental philosophy of a services model approach that takes into account options that exist in applying security. When we overlay the different levels of security that are possible in vulnerability testing with the basic conclusions, we see an approach to delivery scenarios that is already common throughout the security industry today. In this case security may perform a vulnerability scan once a month, a vulnerability analysis each quarter, and an in-depth penetration test annually. Anyone in the security industry today will see this is a typical approach that has been practiced for years. In fact, the increase of depth and granularity over time in vulnerability testing, as an example, has become such a standardized process it is reflected in standards and regulations. Even the PCI DSS differentiates between vulnerability testing and penetration testing.

The approach of performing security in varying degrees of depth and granularity in the vulnerability-testing example represents two interesting characteristics that set the foundation of the proposed service model and how it can be elaborated upon:

1. The security community at large has generally accepted that different levels of comprehensiveness, such as differences in methods, tools, skills, and processes used in the identification of vulnerabilities, can be applied in a manner that helps balance security and business. It is not perfect security or overly lax, but it is an optimal balance for what security is seeking to achieve and what the business can digest. On a more philosophical level, this is security accepting that it is not always possible to do what is demanded by security best practice or a myopic security perspective, but what is needed for that point in time, which is a departure from other scenarios where an "all or nothing" approach to security is deeply rooted in the program.

2. Given that the business does not see a great deal of value in security as it pertains to its mission and goals, and that security is generally perceived as a cost of doing business, it is

difficult to force security upon it by policy and compliance as a must-do. However, the first step in demonstrating value is to make something that is usually unwelcome more palatable. The natural give and take we see in vulnerability testing, such as changing type and depth over time, is an example of structure and options to the business that it can more readily relate to, understand, and see as a compromise.

On the surface, it is quite simple. The service can have "metals," such as bronze, silver, and gold, each representing a different way the customer can use the service. It is important to understand that the delivery model does not imply that there is less or more sophistication and is not dependent on specific tuning of the service for a particular activity. The service's governing elements, such as scope, depth, breadth, granularity, options, and inputs and outputs, theoretically remain intact. Moreover, as this implies, these elements need to exist for each service delivery model.

The metals, as an example of one approach, essentially are several sub-services that can be used independently from one another or in combination. Arguably, when all the sub-services are employed, inherently the overall service is defined, which can be called, for example, platinum (if using metals as a vernacular). To demonstrate, I'll apply the concept to a patch management service using some very basic examples. For this service I'll use the metals bronze, silver, gold, and platinum.

- Bronze—The bronze level of the service acts as an information service to the customer. The results from the service are weekly (or other duration) reports on recently published and applicable security patches, fixes, and service packs accompanied with a list of systems within the customer's environment that are impacted. Included in the report is information about the patch, known issues, where to get it, and known alternative workarounds, as an example. The level of detail in the report is up to the service provider and arguably can be very detailed based on other customers using the entire service offering. In other words, if customer "A" is using the entire service, information from the delivery of the service can provide a great deal of value to customer "B" who may only be using the bronze level of the service.

- Silver—The silver level of the service includes bronze reporting with added features, such as patch distribution services. The security group may provide access to a system that provides patches or patch implementation applications. For example, the security group may create patch "packages" that make the implementation more streamlined for customers. From a cost perspective, this allows the security group to charge for the use of the platform to cover expenses and investments for the platform. Therefore, the value of the tool is directly related to those customers that leverage it. This is an overly simplified statement, of course, but it is one example of tying back to business value and investments related to their interpreted value and employment by the business.
- Gold—The gold level of the service will include bronze and silver, but add to them testing and validation of patches. This could resonate as "certified" patches so that customers are given a degree of confidence that the implementation of the patch has a reduced risk. The certification of patches could be limited to standard builds or commonly used applications. Certifying a patch for a customer system may represent challenges for the security group. Nevertheless, the point is to add value to the security group's involvement by way of the service.
- Platinum—The next level is simply the entire service. This would include everything represented by the previous metals plus complete end-to-end delivery, such as patch implementation activities or whatever the service is prepared to deliver.

As stated earlier, delivery models—or levels—offer some interesting options concerning cost and value to the customer. For instance, it may be elected to provide value-add elements for only certain levels of service. The primary reason for doing this—i.e., limiting value based on level, which contradicts one of the tenets of value—is the level of service does not provide for meaningful information over time. Using the bronze level as an example, what can really be provided to the customer after 20 reports have been delivered? A statement such as, "We provided 20 reports providing information on 321 patches," is arguably meaningless to the customer. Again, all decisions fall back to what is possible, and of that list, what provides value.

A number of other scenarios are supported by delivery models, which can range from deliverable format and reporting to different metrics and measurements concerning delivery. As with tuning options, there may exist conditions under which the customer has to use a certain level of delivery, for example, the first time it employs the service, or when the service is executed at the end of the year it must perform a predefined set of objectives.

Ultimately, it comes down to acknowledging that the customer may have resources and capabilities in support of security. The customer may have a comprehensive lab environment where it can test patches for its specific applications and systems. Or, the environment is small enough that the business has enough resources to implement the patches on its own. There is a wide range of conditions under which a customer may elect to perform certain functions on its own and the security group's involvement may come at an additional—duplicate—cost.

However, scenarios begin to surface in which the customer elects partial service delivery due to its ability to perform certain functions and internally introduces potential for noncompliance with established strategic and global expectations. In some cases the audit group, assuming it is separate from the security group, will provide assurance that the customer is performing these functions as defined. When services are published (service catalog) they contain all the processes, methods, tools, and skill/experience requirements for facilitating the service. By way of this information, an audit group has the necessary information to validate customer self-provided service elements.

Nevertheless, leveraging the audit group is simply one example of a control mechanism. As covered in subsequent chapters, risk and compliance management are critical to the alignment of the service delivery model to broader requirements for security. Therefore, risk and compliance are deeply involved in the development of a service and the various use cases for metals. It is up to the organizational management team in the development of the services to collaborate with customers and delivery resources to identify all the potential options for different models and tuning. Again, it is about providing value and options to customers. From there, risk and compliance are mostly concerned with the delivery model applied.

If a customer elects to employ a certain metal under a condition that actually requires a more aggressive approach, compliance and risk management ensures that the appropriate level of service is enacted. However, it must be added that this is simply not the replacement of one metal for another. There may be combinations that surface that meet the needs of the customer and risk and compliance management. Combinations are also introduced in the cost model and represent scenarios in which greater benefits may be realized for the customer. Nevertheless, this combining of services levels over time acts as an option and value to security.

Consider that a customer may elect to have a bronze service performed monthly for a year. However, over that period the service does not delve deep enough to address risk and compliance needs. Therefore, the silver level of the service may be performed semi-annually and the gold performed annually. As with cost models, there are security advantages to mixing how a service is performed at various points over time to ensure that not only are risk and compliance satisfied, but also there are actually meaningful advantages to the customer.

4.1.1.5 Cost Model Tuning, value-add, and delivery models will have an impact on cost and the options concerning cost models. Assuming that the customer is paying for the service in some form or another, can the service be orchestrated to represent cost benefits? A service may be employed, by default, at certain points within the life cycle of the customer, such as when there are significant changes to an application or a new connection is established with a business partner. However, the service may also contain valuable attributes and benefits if performed more regularly as opposed to event-driven delivery.

If the service is performed monthly the effort—and therefore the cost of performing the service—can be reduced based on economies of scale and predictability in the targeted environment and delivery requirements. This may offer the customer a pricing model that provides long-term benefits and is something the security group may want to promote because it provides more consistency in security and less fire fighting.

For the security group, predictability in future activities can be very valuable when managing resources and increasing efficiency, such as planning. When a customer signs up for a monthly service for an extended period of time, the planning and justification of resources within the security group is much easier. When managers can better predict what resources are needed over time they can more accurately manage resources, budget, and have confidence in controlling costs and capacity. Not only does this help in the management of all services, but it can also play an important role in demonstrating value to the business. Moreover, there is familiarity with the environment. The more often a service is performed the less likely there are significant changes to the environment between times when the service is executed. As more time passes there is an increase in the potential for the environment to change, representing added effort to discover and "relearn" the environment and elongating the delivery time, increasing the potential for errors, and therefore increasing costs. When the service is performed more regularly there is far more predictability in the environment and comfort in performing the service. Resources within the security program that are performing the service become more familiar with the environment and the entire process becomes second nature and therefore more efficient and effective.

Taking these into consideration, it is usually an advantage to the security group to have a customer perform a service more regularly. This is not always the case, and not all services will need to be delivered on a regular basis. But when a service has these characteristics, the security group should formulate a cost model that promotes this to the customer.

From the customer's perspective, some the same advantages apply. The customer may get more core and value-add from the regular application of a security service, and it may bode well when reporting to executive management. However, one of the potential factors, depending on how it is formulated within the security group, is cost advantages. For example, to perform the service on a quarterly basis it will cost $100,000 per year to the business. However, to perform the service on a monthly basis it may cost $120,000 per year.

Of course, there is no limit to the options and it is well within reason that the more the service is performed the less it may actually cost. For example, the bronze level of the service is provided the first two months of each quarter at $5,000, representing an annual cost of $45,000. The silver level of the service is provided the last month in the quarter for the first three quarters at $8,000, representing an annualized cost of $24,000. And given that both of these are performed there is only the need for a gold level to be performed once a year, the last month of the fourth quarter, for $25,000. When combined that is a total of $89,000 per year. When compared to the delivery of four gold-level services performed in a year costing $100,000 that is an $11,000 annual savings to the customer. Not only does this represent savings, but also the value-add elements of the service are greater with monthly activities as opposed to quarterly given the increase in data points that can be acquired over the same period.

Under these conditions, customers are provided value in a manner that exploits economies of scale that surface in the application of the service. Moreover, value-add attributes are far easier to generate and provide more meaningful detail. Finally, and very important, risk and compliance management can be satisfied.

In short, what this basically translates to is something rather significant and should not be lost. This represents a win-win scenario founded on negotiation between the demand of security and the needs of the customer. Customers rarely have the desire for security. It can be disruptive and expensive, and few like having problems exposed. On the other hand, security is very much about exposing problems to ensure they are corrected to reduce risk and ensure compliance. Historically, there have been few options to find the middle of the road. By articulating services in delivery models and relating that to either cost or investment scenarios, it provides the foundation for negotiation simply because there are options to do so.

The above is a very simplified example to make a point. There are several advantages to security and its customers in certain conditions in which the repetition of service delivery provides increased efficiencies. When defining services it is important to formulate a cost model by taking into consideration delivery model, effort, outcome, and advantages to the overall security program. It is predicted that formulating comprehensive cost models will only come with time. As services are delivered management will get more information concerning effort and related delivery conditions that impact effort. For example, in some scenarios consistency in the environment may not have any material influence on the effort required, but other conditions and influencers will surface, exposing options to increase efficiency without loss of effectiveness.

4.1.2 Customers

During service definition it is important to review and become familiar with existing practices the business follows in selecting and acquiring services. For example, many organizations will determine a need and begin to formally define the justification and expectations of a project. This may result in a project plan or in other cases materialize as a request for proposal (RFP) to acquire outside, third-party involvement in the project. Regardless of the type of project or outcome, gaining an understanding of the process is essential to learning how the business evaluates and justifies projects and spending.

At this point is it good to raise the fact that corporate executive management may require that business units employ some or even all of the security services. Every company is different in how demands from corporate resonate at the business level. Some companies allow business units to make their own decisions, some specify justification processes on using a local or regional resource as opposed to a corporate-offered service, and some headquarters simply demand that corporate standards in services be utilized. For example, an office in Milan may have access to less expensive Internet connections than those offered through a provider that has a global contractual agreement as a corporate standard. The Milan office may have to justify this decision, because saving money may also introduce other costs, reduction in service quality, or company risk. For example, the service provider provides firewall and other security services inherent to its Internet services, which may not be obvious or be seen as a value to the office in Milan, but it is to corporate governance and risk. Nevertheless, each company is different as far as how "draconian" they may be in demanding business units purchase services from a corporate entity.

Therefore, if you are in an environment in which corporate demands must be followed, questions concerning the viability of understanding the unique characteristics of how a business unit acquires services may surface. However, there are a few points to consider. First, it is always good practice to know your customer. There is no harm or loss in investigating practices of business units in how they perceive value and define the need for services even if they—technically—have no choice in the matter. Second, draconian corporate practices come and go and are dependent on the existence and types of corporate services. Corporate may have a hard and fast rule that all businesses use the standardized financial system, which is completely understandable. However, it may be very lax about acquiring locally offered services or products, such as Internet connections, VPN (virtual private network) services, applications, tools, routers, switches, servers, or even security services.

The rule of thumb when it comes to business units is to make no assumptions about how, when, and even if they are going to use the service. It is up to the designers of the services model to investigate how security is being addressed and how services are currently consumed by the business. Of course, this all boils down to simply "knowing your customer." Creating services, although it will benefit the security program, is not for the security program, it is for customers. Lacking understanding of your customers could greatly impact the potential value the program is designed to accomplish. In a services model, it starts and ends with the customer. This is not the same as "the customer is always right." This is about understanding your audience and molding your core competencies and needs in a manner that more readily benefits customers as much as it does security.

It is helpful to investigate common gaps across the business units based on common attributes. A very common finding of this nature is security policies and compliance with regional regulations. It is common for large organizations to create a global policy and leave it to the various regions to form a policy to meet their own needs. In many cases, they are left to their own devices and, as a result, regionalized policies are usually poorly defined and rarely enforced. In very bad cases, local policies will conflict with global mandates. This is usually the by-product of a global policy that is loosely defined and open to interpretation. In situations such as these a policy development and management service from the security group may be well received. Given that security policy is a security function, some would argue that this not a service. However, the assumption is that the security group and functions exist at the corporate level, meaning that if regions are left to define their own policy it would be out of the domain of responsibility for the security group.

Another important factor when reviewing various business unit needs is to understand resource requirements and potential gaps in resource capability. This begins to introduce questions about how the security group wants to be perceived within the organization. Nevertheless, we have to expect that when it comes to information security the people within the security group are experts and professionals in the field who represent a valuable educational and advisory service capability. There are a number of security groups in companies today that have limited resources and simply cannot do everything, and they typically employ an advisory-based model. This model is the combination of influence and leveraging outside consultancies to support project-based delivery. A collection of services can be created that include, but are not limited to

- Formalizing influencing security-related activities in business units
- Training and educating resources on security practices and decision-making processes (this is not security awareness training)
- Providing security support within project management

Understanding how the business perceives value in services, what processes they employ in the acquisition of products and services, what challenges they share with other business units in meeting security needs, and helping to close gaps in resources by providing professional advisory and consulting services are some of the things to articulate in the formation of services.

4.1.3 Economics

There are a number of potential scenarios for developing services when it comes to the internal methods of finance and budget management. It is likely that the security group is not in a position to change the fiscal management model; therefore, it is necessary to understand the nuances of internal finances in order to ensure services are correctly employed.

4.1.3.1 Financial Model There are basically two methods concerning internal financing of security: budgeting and chargeback models. Of course, these can be intertwined and combined in different ways to facilitate core security activities and services, such as project budgeting, which takes into consideration security costs that a business unit may have to cover. However, at the extreme, budgeting predicts costs and investment needs for a given period of time. This is usually presented to executive management with evidence for justification in order to acquire funding for the program. Conversely, chargeback models are exactly as one would expect—charging customers for their use of security. Chargeback models can be very specific, defining cost models for time, materials, tools, and other costs incurred in the delivery of security. On the other hand, they can materialize as the overall costs of security that are distributed across the various business units as a corporate "tax."

Clearly, justification for expenditures in either case is one of the overall beneficial results of the ASMA and therefore is inherent to services, risk, compliance, and governance. Here we are concerned with the formation of a service that lends itself to the company's fiscal model. In both cases, either budgeting or chargeback—and in any combination—how costs are incurred in the delivery of a service must be well defined. As this suggests, there must be clear characteristics in the service that produce information concerning costs (e.g., measurable). Moreover, these cost characteristics must be predictable. These may seem obvious to many, but surprisingly this element of services is not always applied effectively and organizations soon come to the realization there is an inherent flaw in the service design.

In addition to how costs are incurred, there is a strategic fiscal model of operations versus services. If we look at the security program in its entirety through cost glasses, we begin to see two fundamental components: security services and the rest of the program. In this discussion, the security organization is everything that supports and drives security and represents a relatively predictable and fixed cost. Security services are the elements of the program that provide targeted people, processes, and technologies to the business and represent an understood cost, but they may be inconsistent in execution due to the nature of service delivery.

If we assume for the moment that a company provides only a chargeback model that maps directly to services, the question becomes, should "revenue" be generated in order to cover operational costs or should budgeting for operations be separated? As one might expect there are several things to consider. For example, you need to define what is operations and what is associated with the service. Is the entire security program—including services, governance, compliance, and risk—going to be financed through the delivery of services, or will only the services themselves (and the direct costs they represent) be supported through chargeback models? If you only charge for the direct costs in delivering the service, how do you pay for the overall program? In short, you have to ask: What is the scope of costs in providing services that are going to be tied—or not—to the charges or budget of a given service?

The core decision is determining if you want (assuming this is an option) to act as a business and all this implies financially, in other words, a cost "overhead" model. Each has pros and cons. Operating as a business within a business means you are essentially running a profit and loss (P&L) center. Therefore, one has to deliver enough services to at least cover the cost of the entire program. Beyond covering costs of the program, one could argue that you have to produce enough revenue (profit) to support program development, internal projects, and other investments to enhance the program. Of course, then the question is, if you produce more money than needed does this flow back into the company, and if so, how? In situations of this nature, such as when business units fund the budget for a corporate group, which is typically based on business unit characteristics including number of users, volume of revenue production, and the like, any leftover monies are given back to the business units using the same model that defined how much they paid.

The advantages of a P&L-based security program can materialize in a number of ways. The executive leadership will likely view the program as valuable in that business units are electing to employ services, thus eliminating concerns related to overhead and budgeting. Additionally, this helps executives manage the security "business" in terms that are consistent across the company. Another advantage is achieving a degree of autonomy. The security group can begin to invest in areas that are meaningful to the organization after convincing executive management to support these efforts financially, which normally would be difficult if not impossible to do.

However, there is a multitude of potential pitfalls with a P&L model. First and foremost, you have to generate revenue to at least cover costs. This makes the assumption that business units will "buy" your services and at a price that supports the model. This alone presents a couple of challenges. For example, you are now competing with external security providers. This puts you in a potentially precarious position of having to get into price wars and competitive differentiation. Now you are also responsible for internal sales and marketing to ensure you are the group the business units come to for security needs. Second is that internal customers will have preferred buyer status, which will drive prices down. Also, the business units are your only customers, which represents a finite and potentially fixed customer base. Last, and arguably the most important pitfall, is the potential impact to security risk and compliance when business units elect not to use your services or only certain services. As a provider, and one that generates revenue, you have a very weak platform for insisting that they leverage the necessary services.

A cost-based, budgeted overhead model also has myriad pros and cons. The obvious first advantage of a budget model is you avoid all the pitfalls of a P&L model. This translates to having greater control over security activities and how these manifest themselves in the business units, because while you may be a service provider, there is less propensity to equate the security group to a profit-driven entity and all that implies. This is founded on a very basic assumption that business units are more willing to pay for (i.e., provide cost coverage or budgeting) services when they know the provider is not profiting from the activity.

However, as seen with a P&L model, the list of disadvantages is longer than the list of advantages. One of the most significant disadvantages of a budget model is that you are limited to a predefined level of spending. This may translate to the inability to deliver services or support the overall security program effectively, or reducing the level of capability maturity or the level of agility and effectiveness. In worst-case scenarios, as the inability to deliver security effectively begins to emerge, business units may not get the level of security needed or look to outside resources for assistance. In both cases, the program will dissolve.

In most cases, for those implementing a services model, a mixture of budgeting and cost recovery will likely materialize. However, the question of scope of costs and their relationship to charging customers resurfaces. Given the diversity in financial models and practices in companies today concerning chargeback and budgeting, there is an endless array of possibilities. It is up to each company and its security group to find a balance between advantages and risks related to the execution, interpretation, and management of funding strategies for security.

4.1.3.2 Model Independent Cost Attributes However, as introduced above, there are service development cost attributes that can be investigated and defined during the creation of services that offer value regardless of financial model. These can be categorized as follows:

- Human resource type—In the development of a service it is necessary to understand the skill requirements of the resources to be employed. Of course, this translates to the number of resources, but also cost. An entry-level security resource will likely cost (salary, etc.) less than someone who has been working in the industry for a decade. Moreover, it is important to include all roles and responsibilities in the delivery of a service, such as managers, project managers, technical resources, contractors, and other people who are involved in the management and delivery of services. Therefore, having a collection of classified skills directly mapped to resources is essential in determining costs.

- Human resource utilization—Performing a service will consume the time of one or more people with potentially different skill sets. Time is a very basic concept and simply requires the prediction, or at least understanding, of initially how much time will be required to perform a service or a given process as part of an overall service. Although quite simple in theory, to be effective a great deal of attention needs to be paid to utilization. For example, it will be necessary to track time, but also consider how time is tracked when a resource can perform multiple functions at the same time, which is mostly related to managers. Additionally, time has to be accurately tied to previously discussed service elements, such as tuning options, value-add, and delivery models. Ultimately, utilization will become a defining characteristic and a core measurement in the governance of service delivery. As such, utilization will reflect the group's ability to deliver effectively and efficiently.

- Tools and technology—Tools can fall into two general categories: those used in the management of services and those used in the delivery of services. In some cases, tools may exist in both of these categories, such as a portal used for tracking service activities that also provides reporting to the customer. The cost of tools that are clearly used in the delivery of services needs to be amortized based on the predicted (or actual) number of times the service or services employ the tool. The more services that use the tool, the less the amount per service execution the cost of the tool represents. Of course, the opposite is also true, such as when a delivery tool is needed for one particular aspect of a single service. Costs concerning tools that support the management of the service, such as time tracking, internal training, and education resources, or tools to manage methodologies and processes, and even other delivery tools, can become slightly more complicated. To avoid such complication, tools of this nature should be simply rolled up under organizational management costs. Nevertheless, this brings us back to the question of scope of costs that are going to be included in the service or services. In these situations it is best practice to determine the role and degree of involvement in delivery support tools and base costs on a percentage across the services related to utilization. For example, if an internal management tool is used 10% of the time for service delivery, then that can act as the basis for cost. That 10% or portions of it can be applied differently across services if one service relies on the tool more or less than others. One may elect to simply take the entire cost of the tool and either equally distribute it across the services as with delivery tools, or use varying percentages of cost based on utilization of the tool relative to each individual service. The rule of thumb when it comes to internal management tools is to ask, "Does it provide tangible value to the customer?" If not, then it should be seen as a cost of performing services in supporting the security services management model.

- Per-use costs—There is the potential for conditions under which the execution of the service requires the purchase of a product or service representing a one-time cost that is unavoidable and cannot be negotiated or managed (or not desired) via a long-term, multi-use contract with a provider. In many cases this is associated with tools, but can also apply to contractors or other similar scenarios. For example, you may find that a service is performed 20 times in a year and always requires the use of a tool. Each time the tool is used it costs the company $1,000. However, for an annual subscription or license, the tool costs $40,000. Obviously, this is a significant savings and justifies an ad-hoc procedure. Therefore, the number of times the cost is incurred needs to be carefully monitored. Additionally, regular negotiations with the provider are necessary to identify opportunities for savings that may surface as changes in licensing structure are communicated. Finally, by experiencing direct cost of goods per service, there is no method for amortization, placing greater emphasis on the purpose and value of the tool in the delivery of the service.

4.1.3.3 Summary You may have noticed certain omissions, such as the cost of products, technology, resource development, and the like. It's important when developing services that you remain focused on recurring costs relative to delivery. For example, let's assume that hard drive encryption is established as a corporate standard for all remote and virtual workers. The cost of the software, maintenance fees, and recurring licensing fees is typically handled outside of a specific service, such as project budgeting. However, there may exist a service in the model, such as end-system security technology implementation and management, that states the security group will manage the acquisition, planning, testing, implementation, administration, and ongoing maintenance of the solution—or some combination thereof based on tuning and delivery models. Therefore, this example service will be concerned with costs associated with the tactical and long-term, ongoing costs in the delivery of the service as opposed to the initial product costs.

Clearly there are a lot of considerations concerning cost in the development of services. Some organizations will find this to be the biggest challenge when implementing services, while for others it may be very simplified. It all depends on how the organization currently funds security activities. Nevertheless, regardless of the financial model, articulating cost information is essential in demonstrating value to the business in the form of effectiveness and efficiency. Cost acts as the foundation for demonstrating efficiency and the reduction of wasteful activities. Therefore, no matter how services manifest in financial terms, understanding, defining, managing, and measuring costs that have been highlighted here is critically important.

4.1.4 Resources

In virtually all cases services will consume resources. There are conditions under which automation represents the bulk of service delivery and other scenarios in which the service relies heavily on manual processes. When developing services it is important to quantify the available resources and capacity to ensure the service is actionable.

As services are defined it is important to ensure that you have all the necessary capabilities required for effective and efficient execution of each service. This directly correlates to tuning options and delivery models, and will impact cost models and value-add scenarios associated with the service. As a result it is necessary to first determine what resources are at your disposal. Next is to evaluate the capabilities of those resources and articulate these as features and benefits. Last, as the initial framework of the service is molded, map the features and benefits of resources against the desired attributes of the service. Once you have a matrix of service attributes and a clear mapping to resources and their capabilities, it will be necessary to rank the intersecting points in order to initially evaluate risks that may surface in the delivery of the service.

To demonstrate using a basic example, assume you have a tool that assists in the automation of application testing. This tool may be the sole basis for the service, such as a bronze level, or play a part in the delivery of the entire service. Nevertheless, the application tool has certain capabilities that will influence the definition of service attributes. For example, the tool may allow the tester to enter up to three different usernames and passwords representing different roles in the application that can be tested. This feature is defined as "testing applications roles" and in turn offers benefits to the customer. Now that you have tool characteristics that represent capabilities as service features and how these benefits can be applied to the customer's needs as options, it is necessary to rank the service element/tool feature combination in order to evaluate delivery risk or potential limitations.

The ranking can be very simple and can consist of any measurement that can be normalized to interpret the level of service risk and applicability. For example, when all the service attributes are combined in a single table that also includes tuning and a delivery model, it will be possible to calculate overall capability and delivery risk for each metal. It should be noted that a scale reflecting capability maturity can be utilized, such as 0–5. Using this as a ranking method can bring consistency to the program and offer greater insights into overall program maturity and delivery capability and capacity.

In our example, assume a scale of 1–5, with 1 being the greatest risk and 5 representing a high degree of confidence in the attribute to meet expectations. We may elect to provide a ranking of 2 because the architect of the service knows—or has investigated—that most applications that are going to be tested have an average of more than three user roles defined. Although the tool can be run multiple times against a single application—such as three tests, each with three different users defined to test all nine user roles—there are fundamental gaps that may surface and cannot be addressed, such as escalation of privileges that may not be thoroughly tested when segmenting tool configuration options. To compensate, a skilled tester may have to supplement the tool and perform these functionality tests manually. This introduces more effort and cost, but also needs to be compared to the ranking associated with that element of the service. If the use of the tool is ranked at 2 and the tester (based on skill, experience, etc.) is ranked at 3, that service attribute has an aggregate of 2.5, which may be enough evidence to do one of the following: move forward as planned, buy a new tool, acquire better testers, outsource this type of testing, or simply not offer that level of service.

In a typical table (Table 4.1) there will be several characteristics that are ranked to determine the delivery risk of a service. As demonstrated in the table, each service and service metal will have resource

Table 4.1   Service Delivery Matrix

DOMAIN	CHARACTERISTIC	SERVICE "A" BRONZE	SERVICE "A" SILVER	SERVICE "A" GOLD
People	Skills	4	3	2
	Experience	3	3	2
	Knowledge	4	4	3
	Familiarity	2	2	1
Process	Completeness	4	4	3
	Applicability	4	4	3
	Input/output	3	3	2
	Organization	4	4	4
Technology	Capacity	4	4	3
	Availability	3	3	2
	Features	3	3	2
	Performance	4	4	4
	Output	3	3	2
Management	Cost	4	3	1
	Utilization	3	2	2
	Goal alignment	2	3	4
	Economies	3	4	4
	Model	3	2	2
	Capacity	4	3	2
Overall		3.37	3.21	2.53

delivery characteristics that can be evaluated for potential risk. In the example, people, process, and technology are the primary delivery domains, with management included as a method to represent overall service delivery risks and business attributes. Clearly, the table can have a wide range of characteristics for each domain and multiple domains can be used. The objective is to closely represent all that is necessary to ensure sound delivery of a service and measure the specific capability to generate an overall perspective of potential downstream challenges or opportunities.

Furthermore, it is possible to expound upon the example to include weighted values and far more sophistication in performing the necessary math to generate a final score. Although not expressed in Table 4.1, different forms of resources (i.e., domains) represent varying levels of relevance to the delivery of the service. For technology-rich services, the requirements for human resources may be of little risk to delivery regardless of score.

What becomes immediately apparent when viewing Table 4.1 is the question, what overall score is acceptable? For example, is an average score of 2 too low, meaning that the risk of delivering the service is too great and represents a potential for failure, or is it optimal? If it is deemed too low, does this negate the existence of the service, or should third parties be introduced to close the gaps? Is there such a thing as a score that is too high? In most cases, an average, unweighted score below 2 can represent challenges in delivery effectiveness and quality. However, this can be directly related to how comprehensive quality and performance measurements are performed. For organizations initially creating services, a table of this nature is more focused on identifying major gaps, such as a ranking of 0, and acting as a baseline to focus improvement activities. Once a service is delivered and performance results begin to be fed back into the program, the delivery risk table can be revisited to determine if the bar needs to be set higher. Although there is no such thing as being too good at delivering a service, for example, one that scores an overall 5, it may be an indicator of overqualified resources. In most cases this is associated with human resources. For example, if Alice is rated a 5 across the service and performance metrics attest to her overall competency, then one may question if she is not being properly utilized in more challenging roles. Overall, it is always good practice to have room to grow, but reaching a very high rating is always a positive.

4.1.5 Ecosystem

In most cases the security group does not necessarily have all the resources needed to manage the organization's security posture directly under its control. It is very common to find that other groups in different areas of the business or third parties are employed to perform certain elements of security.

Firewalls are sometimes managed by security-savvy networking resources within the IT management staff and not someone reporting directly to the chief information security officer (CISO). This practice has evolved for some organizations to a point where the security group comprises only a few resources that act as a policy and standards setting community that provides guidance and is not directly responsible for security implementation and management. Of course, the opposite situation may exist in which the security group is very large with representatives throughout the business being directly involved with everything from day-to-day management and administration to program management and strategic development.

Nevertheless, the growing trend is that fewer resources are specifically assigned to the security group, or will exist in specialist pockets. A large organization may have a security group representing 2% of the entire IT staff. Of that 2% more than half are dedicated to vulnerability testing and research with the rest distributed across policy, risk, and compliance activities. A great number of business, financial, cultural, and political dynamics will have a significant impact on how the security group is structured, the number of resources that are part of the group, and the degree of responsibility concerning their depth of involvement in security activities.

The simple fact is that not all things—even traditional security scenarios—require a full-time security professional. Returning to the firewall example, today's firewalls are a common IT fixture, and once there is a policy, standard, and change control mechanism in place, the day-to-day administration is not complicated. Therefore, the same IT administration staff that oversee servers, switches, and routers can effectively manage firewalls and only needs security's involvement (which is still questionable in some organizations) when changes to the system or rule-set are required that may have an impact on the security posture. This scenario is played out for a number of technologies and processes within IT well beyond firewalls and is based on comprehensive resource utilization and cost management.

For some in the security industry this is a catch-22. On the one hand, the fact that more and more elements of security are moved out of the security group's domain of responsibility is interpreted as the group having less control and therefore increases the potential for errors, poor configuration management, and lack of adherence to security practices. On the other hand, this releases the security group from potentially mundane activities and allows them to focus on risk and compliance and act as an influencer operating at a higher strategic level. Regardless of how this manifests within an organization, there are always situations where the security group must integrate with other internal groups and leverage third parties to ensure security and business objectives are met holistically, representing a security ecosystem.

A security ecosystem is the amalgamation of different people, processes, and tools from various corners of the business and external partners that are leveraged to facilitate a security requirement.

This, of course, is nothing new. It is commonplace to leverage a third-party vendor for management, monitoring, testing, temporarily providing resources to support a project, or utilizing for auditing and assessment activities. Moreover, as discussed above, having resources from other departments manage traditional security technologies or act as extensions to the security group in executing services is a common practice. However, these practices must be clearly detailed when developing security services. The good news is that many companies already have standards concerning setting expectations when using internal and external resources to perform security functions. However, these are typically structured in a way to meet the specific task or requirement, such as consulting services for a project, out-tasking for staff augmentation, or out-sourcing device management. The life cycle is typically determining the need, justifying the expense, procuring the resources, overseeing the project, and either reaching a conclusion or moving into a maintenance cycle.

In most cases, these are usually isolated events and it is left up to senior security management to tie these elements together in a meaningful way for the business. However, within the ASMA, services—in combination with governance and compliance—can help articulate the interdependencies that exist in an ecosystem to ensure they are dovetailed into the program effectively.

4.1.5.1 Case Study To demonstrate, following is an example in which security services management was implemented and utilized to manage a complex security ecosystem more effectively. A large financial organization had a reasonably sized security group that was primarily responsible for performing a wide range of security assessments to ensure various business units were meeting stated policy and standards. The group's activities were mostly focused around preparing for audits, either internal corporate audits or audits to ensure compliance with industry regulations. The group began to naturally form itself into specialty groups. For example, the PCI-savvy resources began to collaborate and form a community of interest as did the people focused on vulnerability scanning, network assessments, system assessments, and the like.

To assist in performing assessments the group created a proprietary assessment process and standard supported by a tool—in this case a comprehensive Microsoft Excel workbook—that was provided to others in IT to complete on its behalf. This was also used with partners and suppliers that required connectivity to the business and, as a result, had to meet a variety of security requirements that would typically define the type of connection or remediation activities that needed to be performed prior to connecting with the business. Adding to the strategy was the use of third parties, such as security consultancies, to perform some of the assessments at remote locations, support the assessment process for partners and suppliers, or perform external vulnerability testing. Professional service providers were evaluated on how effectively they would perform the assessment and meet the established standard process. Finally, as new tools and technologies were introduced, the assessment standard was used as a basis for evaluating the alignment of the technology to the mission of the security group.

To facilitate better management of the assessment program, the organization implemented a service-oriented model. It created a number of assessment services that helped to not only bond the various teams, but ensured meaningful management and options of execution to the business to perform assessments. By implementing a security services management capability it found that it was far more efficient and flexible in meeting the wide range of business needs, while also addressing the demands defined by policy and industry regulations. However, it failed to acknowledge the increasing reliance on other parties to support service delivery and became over-reliant on the standardized process. Establishing a standard and using it as a method for performing activities as well as a basis for defining the use of additional resources is a good practice. Unfortunately, in this case, the services defined did not take into account the governance of others and therefore had limited visibility into the strategic nature of their employment. Slowly but surely stovepipes began to form, and as a result duplicate investments were made and there was limited synergy between external resources and how they were applied.

It wasn't until the costs related to assessments started to skyrocket that the CISO performed an analysis to determine the root cause of the change in costs. What the CISO found was that different services were employing a wide range of resources that could have been easily consolidated. More importantly, not all the capabilities that were made available were being utilized. In one case, it appeared that the reporting capability of one tool was not leveraged, so another tool was acquired to perform reporting activities. Unfortunately, the reporting was not meeting the needs of another group so an additional tool was acquired to provide reporting in the format and structure it needed. Interestingly, the original tool met all these needs.

Ultimately, the root cause was that external resources were not part of the services model and therefore acted as a free radical in the management framework, taking on a life of its own. Once understood, services were redefined and governance and compliance models were adjusted to include the tracking and management of all resources and tools to determine purpose, use, and employment that took into consideration applicability across multiple services. The results were astonishing. Not only were there tangible and immediate savings to the group, but it also found that by deeply incorporating external resources into the services model it gained far more value from the investments. For example, the group found that by providing the service details, expected outcomes, and the overall strategy with its professional services partner it was able to provide additional valuable insights that supported the overall program at no additional charge. Moreover, once exposed to the varying delivery models and the employment of metals in the execution of services, the professional services provider reflected the nuances in their service delivery models, thus creating a far more effective cost and employment model. In another case, in regard to the multiple tools that were acquired to perform virtually the same functions, the company collaborated with the vendor of choice, which resulted in modifications to the tool to support its strategy—again, at no cost—making for a win-win situation.

There are two points to be made by this example. First, and most importantly, security services, if not formed correctly, can inadvertently divide the security organization. Services have the potential of becoming silos and all that implies, which not only can be devastating to the security group over time, but can also undermine the value that is possible. The employment of governance and compliance plays a critical role in ensuring this does not come to fruition. Regardless of the size, diversity, and role of the security organization, the oversight of services definition, evolution, and execution is essential to ensure costs are managed and investments are fully exploited.

The second point is that there is a tendency to isolate resources, such as consultancies, products, or internal representatives from other groups that may be leveraged in the delivery of security activities or services. Regardless of whether a services management model is in place or not, isolation is a consistent theme in security and in other areas of the business. This can usually be boiled down to a "need-to-know" condition in which the manager has a set strategy and prefers to leverage resources in a manner that helps achieve that strategy, but the individual resources are unaware of the ultimate goal and role they may be playing. The ASMA, and all the parts that ensure its function, provides a platform for the better integration of resources and their employment. More importantly, it helps to expose opportunities for improvement given that the entire program's mission is to ensure effectiveness, efficiency, and adaptability.

As stated above, the utilization of resources that are beyond the domain of the security group is not only inevitable, but is a growing trend. Tied to this is the fact that if services are not defined and managed effectively they can act as wedges in the security program, not only creating silos that introduce inefficiencies, but also isolating resources. Understanding the security ecosystem and how it manifests itself in the organization, and using this knowledge to deeply incorporate it into the services, is essential to overall success.

4.1.6 Security

Last but certainly not least is security. Of course, security services development must take into account exactly what the security-related goals of the service are. Understandably, this opens a wide spectrum of options, and there are a number of ways security can be applied to the creation of services. These can be based on security approach, practices, standards, or a combination of these. Regardless of the foundation used or how they may be combined, the services must be unique, actionable, have manageable attributes, be open to tuning and delivery models, and be meaningful to the business, the customer, and to security.

4.1.6.1 Security Approach   Security activities can fall into a number of different groups based on how an organization generally approaches security demands. These can be such things as

- Phased groups
  - Planning—Security services that are directed at planning solutions, controls, or changes in the environment. For example, this may be a security service that is involved in ensuring security is involved in the planning of applications and coding practices.
  - Design—Services may be organized to support the design of projects or other technology-related activities that the customer may be undertaking where security can be applied. This ties back to compliance and risk management, and exists today as security architecture.
  - Implementation—As different solutions are integrated into the environment, security can play a role in the implementation and integration activities. This is analogous to security hardening systems, implementing controls in a new application, providing security configurations for a Microsoft project, and the like.
  - Maintenance—Every environment, or at least a portion of it, will eventually move into a maintenance state. Security's involvement may be in the form of ongoing services, such as firewall management or monitoring.
- Process groups
  - Assessment—This is representative of services that are based on the evaluation and comparison of the environment against best practices, standards, or regulations.
  - Remediation—Once assessments and audits are completed, there are typically actions to remediate findings.
  - Management—Similar to maintenance above, management represents the ongoing processes needed by security to ensure the desired security posture is maintained. A service directed at security in change management or policy management is a good example.
- Monitor—This includes services that are designed to monitor changes to the environment or undesirable activities ranging

anywhere from harmless, unintentional activities to attacks. Examples of services include security monitoring, secure log management, and system policy management.

The above examples are very general, and in some cases organizations will find that services may have all the phases and process groups or only a few so as to target security in a manner that best reflects the typical practices customers have come to expect. Nevertheless, these two basic approaches will either guide the organization of services or help define different delivery metals.

4.1.6.2 Security Practices One of the more common methods for developing services is simply focusing on the practices commonly found in security, such as

- Vulnerability Management—The identification, classification, and potentially the remediation of vulnerabilities. This ranges from scanning to penetration testing of networks to applications.
- Patch Management—The process of identifying, testing, and implementing system patches for security.
- Security Assessment (i.e., compliance audits, etc.)—In security services management this would include rapid risk assessments, but it could include any combination of assessment processes.
- System Hardening—Services that harden standard builds, servers, server systems, network elements (routers, switches, etc.), devices (wireless access points [APs] to on-line printers), routing protocol, and protocol security.
- Code Review—Related to assessment and vulnerability management, but could easily stand on its own as a service, it is the process of analyzing application code to find gaps that could result in vulnerabilities.
- Log Management—This can range from log collection and correlation to storage and review of logs.
- Security Monitoring—Ongoing activities that collect information from various sensors in networks, applications, systems, and databases in order to detect security events.

- Policy Management—Services that focus on the development, management, publication, communication, and awareness activities for policies.
- Incident Management—A service that is initiated upon discovery and classification of a security-related event.
- Forensics—There are conditions that require the collection of evidence. A forensics service can be called upon to perform data collection and analysis activities.
- Security Architecture and Design—As changes to the environment surface, security architecture and design is involved in various elements of the business to ensure security is being addressed.
- Intrusion Detection and Prevention Management—The management of devices that are designed to detect and potentially act upon various conditions in communications.
- Remote Access Security Management—The application of security in providing access to roaming users, virtual office workers, partners, contractors, and vendors.
- Information Security Management—The control of information flow, confidentiality, and integrity. This may include data classification and authorization.
- Authentication and Access Management—The management of the provisioning, removal, and changes to user and system credentials. This is especially important for organizations issuing certificates to ensure people are identified and vetted.
- Training and Education—Security services that are used to expose employees, partners, and vendors to security practices and policies that define and govern security expectations.
- Security Product Evaluation and Testing—As new products and platforms are introduced into the environment, this service focuses on determining the security capabilities or limitations that can be valuable in investment decision-making processes.
- Threat Analysis—A service designed to identify and monitor applicable and addressable threats to which the organization may be exposed. Information from this service is helpful to customers and risk management in formulating meaningful security controls.

- Business Continuity and Disaster Recovery—Represents the security group's involvement in the assurance of system availability and the integrity of information in the face of an event.

As demonstrated, there are any number and combination of security practices that can be converted to security services. The goal herein is to provide a framework to get the most value from security activities, increase efficiency and effectiveness, and provide a meaningful method to ensure adaptability. However, prescribing what services must exist in the model does not provide flexibility, and it conflicts with the fact that there is a great deal of untapped sophistication in existing security programs that can be used to define services. There is technically no limit to the number of services, but of course there is clearly a point where there may be simply be too many. The same cannot be said in regard to the minimum number of security services required. You can theoretically have one security service, but either it would be far too broad or the entirety of the security program and what can be put into services has not been fully investigated.

4.1.6.3 Security Standards   There are a number of security standards in the industry that can be used as the foundation for services. One that stands out is the ISO-27000 security standard series, especially 27002. Using the ISO standards as a guide for the development of services has advantages and disadvantages. Also, there are standards relative to regulatory compliance requirements that may be seen as a source of service development. The advantage to leveraging standards for defining services is that there is inherent alignment with the standard if it is already in use. For example, if the existing security program is based on ISO-27002, having security services that map to this can be helpful to drive consistency and to support certification efforts. However, not all the clauses and categories within ISO-27002 make a good platform for services. Taking a closer look at ISO-27002 we can see only a few areas that map well to services. At the time of this writing ISO-27002 comprises 11 clauses with 39 supporting categories defining security. The clauses and categories for each are

- Security Policy
  - Information Security Policy
- Organizing Information Security
  - Internal Organization
  - External Parties
- Asset Management
  - Responsibility for Assets
  - Information Classification
- Human Resources Security
  - Prior Employment
  - During Employment
  - Termination or Change in Employment
- Physical and Environmental Security
  - Secure Areas
  - Equipment Security
- Communications and Operations Management
  - Operational Procedures and Responsibilities
  - Third-Party Services Delivery Management
  - System Planning and Acceptance
  - Protection Against Malicious and Mobile Code
  - Backup
  - Network Security Management
  - Media Handling
  - Exchange of Information
  - Electronic Commerce Services
  - Monitoring
- Access Control
  - Business Requirement for Access Control
  - User Access Management
  - User Responsibilities
  - Network Access Control
  - Operating System Access Control
  - Application and Information Access Control
  - Mobile Computing and Teleworking
- Information Systems Acquisition, Development and Maintenance
  - Security Requirements of Information Systems
  - Correct Processing in Applications

- Cryptographic Controls
- Security of System Files
- Security in Development and Support Processes
- Technical Vulnerability Management
- Information Security Incident Management
  - Reporting Information Security Events and Weaknesses
  - Management of Information Security Incidents and Improvements
- Business Continuity Management
  - Information Security Aspects of Business Continuity Management
- Compliance
  - Compliance with Legal Requirements
  - Compliance with Security Policy, and Standards, and Technical Compliance
- Information Systems Audit Considerations

From the list there are some elements that provide for a good foundation for services, while others are more programmatic in the management of security, which are arguably covered by the features defined in the ASMA. Using ISO-27002 as an example exposes the fact that while industry standards state operational and management controls, these are directed at a program, not necessarily at actionable services. Again, reflecting back on the first chapter, most security programs focus on security as opposed to the system of applying security. This represents one of the more challenging aspects as well as the fact that it's a shift in traditional approaches to security. Standards are prescriptive of what must regularly occur in security management and define specific characteristics across the program to achieve compliance, such as PCI DSS.

When it comes to regulatory-driven standards, these are translated into activities and controls directed at achieving compliance. If directly applied to a services model there would be a service called "PCI Compliance." Of course, there are situations in which this may be attractive in the development of services. Unfortunately, this does not take into consideration all the areas PCI touches upon in security that do lend themselves to services. For example, annual penetration testing is required as part of PCI. This is a perfect example of employing a service.

The advantage of creating a service such as PCI Compliance is that it can be used to manage the application of security to achieve compliance in a consolidated manner. However, there are two drawbacks to this strategy. First, it does not take advantage of compliance management and begins to isolate compliance, which hinders the ability to demonstrate value and is not scalable. If you are affected by several regulations it will result in a service for each, which is grossly inefficient. Ultimately, what you are trying to achieve by placing compliance in a single service is performed by the compliance management features, which are usually far more effective in doing so. Finally, this does not take into consideration the naturally occurring commonality of security and inherent relationships that exist in all forms of security organizations. By creating a highly targeted service the organization has not only limited value potential, but contradicts the foundation of the intent of the ASMA. The second drawback is the fact that compliance does not equal security. Compliance-based security services are going to focus on the scope that is impacted by the regulation or standard. In doing so this does not provide the ability to apply security effectively across the environment. The result is varying degrees of security posture that may represent weaknesses in one area that can impact the areas that are deemed to be compliant.

When security is organized based on practices and/or approach, compliance is integrated into the services so that they are applied to achieve compliance, but the entire organization has access to these services, which will ultimately ensure a meaningful overall security posture and one that is inherently compliant. Therefore, leveraging standards for the formation of security can be helpful, but if taken too far will nullify the potential value a service model represents and the intent of the ASMA.

5

SERVICES MANAGEMENT

The concept of a services-oriented model in IT is not new. Information Technology Services Management (ITSM), part of the Information Technology Infrastructure Library (ITIL), is similar to services management and has ties to other models concerning process maturity, such as Total Quality Management (TQM), Six Sigma, Business Process Management (BPM), and Capability Maturity Model Integration (CMMI), to name a few. Additionally, these models and others also provide for capability maturity. As introduced, adaptive security management architecture is heavily founded on capability maturity and its integration with service delivery.

One of the similarities that stands out is that ITSM is a platform-based business-promotion-driven solution founded on quality and meeting customer needs. This is in direct contrast to technology-centric approaches in IT management that are more about servers, routing and switching, and bandwidth. ITSM adds a layer of abstraction between the demands of the business and the bits and bytes that make up the infrastructure. At a high level, adaptive security management architecture does exactly this—it provides a mechanism between the nuts and bolts of security with what the business is trying to accomplish, and does so in a manner that provides value through effectiveness and efficiency, and it is adaptable to changing business needs. Although there are other features, the security services are where the rubber meets the road, and services management is the feature that is responsible for how services are applied and leveraged.

Services management is greatly influenced by all the other features within the ASMA. Organizational management develops services to be delivered; compliance management seeks to ensure that service details and how they are applied map to compliance efforts; risk management, much like compliance, influences delivery depth, process, and scope to manage risk; governance seeks to improve business visibility; and capability maturity management is involved to ensure that people and processes are operating efficiently and to improve performance of services. All these features pour into services management as a support structure to ensure that services are applied to address customer and business demands (Table 5.1 and Figure 5.1).

Services management arguably has the most difficult role in absorbing information and direction from the other features, thus making it actionable in interfacing with customers, managing delivery, tracking and managing performance, and reporting metrics and measurements back into the program. This list of responsibilities for services management is comprehensive, but through the use of technology and support from the other features, the act of managing services can become very streamlined and predictable. Although there may be a wide range of services, management of the services is very consistent, and achieving management consistency is essential. Therefore, any changes to the management of services that are based only on a unique service should be avoided if possible. How well services are managed and executed will define the perception the business will have of the security organization on its ability to deliver. Virtually everything will stem from services. The services are not only the interface point with customers, but performance and outcome will also greatly influence other upstream and downstream activities in risk, compliance, and governance, which in turn are designed to enhance service effectiveness and applicability.

5.1 Management Structure

There is a wide range of different-sized security groups in companies, and it is not uncommon to see vast differences in the same industry and with similar companies. Moreover, companies will employ very different organizational structures that align to their business culture and demands. Adding to the complexity is that security groups may leverage resources from other groups as an extension, or engage on-demand resources for security projects. Many security groups are organized into disciplines, such as network security, risk management, compliance, architecture, vulnerability management, and the like, with a manager, director, or team leader overseeing, each of whom directly reports to the security group in some fashion. Of

Table 5.1 Services Management Interconnect Table

ACTIVE FEATURE	AREA OF SECURITY FOCUS	PRIMARY FEATURE INTERLOCK (BENEFICIARY)	INTENT AND EXPECTATIONS	FEATURE INPUT	FEATURE PRIMARY PROCESS	SECONDARY FEATURE INTERACTION	TARGETED AREAS OF THE PROCESS	FEATURE OUTPUT	BENEFICIARIES OF OUTPUT	SUMMARY DESCRIPTION
Services Management	Risk Posture Management	Risk Management	Integration of risk management in the assurance that services are being delivered in a manner that is meeting overall risk posture expectations	Results from rapid risk assessments applied against customer environment and the service management environment	A review of findings and recommendations and comparing them to other expectations and capabilities in meeting the requirements of risk management	Governance	Determine the implications of risk management's input relative to capabilities, capacity, standards, processes, methods, tools, partners and vendors, and customer demands relative to service models and the application of security in the environment	An expression of how risk management's requirements and recommendations will be incorporated, resource requirements, challenges, and expectations	Governance, Organizational Management, Compliance Management	It is essential that security services and the application of security into the business environment are reflective of demands of risk management that will have a broader perspective of overall risk posture. Services management must also report back to risk management

(Continued)

Table 5.1 Services Management Interconnect Table (Continued)

ACTIVE FEATURE	AREA OF SECURITY FOCUS	PRIMARY FEATURE INTERLOCK (BENEFICIARY)	INTENT AND EXPECTATIONS	FEATURE INPUT	FEATURE PRIMARY PROCESS	SECONDARY FEATURE INTERACTION	TARGETED AREAS OF THE PROCESS	FEATURE OUTPUT	BENEFICIARIES OF OUTPUT	SUMMARY DESCRIPTION
										on any material changes to the security posture as a result of security services
	Compliance Posture Management	Compliance Management	Incorporation of compliance management activities in the delivery of services and assurance that the results of services are in alignment with compliance expectations	Results from compliance management analysis of service delivery compliance	A review of findings and comparing to other compliance management's reports on capability maturity management and risk management	Organizational Management	Review the identified findings and recommendations from compliance management and determine requirements for closing gaps	Document a plan for remedying identified findings concerning service delivery compliance to program and corporate compliance, express resource constraints and	Governance, Organizational Management, Risk Management	Services must be applied in a manner that does not disrupt or fall short of compliance needs. Moreover, services management must report back to compliance management on results, findings, and

Performance Improvement and Management	Capability Maturity Management	Collaboration on the identification of gaps for corrective activities and the improvement of processes in service delivery	Capability maturity management's analysis of capability, targeted environment within service management, and scope	Perform an analysis of the assessment findings and compare to services management's service delivery and performance tracking results	Governance	A report on how modifications and/or improvements will be made, what other feature support will be required, and a collection of effectiveness and performance	Governance, Organizational Management, Risk Management	A key feature for adaptation is the ability to identify areas for improvement, promote innovation, and support higher levels of maturity in the application of security to the business. Interactions between
				Specifically, review the capability maturity management and governance to understand findings and collaborate on the areas that can be improved, and what goal and performance indicators		identify issues with plan, and incorporate capability maturity management for process improvement		actions taken as part of service delivery

(Continued)

Table 5.1 Services Management Interconnect Table (Continued)

ACTIVE FEATURE	AREA OF SECURITY FOCUS	PRIMARY FEATURE INTERLOCK (BENEFICIARY)	INTENT AND EXPECTATIONS	FEATURE INPUT	FEATURE PRIMARY PROCESS	SECONDARY FEATURE INTERACTION	TARGETED AREAS OF THE PROCESS	FEATURE OUTPUT	BENEFICIARIES OF OUTPUT	SUMMARY DESCRIPTION
							are expected to change as a result	measurements required to monitor the results of changes to services management and delivery		capability maturity management and services management will be of great importance
	Policy and Standards Management	Organizational Management	Ensure service delivery is in alignment with program expectations for reporting and resource management	Organizational management's review of service management's standards and processes used in the formation of the program	Review the standards and results from compliance management's review of organizational management to ensure alignment in the discrete standards and policies used within service management	Compliance Management	Overall program standards and policies, the standards and policies employed in the application of security, and the role of services management in the enforcement	A report on findings within services management and service delivery concerning applicable standards and policies and how these are being	Governance, Organizational Management, Compliance Management	The goal of services management is to ensure that the overall demands of the security program as defined by organizational management and overseen by risk and

				of stated requirements as they relate to service delivery		addressed or need to be improved in the application of security	compliance management are accurately reflected in the application of security by the employment of security services	Services management will be a prime source—along with governance—in the definition and modification to services relative to evolving customer and business needs. *(Continued)*
Services Management and Orchestration	Organizational Management	Ensure tactical and strategic perspectives from service delivery and management are incorporated into the service catalog and service definition	Service catalog defining service model, type, and structure, change management processes, communications, and customer responses to service organization	Perform an analysis on the service catalog and compare to current service delivery models and type that customers are demanding or demonstrate issues concerning applicability	Governance	Review of the service catalog and model compared to feedback from customers and the application of security. Identification of specific service attributes that	A report on services management's perspective of potential service model improvements, service resource requirements and changes needed,	Governance, Risk Management, Compliance Management, Capability Maturity Management

Table 5.1 Services Management Interconnect Table (Continued)

ACTIVE FEATURE	AREA OF SECURITY FOCUS	PRIMARY FEATURE INTERLOCK (BENEFICIARY)	INTENT AND EXPECTATIONS	FEATURE INPUT	FEATURE PRIMARY PROCESS	SECONDARY FEATURE INTERACTION	TARGETED AREAS OF THE PROCESS	FEATURE OUTPUT	BENEFICI- ARIES OF OUTPUT	SUMMARY DESCRIPTION
							demonstrate efficiencies and higher quality results	recomm- endations on measure- ments for perform- ance and quality		Moreover, services management must be aware of any changes to service structure and have the means to report back to organiza- tional management, governance, and capability maturity management on the performance results of any service definition changes

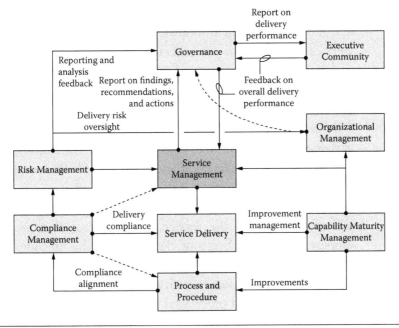

Figure 5.1 Services management interconnect process map.

course, there are variations on this theme that will be reflected by geography, industry, and the number of resources directly or indirectly involved in security activities.

When converting to an adaptive model it is not always necessary to reorganize the group. This can be disruptive and potentially slow the process. Instead, it is an opportunity to show that each feature of the model only defines process groupings and does not have to directly translate to an organizational model. However, nothing demands that these be physically separated with dedicated management or teams. Although this may be helpful, it is within reason to support the services management model as an overlay to existing organizational structures to avoid complete reorganization.

There are two primary groupings of responsibilities for services management:

1. Managing the engagement process—The engagement process includes everything from initiating the service and overseeing the delivery to addressing challenges in quality, timing, and efficiency and the delivery of customer-facing materials. This

is analogous to project management. Engagement management can be summarized as follows:

- Service Coordination—A collection of activities and processes that are used to ensure that all the necessary features in the program are effectively applied in the definition and application of security services.
- Service Planning—Planning represents a collection of activities that ensure the objective, goals, constraints, and concerns are understood and documented. Planning includes scoping activities for the service.
- Delivery Management—Services management is responsible for managing the service and resources that are employed in the delivery of the services. This includes human resources, such as skills, capabilities, and availability; technical resources, such as tools, applications, and systems; process and procedural resources, such as methodologies and other documentation used in the employment of services; and external resource management, such as contractors, third parties, and the utilization of people in different departments that support delivery of security services.
- Closeout—A relatively small but important aspect of managing services that ensures the service is formally ratified with the customer and provides visibility into the role of the service in meeting objectives and goals.

2. Measurements—Although there is a great deal of information exchange between services management and customers, much of this is part of the engagement process. Managing information is directed at tracking, taking measurements, and reporting on the operational integrity of service delivery. This is predominantly information provided to governance for reporting purposes, but includes information for risk and compliance management.

5.2 Service Coordination

Throughout the engagement management process, services management is responsible for coordinating with customers, features, and when other features must interact with the customer. Most of the activities concern customer coordination, but will include collaboration between other groups and features.

The purpose for coordination is to ensure that services management is effectively working with the customer at the beginning, delivery, and completion of the services. As with any feature that is founded on capability maturity demands, all parties in the feature, in this case services management, must be aware of the coordination process. How coordination with the customer is performed must be communicated and agreed upon between services management and the customer.

As demonstrated in Section 5.3.5, Service Initiation Source, there is a great deal of activity between a number of the features in the identification and qualification of service that are to be employed. Without a defined process, these activities can quickly become unmanageable. Although high-level processes are provided, organizations will need to quantify coordination processes that align specifically to the implementation of the ASMA. For organizations looking to implement security services management capabilities, the provided processes will suffice initially, but will need to be modified and customized over time as they are executed. The important attribute of quantification of the process is to ensure that those involved understand the process, even if it is a basic process, to ensure activities are coordinated.

The importance of coordination through the early stages of service definition lies in the fact that interactions between services management and risk and compliance management are one of the key aspects of the ASMA. Failures in communications and coordination between these features and the customer will result in not effectively addressing compliance and risk in the delivery of the service, which can be devastating to the program. Therefore, programs must have defined processes and supporting plans that include the type of information to be shared, meeting times, and what standards are to be used. Supporting materials, such as document templates, tools, reports, and communication standards, need to be defined and managed. Services management will be responsible for managing the detailed processes and support materials for coordination.

Once defined, of course, the coordination processes have to be performed at the right points in time during collaboration between risk, compliance, and services management and the customer. As with any process, there is a plan and an owner of the process's execution. With all customer- and service-related coordination activities, it is ultimately the responsibility of services management. Services management ensures that the service is meeting the objectives of the customer, who is the initiator of the services, and is facilitating information and modifications from compliance and risk management. It's important to note that compliance, risk, and organizational management are not free from responsibility in customer coordination. This is especially true when risk or compliance management is the initiator of the service.

The entire coordination process ensures that the service is meeting the objectives of compliance management and risk management, and the customer. As a result of interactions during the coordination process, decisions and recommendations will flow between the various features and the customer in order to refine the process. This exchange of information as part of the process is critical and as such must be managed, tracked, and documented as part of the service delivery.

Governance and organizational management will be very interested in the flow of information, what decisions and recommendations were made, and how these were managed. These will have a direct impact on interpretations of value and effectiveness and will need to be measured. For example, if the exchange of information concerning decisions and recommendations between features and the customer breaks down, this will cause confusion and reduction in customer satisfaction, and will promote wasteful activities. In this case, governance and organizational management may place certain measurements on customer coordination to ensure such problems are identified early in the process. Governance may learn that certain customers, services, and conditions result in more exchange of information than others. For example, a patch management service is far more predictable in applicability and may have fewer coordination activities than a testing or assessment-based service. These can be measured in the form of time used, number of resources utilized, or volume of materials produced during the process. Therefore, if a service construct exceeds established expectations in these measurements it is likely that something has not occurred as efficiently as predicted.

How services are managed and ultimately performed is directly influenced by how they are initiated, such as by the source of the request for the service, the type of service that is being requested, and, in many ways, the intent and structure of the service. Services can be initiated in a number of ways and how this occurs will affect the flow of activities in services management and in other features in the program. These can be summarized as being initiated by the customer, policy, compliance management, or risk management.

- Customer—Through the publication of the services catalog, customers may initiate a request for a service that will be routed to services management. Within the services catalog are details about the service, such as applicability, use, and delivery models, combined with samples and other information to assist customers in aligning their need to an available service.
- Policy—Corporate policies may exist that define expectations for security, for example, applications must be tested by the security group prior to publication or partners must be assessed prior to connecting to the environment.
- Compliance—Compliance management may need to apply a service (or a collection of services) to a customer to gain information concerning the state of compliance or to perform compliance maintenance activities.
- Risk—Similar to compliance management, risk management may need to employ a service against a customer's environment to ensure controls exist and that the state of its posture is in alignment with expectations in the management of risk. A common example of this is rapid risk assessments.

Other scenarios may surface in the initiation of a service that sometimes can be related to the type of services being provided. Nevertheless, most organizations will find that services are initiated in one of these four ways. In addition to the source of the service request affecting how the service is initiated and ultimately delivered, the type of service can influence these as well. For example, a service may be designed to assess, test, or audit an environment, or to produce designs, such as architecture, or to remediate vulnerabilities or introduce new or additional controls into the environment, or it may be an ongoing service, such as monitoring.

The reason the type of service impacts how the service is initiated and delivered is because of external forces that are out of the control of the security group or may be expected as part of the service to facilitate. This can be related to the scope of the service expectations. The scope of delivery is addressed in scoping an engagement. However, scope with regard to type is what is needed to deliver the service. For example, this can be the procurement of equipment, rack and stacking, or network services that need to be implemented or changed, such as getting a new connection or making changes in routing protocols, which must be performed by other groups. In short, some services are fully encompassed within the security program's ability to deliver, while other services or conditions that may exist in the environment introduce or require prerequisites. The role of the security group, services management, and the services themselves is to understand the scope of involvement that they are willing to take on and to define the prerequisites for which they are willing to either provide support for or direct the customer to work with other groups, such as IT, procurement, and partners, to facilitate.

Another attribute of the service that will influence how it is initiated and delivered is the structure of the service. There are essentially two structures of services:

1. Transactional—This represents services that have a clear beginning and end. Although these services may be employed several times in a year and be tied together to demonstrate value-add, they are employed in specific cycles. Examples include vulnerability testing, forensics, training and education, and incident management.

2. Ongoing—Some services do not have a clear end and represent constant and continually delivered services. Points within the life cycle of the service provide for customer interaction from a management, quality control, customer satisfaction, and value-add perspective, but the service does not have a specific end point until the service has reached the contracted end of life or applicability to the customer. Examples include security monitoring and system management.

The initiation of the services and the combination of the above points will play a role in how the service will be delivered.

5.3 Service Planning

Section 5.3.5, Service Initiation Source, provides information concerning the source of the service request and how this can influence the service through interactions and coordination practices in one of four common scenarios. However, throughout any one of these initiation scenarios, some common activities are necessary in the specific planning of the service.

5.3.1 High-Level Objectives

Regardless of the source of the service, what is consistent in every scenario is that objectives need to be met. Although this may sound obvious, objectives are rarely clearly articulated, documented, and effectively managed. For example, compliance management may wish to initiate a service to ensure that compliance is being managed, or risk management may initiate a service to gain visibility into the control status to measure risk. However, the objective may be general in nature or assumed as part of the responsibility of risk or compliance management. In traditional organizations, risk and compliance management have defined roles and expectations concerning activities, and these are used as the foundation for performing various security activities. Unfortunately, these are typically high-level directives and do not express the specific objective of the activity.

Stating high-level objectives is critical in the employment of the service and acceptable levels must be defined. The root purpose is ultimately to satisfy the business that activities are being performed relative to a goal and are not loosely defined as part of a role or mission. All too often businesses are asked to invest in some form of specific security activity whose only objective is to "achieve compliance." This is too nebulous and does not offer visibility into the activity's specific purpose or potential value that may be realized beyond simply being compliant. Of course, the same is true when a customer requests a service. The objectives of the service must be articulated to ensure the right service is applied in the correct way. Moreover, the objective is essential to guiding risk and compliance management in applying whatever changes may be necessary to help achieve the stated objectives and, ultimately, goals.

Performing this function is not difficult or complicated, but it is an essential step in ensuring security is applied in a manner that aligns directly to goals. Although a service may have standards, processes, procedures, tools, and methods supported by services management and other features that already have measurements and metrics aligning to performance, security, and business goals, without clarity on the objective the intent may be completely incorrect. This is analogous to the perfect performance of services that appear to meet high-level goals of the business but have not addressed the intent of the customer. For example, performing a vulnerability scan perfectly when the objective was more in alignment with a penetration test is ineffective.

In every scenario, the following needs to be formalized:

- Define the objective or objectives concerning the application of security,
- Align objectives with security policy, compliance, or risk requirements,
- Quantify the goals that are the basis for the objectives, and
- Associate objectives and goals to business goals.

In short, any time security is to be applied, the objectives need to be clearly defined, related to other security drivers, and aligned to specific goals, such as customer or business unit goals, and these goals must be related to strategic business goals (see Figure 5.2).

The underlying point is that services consume money and resources and therefore need to be justified for business and security purposes. Moreover, this is not simply about the security organization defining these characteristics for the purpose of articulating business unit or customer goals. The intent is to ensure alignment with the business, and performing security services for security's sake will not facilitate this bond. As introduced earlier, the alignment of goals and continual improvement are the bases of adaptability. Nevertheless, the defining of objectives provides a quantifiable purpose of the security need, which in turn will help not only identify the appropriate security service to be employed, but will also begin to tie tactical needs with stated goals. Services management works with the initiator of the service to help quantify the objective. Through this process an appropriate service is identified that has a pre-established association to process goals (i.e.,

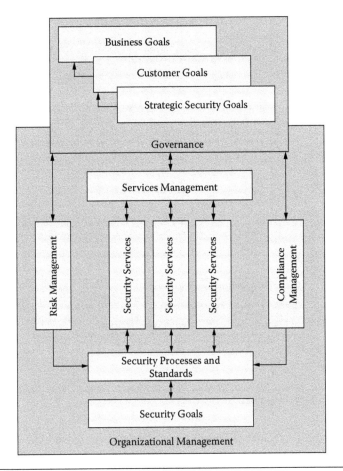

Figure 5.2 Defining objective and alignment to goals.

tactical security goals) and service goals that define how the service is to be delivered and managed by services management and supported by risk and compliance management. Ultimately, governance provides the mechanism to align to strategic security goals, customer goals, and business goals.

Therefore, objectives provide answers to "what is the outcome" and intent for the specific security activity, services definition provides answers to "how it is going to be achieved," and goals in each level help to determine the support of business needs. Figure 5.3 offers a simplified example of the flow of objectives and their relationship to identifying a service and, ultimately, goals. Security can be initiated in a number of ways and for a number of reasons. In the example, a customer has an issue that surfaced due to changes in the business.

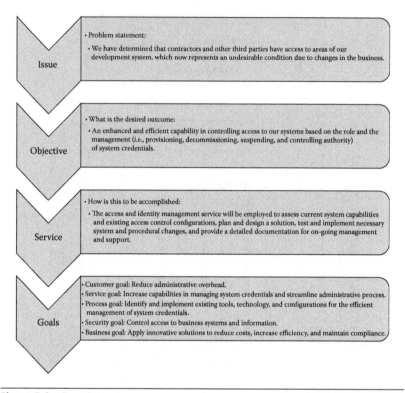

Figure 5.3 Flow of objectives.

For example, a recent change in a system has increased the need for better access control management. The first step is quantifying the objective: What is the desired outcome? What is to be achieved? This is an opportunity to gain insights into the customer's perception of a solution and underlying drivers. In this simple example we see that the customer wants an enhanced and efficient method for managing access. Later we realize that one goal is to reduce administrative burden due to pressures from the business to cut costs, which may result in fewer system administrators. Basically, what the customer is communicating is the need to address the problem, but to do so in a manner that increases efficiency. Using the objective as a guide, services management determines that an Access and Identity Management service is the best fit and has goals—and process goals—relative to controlling access in a streamlined way. These eventually play into more strategic goals of security and the business. Arguably, this is an oversimplified example; nevertheless, the intent is to highlight the importance of defining objectives and how they are essential in identifying the correct service to be applied that also contains service, process, and security goals that align with customer and business goals. For example, if the objective is not clearly articulated, a different service or service type may be applied that does not fundamentally align to goals. It may get the job done, but there may also be inherent misalignment with goals. The importance of applying the correct service type and structure, and the alignment of goals, will become far clearer later in this chapter and in Chapter 9. In short, services are not a "one-size-fits-all" scenario but are tuned to address different demands and conditions. As a result, even one high-level service may have a wide range of variations that may have different goals, measurements, and metrics.

The documentation of objectives and alignment between security, the customer, and the business are essential to demonstrating value and ensuring business alignment, and are absolutely critical to adaptability. All too often security is applied to a business with little consideration for the business's perspective of value and in meeting its objectives. The ASMA is based on the fact that security is valuable and the alignment of objectives is important to ensure value can be proven. As this connection with the business is created, there is greater confidence in the security group to address business dynamics effectively.

Finally, information concerning objectives and goals from all parties feeds into governance to be shared with executive management and supports the justification of an applied service. An objective that is not supported or reflected by a customer is not as valuable and meaningful as objectives that are shared across security and the business. Therefore, these could be expressed as follows:

- The specific goal(s) that the security group is seeking to achieve in the application of security by way of a security service. These can be
  - Identify critical vulnerabilities that may represent a risk to the organization
  - Ensure policies defining user credential management are employed

- The overall goals for security as defined by policy and managed by organizational management, compliance management, and governance. For example:
  - Reduce identified risks
  - Ensure and maintain compliance
- The customer's goals, which have been aligned to the security activity. Arguably, these can and will likely be similar to overall security goals, but security groups should work closely with the business unit to identify its specific business goals and determine alignment. For example, assume a recent acquisition has been completed that provides Web-based services to clients, and the product management group is responsible for integrating business services with as little impact to the new customer community as possible through the transition. Security may provide a number of services (i.e., application testing, code review, system hardening, identity and access management, data security, configuration management, change controls on perimeter devices, etc.) that are in support of this overall business unit goal. The goal of the business unit may simply be:
  - Minimize disruption to the newly acquired customer community and maintain service quality for existing customers throughout the transition process.
- Business-level goals, which can come in many different shapes and are typically general in nature. Nevertheless, it is possible to take security service goals, security goals, and customer goals and align them to one or more strategic goals. In most cases, the business unit's goals will have a clear alignment to a strategic goal. Although this is not always the case, by aligning security activities with the goals of the business unit the likelihood of broader strategic alignment is high. For example, a strategic business goal is
- To ensure customer satisfaction through effective delivery of quality services

The above examples are basic, yet in practice they will be far more detailed. Nevertheless, the basic principle is that a need is realized that drives the demand for a solution, which has a defined objective or outcome. However, there is always a larger goal that must be achieved by the solution. Although this usually happens naturally for large projects, it is rarely practiced for all scenarios, much less documented. In order for security to demonstrate value to a business everything must be approached with the business in mind, and each situation, regardless of size or complexity, must be treated with the same tenacity.

5.3.2 Identify Constraints

In every situation there are constraints that will impact the application of security services. These can materialize as limitations in funding, time, scope, resources, and lines of authority. There is essentially no limit to the conditions that may exist that represent constraints. The identification of constraints will be impossible without stated high-level objectives. Once objectives are documented and an initial quantification of requirements and general scope are understood, these can be used to determine constraints. Additionally, through defining objectives, initial candidate services will be known that when combined with a high-level scope will help expose challenges.

For example, a customer objective is to identify vulnerabilities in an application with the goals of influencing changes in software development and reducing risk to the application. These align well to risk and compliance management and can be tied to strategic security goals and business goals focused on quality. By definition, the application testing service is the most likely service candidate, and the scope is the application in question. This level of early detail is not always possible, but will exist in some fashion. Based on this information, constraints can begin to be investigated. Elements such as timing of the test, access to facilities, resources required, and the environment, which may include third-party providers, can be used to quantify constraints. It is important that services management understands the constraints under which the security group and the customer may be held accountable when conducting security services. In general, governing laws, regulations, policies, standards, and commercial relationships that are well beyond the scope of security's roles and responsibilities can impose constraints.

It is noteworthy to add that constraints can become challenging under certain conditions. It is not uncommon for a customer to state a constraint that is not well founded, especially when it impacts scope or depth of the service. For example, if a service is to be applied to 50 of the 75 systems in the environment and the customer states that it simply doesn't want the service applied to the remaining 25 systems, this may conflict with requirements from risk or compliance management. When these situations surface it becomes a defining moment for the security group in how well the relationship with the customer is managed. This begins to introduce the all-or-nothing traditional approach seen in a number of security programs, which is one of the few root causes of separation between a business and a security group. It is necessary for services management to work closely with the customer to determine options, quantify the importance of the change in scope, and find methods by which the remaining systems can be addressed in a different way or to a lesser depth. The key aspect is to avoid pressuring the customer to do something it doesn't want to do without fully understanding its perspective and with the customer not understanding security's remit. Also, it's an opportunity to avoid a risk acceptance process that is not helpful to anyone and should only be considered as the last option.

As discussed in more detail in subsequent chapters, security services can be tuned and modeled in such a way as to find a balance between what security is attempting to achieve and what the target organization is seeking to accomplish for business purposes. Modifications to what is performed, how it is performed, how often, and to what depth can all be leveraged to create a tighter bond between the business and security that provides the foundation for meeting the needs of everyone involved. The ability to tune and find compensating scenarios through customer negotiations and collaboration is the basis for adaptability and one of the many aspects of the adaptive security management architecture that may be challenging for some. However, the basis of adaptability—optional measures—is deeply ingrained into what security groups do today. The objective is to apply those same concepts at a business level.

5.3.3 Define Concerns

Having established objectives and goals and gaining clear visibility into constraints does not eliminate the potential for concerns. Concerns can come from compliance and risk management and are addressed in the initiation of the service. However, strategic concerns must be investigated at the onset of service planning and will likely come from the customer or the business.

Concerns can be of a technical nature, such as system faults or errors affecting availability of systems during the execution of the security service. They can also appear as quality concerns, such as the use of certain tools and resources that have a known history of issues. Legal and HR concerns may surface due to the nature of the service. Strategic concerns are especially common when the security service introduces new technologies, solutions, and infrastructure in which long-term implications are not fully understood. And there are also management concerns, such as ongoing maintenance and responsibilities of the customer after the service has been performed and security is no longer involved.

Obviously, customer satisfaction can be directly tied to the ability of services management to identify, document, understand, and manage against customer concerns. Communicating concerns is an opportunity for the customer or business to not only convey overall expectations, but to essentially tell the security organization what quantifies its definition of success or failure. Therefore, concerns should not be taken lightly and should act as services management's guidance throughout the engagement on what to avoid or closely track to ensure stated concerns do not become a reality. If managed effectively throughout the process, there will be greater accuracy in the delivery of the service and security can play a meaningful role in ensuring the customer and/or the business is satisfied.

5.3.4 Defining Scope

As with all things, scope is critical. Is the service being applied to a specific network segment or to every server in the data center? Scope will greatly impact effort, timing, and the number of resources needed to deliver the service. There are four primary areas of scope for a security service:

1. Regulatory specifications—Virtually every regulation affecting information security practices defines the scope of what is covered by the regulation. Usually this comes in the form

of defining the target of the regulation, such as information types and activities to which information is exposed. For example, PCI identified payment cardholder information as the defined target and specified that systems that process, store, or transmit this information must meet the regulation (or the data security standard for this example).

2. Environmental characteristics—The target environment will offer a platform for defining scope. For example, if the service is targeted at Internet-facing systems, the infrastructure supporting that environment will act as a starting point for defining scope.

3. System characteristics—A system is a collection of physical or logical devices, applications, and data that provide a function or service to the organization. For example, the financial system may be comprised of several servers, networks, applications, workstations, and data management capabilities. If the objective, goals, and security needs are directed at the system, the system definition will provide initial scope. Of course, this clearly implies that the system must be defined, even at a high level.

4. Service characteristics—Beyond regulatory, environment, and system definitions that help define scope are service characteristics. These are not the characteristics of security services, but rather business services at a number of levels. For example, routing protocols can be seen as a network service that may require security to be applied. Service characteristics can be more complicated than other scoping activities because they are more nebulous and always seem to cross business lines. In most cases, the security group will find that IT is the primary customer business unit of service-based scoping.

The definition of scope should not only include one or more of these attributes, but also set boundaries. For example, a system may be identified as the target for the service, but the boundary may be to exclude a particular application within the system, although all the other applications in the system are included. It is in the definition of scope and boundaries where risk and compliance management's influence and involvement are critical. For example, the customer may define constraints that cause the application to be out of scope, but these may not be enough from the perspectives of risk and compliance management. As stated in the previous section, how security works with the customer to find a method for achieving balance is a large part of adaptability. By reviewing the issue, objective, and goals, and mapping these against constraints and concerns, the security group is provided a great deal of insight to find a solution that meets everyone's needs.

Scope also begins to introduce the depth of the service. Falling back on a liberally used example, it is the difference between vulnerability scanning and penetration testing, or performing forensics that only focus on the data volume and not the swap file or slack space. These represent the slight nuances of security and how security is performed relative to the business needs and security needs. Also, this touches on the fact that there exists a great deal of sophistication in existing security programs to be able to perform these variations effectively and to know when they are or are not applicable or valuable relative to the intent of the service, objective, and goal.

5.3.5 Service Initiation Source

As introduced above, different sources may wish to initiate a service. Therefore, there are different perspectives about the service, its objective, and its outcome. Many of these conditions are identified in the service planning activities, but it is necessary to understand how these may be influenced based on the source of the service request. As a result, services management must capture these characteristics in order to ensure the service is effectively delivered.

In the following sections concerning customer, policy, compliance, or risk initiated services, the information review and validation of a service by risk, compliance, services management, and even customers may resonate in different ways.

- Scope—An increase or a decrease of what is included or to be affected by the services
- Depth—A change in the level of detail, focus, or investigation of the service by employing specific tools, processes, and procedures
- Type—The defined service that is being employed

- Model—How the service is applied over time and in different depths
- Standards, Processes, Templates, Reporting, and Measurements—The modification or addition of one of these attributes in support of the service goals that may be related to scope, depth, type, and model

5.3.5.1 Customer When a customer requests a service it may provide some visibility into the intent it has for the service, but this cannot be the sole source of information to execute a service. Security is always open to interpretation, and although a customer has identified a need and selected a service to facilitate that need, services management must investigate and work with the customer to quantify what the customer is looking to accomplish. Moreover, once the service details are identified with the customer, services management must consult with risk and compliance management.

Services management should consider a service request from a customer as an invitation to collaborate with the customer on learning the objectives and making sure the customer is clear on its options concerning delivery models. During the collaboration and vetting phase, services management is interested in determining the following:

- What has stimulated the customer to request the service?
- What were the processes the customer used to identify the requested service?
- Has the customer had this service performed in the past?
- What are the goals the customer is wishing to accomplish?

While the process of working with the customer is a standardized and relatively simple process, the outcome is very important to governing next steps. As demonstrated, through the collaboration and vetting process with the customer, services management expresses the options in delivery models that meet the needs of the customer more effectively. The refinement of the service for the customer is the basis of demonstrating value. Some customers may assume they need something more than actually may be required, or there may be situations where additional activities may be required to facilitate the need. Services management can help to not only refine the service to the customer's need, but can also explain the reasons and advantages that may surface when the level of service that is required exceeds the customer's original assumptions.

As demonstrated in Figure 5.4, the customer request is routed to services management. Services management collaborates with the customer to identify the best service and service structure that meets the needs of the customer. Services management constantly vets the information collected throughout this process. The process of vetting compares the evolving details of what the customer needs with the goals it is attempting to meet, the security goals of the organization, business goals, and ultimately whether what the customer wants is possible. There are conditions that surface where the customer's demands may exceed what security can do, or services management may not have a service that is representative of what the customer actually needs.

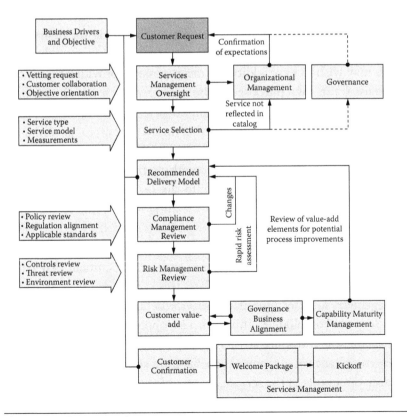

Figure 5.4 Customer service process.

One may ask that if the source of the request is the customer, how can there not be a service within services management? The answer is based on the fact that customers may not always know the exact service, but know what they want. They may have simply selected a service that "looked right" and through interactions with services management the true needs surfaced. In this case, services management consults directly with organizational management to determine if a new service should be created or an existing one should be modified. In turn, organizational management will consult with the customer to determine a solution, and once the customer is satisfied, the process returns to services management.

Once the service is vetted, it is necessary for services management to quantify the service details, such as type, structure, and measurements. Although measurements for performance, quality, and security are integrated into the service, measurements in this case are directed at meeting specific customer requirements that may exist to meet its specific goals. For example, the vulnerability management service may have a number of measurements that are taken during the delivery of the service that ultimately feed into governance. However, the customer may wish to have additional measurements provided that it can put to use for its own purposes. If the measurement is not already part of the service and the customer wants that level of visibility, services management must communicate the measurement to governance. The reason for making governance aware of this new measurement is because not only does it represent something that could be valuable to the program and be incorporated into the security architecture, it is the customer that is requesting it—meaning it has value to the business in some form.

As a result of these activities, the recommended delivery model is formalized. This will usually appear as a scoping document that articulates the service and the overall plan. This is provided to compliance management to determine if the service details in any way conflict with security compliance. This is also an opportunity for compliance management to introduce attributes that it feels are necessary. In many cases, compliance management benefits from any service being applied because the results of the service are provided to it to support auditing and gap analysis processes. The intent of compliance management is to ensure that the organization is not only meeting stated requirements, such as regulation, policy, etc., but also to promote progression and refinement of compliance-related activities and controls. Compliance must also be a continuous improvement process that drives efficiencies in how compliance is realized, maintained, and improved.

There are few situations where the security service would actually introduce noncompliance, but the potential does exist. This potential is based on the underlying complexity between compensating controls and the interpretation of compliance by the customer and services management in the formalization of the service delivery model and method. Ensuring compliance is not always a direct and clear approach. As previously discussed, there are conditions that require compensating controls to indirectly achieve compliance, which in turn can increase the complexity of the environment and make it more sensitive to change. For instance, a regulation may require a seemingly simple control, but to meet the intent of the regulation compliance management may have sponsored the implementation of an array of controls across process and technology, thus creating an interconnected web of apparently small, unimportant items, yet together they achieve compliance and the intent of the requirement. Usually, it is compliance management that has this level of visibility and can rapidly determine if a service has the potential to inadvertently disrupt one or more controls that are part of the compensating web of controls.

It is the responsibility of compliance management to fully understand all the implications—positive and negative—that may result from the delivery of the service. Compliance management's role is to first determine if the service can have an undesirable effect on compliance posture. Again, although rare, it is a necessary step. Second, compliance needs to determine if the service's activities can in some way enhance or improve compliance on a more programmatic level. Compliance management needs to ask, "How can the application of service help improve compliance for the organization?" For example, a security service for a customer must address processes concerning application security in the development phases. On the surface this may be tactical, but from an overarching compliance management perspective it may represent something that can be used for other customers or at least something worth monitoring to determine its role in compliance. Finally, compliance management needs to review the service as a source of information to assist in its role in ensuring compliance. The application of a security service, regardless of type, structure, or delivery model, will produce information. Compliance management must take every opportunity to leverage this information for overall compliance reporting and visibility into the compliance posture.

Once compliance management has reviewed and processed the recommended delivery model and details as well as any changes, it is passed to risk management. Risk management has a significant responsibility at this point. Risk management must determine if the service introduces any risk and if the service is compressive enough. Some may ask how a service can introduce risk if it is a security service. In short, it comes down to the standards, methods, and tools that are going to be used, which may result in an inaccurate picture of the environment. Moreover, if a security service is employed to design, architect, or change an environment or security control, this may be in direct conflict with other controls that are beyond the customer's environment. Risk management must be aware of the overall posture of the organization and through this visibility understand positive and negative impacts that may be occurring in a localized area of the business. For example, assume that the customer, services management, and compliance all agree that a vulnerability scan is the right service. The customer wants to know its vulnerabilities, there is a service model to support this, and compliance management is pleased because vulnerability scans are part of a regulatory compliance requirement. However, risk management may not agree with the methods and tools being used. This is especially true when a vulnerability scan has not been performed in a long time. Additionally, risk management is concerned about scope. Again, the customer, services management, and compliance management are in agreement that 20 of the 50 systems facing the Internet need to be scanned. But risk management knows of new vulnerabilities, tools, or attacks that may affect the other 30 systems and wishes to enlarge the scope.

There are a number of things that will influence risk management's perspective on the service and whether their wants and needs are justified. For example, scanning all 50 systems may simply cost too much or take longer than the customer is willing to accept. In the majority of cases, there is a predictable set of outcomes.

First, risk management may wish to have a better understanding of the environment that is the target of the service to better understand the role of the service relative to overall risk. This decision is based on the current understanding and experience with the customer's environment. If it has been a long time, if there have been a number of changes, or if this is the first time a particular service has been applied, risk management may perform a rapid risk assessment. It's important to note that performing a rapid risk assessment for a 20-system vulnerability scan to use as an example is highly unlikely. However, security services can be quite comprehensive and have many delivery details that are of interest to risk management. A rapid risk assessment will help risk management make informed recommendations.

Second, risk management may not be able to change the scope of the service or type, but it can influence the delivery model. The delivery model determines how the service may be applied differently over time in a way that can benefit security and the customer. For example, risk management may want more than 20 systems scanned, but there may be barriers, constraints, and concerns in accomplishing this. As a result risk management may return with a modified model that states the 20 systems are acceptable, but they must be scanned quarterly, or all 50 systems must be tested within the year. It is difficult to provide examples because the reasoning for risk management's concerns can vary greatly and are unique to each organization. The point being demonstrated is that risk management has options not only in how the service is delivered, but also in the structure and model of the delivery.

Finally, risk management may accept the structure, type, and model of the service, but request that services management provide additional information to risk management in the delivery of the service to help it monitor activities. For example, risk management may not be entirely comfortable with the details of the service, but not to the point where it wants to disrupt the process and the customer. Nevertheless, to satisfy concerns, services management provides additional information from processes and tools used during the engagement to assist risk management in tracking and monitoring the application of the service. An example would be the raw output from testing tools in the vulnerability scan. Although the customer may not be interested in this information, it can be helpful to risk management in identifying scenarios in which a low-risk vulnerability in the customer's environment actually translates to a high-risk scenario in a different area of the business, which may have been the root of risk management's concerns in the first place.

To summarize at a high level, in the simplest of terms, security is about protecting assets from threats and risk management is tasked with finding a balance between them in controls. Within the adaptive security management architecture, risk management plays a key role in assuring that services are applied in a manner that ensures this balance is maintained. However, as opposed to traditional programs in which the security organization may be fully orchestrated and governed by risk management, the ASMA uses risk management as an influence on how security can be applied and as a source of information. Risk management in the ASMA measures risk, and based on these measurements will affect how services are performed. However, compliance management, governance, organizational management, and capability maturity management provide input as well, but for very different reasons. This ensures the program is balanced so that business needs are met, value is demonstrated, and the organization has a meaningful posture. Moreover, this balancing of influence from different perspectives is what enables the program to be adaptable. What is being demonstrated by the interconnectedness of governing how services are applied is that risk management is not the only basis of security decisions, as found in virtually all of today's security programs, and represents a major departure for the ASMA from the accepted standard.

Once risk management has performed any number of activities, or nothing at all, and the service definition is finalized, it is provided to the customer for final confirmation. It is important to note that the customer has been involved in the compliance and risk management review processes; therefore, final customer confirmation is more of an official milestone, ensuring proper closure and helping meet maturity level requirements in the process before moving to the next phase.

5.3.5.2 Policy Conditions usually exist in which security policies may require a service to be performed against a particular customer. Usually, organizational management or compliance management will be the actual source of the requested service. Organizational management is responsible for policy management and may elect to employ a service when the need is identified. However, compliance management, which is responsible for compliance with policy, will be the source of many of the tactical policy requirements. For example, policy may stipulate a strategic requirement that may only be required annually or at major milestones in the evolution of the organization. Organizational management will source strategic policy-related services. On the other hand, policies also imply tactical activities, such as verification of new applications, the assessment of partner requirements, or audit-related activities that occur more regularly as part of standard operations and policy compliance. Therefore, while organizational management is concerned with larger policy considerations, compliance management is tasked with ensuring that policy is enforced at points in the organization's life cycle (Figure 5.5).

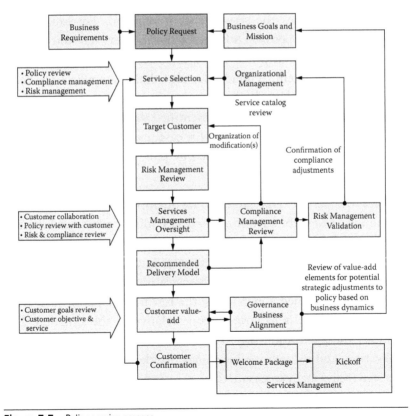

Figure 5.5   Policy service process.

One of two scenarios will occur at the onset of a policy-sourced service:

1. The policy defines a need, which in turn identifies the service to be employed, and then target environment(s) or customer(s) are identified. This is typically associated with strategic policy requirements coming from organizational management that are broad and typically encompass multiple business units. For example, policy states that all Internet connection points must undergo a penetration test annually. Of course, for some businesses, each group, division, or region may have its own Internet points of presence and therefore the policy requirement is broad and the service required is easily matched.

2. The policy defines the need, and there is a condition within a customer's environment that triggers the need for a service to be applied. In this case, the customer is identified through the activity, which is then matched to the policy requirement that determines the service that is required. For example, business units perform different activities every day and there may come a point where one of those activities requires security's involvement. A policy may state that new applications be tested prior to launch. As a result, when a new application is to be launched this naturally identified the customer and then the service to be applied. In this case, customer activities are monitored, and when triggered by policy the service is then identified for that customer.

Once the service and target(s) are identified, risk management again must review the identified service. Unlike a customer-initiated service, risk has far more control over how the service is applied. For example, compliance management is most interested in assuring that an application test is performed against a new application, but it is not equally concerned about "how" the test may be performed. Risk management's role is to govern scope relative to the situation. For example, the application may have several user roles defined in the application, and risk management may decide that all the roles must be tested individually to ensure there is no potential for privilege escalation. This means that more aggressive tactics, different tools, and additional methods need to be used.

Again, risk management may elect to perform a rapid risk assessment to determine if additional service elements are needed. Risk management is not simply focused on doing more, but on doing what is right for the overall organization. Risk management may have a great deal of experience with the particular business unit because it launches several applications a year. As a result, the service type and structure selected by compliance or organizational management may be overkill. Of course, it is equally likely the service is not detailed enough. Risk management is tasked with making this determination and ensuring it is defensible to governance. Recall that governance is the primary interlock with the business. Therefore, if risk management "exploits" a policy to perform excessive services, governance will act as a surrogate for the customer community to offer balance as to how risk management determines what is required.

Once risk management has defined the overall service type and structure it is passed to services management to interface with the customer. As with a customer-initiated service request, services management collaborates with the customer to explain the purpose of the service and the details. If risk management has performed a rapid risk assessment, this process is very short and quickly moves to customer confirmation, and service management's role at this point is moved to the next phases. However, if risk management has not performed a rapid risk assessment, it is likely that this is the first time the customer is aware of this need. Services management needs to work with the customer to ensure alignment and vet the risk and compliance-management-defined service with the targeted environment.

In the event the customer wants changes, it is the responsibility of services management to convey these to compliance management to ensure intent is maintained, and then to risk management to ensure risk is satisfied. If customer changes are confirmed, the process moves to the next phase. If they are not confirmed, it is the responsibility of compliance and/or risk management—whichever is at the core of the dispute—to work with services management and the customer to resolve the issues. In the event no resolution is achieved, organizational management must become involved.

5.3.5.3 Compliance The entire process for a compliance-initiated service is virtually identical to a policy-initiated service with a few changes.

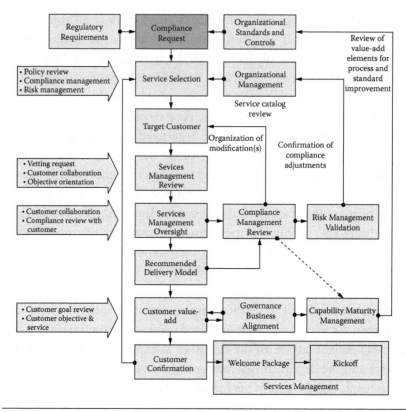

Figure 5.6 Compliance service process.

The first difference is that the purpose for the service may or may not be related to policy, yet it may be related to external forces, such as regulations. This also means that compliance is playing a role similar to organizational management's in a policy-initiated service, as in tactical and strategic. Therefore, one of the two scenarios defined above still applies, but only compliance management will be involved (Figure 5.6).

Second, unlike policy, compliance may require something that may have already been accomplished through another service or activities applied to the target. As a result, after the service and target are identified, compliance management must work with services management to ensure this service is actually needed based on previous activities. This is an important step because compliance cannot be completely aware of all activities all the time and therefore cannot assume that the identified need hasn't already been addressed. Given that services management is closest to the customer, it may have a far more detailed view of the target environment. In other words, compliance management must always collaborate with services management to determine if stated needs can be satisfied with existing documentation and evidence from previous service delivery. If this does not occur, the customer will undoubtedly raise this as an issue and, frankly, may become irate.

If services management cannot satisfy compliance management, the service details are passed to risk management. As with a policy-initiated service, risk management performs the same activities and has the same options in defining details of the service execution with oversight from governance. If changes are needed, the results from risk management are passed back to compliance and services management for review. Services management is included for the same reasons compliance management is, in order to ensure that changes from risk management cannot be addressed without having the service be performed.

If compliance and services management confirm the changes, the process is handed to services management to work with the customer, and from this point the same processes used in a policy-initiated service request apply.

Compliance management and the services it may initiate will play a significant role in adaptability. Compliance management is primarily focused on making certain that the company and the security organization are continually operating in a manner consistent with established external regulations, policy, and security architecture process expectations. As business demands and the environment shift to accommodate new directions, compliance is forced to recognize and effectively address any gaps that may surface. Having the ability to initiate services provides a method for compliance management to gain more information and insights into changes within the organization in order to formulate a solution. Moreover, with governance acting as a conduit to the business, compliance management will typically have a perspective of what changes may be on the horizon. When changes do occur the initial focus of compliance management is to determine gaps and the implications of each gap. For example, if a gap is related to internal policies and standards, changing these to accommodate the business must be reviewed to understand the benefit to impact ratio. If the gap materializes as noncompliance with external regulations, the objective is to find a method to facilitate the business need while ensuring long-term compliance. At this point the value of services to compliance and adaptability begins to surface. Services can act as a tool for compliance to investigate and implement compensating controls based on a full understanding of the environment and the changes that are occurring. Of course, other features in the ASMA are deeply involved; however, compliance management is formulating initial compensating methods.

In a traditional security organization with a compliance management capability, changes are usually received with negativity based on many in compliance having worked diligently to formulate a standard as well as consistency in how compliance is reached and maintained. Changes in the environment will inevitably challenge established standards and therefore disrupt compliance management processes founded on standard management approaches as opposed to those founded on control management approaches. Formulating an integrated compliance management capability that has close operational ties with other features in the program, such as services management, controls can be mapped more effectively so that it is more resilient to change. Services, along with risk management, act as enablers for compliance to constantly relate the current environment to regulatory demands. In addressing regulatory compliance there is a multitude of methods and framework variances that can be employed to achieve compliance specific to the business's environment. However, as a result many build a rigid compliance process once the control framework is formalized. Eventually, it has the potential to become more about compliance to the framework as opposed to the originally intended regulations. This is a pitfall that some have realized, and it greatly reduces the ability to respond to changes in the business. It is far more difficult to change a compliance framework than it is to change controls. The adaptive security management architecture seeks to reverse this by providing a management structure that incorporates all elements of security, governance, and operational management, thus allowing compliance management to focus on the management of controls from a position of flexibility empowered by delivery capabilities and visibility into the security and business dynamics.

5.3.5.4 Risk As will be detailed in subsequent chapters, risk—within the context of an adaptive security management architecture—is concerned with the balance between threats, controls, and assets. This balance is maintained by understanding probability,

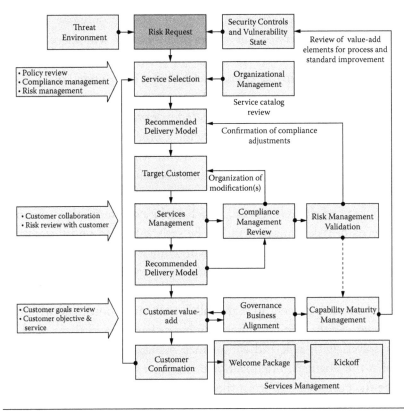

Figure 5.7 Risk service process.

impact, and control capability. Risk management consumes infor-mation of this nature and passes it to governance, which in turn combines it with other information for business communications (Figure 5.7).

There are conditions under which risk management must collect information on control capabilities, such as assessments, or have the opportunity to investigate business unit environments for assets and threats. To accomplish this, risk management may initiate a service targeted at one or more customers.

As seen in policy- and compliance-initiated services, the target or service selection may come before the others depending on the reason for the service initiation. For example, risk management may want visi-bility into vulnerabilities for a given type of system, such as all Windows servers in the network. Of course, this type of activity may touch mul-tiple business units that own and maintain their own Windows servers.

Conversely, risk management may be interested in only one business unit's application, network, or system and therefore will select a target and then the service or services that are needed. Within this context it is assumed that if risk management wanted to perform a rapid risk assessment, they would have done so by this point in time.

Once risk management has selected a service, it must work with compliance and services management. Compliance management is required to ensure they are in agreement, which in nearly all cases they will be due to the inherent common benefits of security activities. Services management performs many of the same tasks as it does in a compliance-initiated service, which includes determining whether the needs of risk management can be satisfied based on information it has from previous activities. As with compliance-initiated services, this is an important step in the process.

As with the other processes, once confirmed internally it is handed to services management to plan, collaborate, and coordinate with the customer. Again, the customer may have changes and these need to be resolved with risk and compliance management. If they cannot resolve the changes, organizational management will resolve them. Once the customer confirms, the service moves into the next phases.

Similar to compliance management, risk management is the cornerstone of adaptability, and the role it plays in the adaptive security management architecture is virtually unchanged from what the core responsibilities of risk management are today. In fact, although risk management is highlighted in the ASMA as a security feature, the context of this is to introduce enhancements to existing risk management programs that are likely already in place. The role of risk management is fundamentally to balance threats and assets through the sound application of controls. These conditions are assessed and measured to communicate what controls need to be considered in order to reduce the risk to an acceptable level. Within the adaptive security management architecture this activity is, for the most part, unchanged. The most predominant changes to risk management are the addition of rapid risk assessments and the placement of governance as the primary interface with the business. Nevertheless, the ability to assess, analyze, and interpret threats relative to controls and the assets of the organization is critical to adaptability. As changes in the business surface they will begin to resonate in how the company operates and how it works with partners, vendors, and customers, and will likely have an impact on technical infrastructure and information life cycle management. These will in some way touch on everything risk management is concerned with, such as data classification, management, and exposure; security controls across people, process, and technology; and they will certainly change the spectrum of threats facing the organization. Therefore, as shifts occur in the business, risk management—as is compliance management—is empowered with services and visibility from governance to interpret the impacts to risk.

Adaptability encompasses a number of capability attributes that must exist to ensure modifications to the environment are achieving a balance between the business and security, which includes compliance and risk, and the integrity of the environment and the operational integrity of the security group to respond and manage change. As previously discussed, one of these attributes is founded on compensation methods in meeting security needs for the business. Risk and compliance management make up the core of determining what controls are necessary within the changing environment relative to what is fundamentally required to maintain the identified risk threshold and regulatory demands. Although this is one aspect of adaptability, it is at the center of adaptation.

5.3.6 Welcome Package

Gathering predefined and specific information from the customer allows the service to be executed to the exact depth and breadth as defined by the customer, risk, and compliance. Each service will have options that govern the use of different methods, tools, and processes. There is no need to have a different service for each scenario, but having varying options for a service will in turn define the type and detail of the information required to perform the service.

It's noteworthy that all the activities that may have been performed up to this point have produced a great deal of information. Interactions between features and the customer to define objectives, constraints, concerns, and scope have resulted in a comprehensive service plan that is specific for that customer and service. This has resulted in the specifics in delivery of the service including everything from what service is to be performed and how-to measurements for security, compliance, performance, quality, and alignment to customer and business goals.

At this point in the life cycle it is necessary to quantify this information and help the customer prepare for the service. This is described herein as a Welcome Package. In nearly all cases, once a service has reached this point of evolution with a customer there is time between when the agreement is made and when the service is to be enacted, which can be exploited to add greater effectiveness, efficiency, and value to the customer.

In summary, a welcome package contains the following:

- Information about the security group
- Information about the security service
- A preliminary project definition plan
- A preliminary work plan
- A list of activities for the customer to perform
- A list of information and documentation that may be needed during the engagement

5.3.6.1 Security Group and Service Information   A welcome package plays two essential roles: professional courtesy and service support. Professional courtesy provides information about the security group and the service. This begins with an introduction to the group's strategy, mission, charter, and objectives as a meaningful member of the business and provides visibility into the leadership team and the organization. Security leadership cannot assume that all customers and business units understand these characteristics of the group or that they have been apprised of any changes. The welcome package is an opportunity to not only build a relationship with the customer, but also to inform the customer of who the group is, what it can rely on the group for, and any changes made to the group in meeting the mission of the business.

The next part is providing information about the service. This is not simply information about the service in how it is being applied to the customer—that is provided by the scoping document—but rather the service in its entirety. This is an opportunity for the customer to see more about the standard service or services than they may have been exposed to throughout the process.

Finally, part of professional courtesy is a welcome letter from the CISO or other executives in the security group. The purpose of this letter is to express the importance of security's role with the customer and its commitment to excellence and quality. The letter should be accompanied by contact details for key people within the organization if the customer wishes to interact directly with management or the leadership team.

5.3.6.2 Preliminary Project Definition and Work Plan   Service support starts with providing an initial project definition and work plan. The project definition plan summarizes all the information collected up to this point, including things such as objective, goals, concerns, scope, constraints, initiator of the service, and information from risk and compliance management. It also includes an initial set of customer contacts collected and the key contacts the customer will be working with. Lastly, a set of assumptions and high-level delivery needs are identified. Assumptions can include those related to constraints, points that have yet to be fully resolved, or attributes of delivery that cannot be fully defined until a certain milestone is met. High-level delivery needs may be as simple as ensuring space to work, access to the environment, and other general aspects.

The work plan is an initial project and resource plan. The goal of the plan is to highlight key activities and the duration expected for them, in addition to the order. For example, the service may start with a document review, interviews, a technical review, a design, and a deliverable. This may occur sequentially or overlap at times and have different durations. A high-level work plan will help the customer gain a better understanding of the general activities and durations.

Supporting elements that should appear in the project definition and work plan include the following:

- Project Overview and Scope
- Communications Plan
- Quality and Risk Management Plan
- Cost Management Plan
- Schedule and Milestones
- Vendor/Supplier Management Plan (if applicable)
- Escalation Plan
- Change Management Plan

5.3.6.3 Customer Activities and Requirements   With every security activity there are things the customer will have to perform. Moreover, the customer can use the time between the service planning and the start of the services to prepare materials to assist in the delivery of the service.

Customer activities include the following:

- Identify resources—The customer will have to identify at least one resource to act as the primary contact for the service. This person will be responsible for addressing the daily activities of service delivery and meeting the needs of services management. Of course, there can be multiple people involved in the service, but one must be assigned as the primary and day-to-day manager representing the customer.
- Prepare environment—Preparing the environment covers two major areas of customer preparation:
  - The first area is preparing a work environment. This can range from providing a cube or a desk for security resources to providing access to facilities, networks, or systems. This also includes identifying communal work areas, such as meeting rooms, and supporting services, such as telephones, that may be required during delivery.
  - The second area is more technical in nature. For example, if a service is going to interact with a system, that system or environment should not be changed while the service is being performed. Therefore, the customer needs to ensure that the target environment has reached a point where changes can be minimized. Moreover, changes that occur in the environment must be provided to the service delivery team so that it is aware and can determine if there are any implications of the change relative to scope and objectives.
- Communications—Except for a few cases in which knowledge of the security service activities is limited to a specific few, the customer must communicate to its internal teams that the service is going to take place. In short, the objective is to reduce surprises. Security delivery resources may show up on site, ask questions, access systems, obtain documentation,

or appear on the network. If the organization is unaware—unless by design—of these activities, they may cause unnecessary disruption.

In addition to things the customer can do to prepare materials, there are also requirements from services management concerning the delivery of the service. Requirements come in two forms:

1. Start engagement requirements—To start a service there are typically specific needs of the security group. A simple example is if the service is to perform log reviews it must have access to the logging system or systems to get started. If the service is an application test that includes authenticated testing the delivery team will need credentials in the application to perform the test. This may be as simple as a username and password combination, or something more complicated, such as a fob or smartcard. In these cases, it introduces more processes that need to be completed. A number of conditions require the customer to perform some activity to start the process, and most of these will be identified by the type and details of the service. Of course, these requirements must be met before the service can begin.

2. In-progress engagement requirements—There may be points in time during the delivery of the service when the delivery team may need information, documentation, additional access, or additional resources from the customer to complete the phase of the service. These requirements are not needed to start the service, but represent areas that can delay the delivery of the service. Therefore, expressing these requirements in the beginning not only allows time for the customer to prepare, but for the customer to fully understand what will be required throughout the service. These requirements must be planned for and it is the responsibility of services management to ensure constant communications with the customer so that the needs of delivery are met at key points in time.

5.3.7 Kickoff Meeting

A kickoff meeting is the formal initiation of a service, and it is an opportunity to ensure that all the activities are communicated and planned. In the scope of activities, after the service planning is complete a welcome package is provided to the customer. At that time a project start time for the service is identified and a kickoff meeting is performed on or before the start date. Of course, all these activities can happen in one meeting or over several meetings. There should be nothing implied that this needs to be complex, just simply comprehensive, and all the elements should be performed. With very small services some may question the validity of having to perform all these steps, but the devil is truly in the details. This is based on the fact that good planning saves money and increases quality. Moreover, when there are good planning practices in place, they become standard and therefore increase maturity and effectiveness, and produce valuable information.

Although there are specifics for a kickoff meeting, at the end of the day it's simply a meeting. As such, there is an agenda of topics to be covered, materials to review, and actions as a result. The ultimate goal is to ensure everyone is pointed in the same direction and expectations are clearly understood. In short, the intent is to

- Officially state the beginning of the service and what is going to occur from this point forward.
- Review and agree upon activities that are going to occur during the service delivery.
- Establish that all those involved are committed to the success of the service and quality of the outcome.

Those required to attend the meeting include representatives from services management, primary delivery resources, and the customer point of contact. Inputs to the meeting are an agenda, preliminary project definition and work plan, and the documented scope. Outputs from the meeting are meeting minutes, action items, and proof that all points within the agenda were covered, such as a checklist. Additionally, it is helpful to have someone document and track sidebar or parking lot points that may not be related to the delivery of the service, yet are pertinent to services management and the customer for future reference.

The agenda should include, but not be limited to, topics such as the following:

- Purpose and Agenda—An introduction to the meeting, its purposes, and, of course, the agenda.
- Customer and Delivery Teams Introduction—Introduction of people involved with the service including not only their job roles and responsibilities, but also their roles and responsibilities within the context of the service.
- Scope Review—Review the scope of the service. This is not an opportunity to review all of what is to occur, but simply what is included in the service and what have been identified as exclusions.
- Project Definition and Work Plan Review—This is an opportunity to review the primary phases and milestones of the project and discuss primary activities.
- Customer Information and Requirements Review—During this portion of the meeting the results from the welcome package are reviewed. The primary focus of this agenda item is to ensure that the delivery team has provided the critical start engagement requirements. If not, an attempt to resolve them in the meeting should be made.
- Change Procedures—There are conditions for both the customer and the delivery team under which changes to the scope and activities may be needed. This is an opportunity to discuss processes and procedures concerning how changes are identified, communicated, and approved.
- Service Risk Management and Escalation Procedures—As with any service, project risk must be managed. Moreover, as challenges surface there must exist a method to escalate concerns. For customers, there is a need to understand who to go to when something goes wrong, and the delivery team needs someone to work with when there are delivery challenges as a result of customer error.
- Information Distribution and Communications Plan—Given that this is a security service, there are a number of scenarios

where the information resulting from the service or even the knowledge that security is being applied must be secured. Plans, processes, and practices addressing how information is to be shared and communicated are important and must be agreed upon.

- Completion Criteria—One of the more rare occurrences in current information security groups in performing security services within an organization is clarity on what constitutes completion. Security has a tendency to touch everything and be a constantly moving target. However, in a security services management model the goal is to ensure there is clarity and value of outcome, and part of this is defining what criteria confirm that the service has met the requirements. Of course, there are ongoing services that may not have finite end points, such as system management, monitoring, log management, and other types of activities continually performed by the security group. In these scenarios completion criteria are typically associated with milestones or key deliverables provided throughout the service life cycle.

At the end of the meeting, everyone should come away with a consistent view of

- The primary contacts responsible for the service
- The scope of the service and what is going to occur
- How to manage changes during the service
- How to address project risk and what resources are available to evaluate problems
- The schedule of events and activities, such as status meetings status reports, preliminary documentation, and the like, and
- Clarity on the criteria that indicate the service has completed all the items

5.4 Delivery Management

Delivery management is responsible for the day-to-day activities performed during the execution of the service. Depending on the type and duration of the service, this may include such things as status meetings, status reports, milestone/phase management, interim deliverables, risk and error management, scope creep, and quality control.

Delivery management ensures that resources show up to work, vacation schedules are managed, backup resources are available if someone is sick, the right tools are available, and representatives from the customer are available when needed to properly facilitate the service's delivery.

The author understands that delivery management is reflective of project management and most organizations have a firm grasp on how they want projects managed. Moreover, there is a great deal of comprehensive information on project management in the industry, including a number of certifications for the profession. This section, and in many ways the majority of this chapter, is not meant as a replacement or a substitute for existing project management standards and guidance. It is provided to ensure that the very basics are communicated and to describe how these may relate directly to the adaptive security management architecture. For those who have comprehensive project management capabilities, the following will likely already be a reality in your environment. For those who may not have a great deal of project management expertise in security, this section will help provide a very basic foundation and show what minimum activities are required to ensure a meaningful program.

Covered in this section are the following:

- Status and reporting
- Deliverable management
- Ongoing management

5.4.1 Status and Reporting

On a regular schedule, typically weekly but daily if required, the delivery team will review progress and the status of activities. This is an opportunity to discuss activities, delivery performance, security goals, issues, risks, and any success stories. This is performed internally first and then with the customer.

5.4.1.1 Internal Status Meetings Internal status meetings are a formal opportunity for the management and delivery team to review activities in service delivery. Management and the type of service define how often these occur and at what level. For small and short-duration projects it may be necessary for the entire team to meet daily. For large services, especially those with multiple delivery groups, groups may decide to meet twice a week and as an entire team once a week. Of course, each case is different. Nevertheless, performing internal status reviews on a regular basis must be considered a requirement to the success of the service and the entire program.

Additionally, there are some services in which risk and compliance management will want or need to be involved in internal reviews. This is especially important if one of these two organizations was the initiator of the service. Moreover, if risk and/or compliance management played a key role in the definition of the service delivery model for the customer based on activities performed during service planning, it will need to be involved at key points within service delivery to ensure that those modifications are a reality. However, it should be added that this may be as simple as providing risk and compliance management the status report or as involved as having them participate in the delivery of the service. It will be up to each organization to determine how this ultimately occurs.

Internal status meetings must accomplish two basic activities: collaborate on the status and progress of the service, and generate a status report to be used internally and act as the foundation for the report delivered to the customer. The best way to achieve this is to discuss what should be in the internal status report, which will expose what needs to be covered by the internal management and delivery team. The status report will likely include the following:

- Overall status in terms of schedule and deliverables with regard to projected expectations at that point in time. Examples include sharing percent complete, remaining items, or items at risk.
- Define progress against defined deliverables. As the service is being performed it begins to produce information and documentation. At certain points within the service there is an expected completion of documentation. The status report needs to reflect if deliverables are on track, lagging, or exceeding expectations.
- Provide a forecast on status and progress of deliverables. For example, show that percentage of completion or outstanding

actions that are due will be completed. Additionally, define what can be expected to be completed in the deliverables.

- Any issues should be identified. Issues are early-stage risks and threats to the delivery of the service. On the surface they may not seem significant, but if not communicated and managed, they may impact delivery.
- Recommendations for change or improvements should be provided. These can range from ancillary recommendations to the customer based on observations acquired during delivery or recommendations for changes in scope if deemed necessary or as a valuable option to the customer.
- Updates to identified risks. As the service is delivered risks may be identified and therefore managed. As a result, a list of risks will be compiled and will need to be updated in each status cycle.
- Action item register management and reporting. Like risks, action items will appear in each status meeting. These may surface as adjustments in activities or actions that must be taken to facilitate the service.

Identified and managed issues, the risk list, and the action item register should include the names of the owners in the delivery team and customer team responsible for addressing these items and a proposed date of reconciliation or closure. The key take-away from internal meetings and the resulting status report is documentation. Documentation is evidence that a process has been performed and provides the foundation for process improvement. Moreover, if status meetings are not performed or are performed and not documented, any downstream issues in service delivery will not be easily defensible. In short, projects can quickly take a turn for the worst for a number of reasons, and without documentation resolution is reduced to a he said–she said debate. Although status meetings and documentation are fundamentally simple, they are representative of a mature program and one that can learn from undesirable results, and, most importantly, rapidly adjust.

5.4.1.2 Customer Status Meetings Once the internal status meeting is completed and a status report is created it must be translated for the customer. In many cases, the internal status report will simply be provided to the customer. However, this is not always the case, being that issues and other information concerning delivery may be relegated to the security group. Nevertheless, it is the responsibility of services management to define the customer status report template or ensure that any customer-provided templates are employed.

Once the customer-facing status report is formalized, the services management team and potentially members from the delivery team plan and execute a status meeting with the customer as agreed in the kickoff meeting. This presents an opportunity to share the status and progress of the service directly with the customer and obtain feedback and direction if necessary. The important aspect of the customer status meeting is to ensure expectations are being met. It's an opportunity to express how the service is progressing, any challenges that need to be addressed by the customer, and any risks that may exist and what is being done to compensate, and to compare overall progress against the project plan. Albeit an obvious statement, it is critical to listen to the customer and take note of indications of customer satisfaction in order to enhance or ensure that those attributes of the service do not waver, and to be keenly aware of initial indications of customer dissatisfaction as well as direct or indirect clues about what security must do to adjust the execution of the service to mitigate challenges early in the process. Listening is especially critical with customers for whom a service is being performed for the first time. Even if there are significant planning and good communication, it is not until the service is being executed that the customer truly begins to experience the approach. For regular customers it is important for the services management team to not become too comfortable with the process. Comfort leads to lethargy and poor predictions, which leads to mistakes and ultimately poor quality. The important message is to take every opportunity to learn from the customer and make appropriate adjustments when possible to promote quality and satisfaction.

Although this is a short section, it is not indicative of the importance of customer status meetings. Services management is about providing value, but it is also about changing the identity of security in the business. Taking the initiative and spending time with the customer to explain activities is an important part of this new identity.

5.4.2 Deliverable Management

As previously stated, every service will result in some form of deliverable. Even such things as status reports, meeting notes, tool output, and e-mail should be considered part of the deliverable. In short, there are always work products as a result of a service.

As such, deliverables need to be tracked and managed, and this was demonstrated in the status report section. Once they have been measured against the planned scope and activity of the service and quality expectations, they can be delivered to the customer. It should be noted that deliverables may be provided in various forms and stages to the customer throughout the delivery process. Nevertheless, the same rigor must be applied to all materials, regardless of stage, before being provided to the customer for review.

All materials that are to be used as part of the deliverable must be formally reviewed internally for quality control. Internal quality control should be a constant in service delivery, and those who are responsible for the generation of materials, which includes everyone involved with security, should always be focused on the quality of their work product. Doing so simplifies the formal quality review and makes for a delivery team that is much more responsive to customer requests.

Overall, the process is relatively simple. First, the producer of the materials must perform a regular review of the material for quality and accuracy. Others in the team should review the materials, and then management does a final review. During the management's review of the deliverables, the primary objective is to ensure that the deliverable meets the customer's quality requirements as defined in the kickoff meeting. This includes everything from document format and language to file format and structure.

Also, resources that are not involved in the delivery of the service, including, but not limited to, compliance and risk management, should be included in the review process. Finally, the quality review process must be documented, tracked, and managed. This is a requirement for capability maturity and ensures there is consistency in delivery products.

Once the deliverable review is complete, it is provided to the customer for review. The customer may define the process for delivery and services management, depending on the criticality of the delivery, and security may wish to formalize completion of the deliverable by conducting a review meeting with the customer.

5.4.3 Ongoing Management

Services management is responsible for all aspects of delivery, and a number of different services may be performed at any given time. Depending on the size and complexity of the organization, this may require one manager or project leader, or a small team if the environment is very large. The following sections touch on areas of overall management activities that must be performed as a minimum and apply to a services model.

5.4.3.1 Schedule Management
Scheduling plays a key role in the definition and delivery of services, especially with regard to service granularity and the number of proposed services that will be maintained in the services management model. Therefore, scheduling resources begins in the service definition. The number of resources and type of skills required will be defined within the service and act as a guideline for services management. These service attributes are only guidelines because dynamics may force services management to adjust to compensate for specific conditions.

Discussed in more detail in Chapter 9, organizational management, resource skills, certifications, and capabilities are measured to build an overall service delivery capability. Measurements of this nature will assist services management in determining how to apply resources, especially in those cases in which the resources defined in the service are not available. For example, the service may call for two resources with specific skill levels, but one of these resources may not be available. As a result, and empowered with the skills and capabilities tracking and management tools from organizational management, services management may elect to fill the open position with two lower-level resources to compensate.

Beyond assigning resources, schedule management ensures that resources are made available for the duration of the service based on the project definition and work plan. There may be different numbers and types of resources needed at various stages of delivery, and it is the responsibility of services management to ensure these needs are met.

Last is the utilization of resources from other groups or external third parties. In many cases services management will not have the final say in how resources from beyond the security group are applied. Much of the control of resources is determined by agreements and, frankly, the flow of money. With regard to the flow of money, if the security group has directly procured third-party support for the delivery of the services, it is in control of those resources. However, there may be conditions under which resources beyond the direct control of the security group are required to meet the objectives.

In the development of services and identification of resources this process includes the identification and acquisition of resources that may be required from other groups, such as IT, development, or even human resources (HR) and legal. It is necessary for organizational management to establish agreements and expectations with these other groups so that services management is provided a degree of control to ensure the service is effectively delivered. This is a critical responsibility of organizational management, and any failures in addressing resource requirements will manifest themselves in delivery and greatly impact the quality and value of delivery. In many ways, when the security group relies on resources beyond its control the risk of poor delivery is dramatically increased. As a result, these activities must be thoroughly planned.

Within the context of adaptability, resource management and scheduling become essential in determining how to compensate for changes within the business. A simple example is budgeting. The business may demand cuts or reallocation of funding from operational expenses to capital expenses in order to acquire much-needed technology. Given that third-party providers or contractors may support a number of services, this may represent the best area for temporary cost reductions. However, without clear visibility into the costs associated with the service, how often the service is utilized, the role of the service in supporting the overall security posture, and how the service is or can be affected by the increase or decrease in other security services, the decision may have unpredictable results. This raises questions concerning training of existing staff to perform the same duties as a contractor, or the utilization of multiple other, less expensive services to compensate for the reduction of a specific service. Finally, with clarity on the affected service's objectives, processes, and outcomes it will be possible to tie these to the newly introduced technology or other emerging capabilities as compensating methods.

The key point is to understand that resource requirements and project plans specifically associated with a service play heavily into the adaptation of the overall security program when business needs instigate changes in operations. Although other examples and processes concerning adaptation are discussed in greater detail in subsequent chapters, it is also worth noting that some of the balance between business and security activities is being performed naturally today, yet this is predominantly based on intuition, experience, management skill, and institutional knowledge. The goal of the ASMA is to codify this and make it tangible with information, processes, and evidence so that decisions have greater merit, are defensible, and have measurable and predictable outcomes.

5.4.3.2 Scope and Change Management Throughout the delivery of services and status meetings, adjustments to scope and changes in the customer or delivery environment may surface and must be managed. Again, there are well-defined processes in project management that address these activities, but within a services model there are additional considerations.

When scope and other changes surface it is necessary for services management to reconvene with risk and compliance management to ensure those changes are not detrimental or somehow conflict with influences that were introduced during services planning. This is especially important if risk or compliance management was the initiator of the service. Depending on the level of change, in many cases services management will be able to effectively address changes due to its involvement and the customer management it performed in planning processes that defined objectives and goals. Nevertheless, there are conditions that will require the involvement of risk and compliance management.

It is difficult to set metrics to assist in the decision criteria. Even small changes to scope can have a dramatic impact on intent, whereas large changes may have none at all. Making certain that risk and compliance management are, at a minimum, provided status reports will ensure they always have the opportunity to comment on changes.

5.4.3.3 Information Management   Part of ongoing management is the control of data and information as a direct result of the service. This applies to operational and management information and delivery information. Although the information may be of different types, the consistent theme is how this information is secured and communicated. This can be as simple as having an engagement site with all the deliverables secured to only allowing access for customer representatives and the delivery team to having comprehensive controls and data classification for sensitive materials.

Operational and management information involves data that is collected about the performance, cost, and quality of service delivery. Examples include performance and cost measurements, quality control activities and resulting information, and resource information, such as tool configurations, procurement contracts, and billing and invoicing data. Access to this type of information should be limited to those who require it. Also, how the information is communicated, tracked, and documented will need to be addressed relative to security policies and existing data classification standards. Lastly, information related to the execution of services, such as how processes were employed, any changes made in processes and standards during delivery, and any data relating to how changes were managed, is important, especially for capability maturity and compliance management.

Delivery information essentially includes the customer deliverables and supporting materials. In short, it is anything that is a result of the service that can be directly tied to the customer and the activities performed. Clearly, this information must be protected on behalf of the customer. Any customer-specific requirements will be identified during the service planning and kickoff meeting. However, services management must establish a baseline policy and supporting processes and procedures that are to act as the minimum controls concerning all customer-related information.

5.4.3.4 Cost Management   Managing the costs incurred by the service is paramount and is an activity with which governance will be closely involved. Clearly, for the model to demonstrate effectiveness and efficiency and be valuable to the business, it must be highly tuned to how investments are applied. Cost management not only has tactical meaning, but also considerable strategic meaning.

Tactically, exceeding established cost forecasts in the delivery of the service might be a highly unwelcome occurrence for the business. Based on the planning, service structure, and oversight of scope, the potential should be minimized. Moreover, through scope and change management, if performed correctly, changes that impact cost should be documented and put through an approval process to make certain that increases in cost are justified.

Cost should be a predominant factor in decision making as opposed to other characteristics of delivery. For example, if services management underestimated the effort and committed to a completion date that is not possible, it may seek outside support—at a cost—to ensure the date is met. Of course, this is not a simple decision, even if the monies exist. All the other features, especially governance and organizational management, which are responsible to the business, are essential to understanding and managing decisions of this nature as they occur.

Strategically, cost management plays a key part in reporting, trending, and adaptability. The first of these, which measures performance against costs forecast, will be a prominent attribute in reports to the business by governance. Demonstrating cost-effectiveness and good management of financial resources is paramount. Governance can use this information to express operational integrity and combine it with other data to articulate the effectiveness of the security organization as a meaningful part of the company.

Second, governance will use cost management information from each service to monitor overall performance and delivery activities to identify trends. For example, governance may find that certain services consistently run over budget, which means these services are not well defined or well scoped. Governance may find that certain managers on different types of services result in tighter control, leading it to conclude that those individuals or the processes they are using are better than others. Some services may come in under budget consistently, but exceed performance goals—or vice versa. Finally, governance will tie performance of this nature to demands and security goals. For example, a particular service may be in high demand, but is constantly running over the budget and is not addressing key security goals. On the other hand, a service may be underutilized, but aligns well to several strategic security and business goals and is always on target with cost forecasts.

Cost management, or certainly the information collected from managing costs in services management, will play a critical role in adaptability. Understanding overall costs of services and their relationship to performance and security and business goals is one of the key ingredients to promoting adaptation to business dynamics. To elaborate, understanding the costs related to a service and how that service is performing relative to business and security goals will provide indicators on how that service can be adjusted or prioritized in the event of environmental, budgetary, or resourcing changes. Each security service provides a method to apply security in a specific way that ultimately forms the security posture. Everything from vulnerability tests and patch management to log management and network security represents a consolidated and focused effort that defines the layers of the security program. As layers, which are in many ways analogous to defense-in-depth strategies, services provide integrated security controls that may have overlaps and compensating factors that reduce exposure and risk as well as ensure compliance. As such, from the perspective of the security posture, services—in their entirety—can be adjusted relative to one another to manage changes in the business, but without dramatically impacting the posture or reducing effectiveness.

In general terms, the concept is not unlike making adjustments to an equalizer for a stereo, such as adjusting bass, gain, tone, and the like. The music still plays, it simply sounds different and draws more or less from different system components to produce the sound. Through services and the existence of the adaptive security management architecture in support of how security is applied, managed, and measured, there is a wide range of characteristics that provide for adaptation; one of the primary ones is related to cost management. By relating costs to goal attainment, managing risk, and ensuring compliance, and understanding the inherent relationships that exist between services, costs can be used to emphasize or de-emphasize one service as it may relate to another. For example, there is a relationship between patch management and vulnerability management, which are two different approaches to managing exposures. Vulnerability management may be focused on the identification of vulnerabilities and developing recommendations that may include configuration changes, policy changes, code changes, and the application of patches. Patch management seeks to ensure system stability and security by applying patches that may eliminate vulnerability for which tests were not performed. This represents a security overlap that can be exploited. If patch management is far more cost-effective than certain vulnerability management activities, this may be an indicator that it can be used more often and still achieve the desired level of security. Of course, cost is not the only decision criteria used in adjusting services, but the association between cost, effectiveness, goal alignment, and role in security posture provides for adaptability.

5.4.3.5 Performance Management An essential responsibility of services management is managing performance. Capability maturity management will act as a supporting feature for services management and provide input and support in identifying performance challenges as well as opportunities to increase performance. Interestingly, this real-time interaction between these two features is representative of a level 5 in the capability maturity model.

Performance management acts as the compensating delivery control in relation to cost management. Cost management is focused on the effective management of resources and fiscal responsibility throughout delivery. However, just because the delivery is meeting cost requirements does not imply that performance is optimized. Without performance management there is a propensity for every service to simply meet or run over budget, and not necessarily exceed expectations. It is human nature to consume what is available. For example, if a resource is provided one week to perform a function that can be completed in three days, it's likely the activity will consume the available time.

Services management has the additional responsibility of managing performance, and it does so by ensuring that resources are doing their best to achieve goals in an efficient manner. The idea is to reduce wasteful activities and push the team to meet or exceed expectations. Not only does this require the close management of activities, it also necessitates monitoring processes for opportunities for improvement.

In many ways, services management will collaborate closely with capability maturity management and will also receive input from compliance management, given that it is focused on ensuring the program is following stated processes and using defined standards.

Performance is critical to the overall success of the program, and capability maturity management exists to work with governance at a strategic level to ensure process faults are corrected and indications of performance activities result in process improvements. It is the responsibility of services management to monitor and track performance measurements and provide these directly to governance for oversight and business-level communications.

5.5 Closeout

When the service is complete there is a final delivery of the work products. Unlike other deliverable reviews that may or may not include a meeting, the final deliverable should be provided in a meeting. This provides the opportunity to ensure that all the criteria for completion have been met and the customer can confirm acceptance.

In a perfect world a service has a distinct beginning and end. However, this is not always possible or necessary. For example, a service such as patch management or policy management may appear as ongoing, but will typically occur in cycles. This is characteristic of typical services. However, services such as security monitoring are constant, and starts and stops can be detrimental to delivery. As a result, closeout activities will manifest in two different ways, but will likely be very consistent in delivery. For services that have a clear end point, a closeout is an opportunity to meet with the customer and provide all the final documentation and materials generated throughout the service, from status reports to configurations; discuss the process; summarize the outcome; answer questions; and present a quality survey for the customer to complete. It is important that closeouts be performed regardless of the size of the engagement. It's about quality, satisfaction, and learning from the entire process.

For ongoing services, closeouts are more of a milestone quality check. These can be performed quarterly, for example, and are an opportunity to summarize activities, findings, and recommendations that have surfaced from the onset of the service or since the last meeting. This is an opportunity to demonstrate value to the customer by expressing what has been accomplished and what trends have been identified, and generally exposes the customer to an executive-level summary to validate its investment in the service. The process is usually similar to a standard closeout, but with the addition of forward-looking statements. At the end of the meeting the customer is encouraged to complete a quality survey.

A closeout meeting represents the end of a service, phase, or a milestone. Depending on the type and size of the service provided, it is good practice to summarize the service in a formal presentation. The goal is to provide a crisp summation of the service, accomplishments, lessons learned, and outcome. It is also an opportunity to highlight those individuals within the customer's environment that assisted in the delivery. Finally, the closeout must contain the achievement of metrics. These should include any expectations set by the customer, risk, and compliance management (if applicable) at the beginning of the service. However, what should also be included are general security and performance metrics. It is assumed that the customer would benefit from knowing that another group within the company has met its own expectations for performance.

Finally, and a very important addition, is the impact of the service on the organization as a whole, specifically with regard to security and business goals. This assumes that every security service had some positive impact on security for the organization. At the initiation of the service, and all that was implied, a great deal of energy was expended to ensure that the service related to the stated objectives, the goals of the customer, the security group, the business, and compliance and risk management. The term customer has been used throughout this chapter to instill a sense of service ownership in the program. However, the reality is that the customer is part of the business, and as part of the business it should have visibility into the security group's performance and how the service plays into the bigger picture for the company. All the objectives and goals outlined in the service planning and those that exist within governance and services management for service delivery should be reviewed with the customer.

As the last act of the closeout, the customer is formally requested to complete the quality and satisfaction survey. It is highly recommended to use a third-party system and process for surveys to ensure complete autonomy; however, this is not always possible. Another option is to provide the survey on-line via an internal system. Most people prefer to complete forms on-line and this streamlines the process. At a minimum, if on-line surveys are not available, a survey form must be provided and with it a self-addressed, stamped envelope or internal mail folder to ensure the customer is not overly burdened with submitting the form. Ensuring that a satisfaction and quality survey is completed is of great importance. It is a simple yet extraordinarily important feedback mechanism that can help the security organization increase quality and business alignment. The questions should focus predominantly on the customer's experience in working with the security group and not necessarily on what was specifically performed, although certain aspects of a given service should be included. Responses should be organized based on customer, rating, and service to expose trends, such as the same customer having varying degrees of satisfaction with the same or different services. There is a science to quality and satisfaction surveys that is well beyond the scope of this book; however, there are a few points worth highlighting. First, take advantage of high scores to generate success stories sponsored by the customer. Of course, move rapidly to address low scores. An organization is often judged on its response to poor satisfaction results, and if there is no response the ability to regain trust and confidence is significantly reduced.

5.6 Measurements

As the primary method for applying security to an environment, security services produce an array of information concerning delivery that can be combined with the measurements from other features to obtain a holistic view of performance. Although information produced by the other features is valuable, organizations will seek out the opportunity to obtain a wide range of granular information from services management. In fact, the most challenging aspect of measurements taken from service delivery and services management is determining what information is worth formalizing as an indicator of performance. On the surface, having too much information may not appear to be problematic, especially when compared to the lack of measurable information in other forms of security management models. However, this raises a strategic issue that will require time and attention.

First, it must be acknowledged that measurements are, in part, service dependent. Although there is a set of measureable, performance-related pieces of information that are consistent across all services regardless of type, each service will have a unique collection of information that can be made available to the measurement process. With that in mind, it must also be understood that you are what you measure, and the act of taking measurements will fundamentally change the context of the environment. In theoretical terms this can be related loosely to the Heisenberg Uncertainty Principle, which in layman's terms implies that you cannot measure something without changing what you are measuring. More specifically, the principle states that while you can measure the position of a particle you cannot also accurately measure its momentum or velocity. Translated to the comparably simple world of security and performance measurements, this means that when you measure activities you set in motion an environment relative to those measurements, and by measuring one set of attributes inevitably you are not going to measure others.

Assume you own a car lot and have salespeople working for you. Their commission is based on the number of cars sold, and as a result salespeople are selling cars at a high volume. However, it is not necessarily just volume that makes the company money, but also the margin. You find that a large percentage of sales have low margin, meaning the salespeople are cutting great deals to ensure customers drive out with a new car. Technically speaking, salespeople do not care about margin because they are paid based on volume and as such will operate in a manner that may conflict with the profitability of the business. The influence of measurement can have a profound impact on the business, both negatively and positively. For example, if you are experiencing issues with quality you start to define quality metrics and tie these to employee performance, such as pay, commissions, or bonus. These are examples related to the first attribute of the Heisenberg Uncertainty Principle. However, to the latter attribute, you cannot measure everything. If that were the case every company would have perfect quality and performance, but in reality something will always slip through the cracks or be misinterpreted, or worse, you'll lose all your employees because they cannot achieve stated goals. In short, you cannot measure everything, and what you do measure will define the organization. There is an excellent paper that I highly recommended you read, "Metrics: You Are What You Measure," by John R. Hauser and Gerald M. Katz (published in April of 1998). The paper expresses the meaning of measurement within the context of business and defines seven pitfalls and seven steps to good metrics that, when viewed in their entirety, provide the basis of a measurement strategy. Following is a high-level overview of the pitfalls and steps with commentary that ties it back to the ASMA:

Pitfalls that lead to counterproductive metrics include the following:

1. Delaying rewards—Companies must accept that things change and people change jobs or are promoted, making it difficult to fulfill long-term-oriented metrics-based rewards. The authors summarize this as looking for metrics that can be measured today but which impact future outcomes. Within the ASMA, specifically services, if you measure delivery team members on aspects that will not come to fruition in a meaningful amount of time, it is likely they will not resonate with the metric.

2. Using risky rewards—In short, what is the risk to the business or to the manager/employee? Companies can diversify risk, but employees cannot, making them risk averse to vague or uncertain outcomes that are beyond their control. Measurements have to be applicable and clear to the community they are addressing. Moreover, within the context of service delivery there must exist a balance of accountability to metrics and authority to make a difference. If a security resource is measured against things employees cannot influence or that are not clear, it will have little meaning.

3. Making metrics hard to control—A simple interpretation of this pitfall is that while metrics at one level can have significant downstream effects, it is important that they are focused on the specific area and are measurable today, yet align with long-term goals. This is similar to the first pitfall but from the perspective of what to measure and what level of activity. This aspect is critical in the ASMA. Measuring services in a manner that is not reflective of the team delivering the service but has meaning farther up the food chain may completely lose meaning to those responsible for the delivery of security.

4. Losing sight of the goal—Conditions arise in which the original intent of a metric becomes out of character with the goals of the company and needs to be modified to obtain better alignment. Within the context of the ASMA this relates to doing more than is really required and expresses the importance of service delivery models and ensuring that what is needed, not what is wanted or implied, is applied to the business.

5. Choosing metrics that are precisely wrong—In summary, although you may have exceedingly accurate measurements and metrics, these characteristics do not imply that they are meaningful. Unfortunately, this is all too common in information security in which vast details concerning an aspect of virus controls or firewall change management are highly detailed, but have virtually no relevance to the program or the business and security goals. This is generally understood as "just because it can be measured doesn't mean that it should."

6. Assuming your managers and employees have no options— The authors express this as the goal of metrics that is to make people work smarter, not necessarily harder. Moreover, the best people are already working hard. Therefore, if the metrics system demands they work harder as opposed to smarter, you will have to pay them more or lose your best employees.

7. Thinking narrowly—The authors provide an excellent example in which an executive of a software firm utilized telephone service representatives to gain visibility into customer questions and problems and created a metric/reward system to ensure this information was fed back into the development team. The end result was greater quality and customer satisfaction. In this example, the theory that you are what you measure was used to the advantage of the organization.

Taking into account the pitfalls, the authors accurately state that while it may be easy to select a metric, it is hard to select a good metric. Steps towards good metrics include the following:

1. Start by listening to the customer—As stated by the authors, this first step appears to be a naive approach, but it is remarkably overlooked. Unfortunately, this is exceedingly true within

the information security space. Many in security see elements of the business (customers) as a target for control, just as the business sees no value in security. Few in the security industry stop to understand the different pressures placed on different groups. Admittedly, this is starting to change in the industry, in some ways as a result of the shift that has occurred in IT and service-oriented IT delivery models.

2. Understand the job—Once you understand the customer you must understand the managers and employees. The authors provide insightful questions: What do managers and employees value? How do their decisions and actions affect the metrics and the desired outcomes? This is very compelling in security due to the technical nature and arguably uniqueness of the security community. On September 9, 2009, Jeff Ello of *ComputerWorld* published an article that also appeared in *CIO Magazine* titled, "The Unspoken Truth About Managing Geeks." It was an insightful perspective into the fundamental divide that exists between management and technical resources, and provided ways to embrace these differences to create a sound and valuable environment. The point that the authors are making in this second step is that knowing your people is as important as knowing your customers.

3. Understand the interrelationships—Understanding interrelationships enables you to interpret the potential outcome of measurement, which may not be obvious due to other communities, such as suppliers, vendors, peers, and the like. Therefore, through this step we now understand customers and employees, and we are now looking at other features such as partner, supplier, and vendor interactions with the company that may influence outcomes.

4. Understand the linkages—Here the authors introduce the House-of-Quality Metrics matrix. In short, this involves linking efforts to metrics and to desired outcomes.

5. Test the correlations and manager and employee reactions— Related to the car sales volume versus margin example, the authors convey that companies will hire bright people and those people will find methods to maximize their own well-being under the system. Of course, the company hopes the

decisions and actions of these people are in the best interest of the company, but this remains uncertain. Therefore, a metrics system has to be tested. There is a rich culture in security and many professionals pride themselves on finding "alternatives," and within this step these professionals may find ways of exploiting the system. Moreover, as alluded to in "The Unspoken Truth About Managing Geeks," technical people are very logical, and metrics that are not logical will not resonate with them. In both cases, testing how measurements and metrics are interrelated and their impact on the team is paramount to ensure they will have meaning to the security program as designed.

6. Involve managers and employees—The authors wisely state that those who are subject to metrics systems should be part of the team responsible for developing them. While this may seem obvious, it is not common. In identifying measurements in the security program, organizations would be far better off in collaborating with the delivery and management team. Although delivery and management may have a more tactical view of the world relative to their activities and role, this too is a part of the management of a metrics and measurement system and will always provide value. Also, involvement of the target community will streamline testing of the system.

7. Seek new paradigms—The authors state that the final step is one of caution and to use the previous steps creatively. Metrics are to be used to get the most from your managers, employees, and work processes, but this should not limit the development of metrics. In many ways this is the antithesis of the last pitfall. Do not get too comfortable with the system; instead, find methods to use the system to drive objectives and meet goals in imaginative ways. This one aspect alone is essential to the ASMA. The existence and role of governance and capability maturity in the system is a testament to the underlying value of driving innovation and improvement.

There is a great deal of information and guidance concerning measurements in business and security that will be helpful in formulating a methodology. However, few address the underlying theories and impacts of measurement to the business that the Hauser and Katz paper does.

As previously alluded to, organizations will find that the ASMA provides the opportunity to collect vast amounts of different kinds of information that can be used to gain visibility of performance, and the challenge will likely be what to measure. Although somewhat obtuse, for security groups entering into measurements of service delivery, it is typically best to capture as much information as possible and then base formal measurements on primary goal indicators. This approach flies in the face of several strategies that state, once again, that just because it can be measured doesn't mean that it should be, and this is quite accurate. However, in the early stages of service delivery it is helpful to gain a view of the spectrum of information flowing from the application of security services and from that develop a more fine-tuned method. Taking this approach ensures that important measurements are not overly preordained. For example, some may approach a condition with a set of predefined expectations and work to extract (or forcibly pull) from the environment the information that they feel best reflects their expectations of measurement, which in some ways relates back to the last pitfall and final step in the above list. This approach ignores the value of other information and in fact may be focused on the wrong, less meaningful information.

5.6.1 Overview of Measurements

As introduced above, measurements, or more accurately, what can be measured, will materialize in two ways: information that is applicable to all services and information that is specific to a service. Taking this into account it is virtually impossible to express service-specific information due to the fact that services may take on a number of different forms in your organization for all the reasons covered in Chapter 2. The above should act as guidance in formulating a system related to information stemming from the services developed specifically for the organization. Nevertheless, it is reasonable to offer some examples of measurements that are general in nature, and though these may be obvious, it is up to the organization to build on these simple examples to develop a system that best works within its environment.

With regard to service and service delivery, as one might expect it is the responsibility of services management to collect, document, and track the information for later analysis. It is noteworthy to add that all features in the model must perform measurements of this nature. Costs, performance expectations, process management, and quality of activities are unique to each feature as well as how that feature may interact with other features of the model. Therefore, although this section is dedicated to services management, it is an introduction to what all features must perform. Measurements concerning not only the operations of a feature, but also how features interact are equally important. All measurements are provided to governance for processing and influence. At a high level, these include, but are not limited to, the following:

- Cost measurements—Gaining an understanding of costs related to performing a service, or any feature for that matter, should not be complicated or difficult. In some service delivery scenarios the scope and type of service will provide a baseline of costs and what can be expected, whereas in other situations there will be general measurements that are consistent and act as a standard. The challenging aspect of determining costs will be defining what is directly applicable to the delivery of the service. As discussed in the economic section of the Chapter 4, there are levels of depth as to which costs are directly related to delivery as opposed to more general costs, such as those that may span services. In most cases, costs should be initially focused on those that are directly incurred by the service, such as time resources employed, any tools that may be required to perform a function, and any external resources used that consume money, such as a contractor or consultant.

- Performance measurements—Performance is usually related to an established set of expectations. For example, a service is projected—based on scope, etc.—to take 200 man-hours to complete, which was determined by the last several times the service was employed, creating a baseline. If the next time the service is employed it exceeds the projected time to complete, this may be an indicator of poor performance. However, this does not preclude that other supporting elements of service delivery—beyond the service—did not influence the outcome. The objective is to expose wasteful activities and acts that may surface later as poor quality. Moreover, performance provides a view into efficiencies that are being realized or areas needing improvement. Performance measurements are going to be of great interest to governance and organizational management and will reflect on the performance of services management.

- Process measurements—Very much related to various performance measurements, process measurements seek to gain visibility into whether processes were executed at the right point in time, how well the process was applied, and even how well the process is defined. Services are process intensive and cover everything from customer interactions, service management, and service delivery. As such, there is a great deal of data that can be gathered. For example, were processes executed in the right order, how long did the process take to execute, and why did it take more or less time than expected? Did the execution of the process result in projected outcomes? What resources were used in the execution of the process, and did they meet expectations? The objective is to extract a view of the effectiveness of processes. As such, the information will be valuable to capability maturity management and will be used to isolate areas of process improvement.

- Quality measurements—It can be argued that quality is a perspective of work products that is an amalgamation of performance, cost, people, and process, and therefore is an outcome as opposed to a specific measurement. This perspective is mostly associated with a services structure, and those in manufacturing who perform tests specifically to determine product quality would naturally disagree, and rightly so. However, security services rarely result in a final "product" that can be accurately measured to express its specific quality beyond a point in time. This is partly rooted in the dynamics of threats, meaning that although a resulting control (e.g., product) implemented by a security service may be of high standing, it may change overnight with the ebbs and flows of the threat environment. Therefore, quality in service delivery can be difficult to home in on and will usually comprise a set of quality indicators. In addition to the above, these may include quality and satisfaction surveys to customers, percentage of time or number of times the security group was called back to the customer to correct a feature, or the amount of time consumed in compensating for faults and errors in the service delivery framework. For security, quality is typically about looking for the answers to such questions as, were the expectations of the customer met? Did the service provide value and meet security and business goals? Are customers satisfied with the service performed? All features of the ASMA, from compliance and risk to governance and organizational management, are going to be interested in quality indicators.

Each organization will have its own approach to what measurements are taken and may develop many more common platforms for measurement than presented here. The definition of measurements may be supported by the organizational model, operational model, and financial model that the security group is held to. Moreover, different security and business goals will drive many of the measurements. The important part is to ensure they are measureable, they are associated with goals, and that there are processes that can be employed to influence the measurement.

5.6.2 Tracking

Although service execution management is involved with the day-to-day and all that implies, tracking and measuring is focused on the business elements of delivery. The results from this activity will feed directly into governance to be processed in order to determine effectiveness and efficiency, and to be mapped to overarching key performance indicators (KPIs).

There is a broad spectrum of what can be measured and monitored, and this will in some ways be defined by the service itself. The goal is to determine what measurements are consistent across all services, which ones are unique, and the specifics on how the measurements will be taken. It should be noted that this element of delivery management is critical to the overall objective of security services management. Without this information, governance cannot obtain the evidence necessary to interface with the business and will not be able to convert feedback from the business into meaningful adjustments in delivery.

Tracking is used as the basis of activity monitoring, for instance, are status calls being performed, is everyone needed on the calls, are meeting minutes taken, are action items documented and tracked, have issues been properly escalated, and has the scope changed? These questions and many more are used to ensure processes are being followed and to identify wasteful activities. From this measurements can be taken (indirectly) and direct measurements can be made of standard processes, such as from time entry systems, expense management systems, invoicing, budget management, resource utilization, risk and incident management, action item completion rates, and a number of other scenarios that not only ensure the service is on plan and on target, but it is operating in an efficient way.

The issue of quality, or rather, indicators of poor quality, will likely surface during service execution management and tracking and measuring activities. Nevertheless, quality must be addressed throughout the engagement. Deliverables must be reviewed for completeness and accuracy as they are developed, and developed technologies, such as configurations, scripts, applications, and other things generated within the technical domain from the service, must be tested and reviewed. This can range from very simple things, such as ensuring scripts are commented on and have version numbers and correct spelling and grammar, to complex situations such as architecture design.

6

RISK MANAGEMENT

Risk management is the cornerstone of security and can be seen as the predominant force in virtually every organization. There are numerous books and materials that delve into the inner workings and methods related to managing risk. Therefore, within the context of the adaptive security management architecture, any existing risk management program will dovetail directly into the model presented herein. However, given that risk management is part of the model and must work with the other features, it is important that we explore the interconnections that must exist as well as the new role for risk management in the ASMA.

Risk is a very large topic and there are many resources available that detail the different approaches and methods for managing and monitoring risk. There are nearly seventy established risk assessment and management models and hundreds of tools and applications available in the industry today. As such, this book does not detail or cover risk management methods specifically. It is assumed that risk management is fully understood and even employed in your environment. The objective herein is to discuss an enhanced role of risk management as it relates to the adaptive security management architecture. Attention has been given to ensuring that regardless of what risk management model or standard that is currently employed, it will successfully interlock with the adaptive security management architecture. The model assumes that every risk management model is based on the same basic principles and is not concerned with what particular methods and tools may be employed. Therefore, the ASMA seeks to leverage risk management's core principles as opposed to the various methods in an effort to ensure overall security objectives are achieved.

However, what will be revealed by this high-level integration of risk management is the role risk management will have in support of the ASMA. Characterizing risk as a supportive feature of the ASMA—as opposed to being "the" program—may be difficult for some, especially those who have founded their entire program on risk and all this implies. In an effort to summarize this new role of risk and what it may mean to existing programs, consider the following points:

- It is exceedingly likely that what is being performed in the management of risk will not have to change. How risk is evaluated, managed, and monitored today will not only remain intact, but will greatly benefit from the ASMA.

- Assessing risk as part of a risk management program is usually comprehensive and utilizes a vast array of security capabilities, tools, and methods from a number of security disciplines. Within the ASMA, some of these activities materialize as a result of the delivery of security services. Not only do existing risk management practices have an influence in the delivery of services, but they are key to ensuring the correct services are employed in a manner that is reflective of managing overall company risk. This is used as a method to take advantage of risk assessment capabilities and oversight by incorporating them into a business-aligned and measured services model.

- For some organizations, risk management is an overlay comprising key resources that leverage other areas of the business and providing visibility into information risk scenarios for the modification of controls. The role of risk management in the ASMA is virtually the same, with services and services management acting as the arm that applies security and feeds risk management. For organizations in which risk management is the entire security program, from high-level management to tactical activities, the ASMA again provides a method that ensures specific assessment and remediation activities are performed effectively.

In short, the basics of risk management virtually remain the same. However, there is a change in the role of risk relative to the business and as it relates to the services model compared to common risk management. In summary, these are as follows:

- Risk management is traditionally used as the platform for the justification of security investment. Moving forward, governance will play the primary role in articulating security to the business, and risk management will be focused on ensuring services are applied in a manner that does not introduce unacceptable conditions. The role of executive interactions on the state of the security program, activities, compliance, and risk is the sole responsibility of governance.

- It is typical for risk management to determine specific security activities in the implementation of controls in order to reduce risk, and it will have standards for how this is performed. In the ASMA, this is a collaborative activity between risk management, services management, compliance management, and the customer. In other words, the final decision on security activities is not simply that of traditional risk management but will be the result of all features working together.

- Risk management is augmented by the addition of rapid risk assessments. The concept of performing rapid, highly focused assessments is not unique, and many companies perform these types of activities as part of existing risk functions. However, in an adaptive security architecture, a rapid risk assessment capability is required as part of the ASMA. Without this element it would be very difficult to realize several advantages intended by the overall model to balance adaptation with managing the security posture.`

As revealed, the implications concerning existing risk management functions and how these relate to architecture are minor and can be easily addressed. The intent is to ensure the ASMA can easily incorporate existing risk management practices. Without this openness for risk it would be very difficult for organizations to adopt the ASMA given the pervasiveness of risk management as the dominant characteristic of security programs. However, as defined, the arguably dramatic change in role from the foundation of the security program to simply one of many voices feeding into the business through governance may not be well received by some who hold risk management in high regard. Nevertheless, changing the role of risk management and fine-tuning its involvement in the application of security, while simultaneously bringing more to the business discussion with governance having oversight of all the features, is an absolute necessity to achieve adaptability and change the value security can offer.

6.1 Risk Management as a Feature

Risk management is a very comprehensive system comprising of methods, processes, tools, and, in many cases, dedicated resources tasked with understanding threats, weaknesses, the potential for incidents, and the impact in the event an incident materializes. It uses this information and related analysis to express controls needed to reduce or avoid the risk altogether or simply accept the risk.

Risk management, and all that it implies, is essential to a business. In fact, many companies will have a Chief Risk Officer (CRO) or equivalent who is responsible for all risk and usually acts as chairperson for a risk management committee comprising executive leadership from all parts of the business. All types of risk information and analysis may be fed into the program to help the company make meaningful, informed decisions. Risk can manifest in a number of ways, including such areas as legal issues, facilities (fire, acts of God, etc.), fiscal performance, investment management, materials management and logistics, equipment, personnel and safety, regulatory, pollution and waste management, unions, and many others. Frankly, the list is infinite and is governed by the structure of the business and industry. Risk is found more commonly in some areas among different industries than others, such as information risk management, which is an area of interest for adaptive security management architecture.

As introduced above, as part of a holistic risk management program, information risk management can be quite complex. For a far more detailed explanation of information risk management I recommend reading anything on this topic by Thomas R. Peltier. Usually, information risk management is a combination of several processes. For example, a risk assessment is performed to determine vulnerabilities and the state of controls and that information is overlaid with identified threats. From there, work is done to determine the likelihood of exploitation of vulnerabilities by threat agents and ultimately compare that potential to impact. Other attributes of risk management apply as well, such as understanding the valuation of digital assets, influencing policy and standards, articulating controls and their status and capabilities, and performing a comprehensive analysis from which to draw conclusions. Ultimately, information security is as much an art form as it is a science. As a result, there are several standards, approaches, methods, and tools that permeate the security industry. Again, as far as security services management is concerned, it is most interested with the interconnects and its role in service delivery. However, it is necessary to define information risk management as it relates to the ASMA in the facilitation of an adaptable security capability.

Incorporating risk management as a feature of the adaptive security management architecture provides several advantages with very little impact to existing risk management models. The predominant reasoning is to acknowledge that, moving forward, companies want more from their security group besides simply managing risk. Obviously, compliance is of great importance and as such exists as a feature, too. However, some organizations incorporate compliance into risk management, approaching compliance gaps as a "threat." Although having risk management as the predominant security identity is not an entirely negative position, it does not necessarily directly address what businesses will demand in operational integrity, capability maturity, and the sound and balanced application of security. The objective of the adaptive security management architecture is to achieve better business alignment and demonstrate to the company that security can operate in an effective and efficient manner, thus enabling the business to reach its goals. Programs founded solely on risk may not be well positioned to provide a truly comprehensive picture of security as an enabler, given their focus on protection.

Today we see trends of what risk management's role is becoming and this is reflected and promoted by the ASMA. For example, many organizations are beginning to produce operational layers in security, from high-level strategic roles and responsibilities to tactical activities. As an example of the former, security groups will address risk with a small group of resources whose primary purpose is to identify risks, work with other groups to facilitate change, and report findings and plans to the executive community. As to the latter, the other group's risk management resources may range from those in IT and legal to HR and procurement, in addition to other delivery agents in the security group managing day-to-day security processes. This has materialized as risk management in an advisory role to other elements throughout the company and providing information upwards to executives, such as a CRO. In other words, risk management isn't "in the trenches," but rather collecting information and using risk management models and methods to ensure the overall optimal security posture is maintained by guiding resources throughout the environment to implement security controls or to ensure that visibility into the state of security is maintained. In fact, organizations that have modeled their risk management in this way have done—or are doing so—with compliance management. They create a group responsible for ensuring compliance, but do so through the interaction and leveraging of multiple resources from various groups throughout the company. These strategic groups are usually represented in a governance model that seeks to incorporate information about the state of the security posture and build a connection with the business leadership community. The adaptive security management architecture fully embraces this philosophy and provides the structure to exploit the potential that exists to drive value and adaptability.

Based on this, the focus is to place risk and compliance management on the same operational plane with services management and capability maturity management in order to drive a tighter bond between strategic visibility and influence and the actions taken to apply security and how well these are performed. Governance will act as an agent for change based on information flowing into and out of the executive community with the intent of improving value and ensuring security is in alignment with business demands and goals.

6.2 Risk as Communications

In many organizations, and understandably so, given the omnipresence of risk and its importance within today's security program, risk management and the results from risk management activities are used as the sole mechanism to communicate with the business. Unfortunately, this is not as effective as it could be and not always as successful as some assume.

First and foremost, speaking only in risk terms sets a foundation of negativity and puts executives in a precarious position. Risk conveys a "do this or else" message, and most executives prefer to not be trapped or forced into decisions, preferring a proactive, solution-based discussion.

To be clear, executives do not fear risk or challenges and are very apt at digesting complex information to make informed decisions. However, executives are most concerned about the business, which encompasses a vast array of moving parts that are exceedingly complex, making information security appear, frankly, small but important. Exacerbating the issue, and as an indirect result of the negative posture that risk presents, security is perceived as a pain point and uninteresting in the larger business environment.

Security competes with many other areas of the business for executive mindshare and attention, not to mention money. Executive time is limited and executives are a demanding audience. Security must be engaging, proactive, and applicable. Additionally, the ability to communicate security in a manner that resonates with the mission, goals, and charter, and takes into serious consideration current business challenges and events, makes the process far more valuable to the audience.

This is not to convey that risk is absent from the discussion. But what is being stated is that risk alone is ineffective at garnering the true attention of the business owners and bringing to bear multiple points about how security is functioning, and its role, activities, effectiveness, efficiency, capability, and how they relate to the business, and ultimately how risk is being addressed. In other words, risk as the basis for communications with the executive community is one dimensional, has a negative tone, and as such places barriers to success in bonding more closely with the business. Moreover, the security mindshare of that executive community is minimal because there are many other things on executives' plates and, most importantly, security does not provide an engaging argument that demonstrates value beyond risk.

Therefore, the challenge is determining how security can communicate with the executive community in a manner that garners more attention and does so in a way that promotes value. The key is translating the role of security into a solution-based, value-add discussion that offers better visibility into its alignment to business goals and in terms that are more readily digested. The method to facilitate this translation exists within the relationships between the four major features in the ASMA and relies heavily on governance as the final communication mechanism. It will be demonstrated that the results from risk management activities will have far more value when directed into the model as opposed to out into the business community. Risk management is a powerful tool, but it's not the only tool. And this is one aspect of the adaptive security management architecture, among others, that may be difficult for some to embrace, but will become clearer as the adaptive security management architecture takes shape.

6.3 Role of Risk Management

The role of risk management within the ASMA is to provide several key capabilities to the security organization, one of the most important being the ability to maintain posture stability as security adapts to shifts in the business and environment. The adaptive security management architecture seeks to create an operational environment for security that inherently provides for a predictive adaptation to business needs. To get to this point, there must be a degree of uniformity in how security is applied, resources are utilized, compliance is attained, risk is managed, and how security interfaces with the business. As the foundational elements begin to work together the ability to adapt—and do so effectively with greater visibility of outcome and impact—begins to introduce its own form of risk (Table 6.1 and Figure 6.1).

The basis of adaptation is having clarity in all the details of security as an operational unit of the business and as a function of the business. It goes beyond risk and compliance and injects services and maturity as peers in the security architecture. When all the security features are working together, security is well positioned to predict and adjust rapidly to challenges—security or otherwise—and provide a high degree of confidence in the outcome without exposing the company to undue security risks, drops in performance, or spikes in investment needs. To accomplish this each feature is focused on a specific area of the security program to ensure gaps do not surface. Although all of the ASMA features have a responsibility to the organization and have overall visibility and influence, risk management is unique in that the successful realization of adaptability is only possible when acceptable levels of risk are established, understood, and maintained. Essentially, the capability of adaptation is meaningless if adaptation introduces unacceptable risk. If introducing risk were of no concern, then changes to the organization would be simple and commonplace.

Table 6.1 Risk Management Interconnect Table

ACTIVE FEATURE	AREA OF SECURITY FOCUS	PRIMARY FEATURE INTERLOCK (BENEFICIARY)	INTENT AND EXPECTATIONS	FEATURE INPUT	FEATURE PRIMARY PROCESS	SECONDARY FEATURE INTERACTION	TARGETED AREAS OF THE PROCESS	FEATURE OUTPUT	BENEFICIARIES OF OUTPUT	SUMMARY DESCRIPTION
Risk Manage-ment	Risk Posture Manage-ment	Services Management	Ensure that the scope and definition of services to be applied are addressing risk as needed	Service model, type, and approach based on source of initiation	Rapid risk assessment against the targeted service environment	Compliance Management	Evaluate the state of the targeted environment to ensure that the applied service structure is in alignment with risk demands for the customer	Clarification on the state of the target environment used to modify the service approach and delivery model if necessary	Governance, Organizational Management, Compliance Management	Risk management is focused on ensuring that services are applied in a manner that supports the overall business demands concerning risk posture. Governance will play a primary role in the interpretation of risk and demands of the business *(Continued)*

Table 6.1 Risk Management Interconnect Table (Continued)

ACTIVE FEATURE	AREA OF SECURITY FOCUS	PRIMARY FEATURE INTERLOCK (BENEFICIARY)	INTENT AND EXPECTATIONS	FEATURE INPUT	FEATURE PRIMARY PROCESS	SECONDARY FEATURE INTERACTION	TARGETED AREAS OF THE PROCESS	FEATURE OUTPUT	BENEFICIARIES OF OUTPUT	SUMMARY DESCRIPTION
	Compliance Posture Management	Compliance Management	Evaluate compliance demands relative to managing overall risk posture	Compliance requirements for the targeted environment, which can be the customer, security program, or organization	Rapid risk assessment against the targeted environment and evaluation of compliance requirements that are being applied	Services Management	Services, methods, standards, and policies related to the customer, program, or organization	Assurance that compliance requirements are in alignment with maintaining the desired risk posture	Governance, Organizational Management, Services Management	Risk management needs to be satisfied that controls (and compensating controls) that are accordance with external and internal compliance forces are in alignment with risk posture expectations

Perform-ance Improve-ment and Manage-ment

Capability Maturity Management	Evaluate the implications of maturity relative to maintaining and managing risk	Materials and reports from the capability maturity analysis on service(s) that are of interest to risk management	Analysis of findings within the capability of service delivery focused on trends, performance, and effectiveness of applied services
Services Management	Services management processes, service delivery processes and tools, reporting, status reporting, performance metrics, findings and classification, quantity, location, and environment	An analysis of risk posture relative to changes in identified capability in the delivery of services relative to target environments, which may include the execution of a rapid risk assessment	
Governance, Organizational Management	The impact to risk in changes in capability maturity can have a profound impact on the risk posture and the ability to ensure controls are realized in a manner that ensures the intended objective		

(Continued)

Table 6.1 Risk Management Interconnect Table (Continued)

ACTIVE FEATURE	AREA OF SECURITY FOCUS	PRIMARY FEATURE INTERLOCK (BENEFICIARY)	INTENT AND EXPECTATIONS	FEATURE INPUT	FEATURE PRIMARY PROCESS	SECONDARY FEATURE INTERACTION	TARGETED AREAS OF THE PROCESS	FEATURE OUTPUT	BENEFICIARIES OF OUTPUT	SUMMARY DESCRIPTION
	Policy and Standards Management	Organizational Management	Involvement in the establishment of policies and standards as part of the overall corporate risk management	Standards and policies that define the security organization and the overall requirements of the company	Rapid risk assessment of the program management processes concerning the definition, oversight, and specifically the enforcement of standards and policies	Governance	Understanding the implications of changes to policies and standards as defined by governance and the relevance to risk posture and the ability to incorporate into future rapid risk assessments and modifications to service delivery	An analysis of risk posture relative to changes and/or status of standards and policies from organizational management and governance expressing specific areas of enforcement and how these will materialize in service delivery via rapid risk assessments	Governance, Compliance Management	Gaps in alignment to policy and standards represent a threat to the overall risk posture. Risk management will work with Organizational management in the management, communication, and enforcement of stated corporate security expectations via services management and delivery

Services Management and Orchestration	Services Management	Identify areas of service models and structures that enhance or can potentially destabilize risk posture	Service model architecture, service type, delivery specifications, resources, and catalog	Rapid risk assessment of the service delivery models and types concerning organization and structure to ensure security controls and activities are represented for achieving the desired risk posture	Organizational Management	Service descriptions, the necessary inputs to services for determining what models and types are to be employed, the expected outputs from the service and how they are to be generated, tracked, and measured concerning applicability to risk management	An analysis of service structure and relevance to overall risk management in how services are communicated, published, identified, and employed in meeting risk expectations for ensuring security is applied effectively	Governance, Services Management, Compliance Management, Organizational Management	How services are formed, defined, and the models in which they may be presented to customers will have an impact on how security is realized and therefore the implications—positive and negative—to the risk posture

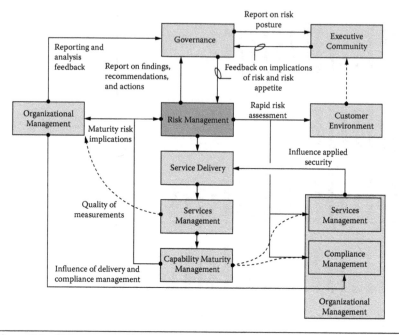

Figure 6.1   Risk management interconnect process map.

6.4 Rapid Risk Assessment

Security services embody what is possible in the application of security practices. Introduced in the previous chapters, services provide not only the means to apply security effectively and efficiently, but more importantly they offer the ability to tune attributes within the service to govern their execution in accordance with many other factors. One of those factors is the needs of the business unit, group, or target of the service. For example, assume a business unit is launching a new customer-facing, Web-based application to generate additional revenue from an emerging market demand. Historically, security policies would stipulate which security practices are required by the business to launch the application. For demonstration purposes, let's say policy states that an application code review must be performed to ensure compliance with corporate policy and industry standards. However, this assumes a great deal and is founded on established policies and standards that may not reflect nuances in the demand; or the state of the business at that point in time, such as risk appetite; or other dynamic conditions relative to the specific situation that would influence the execution of the security services.

This is where the power of risk management can be wielded with acute precision. Again, security services management assumes that a risk management capability—of any kind—exists in some fashion. Based on this assumption it would be logical to conclude that several standards and reference materials exist, such as a threat table, asset valuation database, vulnerability criticality matrix, and actuarial data that has been collected from previous risk assessments. Therefore, we can leverage this sophisticated tool to help tune security to the specific environment for the application of the service.

A rapid risk assessment is a highly focused assessment that is performed by risk management to gain visibility into the specific conditions that may exist in the targeted environment, which may influence the delivery model of the service. Returning to the above example, the launch of a new application by the business has initiated a core review service and services management works with the customer and risk and compliance management to ensure the service is applied in the most effective manner. Therefore, as risk management becomes involved it may be necessary to learn more about the customer's environment and the larger, broader implications of the application relative to the security posture. For example, is the application exposed to the Internet or is it for internal purposes? Is it for partner and vendor interactions? In what systems will the application reside, and what other system services will be accessed or utilized by the application? There are a multitude of other questions and concerns that may surface that risk management must understand in order to drive the necessary modifications to the service before it is deployed.

A rapid risk assessment is not always needed due to the potential familiarity of those within risk management with the target environment. However, there are always situations where there isn't enough information for risk management to work from in order to draw reasonable conclusions to advise services management in the application of the service. Nevertheless, it is the responsibility of those in risk management to become educated about the targeted environment. Part of this educational process will be supported by information from past services that have been performed for the customer. Although the information from previous services may not be directly related to the specific activities laid out in the service that is being reviewed, risk management can extract a lot of valuable information that can be used in creating more familiarity with the customer's environment, expectations, mission, and other forms of security that have been applied or implemented.

Nevertheless, there are times when risk management decides that performing a rapid risk assessment is necessary to accurately drive input into how the service is executed. As the name implies, assessments of this type are highly targeted, use prescribed processes, and should take very little time. However, this is based on the assumptions made above that an existing, comprehensive risk management capability exists and there are meaningful tools and information concerning threats, controls, and assets that assist in streamlining the process. Therefore, although rapid risk assessment features are prescribed herein, their ability to facilitate as offered relies heavily on the maturity of existing capabilities and tools.

6.4.1 Making the Decision

As critical as performing a rapid risk assessment is to the viability of the service and the overall goals of the services management program, it is equally critical to know when not to perform the assessment. Again, the ultimate goal is to demonstrate effectiveness and efficiency, and blindly following a standard process achieves neither of these. Returning to the code review example, if this were the first time working with this business unit or it had been a long time since supporting this unit, or the application was very different from previous applications, then performing a risk assessment would be a good idea. Of course, the inverse is also true. When there is a great deal of intimacy with the environment, performing a risk assessment is questionable. This involves simply knowing the difference between when to follow standard processes and when to apply common knowledge.

To help create a foundation for the decision processes it is important to create a decision matrix that is based on easily obtainable information and can be performed quickly to reach a decision in short order. In the early stages of development this might exist as a worksheet used during a short interview with key staff from both the customer and services management. Nevertheless, over time, historical data from the application of previous services and broader risk management data, along with other information collected from performing these activities, need to be incorporated to make the decision process meaningful. It is worth noting that given the intent and targeted nature of the assessment, the decision-making process to perform or not perform the assessment must consume no more than 5%–10% of the time and resources that would be required to perform the risk assessment. The percentage range is ultimately up to the CSO or team leader responsible for the services management implementation. Moreover, the decision process can be automated to a high degree, if not completely. It is well within possibility to create a simple Web-based application or survey-like capability where business units and the security group can answer simple questions that are compared to an established methodology producing a go or no-go result. In fact, automation will play a key role throughout the architecture. In one test scenario, the decision process to perform the risk assessment, the risk assessment itself, and the criteria concerning service attributes resided in a single application. Information from different groups was entered, and if it was determined that an assessment was needed that information was then used to inform the team. Based on information collected from the assessment, along with other specific details, the service delivery elements were produced. The ability to automate these functions is not only a testament to the implied simplicity of what is being discussed, but is arguably a requirement for a meaningful and highly productive services management system.

The criteria for the decision-making process can be anything and are predominantly guided by the business environment, the existing security culture, the overall corporate demands across risk and compliance, the service that is being performed, and ultimately the budget. When developing the decision criteria the overriding principle is that the execution of the risk assessment, such as what methods and tools are to be employed, input required, and output from the exercise, are directly tied to the service or services that are planned to be performed. From this statement, the first thing that should become obvious is that there are potentially different risk assessment methodologies, tools, and so on, for each service, and there are likely going to be many services in the ASMA. Again, this is why automation is important and we're striving for effectiveness and efficiency. Therefore, the decision criteria will be reflected in the risk assessment process and the service it is supporting. Given that the purpose of the criteria is simply to determine if a risk assessment is to be performed or not, all you need to investigate is the delta between security's understanding of the environment, the business objective, and the current state of the target environment.

6.4.2 Rapid Risk Assessment Requirements

As introduced above, the rapid risk assessment relies heavily on the existence of existing risk management capabilities and broader risk management information to facilitate a speedy process, which will become increasingly evident as specific activities are provided. In some cases there are gaps or misalignments between the prescriptive rapid risk assessment approach and existing risk management capabilities. Most commonly it is the lack of a meaningful threat table, which is the meaningful organization of threats and threat agents that provides a fundamental understanding of what they represent to the company. Surprisingly, this is not a feature commonly found in security organizations today.

6.4.2.1 Defining Threats
Given the importance of understanding threats relative to any determination of risk, and the fact that some risk management organizations do not have a defined threat table or matrix, it is helpful to explore this topic briefly. First and foremost, if we accept that there is no perfect security, by very definition we accept that there are threats that cannot be stopped. Therefore, threats come in several forms, and as such there surfaces a spectrum of applicable threats. These are the threats that apply to your business. For example, if your company performs testing on animals it is likely that animal rights activists will be a realistic threat as opposed to a company that does not do animal testing or impacts animals in any way, such as making shoestrings.

Within the spectrum of applicable threats there are two basic characteristics: the threats we can address and the ones we cannot. There are fundamentally two factors that determine whether threats are addressable or non-addressable. Of these, the predominant force is the cost to reduce the likelihood of success of a given threat. Of course, cost is related to impact, and when there is a meaningful ratio between the two, a control may or may not be implemented, and the latter is simply accepting the risk. The other far less articulated factor is the "impossibility" of the threat. This is an applicable threat that is not addressable, yet it exists and is applicable. In other words, there are no meaningful controls that can be implemented to reduce its likelihood, or the cost is so great or the controls so restrictive that operations would cease to function.

This can be summarized as a set of threats that applies to a business, and of those there are ones it can process to determine if it should invest in a control or not and then there are applicable threats the business can do nothing about. These will be referred to, respectively, as "applicable addressable threats" and "applicable non-addressable threats." If we accept these as fundamental principles, we also accept that controls are inherently related and inexorably tied to the threat. Of the controls that have been defined, justified, and implemented, these typically represent only a fraction of the applicable addressable threats due to the fact that some of the applicable addressable threats identified were deemed too expensive to compensate for. As a result, we have a new spectrum of threat definitions specific to the company and acceptable risk posture: the threats that we have controls for and the ones we do not. Within the group of threats that we have not compensated for are included applicable addressable threats and applicable non-addressable threats; these will be called "accepted threats." Of course, the ones for which we have established controls will only include applicable addressable threats; these will be called "addressed threats." Obviously, addressed threats are simply a fraction of applicable threats and an extraordinarily small percentage of all threats.

With the spectrum of threats refined to a workable and manageable scope, these can now be placed into a table that quantifies them. In most cases, an organization in the process of creating its first threat matrix will likely start with applicable addressable threats and applicable non-addressable threats, and even a few non-applicable threats until they can be weeded out of the system.

First, the threats are organized into groups, as follows:

- Natural threats—This includes "acts of God," such as flood, fire, earthquake, dam failure, epidemic, sinkhole, tornado, hurricane or typhoon, mudslide, landslide, blizzard, and just about any naturally forming condition that can threaten lives and assets.

- Human accidental—These are conditions in which people simply make mistakes, such as fire, explosion, crash (plane, train, automobile, etc.), operational errors, maintenance errors, programming errors, medical emergencies, exposure to hazardous material, and the like.
- Human deliberate general—These are examples of where people simply perform disruptive or harmful acts to others and organizations, such as terrorism, sabotage, bombing, arson, hostage taking, vandalism, strike, riot, extortion, assault, murder, and the like.
- Human deliberate technical—This is the manifestation of human activities in the technical domain, and the thing security organizations focus on the most. It can include hackers/crackers, script kiddys, cyber criminals, cyber industrial espionage, hacktivists, cyber warfighters, cyber terrorists, and even technical developers, representing those who write programs that enable others to perform attacks.
- Technical—Represents the separation of humans from automated attack scenarios, which is becoming increasingly important, and can include worms, viruses, spam, Trojan horses, spyware, phishing, and other attack vectors that are automated.
- Environmental—These are generally associated with the threat of failures, such as power outages, water leaks, temperature control failure, telecommunications failure, emergency response failure, and other forms of utility that are essential to operations.

Although not a comprehensive list, the above should provide some perspective for identifying threats. From this point it is necessary to associate characteristics of the threat. In general, this can start with basic characteristics, such as

- Scale or measurement—Virtually any threat can be quantified. Hurricanes have categories; tornadoes use the Fujita or "F" scale; blizzards, snow storms, and rain are measured by inches or centimeters per hour; bombings have radii and the like. However, when it comes to humans and especially those related to technology, Donn Parker's SKRAM (skills, knowledge, resources, authority, and motives) represents the best characteristics for measuring the human threat.

- Time or rate of occurrence—Something that many within the security community resonate with is simply how often the threat manifests itself. This is mainly associated with season scenarios, such as floods and the like. However, it can also relate to terrorism, which has proven to be sensitive to meaningful dates. Even hackers have cycles and some areas have seen in increase in attacks from this community during such events as spring break or after a natural disaster.

- Geography or location—This is representative of a threat characteristic that is mainly associated with acts of God and can expand to include cyber warfare and cyber terrorism. In the latter case the threat may be identified geographically, but this may have little significance as to where the attack materialized. It can be a little helpful to block IP addresses, but that is typically the extent in the digital domain.

- Enablement—This is an objective perspective, but it is helpful to increase the granularity of information relative to a threat in at least expressing what is needed by the threat to form an attack. This elaborates on SKRAM, specifically in regard to resources and interestingly, in some cases, will include motive.

- Threat action—In simple terms, this is an oversimplified definition of the results of a threat or threat agent. In some cases, organizations will go as far as to break these down by severity. However, associating severity with regard to the environment and assets later in the risk assessment process is recommended. Moreover, threat action has been used to articulate the sophistication of the threat, elaborating on the definition, such as expressing the difference between a script kiddy, a hacker, a sophisticated hacker, and a well-structured cybercrime organization.

It is important to simply focus on the threats and their characteristics. Microsoft's threat modeling process has five steps: (1) Identify Security Objectives, (2) Survey the Application, (3) Decompose It, (4) Identify Threats, and (5) Identify Vulnerabilities, which is more of an inside-out approach and represents the identification of applicable addressable threats based on the state of a system. Additionally, this model is more about quantifying risk as opposed to isolating threat characteristics. A similar model is DREAD, or Damage, Reproducibility, Exploitability, Affected users, and Discoverability, which are used in a basic formula. Again, this is the association of threats based on impact and environment. Practices such as this become confused with the broader aspects of determining risk, are not scientific, and can inadvertently highlight the wrong threats and completely miss the ones an organization may need to be concerned about. Granted, models of this nature have arguably stemmed from the fact that threats are difficult to quantify, and therefore working from the inside out helps to reduce the potential scope of threat.

Another approach is STRIDE, a threat classification scheme based on known threat attack vectors and practices. STRIDE stands for Spoofing Identity, Tampering with Data, Repudiation, Information Disclosure, Denial of Service, and Elevation of Privilege. It is a compelling model that can be focused in the software development life cycle and loosely applied in other security domains. It can be said that SKRAM represents the capability and STRIDE represents the employment of that capability, and together they can be very helpful in quantifying threats.

There is no lack of other models that provide other perspectives of measurement. However, most define threats based strictly on the environment, which is related to the concept that a system attracts a certain type of threat, and incorporates impact relative to vulnerability. Technically speaking, when impact and vulnerability are introduced this is assessing risk, which is a more comprehensive method, not assessing threats, which is something highly targeted. Although it is tempting to define a threat based on its relation to the environment, the problem is that threats change and so does the environment. This is also known as threat environment, taking into consideration known threats and the ability to defend against them, which is meaningful in a relatively static condition. Conversely, by creating a threat matrix that characterizes threat as those listed, incorporates capability (i.e., SKRAM), and the potential employment vectors, for example, STRIDE, there is a basis for comparison to the environment in the form of a risk assessment. This is helpful in that threats can and do govern security controls, whereas other inside-out methods apply the controls and attempt to align the threat. However, when using a strategy in which threats are articulated and then mapped to the environment, it becomes critical to monitor threats just as you would monitor the environment for changes that may affect the security posture.

6.4.2.2 Understanding Controls State Performing a rapid risk assessment, or even a more comprehensive and traditional risk analysis, requires a keen view of the reasonable capabilities of security controls. In many cases, traditional risk management will perform vulnerability assessments to interrogate the capabilities of controls when faced with a structure testing methodology. Moreover, technical system assessments are also performed to review adherence to stated policies and standards that were defined and implemented to establish security controls.

As with defining threats, it is necessary for organizations to have consolidated and accurate information concerning the state and capability of security controls within the environment. Interestingly, and unlike threat matrices, organizations will typically have this information. However, one of the challenges that many face is a view of security controls relative to the customer's environment. Rapid risk assessments are highly targeted to the environment and service in question. Therefore, having a view into the state of controls of, for example, the marketing business unit, or research and development, sales, engineering, product management, facilities management, HR, legal, and any number of divisions that exist within the company, can become challenging. The challenge stems from the fact that security is predominantly seen horizontally or as a common feature across the business. This is an obvious result of the association security has with IT and the fact that there are shared IT systems, services, and infrastructure, so it is natural to have a broad-spectrum view. This is best seen in perimeter security in which many business units use the same Internet-facing infrastructure; therefore, any controls in that environment naturally apply to all business units. Of course, this makes the assumption that one business unit doesn't have special rules or services features that are unique to it, which in turn can represent a different collection of control capabilities.

Although this is a simple example, the ability to at least categorize and group controls—and their state—based on the specific target environment is important to a rapid risk assessment. Additionally, once a level of completeness in alignment of controls, state, and environment is achieved, at least at a high level, organizations should begin to associate groups of controls to security service attributes. For example, the security service to be applied is focused on one aspect of the environment. When risk management decides to employ a rapid risk assessment it needs to start with the area of the customer's environment that is in question. From there a broader view can be taken to help risk management advise the customer and services management in the tuning of the service. Having controls grouped and cross-referenced against the services will greatly streamline the initial phases of the rapid risk assessment.

As you can see, the solution is not as simple or as obvious as some are led to understand. Conversely, some environments are not complicated and do not have overly specialized controls that do map across the business. Nevertheless, fully understanding the details of the environment and services is yet one more step to effectiveness and quality. More importantly, the fundamental goal is having information about the state of controls readily available to increase the efficiency of the risk assessment process.

6.4.2.3 Quantifying Assets Without a doubt the most challenging aspect of security and risk management is the identification and valuation of information assets. Information is highly dynamic in state, location, context, and value, and in many cases it is very unstructured. For many in security this is viewed as impossible, and therefore they take a position of securing the system based on its role in the business, implying importance of information. Of course, this involves a number of approaches that are arguably indirect and deal with information systems and not specifically with the actual information. Data Loss/Leak Prevention systems are becoming more common, which is a meaningful step toward closer control over the flow of data from one security domain (trusted) to another (untrusted).

One cannot deny the security irony: How can a company ensure a meaningful balance of security controls between threats and assets when the assets are so elusive and dynamic? The answer is simple: we do the best we can. And the same holds true within the context of requirements for a rapid risk assessment. It may be impossible to reasonably evaluate the value, state, and location of information assets within a customer's environment when assessing conditions to drive the accurate application of a security service. Again, taking into consideration the intent and timely execution of the assessment, there are simple methods for gaining a general, albeit imperfect, view of valued assets.

In a process used extensively by the government, which can be seen in the Department of Defense Information Assurance Certification and Accreditation Process (DIACAP), the information is generally described, and the organization applies perspective of the impact if information is lost, damaged, stolen, etc., and identifies the system that is responsible for that information to apply security controls. Of course, DIACAP is far more comprehensive and provides a classification of information relative to mission criticality. From this point the system is identified and a Mission Assurance Category (MAC) is assigned that ultimately is associated with specific security controls, which are further defined in the Security Technical Implementation Guides (STIGs). This is a gross oversimplification of a comprehensive process, but the point is that the system can be the target.

In other words, information is not specifically identified, but rather the role of the information in the business is identified, which translates to criticality, which in turn defines the security needed for a system. Although this works well for the government, it can be challenging for those companies in the private sector because a "system" is hard to draw a line around. There are shared technologies, and service-oriented technologies blur the line between systems. Again, there is no perfect method, but this approach lends itself to the overall intent of a rapid risk assessment: targeted, simple, fast. Therefore, a requirement to perform an assessment is to have the ability to quickly define—at a high level—what information is important to the customer, what is its general criticality, and a general understanding of what in the customer's environment is responsible for or is interacting with that information.

As a basic example, the process can be expressed as follows:

- What major groups of information are important to the operation of the business? A response may include customer information, product pricing, and shipping logistics.
- What would be the impact to the business's ability to perform if the information were to be unavailable? The customer may respond with, "We could survive a few days without customer

and pricing information because it does not change daily, but shipping logistics are very time sensitive. Our operation would virtually come to a halt in a few hours if we lost logistics information."

- What would be the impact if information were stolen? The loss of pricing information, especially to a competitor, would have short- and long-term implications to the business. The loss of customer information introduces legal and regulatory concerns, not to mention customer satisfaction, retention, and future acquisition. Logistics would have little or no impact.

Table 6.2 is a very simple table that can be created that compares information impacts across confidentiality, integrity, and availability to determine criticality.

The next step is identifying the systems involved, again at a high level. For example, you find that the customer is using two systems: customer relationship management (CRM) for customers and pricing and event log management (ELM) for logistics. From here the information criticality to the system is mapped to gain a perspective of the importance of the system (Tables 6.3 and 6.4).

Table 6.2   Information Criticality Matrix

INFORMATION	CONFIDENTIALITY	INTEGRITY	AVAILABILITY
Customer Data	High	High	Medium
Logistics	Low	High	High
Pricing	High	High	Medium

Table 6.3   CRM System Criticality

INFORMATION	CONFIDENTIALITY	INTEGRITY	AVAILABILITY
Customer Data	High	High	Medium
Pricing	High	High	Medium
Overall System (high water mark)	High	High	Medium

Table 6.4   ELM System Criticality

INFORMATION	CONFIDENTIALITY	INTEGRITY	AVAILABILITY
Logistics	Low	High	High
Overall System (high water mark)	Low	High	High

6.4.3 Performing a Rapid Risk Assessment

A rapid risk assessment is performed using the standard approach found in large, more comprehensive risk assessments, but as implied in the previous sections there are requirements to ensure the process is not overly time-consuming. Moreover, focus is important. This is not an opportunity to perform a deep analysis to set security strategy, but rather a tool used to make informed tactical decisions concerning how a service may need to be tuned. Although granularity is lost to gain efficiency, this is an acceptable trade-off considering the overall intent and role of the assessment. Fundamentally, this leads us back to the broad assumption that a risk management capability exists and that more comprehensive and broad risk assessments and analysis will be performed as normal.

The approach is broken into the basic areas of assessing risk (note that portions of the following can be found in the IAM, NIST, DoD, and other risk models, such as OCTAVE):

- Assess threat
- Assess vulnerability
- Assess impact
- Determine risk
- Quantify service adjustments

6.4.3.1 Assess Threat Using the threat matrix discussed above, it is necessary to begin by identifying the applicable threats to the target environment. Depending on the comprehensiveness of the threat table and how well it is organized and managed, this process is short and concise. Note that this involves identifying applicable threats from the table based on general definitions of the environment and not security control capabilities of the environment as a basis of identification. In other words, at this point it is not an inside-out approach.

Next is to identify and assess the threat impact potential. Again, using the threat table as defined, we can use the various characteristics of the threat. Moreover, NIST's SP-800-30, section 3.2, and the OCTAVE threat profile materials can further assist in interpreting impact potential. With this as a basis it is necessary to assess threat agent capability. As shared, SKRAM combined with STRIDE is a meaningful method to equate impact and threat agent capability. Using this as a platform it is helpful to determine the likelihood of the threat coming to fruition. This begins to reintroduce applicable addressable threats and applicable non-addressable threats and their relevance of occurrence. For example, if an applicable addressable threat is a virus or worm (malware) the likelihood of occurrence is quite high.

Finally, and more directed at performing rapid risk assessments regularly, when the assessment of threats for a specific customer's environment is complete, it is necessary to document and prepare for monitoring the identified threats. Although this has greater importance over the long term of performing assessments, its applicability in the short term is important as well. For example, an identified threat may have a change in status or characteristics during the rapid risk assessment or during the time the service is being employed, which may have an impact on how the service may be delivered with real-time changes.

6.4.3.2 Assess Vulnerability The process of assessing vulnerabilities, if not done carefully, can become very time-consuming. It can include everything from performing vulnerability tests, such as scanning and analysis, to system configuration review. It is noteworthy that risk management can gain substantial information from previous security services applied in the past that were originally targeted at assessing vulnerabilities. Moreover, and to state the obvious, if the security service in question, which has initiated a rapid risk assessment, relates to assessing vulnerabilities, this aspect alone may negate the need for a rapid risk assessment. Nevertheless, risk management will remain interested in the outcome of the service for future purposes.

Part of the process includes determining applicable vulnerabilities. This relates to identified threats and what is important to tuning the service. It can be argued that all vulnerabilities are applicable in some way, but have different levels of criticality. Nevertheless, this is an attempt to bring additional focus to downstream activities and streamline the overall process. With a set of identified vulnerabilities, these can be further compared to applicable threats and overall environmental characteristics to determine exploitation potential. For example, a system within the customer's environment has an applicable vulnerability, and when related to identified threats represents some-thing of interest. However, the exploitation potential may be virtually nullified because the system in question is deep within the environ-ment and not exposed to the threat. The process of evaluating exploi-tation potential is important in determining risk, and within the context of a rapid assessment may require "leaps of faith" to ensure the exercise is not overly time-consuming.

As discussed above, there is an overall system aspect to defining controls and asset identification. Therefore, once all the applicable vul-nerabilities and their characteristics are refined, they are then related to the systems utilizing the simplified system tables provided above. Just as information criticalities were mapped to identified systems, so are the vulnerabilities, which may map to one or more systems. This offers risk management a holistic view of the vulnerability, threat, and control condition tying back to what is important to the customer.

Finally, as with threats, identified vulnerabilities need to be moni-tored for the same reasons—things change that may affect the appli-cation of the security service, resulting in real-time adjustments, or become important to the overall security posture over time. Risk management can become the basis for initiating a service because it is monitoring threats and vulnerabilities. Therefore, the aspect of moni-toring the threat and vulnerability environment is very valuable to risk management. Although there may be no system changes, vulner-abilities do surface regularly. A new vulnerability may be discovered based on the assessment and risk management determining that pre-viously assessed systems are affected. This is a very common practice in security and should be no surprise. Even hackers are known to keep a database of targeted system characteristics so that when a new vul-nerability surfaces they do not have to interrogate the system again, but simply compare it to their database. The same holds true for risk management.

6.4.3.3 Assess Impact The section above concerning quantifying assets introduced the relationship between valuation and impact. This is built upon by combining that information and the information from assessing threats and vulnerabilities. The process is focused on taking a relatively comprehensive look at all capabilities—those of threats and controls—and drawing a broader picture of impact. Once overall capabilities are articulated and compared, it is necessary to identify potential impacts. This is essentially validating and refining the customer's perspective of impact and converting these interpretations into actionable features.

Finally, again we add monitoring impacts. This is simply an extension of monitoring threats and vulnerabilities because they will inevitably resonate in the form of impacts. Although this is not always a result, and changes in the threat and vulnerability space may have minor implications for impacts, the fact that changes can occur while the service is being applied demands that impacts be monitored relative to threats and vulnerabilities.

6.4.3.4 Determine Risk and Quantify Service Adjustments　At this point risk absorbs the information produced from previous activities to relate to threats, vulnerabilities, and impact. This process is very well defined within the industry of risk management and as such there are many different approaches. One of the potential pitfalls to avoid with respect to ensuring a rapid approach is in overcomplicating the process. Within the context of a rapid assessment the goal is to take what was learned to determine what adjustments may be needed—if any—in the service that is planned to be executed.

In traditional and more comprehensive risk determinations the goal is to identify potential countermeasures to address the risk. However, although the same basic principles apply, the end result is different. In traditional risk assessments (i.e., those that will continue in some form despite the existence of the rapid risk assessments) the result is the specification of controls that may materialize as changes to the environment, the addition of new technology, or changes in processes and standards. At this point this list should look extraordinarily familiar to the responsibilities of other features, such as capability maturity management, services management, and organizational management. Therefore, the results of a rapid assessment are used to guide services management in the tuning of the specific service and will typically include providing guidance to all the other features to promote changes to controls, technology, standards, and policy.

As introduced at the beginning of this chapter, the role of risk management will change relative to the features used and this is most evident in the final results of risk assessments. In traditional programs risk management would not only identify countermeasures, but also drive these changes into executive management and throughout the environment to implement changes. Conversely, in the ASMA risk management takes an advisory role as a peer to the other features to ensure balance in the approach to changes.

7

COMPLIANCE MANAGEMENT

Ensuring compliance for an organization is an essential requirement for any security group. Virtually every company is impacted by regulatory oversight that stipulates demands that resonate in information security. Even organizations that are not affected by external demands will want to ensure they are in compliance with internal requirements, such as policy, standards, and processes.

Compliance management within the ASMA is responsible for ensuring the company is compliant with external industry regulations and standards as well as internally defined policy and standards as they relate to information security. These activities not only address compliance throughout the organization, but also include compliance within the security group and the adherence to established expectations in managing information security services, risk, organizational oversight, governance, and ensuring capability maturity. As implied, this responsibility has a broad scope. Compliance management has to address potentially multiple external regulatory forces, internal standards, and policy compliance, and is responsible for the adherence to established processes and standards that define the ASMA.

Traditionally, the role of compliance management has been focused on making certain that the company is in compliance with industry regulations. For example, the compliance manager in a security group working in the healthcare industry is keenly focused on making certain the company is meeting the requirements defined in the Health Insurance Portability and Accountability Act (HIPAA) of 1996 and the Health Information Technology for Economic and Clinical Health Act (HITECH Act), enacted as part of the American Recovery and Reinvestment Act (ARRA) of 2009. In many cases, this is reactive and compliance requirements are determined upon publication of the applicable standards, a gap analysis of the existing environment, and interpretations from audit. Some organizations are proactive and seek to ensure that compliance is addressed early in new projects or security program management and also take into account early development of emerging regulations and standards (Table 7.1 and Figure 7.1).

Existing compliance management activities will likely need to be modified to address how compliance is integrated into services as well as having its role expanded. In many cases, compliance is a separate function, and in some scenarios it is not part of information security. Compliance will typically set standards in reference to a particular regulation and perform audits against the environment to ensure requirements are being met. Additionally, compliance will interact with evolving projects and activities to assist in reducing gaps over time. It is this second aspect of compliance that the ASMA seeks to exploit. The objective is to integrate compliance throughout all security activities so that it is inherent in the way security is applied to the organization. This does not replace the need for audits and verification practices, but allows for the utilization of services by compliance management, reduces the number of findings, streamlines the effort required to close gaps, and allows organizations to address multiple regulatory demands through a single framework.

7.1 Adaptive Architecture Compliance

As stated, compliance management has two characteristics that are closely intertwined to achieve compliance. The first is its role in ensuring that the processes and standards that define the ASMA and all the features are adhering to expectations. Fundamentally, security compliance is targeted at making certain that policy, standards, and processes that are designed to establish a specific posture are being enacted correctly.

Compliance interprets the requirements in order to facilitate specific actions and controls. For example, a regulatory requirement may state that passwords must be complex enough to reduce the potential for a threat to determine what they are and they should be changed regularly. A supporting standard may state that passwords must have a minimum number of characters, contain alpha and numeric characters, and be changed every 60 days. Compliance seeks to convert these demands into controls in the environment that can be managed and may regularly audit systems to ensure the demands are being met.

Table 7.1 Compliance Management Interconnect Table

ACTIVE FEATURE	AREA OF SECURITY FOCUS	PRIMARY FEATURE INTERLOCK (BENEFICIARY)	INTENT AND EXPECTATIONS	FEATURE INPUT	FEATURE PRIMARY PROCESS	SECONDARY FEATURE INTERACTION	TARGETED AREAS OF THE PROCESS	FEATURE OUTPUT	BENEFICIA-RIES OF OUTPUT	SUMMARY DESCRIPTION
Compliance Management	Risk Posture Management	Risk Management	Gain visibility into risk management's interpretation of the application of security relative to maintaining and improving compliance	Results from all forms of rapid risk assessments against services management, organizational management, and capability maturity management	An analysis of risk management findings, changes, and recommendations concerning the overall risk posture to determine implications to program, corporate, or external compliance requirements	Services Management	Risk management's analysis containing interpretations, recommendations, and actions and how these have materialized in delivery standards, processes, and scope of how security is applied to the environment	Identification of areas of risk management modifications that are determined to be misaligned with compliance efforts relative to the application of security services or areas where risk	Governance, Organizational Management, Services Management	The goal is to ensure that compliance activities and results are having a positive effect on managing risk and ensuring meaningful security. Compliance alone does not equate directly to security that may be

(Continued)

Table 7.1 Compliance Management Interconnect Table (Continued)

ACTIVE FEATURE	AREA OF SECURITY FOCUS	PRIMARY FEATURE INTERLOCK (BENEFICIARY)	INTENT AND EXPECTATIONS	FEATURE INPUT	FEATURE PRIMARY PROCESS	SECONDARY FEATURE INTERACTION	TARGETED AREAS OF THE PROCESS	FEATURE OUTPUT	BENEFICIA-RIES OF OUTPUT	SUMMARY DESCRIPTION
								management's modifica-tions have supported compliance efforts		of great interest to the organization
	Compliance Posture Manage-ment	Services Management	Ensure services management and service delivery are being performed in accordance with compliance demands	Results from service delivery and the application of security services throughout the environment, including deliverables, processes, and standards	An analysis of services management's oversight of the delivery of security services to determine adherence to established expectations of compliance demands	Risk Management	Services management's overall management of service delivery specifically focusing on customer interactions, materials and deliverables, application of resources, and role concerning the enforcement of standards and policies in how security is applied	Identified areas of noncompli-ance, areas for improve-ment in executing against compliance expecta-tions, and specific areas where services manage-ment is	Governance and Organiza-tional Manage-ment	Compliance management is tasked with ensuring that overall compliance is achieved and a large part of this responsibility is ensuring that security is applied—via services

Performance Improvement and Management			
Capability Maturity Management	Ensure that services management is operating in a manner that promotes the improvement of compliance-related activities	Results from capability maturity assessments and related documentation concerning findings, recommendations, and specific areas of improvement	An analysis of capability maturity management's findings and how these have resonated with governance in communicating activities to the executive community
Services Management	Capability maturity management's compliance with established standards and processes for performing maturity assessments, reviewing results, documentation, tools, methods, and resources	Documented findings concerning how capability maturity management is performing against expectations, how these are related to changes in services management, and assurance that capability exceeding or ensuring compliance through innovative activities	
Governance and Organizational Management	Compliance management wants to ensure that process improvements and changes do not disrupt compliance expectations in the application of security as well as working with capability maturity management—in a manner that is supportive and promotes compliance demands		

(Continued)

Table 7.1 Compliance Management Interconnect Table (Continued)

ACTIVE FEATURE	AREA OF SECURITY FOCUS	PRIMARY FEATURE INTERLOCK (BENEFICIARY)	INTENT AND EXPECTATIONS	FEATURE INPUT	FEATURE PRIMARY PROCESS	SECONDARY FEATURE INTERACTION	TARGETED AREAS OF THE PROCESS	FEATURE OUTPUT	BENEFICIARIES OF OUTPUT	SUMMARY DESCRIPTION
								maturity management is providing ongoing monitoring of capability and modifications to delivery		management to identify opportunities for more efficient and effective compliance efforts
	Policy and Standards Management	Organizational Management	Ensure the entire security program is compliant with established policies and standards	Industry standards that are employed, standards that have been defined by organizational management, and standards defining the program	A review of organizational management's oversight and governance of the policies and standards relative to the program and corporate compliance, and the	Governance	Organizational management's processes, deliverables, communications, documentation of changes, program monitoring and reporting, organizational integrity management,	A report on the integrity of overall program alignment to established standards, interactions, reporting, and	Governance, Services Management, Risk Management	Compliance management is responsible for the security program's compliance to self-imposed policies and

Feature	Purpose	Artifacts	Artifact Analysis	Related Features	Compliance Management Activities
Services Management and Orchestration	Ensure that the overall management and oversight of service definition, structure, models, and communication are in alignment with established expectations	Service catalog, service model descriptions, service catalog management processes, change processes, and documentation concerning feature input	An analysis of organizational management's management of the service models, types, and catalog, supporting materials, and processes	management of the security organization; performance management, and change management; Organizational Management	management practices and how they relate to program and corporate compliance standards, and as such will work closely with organizational management and all the other features to ensure this is a reality
Services Management		Service catalog management practices; evidence of how other feature interactions are performed, managed, tracked, employed, and monitored; team management; customer management; quality and performance management and reporting	Identification of gaps in organizational management's adherence to established practices and standards concerning feature input management,	Governance, Risk Management, Services Management	As services are defined, managed, and modified to meet the needs of the business, compliance management will perform regular reviews of service models and definitions and monitor how and when they are

(Continued)

Table 7.1 Compliance Management Interconnect Table (Continued)

ACTIVE FEATURE	AREA OF SECURITY FOCUS	PRIMARY FEATURE INTERLOCK (BENEFICIARY)	INTENT AND EXPECTATIONS	FEATURE INPUT	FEATURE PRIMARY PROCESS	SECONDARY FEATURE INTERACTION	TARGETED AREAS OF THE PROCESS	FEATURE OUTPUT	BENEFICIA-RIES OF OUTPUT	SUMMARY DESCRIPTION
								change control of service models and types, and customer feedback and quality control relative to service catalog		applied to the business through services management

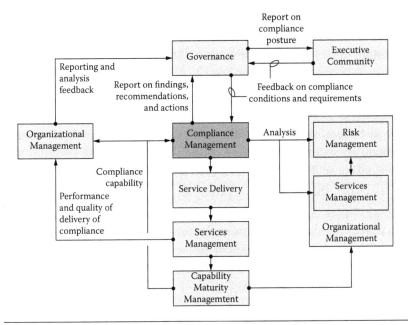

Figure 7.1 Compliance management interconnect process map.

This may result in the use of tools and other methods to accomplish these tasks. Moreover, there may exist conditions in systems that do not support the standard, and compliance must identify compensating controls that meet the intent of the requirement.

The processes and standards defined within the security program act as the basis for compliance management to perform similar actions. For example, risk management will have a set of processes that define how rapid risk assessments are performed, the standards to be used, and how the activity is managed. These set the tone for risk management and its interaction with the business and other features within the model. Compliance management's role is to ensure that risk management is in compliance with its own policies, standards, and process, and with those of the rest of the features.

This activity implies two things: (1) risk management, as with other features, has a set of defined processes and standards, and (2) compliance management performs audits against the internal program. The results from audits will go to organizational management for review and if changes are deemed to be required, will oversee the implementation of modifications. The concept of exploiting compliance management to ensure the program is in alignment with its own internal policies and standards is not new. This is especially common in organizations that are ISO-27001 certified. In order to maintain certification there must exist a method to ensure that defined practices and standards are being implemented and managed correctly. The importance of performing self-audits is based on several factors, most important of which is adaptability. To ensure adaptability you must first have confidence that current activities are functioning as designed. If you do not have this visibility, there is no assurance that changes in processes and standards will have the desired impact. Compliance management is focused on making certain that defined requirements in the program are being met, whereas capability maturity management is focused on how well these are being performed and is forward looking. However, if internal activities and management controls are not audited, the organization is unclear on what is currently being performed, which makes any improvements or changes to the program far less accurate, ultimately resulting in the inability to predict the impact of changes.

Compliance management and capability maturity management work hand in hand to promote effectiveness and adaptability. Nevertheless, in many ways capability maturity management is heavily reliant on compliance management to ensure that the purpose for the processes and standards is being met. This role has far-reaching implications. For example, if a feature of the program is not compliant with its own standards, results from its activities will likely produce skewed measurements that are ultimately fed into governance and then the business. When governance reaches into capability maturity management in order to influence improvements it will be working on a foundation that is at best misaligned, and at worst, dysfunctional.

To demonstrate, compliance ensures that a standard and process is being executed specifically as defined. It is not necessarily concerned about the outcome, but simply that the standard is being applied as defined by policy and other directives. Activities resulting from the audited process provide measurements to governance that will help to expose any gaps in performance. From this information, governance may interact with capability maturity management to improve processes to make a meaningful difference in future activities that will once again resonate through measurements and into the business via governance. If we remove compliance from this cycle and measurements are once again passed to governance, changes and improvements are passed to capability maturity management. Unfortunately, it may make changes that are completely irrelevant because the process or standard identified as the target for improvement is not being used as designed. In short, nothing of substance may be achieved—only wasting time, effort, and money.

The results can be devastating. Each feature in the model plays an important strategic role in the overall program, and any gap in one of the features will have a cascading effect. In the above example, several things are impacted, for instance, inaccurate measurements are passed to the business, wasteful activities are undertaken in governance and capability maturity management to correct or improve something that may have virtually no impact, and there is confusion as to why identified issues remain. However, more importantly, the lack of critical visibility provided by compliance greatly hinders adaptability and the entire program becomes stalled. In short, if you do not know exactly what you are doing, there is no way of knowing what the exact problem is, much less make changes in order to increase performance. Clearly, this translates to adaptation. Although much of this discussion has been about improving performance, the core of adaptation is founded on accurate adjustments to address business dynamics, which is essential to enhancing performance.

Based on this, there are several summary considerations in the primary activities of compliance management and its role concerning the ASMA's features:

- Involvement in the determination of how attributes of a security service may be tuned to achieve the needs of the customer while ensuring the customer and the organization as a whole is meeting external and internal compliance requirements. Tight coupling with services management is required.
- Complete and consistent visibility into the operational conditions of all the features. Moreover, compliance management will require that all the features of the program have consistent methods of producing information relative to performance against established standards and processes.

- Compliance management will need to create an assessment and audit capability, such as a tool and necessary processes that are geared specifically to the verification of process and standards execution and adherence.
- The formation and organizational management approval of a compliance reporting structure and tracking mechanism that is made available to the other features. The key is to ensure that each of the features has equal visibility into compliance management's interpretation and status of compliance.
- Compliance management will need to facilitate an understanding, with the support of organizational management, on the methods of enforcement and key responsibilities of the representatives from each feature to ensure necessary changes are integrated.
- A close interlink is formed with capability maturity management, with oversight from governance, to ensure that there is clear agreement on the scope, depth, and breadth of changes or improvements to processes and standards that meet compliance management's expectations, but not hinder or impede the delivery of services, the role of risk management, or process improvement methods or objectives.

It is important to know that most, if not all, security programs today have ample capability in managing compliance. Therefore, this is not a complicated process, and in fact it takes advantage of existing capabilities and applies them to offer adaptability. As introduced above, some organizations already direct compliance efforts inwardly to ensure they are in alignment with their own expectations. However, this activity is far too rare, and only a handful of organizations have tied compliance efforts to process improvement and even fewer have tied them to adaptability. Through the looking glass of a service-oriented model, compliance represents a vastly untapped opportunity to gain better alignment with the business and is core to demonstrating value.

For some, this may seem ironic. Historically, and understandably so, compliance and especially audits have been part of corporate policy and typically an unwelcome presence that reminds companies they are being forced to meet external forces that have little or no bearing on the success of the business. Interestingly, this provides an opportunity for compliance to have a direct impact on the value of security within the organization and its ability to demonstrate value.

7.2 Corporate Compliance

In alignment with traditional compliance management activities, groups and individuals responsible for compliance interact with various areas of the business to ensure that controls, processes, and standards are compliant with external regulations and internal policies. These individuals achieve compliance by performing activities such as gap assessments and audits. Compliance groups will establish standards, processes, and tools, which are made available to other parts of the business to follow and implement in order to ensure a degree of consistency in how security is realized. For example, a regulation may stipulate certain security controls, and compliance provides interpreted materials, such as approved standards, specifications, and tools, that help ensure that the unique business environment—people, process, and technology—is meeting the demands of the regulation. Additionally, compliance will establish practices concerning the verification of controls. This may materialize as a formal audit checklist or assessment templates that other groups can employ to ensure their activities are addressing applicable compliance demands. Moreover, it may be determined that specific security services may be developed on behalf of compliance management to facilitate the assessment and audit activities. Again, compliance management's mission is to ensure compliance, which under normal circumstances does not mean performing actions directly with the customer, which is the role of services management. Although risk management has the means to apply a rapid risk assessment, this is unique in the ASMA and many organizations may find it much simpler to have rapid risk assessment as a defined service. However, it is typically in the best interest of risk management to have direct ownership of performing assessments of this nature. Conversely, compliance management has a broad scope of responsibilities and will typically have services developed to ensure overall corporate compliance. It is the responsibility of compliance and services management to determine which services feed information to compliance management to reduce the need for a specific service.

Nevertheless, as a result, companies have created compliance frameworks that allow them to address multiple regulations through a common compliance approach. For example, compliance groups will usually create a mapping of security controls and their applicability to multiple regulations. By doing so audits are more streamlined in addressing several regulatory demands and gaps are quickly identified. This is a growing practice in several industries, and there are strong indicators that more and more companies will be required to meet a broad range of regulations in the future. In the ASMA these inherent activities are built upon and codified. As introduced in Chapter 5, "Services Management," compliance management plays an important role in ensuring that security activities performed within a service are proactively addressing compliance demands. This also provides the opportunity for compliance to be involved in the delivery of the service or have access to the resulting materials to support broader compliance demands. The ASMA seeks to take advantage of current compliance practices or provide a mechanism to support greater efficiency in addressing multiple regulatory demands in the future when they emerge. In summary, how this is performed in a services management model and the relation between external regulations and oversight of services management is based on the following general interpretations, each building on the next:

- Many companies are currently faced, or will have to face in the future, compliance with several different regulations.
- Different regulations affecting a company's information security controls and program are going to have inherent similarities, such as perimeter security, authentication and authorization, encryption, anti-malware, and the like. This represents the natural consistency that is found in information security regardless of how it may be organized.
- Given the inherent similarities across regulations, to address multiple regulations organizations have, or will have to develop, common security controls mapping to the applicable regulations. This is the process of identifying security processes, procedures, and technical controls that can be applied to more than one regulation's requirement.
- Given that common compliance control mappings are unique to the organization and touch on security processes,

procedures, and technology, they directly influence or even govern the application of security.

Therefore, taking these four points into consideration, compliance management's role in the ASMA is critical in ensuring that actions performed in the delivery of services meet established expectations (i.e., common compliance framework) to addressing overall compliance of the organization not only in meeting multiple regulations, but also ensuring the enforcement of policies. Within this model, compliance management becomes actionable and integrated into everything that security services perform. In short, the ability to ensure overall corporate compliance rests predominantly in the ability to influence and exploit security services supported by an overall compliance framework managed and reported on to governance by the compliance management group.

By incorporating compliance into services the results can be far reaching and can dramatically change how companies address compliance. Achieving compliance with regulations becomes, for lack of a better term, a by-product of security. Moreover, as new regulations are imposed on the company the process of integrating the regulation's demands into the security program is made much easier.

7.2.1 Standards, Processes, and Procedures Compliance

One of the interlocks between compliance management and services management to ensure that compliance is integrated into service execution is related to standards, processes, and procedures. Standards, processes, and procedures provide the foundation for security services: how they are performed, focused, and measured. In order for compliance to be achieved with either regulations or policies there must exist a mechanism for compliance to not only introduce or modify standards, processes, and procedures for one or more services, but also to make certain they are being followed. This introduces two key points:

1. Compliance management must work very closely within organizational management to oversee standards, processes, and procedure development and management as it relates to security services, and have them incorporated into the activities of capability maturity management.

2. Compliance management's role in the oversight of adherence to established practices performed in services management is crucial to ensure standards, processes, and procedures are being followed in the delivery of security services.

In short, not only is compliance deeply involved in the definition of core attributes of service delivery, but it is also responsible for ensuring that services effectively employ them as intended.

To demonstrate, assume a new regulation is published that specifies that code for applications must be reviewed for security purposes. Accompanying the regulation is a set of standards that defines the high-level characteristics of reviewing code for security flaws, such as input validation. There is an existing "Secure Code Review" service in the services management model. Compliance management assesses the security services to find that it does not effectively address input validation code. Compliance management introduces the standard (a portion of the standard or a modified standard), processes that must be followed in the employment of the standard (such as those to be followed based on type of code), and the procedures to be acted upon (such as proper configuration of a code-scanning tool to identify input validation flaws). Once integrated, compliance management works closely with capability maturity management to ensure they are both reflected in those elements driving the application of the security services. Services management monitors the employment of standards, processes, and procedures for compliance management to ensure the feature is operating as designed. Compliance and capability information on compliance performance of the service is passed back to compliance management from services management for review and ultimately to governance.

7.2.2 Corporate Compliance Considerations

It may not always be possible to achieve compliance through the incorporation of compliant standards, processes, and procedures in security services. This is because some regulations may go beyond typical information security controls and touch upon other corporate services, such as HR, legal, and finance. For example, Sarbanes-Oxley (SOX) is a broad regulation impacting many areas of the business, with information security and information systems being a small part.

The ability to address this depends in many ways on how a company currently manages overall compliance for broad regulations, such as SOX. Given that the ASMA is within the information security domain, organizations employing a security services model will find that all of the regulatory demands that affect information security can be effectively realized through services management. However, given the scope and purpose of the model it may not address an entire regulation.

Unless an organization decides to hand over all compliance to the security group, compliance management's role is to report on information security compliance to a compliance committee or the organization responsible for overall compliance. If in a rare case in which the security group is responsible for the entire regulation—one that goes beyond traditional security domains—administrative and operational connections must be created with the various business areas to enable the program to manage that broader scope of compliance.

8

GOVERNANCE

There is no shortage of definitions for governance, especially within the security industry. They can range from executive oversight committees to policy enforcement. Nevertheless, the one provided by the Information Systems Audit and Control Association (ISACA) stands out and reflects the general purpose and role of governance within the ASMA:

> Establish and maintain a framework to provide assurance that information security strategies are aligned with business objectives and consistent with applicable laws and regulations.

Admittedly, the supporting elements as defined by the ISACA do not necessarily explore the potential of governance in the security space to the level the ASMA will. Nevertheless, the definition above is quite pertinent in focusing on the alignment with business, yet consistent with laws and regulations. Not only does this embody the overall intent, but it also rightly implies that governance is the best point of interface with the business on strategic topics concerning security posture.

Within the ASMA, governance acts as a bonding agent between the business and security communities. One can liken governance to an interpreter of information flow in and out of the security program to the business owners and executives. It provides a method for the collection of specific operational and security information and the ability to articulate that information in an agreed upon structure. More importantly, governance provides a critical service to security by absorbing business strategy from executives and ensuring that they are fully digested by the security program. Governance also provides the means to take into consideration all elements of security and business to ensure that dynamics coming from the business to security and from the security organization to the business are well formed, comprehensive, and meaningful. Following is a summary list of responsibilities and activities for governance:

- Ensure that information from all the features, such as measurements and metrics relative to operational performance, security performance, and meeting security and business goals, is managed, monitored, and reported to the business in a comprehensive and accurate manner that resonates with the business.

- Have the ability to effectively absorb and process information from the business concerning security's ability to meet expectation of performance, quality, and goals, and ensure the information is equally understood by all the features of the program in order to address business needs.

- Act as a source of information and guidance in the awareness of strategic business activities to promote adaptation or the validation of proposed adaptation processes. Governance is expected to not only interpret business dynamics based on the relationship with the executive team, but also to have the necessary visibility to vet proposed modifications to the program that are designed specifically to adapt to the identified business trajectory.

- Act as a customer representative prior to and during the application of security services that are initiated by compliance or risk management. Given governance's view into the interpretation of security's value by the business, it will also ensure that security activities are in the best interests of the business. By providing this service to the other features, governance assists in promoting balance between security objectives and intent and that of the business or business unit.

- Provide the primary interface to capability maturity management in the improvement of processes and standards relative to targeted levels of maturity in the security program. Moreover, it is governance's responsibility to ensure that information flowing from risk, compliance, and services management concerning measurements of performance is evaluated with capability maturity management to ensure that changes to the foundational elements of service delivery had the intended outcomes.

- Governance is responsible for acting as the primary force in the establishment of measurements and metrics as they relate to operational and security performance in meeting security and business goals and objectives. Governance is expected to collaborate extensively with the other features in the formation of strategic metrics into the business. It is important that governance is the central point of the metrics strategy and design so that inputs from the business concerning performance and inputs from the features remain aligned to stated goals and as such have the ability to determine the positive or negative impacts of process changes or improvements, or the outcome of adaptation.

To accomplish this, governance is not only an observer, but also an agent of influence. Observation is the collection of information within a defined framework that can be used as supporting material for the formation of upward communications. Of course, the opposite is true in the absorption of information, direction, and demands from the business, which may range from "great job" to "you dropped the ball" and everything in between. Governance seeks to map business level interpretations of success, failure, and direction to actionable changes within the security architecture across all the features.

As an influencer governance plays an essential role in how measurements of performance, security, and quality are performed and modified to ensure they are actionable and accurate. Through observation and the exchange of information with executive management, governance is in a unique position to define what measurements are resonating with the business and which are not. From this governance can greatly influence not only what measurements are being taken, but also how they are taken and how they are used to incorporate executive direction and the ability to respond effectively to that direction (Table 8.1 and Figure 8.1).

Governance is key to adaptability. Governance has all the pertinent security and operational performance information as well as visibility into business dynamics. By way of services management, governance has intimate visibility into performance, security, and quality measurements that help in understanding how security is being performed. Compliance management ensures that the information being generated is accurate and in alignment with defined processes and standards within the program and that services are ensuring corporate compliance. Capability maturity management identifies areas of weakness and opportunities for improvement in the program to drive

Table 8.1 Governance Interconnect Table

ACTIVE FEATURE	AREA OF SECURITY FOCUS	PRIMARY FEATURE INTERLOCK (BENEFICIARY)	INTENT AND EXPECTATIONS	FEATURE INPUT	FEATURE PRIMARY PROCESS	SECONDARY FEATURE INTERACTION	TARGETED AREAS OF THE PROCESS	FEATURE OUTPUT	BENEFICIARIES OF OUTPUT	SUMMARY DESCRIPTION
Governance	Risk Posture Management	Risk Management	Obtain clear visibility into the state of the customer, group, and overall risk posture of the organization in order to effectively report to the executive community	All of risk management's reporting from rapid risk assessment across the program and customer environments	A review of risk findings concerning overall risk posture, customer risk status, and how recommendations have been articulated and/or implemented and measured	Compliance Management	An analysis of specific risk management reports on risk posture, recommendations, the basis of findings, relevance to specific areas of the business, basis of recommendations, and how risk management will measure changes in the environment	A report on risk posture, findings relative to other activities in the security program, a review of implications relative to business goals and objectives, and recommendations on overall performance related to corporate risk	Executive Committee, Board, Customers	The objective is to ensure that governance has clear visibility from risk management's perspective on the overall risk posture, risk related to service delivery, and other risks that need to be translated and combined with other performance information for reporting to the executive community

Compliance Posture Management	Compliance Management	Gain an understanding of the compliance of the organization, program, and services relative to communicating with and addressing demands from the executive community	All of compliance management's reports as a result of performing assessments and analysis across the other features	An evaluation of compliance findings relative to program compliance, corporate compliance, and regulatory compliance	Risk Management	Specific recommendations to risk, service and capability maturity management features concerning compliance, identified areas for improvement and areas of innovative approaches to meeting compliance expectations	A report on the overall status of compliance, indications of future compliance demands, gaps and remediation activities, areas demonstrating effective compliance activities, and associated performance of compliance activities	Executive Committee, Board, Customers, Organizational Management	Governance wants to ensure that the program is compliant with established program standards, external regulatory demands are being met, and corporate policies and standards concerning overall security are in alignment with expectations. This information will be combined with risk management data to convey overall security posture to the executive community

(Continued)

Table 8.1 Governance Interconnect Table (Continued)

ACTIVE FEATURE	AREA OF SECURITY FOCUS	PRIMARY FEATURE INTERLOCK (BENEFICIARY)	INTENT AND EXPECTATIONS	FEATURE INPUT	FEATURE PRIMARY PROCESS	SECONDARY FEATURE INTERACTION	TARGETED AREAS OF THE PROCESS	FEATURE OUTPUT	BENEFICIARIES OF OUTPUT	SUMMARY DESCRIPTION
	Performance Improvement and Management	Capability Maturity Management	Ensure the effectiveness and efficiency of the program, service delivery, and services management to report to the executive community	Results from capability maturity assessments and analysis, identified areas for improvements in processes and measurements	An analysis of performance and quality measurements, findings, improvements, innovative activities, and program requirements	Services Management	Specific activities concerning performance measurements on the delivery of security services, risk management activities, compliance management oversight, and implementation metrics	A report on program and security performance covering organizational integrity, security integrity and posture, risk and compliance posture, and related performance against stated goals and objectives	Executive Committee, Board, Customers, Organizational Management, Compliance Management, Risk Management	Key to adaptation is expressing what areas of the program are improving, areas that represent gaps in maturity (especially with interlocks), and how well improvements to the underlying features are impacting overall performance and quality of the security program

| Policy and Standards Management | Organizational Management | Ensure alignment to business expectations of the program relative to performance and organizational excellence in support of the interactions with executive communities | Organizational management's reports and results from feature management concerning the oversight, incorporation, and enforcement of policy | An evaluation of standards and policy management and how this has resonated within service, risk, and compliance management concerning modification of delivery and activities | Compliance Management | A review of standard processes and policies focusing on interpretation of intended demands from the business, external regulatory features, and customer feedback on performance of applied security services and activities | A report on the status of standards and policies, how these are being managed and incorporated into the program and the business, how they are updated and measured for results, and the performance in assuring compliance to stated requirements | Executive Committee, Board, Customers, Partners and Vendors, Organizational Management | Governance wants to ensure that skills, resources, reporting, and overall corporate and program policies and standards are being employed as defined and managed by organizational management. Information from risk, compliance, and capability maturity management will be combined with capacity and capabilities of |

(Continued)

Table 8.1 Governance Interconnect Table (Continued)

ACTIVE FEATURE	AREA OF SECURITY FOCUS	PRIMARY FEATURE INTERLOCK (BENEFICIARY)	INTENT AND EXPECTATIONS	FEATURE INPUT	FEATURE PRIMARY PROCESS	SECONDARY FEATURE INTERACTION	TARGETED AREAS OF THE PROCESS	FEATURE OUTPUT	BENEFICIARIES OF OUTPUT	SUMMARY DESCRIPTION
										resources, and alignment to overall corporate policies and standards
	Services Management and Orchestration	Services Management	Ensure the alignment between business needs and demands and the formation, management, and communication of services	Results from organizational management, executive community interpretations of service applicability, and customer concerns	Evaluate the business's overall perspective and interpretation on the formation, structure, and available models used in the application of security	Organizational Management	A review of information collected from the executive community and customers concerning service models and catalog and compare to the results of services management and orchestration analysis from all the other features	A report primarily to the security organization on the executive and customer expectations concerning services, delivery activities, and measurements and compared to current and planned modifications to the catalog	Executive Committee, Board, Customers, Organizational Management, Capability Maturity Management, Risk Management, Compliance Management	By absorbing information and direction from the executive community, governance will influence the structure and definition of services, how they are managed and communicated, and ultimately how these resonate in the

application of
security
through
services
management,
risk
management,
and
compliance
management,
with
information on
effectiveness
and efficiency
from capability
maturity
management

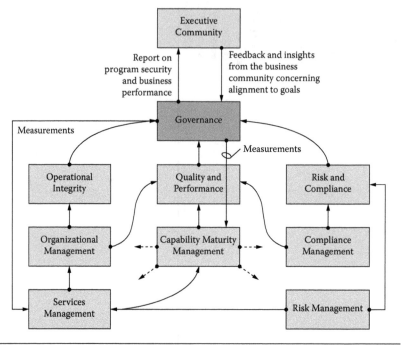

Figure 8.1 Governance interconnect process map.

greater effectiveness and efficiency and oversees the overall development of processes and standards. And risk management provides much needed information concerning the security posture, visibility into threats, security controls, potential, and impact.

All this information allows governance to paint an accurate picture that stretches the spectrum from security to operational integrity. Through this information governance, in collaboration with organizational management, can begin to better understand what is at its disposal for addressing business dynamics. Of course, the primary target for information from governance is for the business to gain awareness of security's capabilities and impacts. However, the information will also expose what is possible and act as a predictive model. As information is organized it can be used as the basis for comparison to emerging business demands or even "what if" scenarios.

8.1 Governance Observation and Communications

Governance provides the foundation for upward communication of the overall performance of security and its role within business operations. Historically, information risk management has been the platform for demonstrating the role and purpose of security within an organization. Risk management is used to quantify the need for security in order to stimulate discussions concerning investments or actions that are necessary by the business to reduce risk or accept it. However, within the ASMA, governance takes on this role, which represents a significant shift in established expectations of risk and governance. Within this context risk management is no less important, but the information it provides is combined with compliance, services, and capability maturity management to give a complete picture to the business on security as an organizational unit, not simply a one-dimensional security perspective founded solely on risk.

Each feature provides information to governance. Information will typically be provided in the form of metrics, which are related to specific processes and business and security goals as understood or defined by the feature. The specific measurement data, or supporting evidence of the information, is maintained by the feature and made available to governance regularly or upon request, such as audits or verification of what is being measured and how it is being measured. The objective is to initially provide governance with enough information about the performance of the feature and allow the feature's management to process all the data into salient information that governance can then combine with information from other features to build a meaningful executive-level representation. However, it is equally important that governance has the ability to interrogate the source of information provided. This is critical when governance needs to absorb information from the executive community and influence how measurements are performed to support change. As discussed in the section above concerning measurements, you are what you measure, and therefore changing what features are measured and how can have tangible results in ensuring change that meets business needs. Without visibility into the details, this is not possible and will undermine adaptability. To illustrate, governance may receive a report on various metrics from each feature monthly and from this prepare an executive report. Reponses from the executive community are collected and identified as opportunities for gaining more visibility in a particular feature. At that time it will be necessary for governance and the feature management to collaborate on what and how measurements are being taken in order to either change, enhance, or add measurements to improve reporting accuracy and to meet the needs of the business. It's noteworthy to add that capability maturity management will likely be involved to assist in the investigation and support implementation of modifications.

Governance observation and communication is predominantly focused on collecting the necessary information and processing it to a point that it is in alignment with executive expectations. Of course, this in turn requires several things:

- Acquire all the security and operational details from the other areas of the security model and summarize them into a collection of specific points on performance, security, and quality.
- Ensure that information is accurate and reflective of the environment. Governance must be certain not to unintentionally skew information through summarization activities.
- Provide information to the executive community in an agreed upon structure and format to ensure it is readily consumable, understandable, and poignant.
- Governance must be fully apprised of and educated on the information being provided in order to ensure clarity in discussions and to effectively address questions and concerns.
- Ample preparation has been performed prior to the meeting. It is necessary to look at the information objectively and identify trends and potential interpretations beforehand in order to have prepared responses.
- Establishment of a clear agenda with ample time allotted for addressing questions and receiving direction.

One of the mistakes made by many in the position of communicating with the executive team or committee in reporting on security status is attempting to explain or fix the problem in the meeting. If the information is not presented effectively, it will result in a number of questions that have the potential to derail the meeting and make the security group appear unprepared, which in this case would be true. There are a number of examples in which the discussion degrades to a point where it is more about the content of the report versus the intent of the report, and the presenter from the security group is left explaining the graphs and charts as opposed to the information he or she is attempting to convey. As a result, many are forced into explaining a wide range of potentially confusing subjects in response to questions that could have been avoided with proper preparation.

Nevertheless, even when information is well understood, there are likely situations in which the executive community will aggressively interrogate the information. In many cases, questions may be rhetorical and asked to simply make a point, whereas others are meant to determine specifically what is going wrong or how the improvement was realized and whether it is sustainable. Moreover, many questions may be leading or used to either undermine the proclamations or convey to security that conclusions are not well founded, or they do not have enough evidence to convince executive management. For the presenter, there is a tendency to explain in detail the situation or offer insights on plans that may not have been formalized in an attempt to manage the interrogation. In reality, the role of governance is to take this information back into the security group to form a solution, not to create one on the fly in the meeting. Generally, the rule of thumb is to answer questions that you have prepared for and do not try to correct issues in the meeting. This should be seen as an opportunity to learn and obtain direction, not set in motion ad hoc solutions that may fail or have a short lifespan.

There have been many situations in which the information presented is interpreted by the audience in a manner that was not predicted, which brings us to the point above—preparation. Everyone has different styles in preparing for an important meeting, and the audience and the presenter's knowledge of how the audience responds to different information influences this. Regardless, the one consistent thing separating those who have successful meetings and those who tend to have challenges is reviewing the information objectively. Once the report or presentation is complete, review it from a completely different perspective and determine what the information is saying and what can be interpreted. This isn't finding different ways to give good or bad news, it is attempting to view all the information empirically in order to discern what conclusions could be drawn that may not have been intended—for better or for worse. There have been many unfortunate meetings in which the information was assumed to be positive only to find that when presented to executives, who know how to effectively interpret complicated information, they rooted out gaps and even conflicting data points that undermined the entire meeting. Governance must be fully prepared for any situation because regardless of how well the security group is performing, the impression of the group in executive meetings will have long-lasting effects.

Of course, effectively communicating information to executive management is only half of the equation. The real value of the security group will be demonstrated by the ability to collect information and direction from the executives and make it actionable. As with presenting information, much of how this occurs will be defined by how the executives communicate their thoughts, interpretations, and direction. However, it is helpful to know that how data is presented can help extract valuable input from the meeting. As each meeting is performed, lessons learned from the process need to be reviewed, internalized, and used as the basis for improving communications in the future. Nevertheless, the goal is to improve business alignment, interpretation of value, and create a platform founded on adaptability so that as information and directives are provided from the executive community, they can be enacted in a meaningful way and demonstrated in future meetings. The key, of course, is capturing the information and converting it to actionable items. Therefore, this requires the following:

- Ensure that the direction is clearly understood. This can be more difficult than expected. Some executives provide well-articulated direction, while others may convey their wants and needs in a more roundabout manner. The advice is to never assume and always validate what was communicated.
- All information from the executive community, regardless of how benign it may seem at the time, must be recorded and logged for future reference and used as a method to communicate back into the security program.
- To state the obvious, document the direction. This can be simple notes, or a parking lot or whiteboard where actions are collected. As far as advice goes, take the time to write down the important points and do not overly rely on the meeting secretary to capture your interpretation of comments in the meeting.
- Collect and manage information flowing into the security group from the executive community to ensure business alignment.
- Convert the direction provided into action items, which includes assigning resources, dates of completion, and activities and work products as a result.

Many of these points on observations and communications are certainly not new, but they are worth expressing as an introduction to the importance and nuances of communication. Nevertheless, there are some additional attributes that are important to consider.

- The ASMA is founded on broad collaboration. Collaboration within the security group, with customers, and with the executive community is important to ensure information is flowing, needs are being met, and changes in the program are effectively communicated. Transparency is essential to the success of the security program, even when you don't want it.
- As stated, governance is responsible for providing detailed reporting to the executive community as the primary interface. This is an ongoing process, and as such governance is expected to articulate applicable trends to assist in strategic decision making.
- Regardless of how large or small the security group, there is potential for miscommunication. There are a number of potential scenarios in which lack of meaningful communications can have disastrous effects. For example, when two or more different services are being performed for the same customer, and actions in one area are not known to others working in different yet related areas, errors may be introduced or wasteful activities may result. Moreover, given that governance involves obtaining insights from the executive and customer communities, it must ensure that this information is incorporated into the program and monitor how it is resonating in and between the different features.
- Connecting with customers is essential. It's not enough to collaborate for the delivery of a service. Although doing so is important, it is also very tactical. Governance connects with the customer base regularly and compares feedback to information coming from the executive community. All this information is used to enhance the program at a strategic level.

It should also be noted that customers can be an enormous asset when interfacing with the executive community. Case studies, success stories, and other customer-supported evidence can be very valuable in demonstrating the business value that security is providing.

8.1.1 Role of Communications in Adaptability

The process of adaptation can be as much a reactive process as a proactive one. In either case it is about how information is obtained and used to instigate change. Of course, the differentiating factor is the type of information being used. For example, information about an impending business change can be used to be proactive and make adjustments to the program so that when the change occurs you are established, or at least prepared. Conversely, if the information is received after the fact, the ability to adapt and the time required for organizing efforts to come in line with the change will ultimately reflect on value. Having an adaptive security model ensures that the security organization is not only poised to align to emerging demands, but to rapidly retool in order to maintain or even increase effectiveness in a changed environment. It is the role of governance to ensure this information is fed into the security program and that the program's response to it is provided back to the business.

For many organizations security is generally in a reactive state. This applies to its role in business as much as it does in traditional security. When a new regulation is published, the security organization reacts, or when a new threat or vulnerability is discovered, the security organization reacts. In many ways, this is the nature of security in today's world. However, what separates a good security program from a great security program is its time to respond and doing so in a manner that is effective and repeatable and not fire fighting. Moreover, the nature of reactive security does not necessarily have to exist at the business level, and this is the role of communications in adaptability.

Governance working as the interface to business and empowered with the knowledge of security operations and the ability to influence change in the alignment of security is the tipping point for adaptability. While other features throughout the ASMA are refining and enhancing capabilities and increasing the effectiveness of how security is applied to manage risk and achieve compliance, they are also inherently creating potential. As capability maturity management seeks to improve and innovate in working with services management, and compliance and risk management tune and modify advances in how security is applied, there is an increased awareness of potential barriers. As discussed above, the information collected by governance from the security organization can act as a predictive model. More importantly, over time there is increased knowledge about what can and cannot be accomplished easily. These act as a performance envelope encompassing what is being done today and presenting what could be accomplished.

As governance obtains highly valuable information from the business there are natural indications of tactical and strategic business demands. Through communications with those beyond the security group, governance, along with organizational management and other features, can compare its performance envelope to potential business directions. This is only possible when there is a high degree of visibility into the operational integrity of the security program. Once achieved, identifying what can be changed and, more importantly, accurately predicting the outcome of the change are well within reach.

There have been conditions in which the business needs to change and security is one of the many areas of the organization that is looked at to support the change. In nearly all cases, when walking out of an executive meeting about change the CISO will say something to the effect of, "Well, now we just have to figure out how to do it." Albeit completely understandable, the "figuring it out" part can be incredibly streamlined when there is clear visibility into the program and what is possible. All the features in the ASMA produce information that helps to create a comprehensive view of the security organization from a performance capacity and effectiveness perspective.

8.2 Governance Influence

As observations from both the business and security are processed, changes in the way things are measured will likely surface. For example, security experts may define metrics that make perfect sense to them, but are not translating effectively to the executive community. Governance can be used to either modify or introduce new forms of measurement to help close the gap. Clearly, this has to be done so that not only is the information meaningful to both parties, but actionable items can be afforded.

Another primary role of influence for governance, and arguably one of the unfortunate failings of some security programs, is ensuring the ability to apply changes relative to what is being measured. When measurements are taken over time, whether security related, performance related, or business related, there must exist the ability to manage changes to influence those measurements over time. This may seem obvious, but there are a number of scenarios in which information about the state and direction of security are provided where there is no ability to manage distinct elements of the measured environment to influence those results. In these situations reporting on the condition of security is undermined and gives a poor impression of the program.

As a simple example, let's assume that you're measuring the number of system vulnerabilities in an environment. Added to this measurement are criticality of vulnerabilities, applied patches, and other information that helps communicate state. First and foremost, this is a very good practice for security. However, the question is, should this be a metric presented to executives? To put it succinctly, you technically have very little control over the number of vulnerabilities in your environment, but rather control in how they may be managed or addressed. At any point in time a collection of new vulnerabilities can be published, dramatically changing the state of the environment overnight. Although this is understood within the security world, a report to executives that vulnerabilities have increased 27%, regardless of criticality and other conditions well beyond your control, may not be well received.

Knowing when there is a spike in vulnerabilities is important to security so it can be managed effectively, such as rapidly applying a new patch. Therefore, security measurements are essential to the model and will resonate deeply in risk, compliance, and services management. But these are the inner workings of security, and peaks and valleys in a security metric may result in confusion for executive management on security's capabilities when in fact it's a typical cycle as new vulnerabilities are discovered, published, and mitigated.

What many organizations will find when they implement a model for adaptability is the ability to show overall trending or stable activities in the midst of dramatic environmental changes. Although executives may not fully understand why there are increases and decreases in the number and criticality of vulnerabilities over time, they do resonate with the ability to manage these things effectively. To offer an example, a monthly report was provided by the CISO on various security metrics that essentially showed the number of vulnerabilities and their criticality. In the report were peaks and valleys over the year with the overall trend moving up slightly. This was not well received by the executive, who saw the report as security's inability to address vulnerabilities when in fact the opposite was true. What the CISO failed to demonstrate was that although there were increasing vulnerabilities, the time to correct them was dropping rapidly and the methods used were increasing in effectiveness and efficiency. The real state of security was that although it could not control the number and criticality of vulnerabilities that were obviously increasing in volume due to a number of environmental factors, it was increasing its capability in managing them effectively. Unfortunately, there were no measurements to support this claim and therefore no hard data in the report to support the CISO's claim of greater operational integrity. No matter how hard the CISO tried to explain, the data presented were used as a counterpoint. "How can you suggest that you are effective in addressing these security issues when they are clearly increasing?" Therefore, measuring something you cannot control without other measurements that demonstrate your ability to manage diversity is ineffective and will undermine the security program in the eyes of the business.

8.2.1 Control and Accuracy

This scenario has played out for many CISOs in the last several years as security metrics and dashboards have become increasingly popular. As a result many have learned from these lessons and begun measuring other performance features to demonstrate that there are compensating activities. However, this has presented two more problems: control and accuracy.

Control, or the lack thereof, as demonstrated with security metrics and vulnerabilities also applies to operational capabilities. Once you have accepted that you cannot control certain aspects of security it demands you provide additional visibility into your ability to manage them effectively, and you soon realize that you may not have as much control over managing such things as vulnerabilities as you may have assumed. For example, there was a set of security reports that was generated weekly and provided to executive management monthly. In the report there was an overlay of two measurements: vulnerabilities and time of remediation. Although the number and type of vulnerabilities fluctuated and increased over time, the time of remediation was dropping consistently. The CISO has predictive trends demonstrating a targeted time of remediation and aligned these to the ability to address increasing trends in vulnerabilities. The objective was to illustrate that there were enough resources to meaningfully handle a certain volume of vulnerabilities, but only to a certain point. Unfortunately, the association of per-vulnerability correction time and volume backfired. What occurred was the CISO did not have accurate performance information on the capability of the team to remediate vulnerabilities, and as a result the prediction was woefully incorrect. As each report was provided the time of remediation began to stall, became flat, and even had spikes, all of which were well short of the targeted level. The truly damaging part was that some of the increases in remediation time coincided with increases in vulnerabilities, essentially demonstrating that it took longer to remediate on a per-vulnerability basis as the volume increased.

From a performance perspective one might assume that the more problems there are the longer it will take to fix them. Although this is true in overall time consumed, the time metric was based on a per-vulnerability number, not volume. Of course, from a security perspective this dynamic can make perfect sense simply because the time to remediate is, in many ways, tied to the vulnerability. A vulnerability in application code logic will likely take longer to correct than one that can be repaired by applying a patch. Adding to the malaise demonstrated in the previous paragraph, there were no defined processes for remediation; it was, for the most part, ad hoc and predominantly reliant on individual expertise. As a result, there were no direct or meaningful measurements being taken to support the projection, much less provide the ability to improve processes of remediation. The basis for the problem is that the CISO did not have enough program control to influence time of remediation, a critical metric being used in the report. Moreover, the time measured did not take into account different types of vulnerabilities and how they influenced time of remediation. All this stemmed from oversimplification of the information and the inability to effectively control the operational characteristics of vulnerability management to achieve projections. Of course, the results were not well received by the executive community.

This and the previous example are provided to convey a very simple message. When measurements and metrics are based on information flowing from the security program and there is either (1) no method for implementing modifications to the program to influence those measurements, or (2) measurements are being taken from characteristics of security that are completely out of the control and beyond the influence of the security group, then the resulting perspective of the metrics to executive management will fail, and fail catastrophically. Again, although this may seem painfully obvious, there are unfortunately many examples of security and performance metrics not being viewed objectively and interrogated from this position. The result is information on the performance of security being presented and there is nothing the security organization can do to actually make a line in a report change direction. Although the ASMA is primarily structured to ensure business alignment and business value, many will find that the first form of value to the security organization will be clarity of performance and the means to take ownership of that performance.

Next is the challenge of accuracy, which can become an Achilles' heel for a security program presenting metrics and projections to the executive community. In the above examples the problem was founded on not presenting meaningful data due to the inability to control vulnerabilities and operational aspects of managing vulnerabilities. However, as organizations look to provide ever more valuable insights in the form of metrics the second challenge of accuracy begins to surface. Accuracy is representative of the condition or quality of being correct or exact and free from error or defects. As such it implies that measurements are taken correctly, and that measurement data is defensible and supported by evidence proving the end report's characteristics. Therefore, as one would assume, great care in how measurements are taken and recorded must be applied and documented. This is based on the fact that at some point measurements will be interrogated. In fact, with regard to changing business demands, this is likely going to increase substantially as executives dig deeper into operational integrity measurements to ensure their investments are being applied effectively.

As a result, a degree of science must be applied in the act of measuring a condition or process. Without a supporting process and evidence of the measurement, all upstream information is open to question, which will put governance in a precarious position if questioned—and there will be questions. The process of ensuring accuracy does not have to be complicated. As with many elements within the model, organizations need to be more concerned with the quality and less with the complexity. In fact, the greater the simplification of processes and management of measurements the greater the opportunity for adaptability. This is a conclusion based on the role of governance in monitoring, through measurements and metrics, whether changes in the program have the intended outcome. The same holds true for every feature. Therefore, the simpler and more accurate the process of measuring, the fewer the opportunities for errors and the more efficiently the measurements will reflect changes in the program.

Accuracy not only applies to how data is collected, but also to how it is processed. As the number of variables increases, the potential for different interpretations of that information increase exponentially. How these perspectives are generated can have an impact on how they are perceived. Building on the above example, many organizations will combine different metrics to demonstrate performance, such as number of vulnerabilities compared to time of remediation mentioned above. In the example, the association of time per vulnerability and number did not expose the difference in time based on type of vulnerability. It is likely that an average was used across all different times reported in the period. Therefore, the math used to compile information can have a dramatic impact on the accuracy of what is being presented and send a very different message.

For example, in working with an organization by performing an analysis on security effectiveness in addressing constant security activities, all the metrics were consistently moving up and to the right—a positive trend. There was an emerging concern on the sustainability of such performance and seeking direction on investments that would improve scalability, mostly targeted at technology due to the interpretation of the results. However, upon deeper analysis, out of the thirty-plus measurements being taken, only a portion were being calculated and the formula was not taking into account inherent relationships that existed between people, processes, and technology and the overall operational integrity of the group. When the data was processed against a different model that exploited these inherent, and to some degree obvious, relationships, the result was illuminating.

Although the ultimate trend of performance was virtually the same, the problem of scalability was that not all employees were using established and proven processes and tools. The averaging of limited information was masking the fact that certain individuals were grossly outperforming those who didn't use a particular process or tool at the right time or at all. Although these measurements were taken, there was no association to other more mission critical measurements that ranged from time-per-ticket or number of patches applied to number of communications, such as calls and e-mail, or gaps in audit results. Moreover, the quality metrics were different and although performance was up, quality was flat and in some cases declining. In other words, everything appeared to be running as designed, but advances in other related areas of the program were not being experienced. All the measurements pointed to technology as the problem and as the organization invested in technology it didn't realize all the expectations of projected improvements.

As a result of the exercise, investments allotted for technology were redirected into a pilot group in which one of the three shifts was reintroduced and retrained on the entire set of processes. As each problem was managed all the processes were applied; those not applicable were eliminated and eventually the problem or action required was corrected or completed. The overall number of activities accomplished in the pilot dropped due to the added steps, but it allowed the shift team to learn what processes and tools were most effective for a given scenario. Eventually the pilot group dramatically outpaced the others and the change was implemented program-wide. The end result was that far more efficiencies and greater effectiveness was realized for a mere fraction of what was being planned to increase technical capacity. If the methods of measurement were not interrogated from an objective standpoint, the company would have wasted a vast amount of money.

In this scenario, the measurements were sound, but the accuracy in how they were used to portray what was really occurring was incorrectly managed. The result directed the company's attention away from the real problem and it could have expended a lot of energy and money in directions that would have had virtually no impact. There are two lessons that can be gained from the example. First, measurements have to be accurately taken and accurately processed to convert the data to meaningful information that is reflective of the condition. The second lesson is that the relationship between people and processes is powerful. When the capability maturity is increased far more effectiveness can be realized.

8.3 Operational Characteristics of Governance

Governance is one of the more complex topics in the ASMA because it touches everything and is the basis of connecting the program's value to the business—a critically important responsibility. Although covered generally above and in preceding chapters that touched upon governance, the following sections will highlight important points.

8.3.1 Performance Management

Performance management exists in some form or another in every feature of the model and is critical to achieving the mission of the ASMA. Governance is responsible for not only collecting performance information from all the features, but it must also ensure that these are communicated effectively to executives, customers, and within the security group. Additionally, based on governance's involvement with the executive and customer communities, and having deep visibility into performance measurements, it is also in the position to influence change. Change can occur in two basic ways:

1. Changing the metrics or reporting of metrics to better service the larger community
2. Changing standards, processes, and procedures in how various security services are performed and managed to ensure that performance is increased and therefore reflected in the reporting

8.3.1.1 Measurements Throughout the program information is being collected. Not all of this information is required to facilitate the need of governance in communicating performance achievement and improvement. Nevertheless, all the measurements taken in the program act as a pool of resources for governance, and it is up to governance to determine which ones are necessary to ensure alignment with the business. Typically, organizations will have key performance goals (KPGs) that state strategic goals of the company and are supported by one or more key performance indicators (KPIs). Key performance indicators are quantifiable measurements that reflect the critical success factors in meeting stated goals.

Key performance indicators can materialize as or be supported by a number of metrics that express measurements over time. For example, some may choose to define a number of specific metrics that roll up into one or more KPIs that in turn support a KPG. On the other hand, many will find that KPIs and metrics are synonymous and simply have two levels in the measurement hierarchy. Nevertheless, when employing all the features many organizations will find that a number of metrics surface in the various features that lend themselves to being summarized into KPIs. It is the responsibility of governance to define or map security to key performance goals and determine what KPIs and metrics are necessary to best track success in meeting those goals.

There are two fundamental targets for measurement that must be performed:

1. Security measurements—These are KPGs and KPIs (and potentially metrics) that are specific to security. These will encompass everything from risk and compliance to technical controls and security management.
2. Operational measurements—These are measurements that are targeted at measuring the operational integrity of the security organization. These address effectiveness, efficiency, and adaptability, in addition to capability maturity, financial performance, and quality.

In the Measurements section of Chapter 5 "Services Management," the overall consideration of forming measurements and a metrics strategy were provided. Added to this and the fact that governance will be the center point for the metrics strategy, there is specific guidance that can be offered. In basic terms, this is the SMART model used in project management or in setting the goals of individuals and other forms of performance management:

- Specific—Also includes significant, stretching, and simple to ensure that measurements concerning performance are meaningful to the intended audience that will be measured, not complicated, and represent an opportunity to push what is possible.
- Measurable—Also includes meaningful, motivational, and manageable to promote the fact that measurements are an accurate reflection of expectations and demands. More importantly, there exists a foundation to produce the information driving the measurements.
- Attainable—Also includes appropriate, achievable, and actionable to ensure that performance measurements are capable of being met within reason. Of course, there are stretch measurements that help to promote better performance and acknowledge those that overachieve.
- Relevant—Also includes realistic, resourced, and results focused, which ensure that measurements are applicable to the community and environment being measured.
- Time-bound—Also includes time-based, time frame, and time limited to express that not all measurements should be open-ended and have a finite period of measurement and, in some cases, relevance. This is also to ensure that rewards (or corrective measures) associated with performance are applied in a meaningful time period.

Although there are a number of methods and criteria for setting objectives, whatever model is employed must promote alignment with setting goals. This aspect—alignment of measurements to goals—can be difficult in security and has challenged many. Basically, assume that a business goal is to increase customer satisfaction. How does one translate that to a security goal or an objective that will ultimately define performance and operational measurements? Of course, there is no easy answer and there is vast material available that attempts to provide one. However, the reality is that goals are unique to each organization. Although goals from different organizations may appear similar, such as in the example, how they relate to activities within the business will vary dramatically simply because all businesses have different approaches, management styles, and culture. This is the reason that KPGs and KPIs are so important—they help to provide a view into the interpretations of goals relative to how they materialize in the business. For example, the goal of increasing customer satisfaction will begin to take shape in KPIs, which in turn will begin to isolate business practices and processes. It is critical for security to interpret business and operational KPIs in order to find a method to intersect security activities and processes with overall business goals.

The importance of this exercise cannot be overstated and is essential to not only ensuring alignment with the business and changing the identity of security in the business, but is an avenue for security to truly enable the business. Building on the example, assume a KPI looks closely at one of five programs created to increase customer satisfaction. Further assume that the program in question deals with the accuracy, effectiveness, and efficiency in the company responding to customer requests for information that is the basis for sales and customer management activities. Contained within the program are several measurements, such as time to respond, number of errors, resources utilized, involvement of the quality organization, and the like, all feeding into a KPI that expresses the program's overall performance and role in meeting the overall goal. From these measurements and their relation to the KPI it is possible for security to investigate the methods and services the organization may be using to ensure the measurements are moving in the right direction. A simple example may be to start looking at the systems and processes that actually provide the measurements into the KPI. For example, there may be a portal that is for internal uses or is customer facing where information can be provided. This may provide further evidence into the role of tickets and ticket management contained within the portal. One can start to look at how security can influence that system. For example, can identity management assist in better ticket routing? Are customers not using the portal because of a concern for exposing private information? In short, what can security do to participate in the company's achieving its goal?

In some rare cases, an opportunity is presented to a security group that offers yet another example of why governance's interface with the business is so important. For example, there was a large firm that had aspirations of dominating the market and becoming a leader, which was a realistic goal and well within reason. Part of the strategy was a combination of acquisition and deep partner and vendor integration, which represented challenges for everything from business process to IT. As the business executed the plan there were gaps and delays that hindered the process and caused other board-level issues in strategy. Under deeper analysis it was found that integrating partners was slowing due to the inability to demonstrate due diligence in processes and technology integration. Eventually it was determined that sections of the organization were not meeting audit expectations. The security organization quickly identified the areas it could influence to change this relatively low-level condition, which once corrected began to resonate at the highest levels of the strategy. In this real-world example, security identified an opportunity and applied itself to an area that was normally not within its remit to have an influence on the audit results.

8.3.1.2 Monitoring   Given that governance is intimately involved in the collection and maintenance of performance measurement, there must also exist a method to monitor what is being measured. Some measurements must be taken in very short intervals to be meaningful, whereas others need to be checked only over long periods of time. Validation is also a part of monitoring. It is not always a matter of simply absorbing information; there must be a method to occasionally ensure that the measurement process itself is functioning as expected. For example, one measurement may be tracking the number of logs collected from a system. Of course, this is inexorably tied to the configuration of the system to send logs deemed as important. If the system is not configured correctly, the measurement is questionable at best and rendered useless at worst.

It must be understood that the integrity of measurements must be defensible. Any weakness in the foundation becomes exponentially magnified as the information is processed. Governance, by way of its role, is indirectly responsible for monitoring measurements and environmental conditions that may impact the measurement process. In reality it is the other features that must perform the heavy lifting of monitoring, but governance is responsible for understanding and managing conflicts or other forms of misalignment.

8.3.1.3 Improvement Management   Very much related to all the characteristics of performance management is the ability of governance to influence the improvement of processes. This is also very similar to compliance management's role in influencing standards, processes, and procedures to ensure compliance. As with compliance management, governance—as the information gateway to the executive and customer communities—needs to have interlocks with compliance management, services management, and ultimately capability management to ensure that perspectives of quality, satisfaction, effectiveness, efficiency, and adaptability are being integrated into the operational aspects of service delivery.

This represents a unique interchange and partnership with compliance management in the modification of standards, processes, and procedures. Of course, risk management is the final stage in vetting the changes to ensure that well-intentioned changes from governance and/or compliance do not result in adverse affects on service delivery that may result in increased risk. Ultimately, capability maturity management will perform the work of integrating changes in improvements.

With governance's visibility into measurements and the state of the security program as interpreted by the executive and customer communities, it is in a unique position to influence the improvement of a number of processes throughout the program. These will typically surface as high-level changes, and it is up to other service model features to translate to their respective areas of responsibility.

Governance, along with organizational management, is best positioned to understand the overall quality of the program. Specifically, governance obtains valuable feedback from executives and customers that must be acted upon if there are issues. As with process improvement, governance's role is to ensure that information from beyond the security group is interpreted and passed to the respective security features to ensure that it is addressed. This is based on the fact that customers may not articulate concerns in a manner that resonates within the security group in order to know exactly what changes are necessary. For example, a customer may state that the results from the test were not actionable and it did not know how to put the results to use. It is up to governance to interface with the customer to explore the problem more deeply and convert that information into specific guidance for the security group.

9

ORGANIZATIONAL MANAGEMENT

As introduced above, organizational management provides the executive and leadership team with the oversight that is necessary to ensure the entire security program is meeting expectations. As such, this embodies a number of strategic and tactical elements of security management that are important to the overall program, and also support elements of security that are necessary but not addressed directly by other features. Moreover, organizational management has the responsibility of establishing a coherent security strategy, one that is supported by a mission statement, charter, and objectives. It is important because it defines the security organization's identity to others, helps those within the security group to understand their role and the direction of the group, and acts as a reference when the group is challenged to take on something different that may or may not be in alignment with the intended role of the security group. Clearly, this goes beyond just the ASMA; it should be reflected at the strategic level so that the business can resonate with the service delivery identity of the group (Table 9.1 and Figure 9.1).

9.1 Organizational Structure

The structure of the organizational management team can take on many different forms, and each CSO will have a different approach. However, the following are organizational characteristics that should be considered:

- Feature representation—The leaders of risk management, compliance management, governance, services management, and capability maturity management should report to the CSO and have a formalized forum to meet on a regular basis. Of course, each representative should have an opportunity to report on activities and needs from the others.

Table 9.1 Organizational Management Interconnect Table

ACTIVE FEATURE	AREA OF SECURITY FOCUS	PRIMARY FEATURE INTERLOCK (BENEFICIARY)	INTENT AND EXPECTATIONS	FEATURE INPUT	FEATURE PRIMARY PROCESS	SECONDARY FEATURE INTERACTION	TARGETED AREAS OF THE PROCESS	FEATURE OUTPUT	BENEFICIARIES OF OUTPUT	SUMMARY DESCRIPTION
Organizational Management	Risk Posture Management	Risk Management	Ensure that the overall program and all the features are contributing to the management of the risk posture	Results from the rapid risk assessment and related documentation provided to governance on the overall risk posture and methods for measuring and managing via security services	Perform an analysis of the findings and activities and how they are being applied by compliance and services management	Governance	A review of risk management's rapid risk assessment processes and reporting standards to the other features, and the methods for monitoring risk posture in how services are executed	A report on the alignment of risk management's activities to the intended role and the level of effectiveness and efficiency in monitoring and addressing dynamics in risk relative to feedback from services, compliance, and capability maturity management	Governance, Compliance Management	Organizational management must have an understanding of risk posture and the interpretations of risk relative to service delivery. This is needed for policy, standards, and resource management and to ensure risk management is performing as expected and collaborating effectively with other features

Compliance Posture Management	Compliance Management				Risk Management			Governance, Risk Management	
		Ensure that the program and features are promoting compliance activities and meeting business demands for compliance and are being communicated effectively to customers	All the results from compliance management's analysis of the other features, recommendations, activities, and methods for measuring compliance status	A review of compliance management processes, methods, interactions, reporting processes, and interactions with the other features		Compliance management's processes and standards concerning management, reporting, tracking, and interactions, and includes specific methods for determining and monitoring improvements	A report on the overall management of compliance, compliance management's adherence to processes, standards, and policy, role in the enforcement of compliance by collaboration with service and risk management		Assurance that the overall program is compliant and the security program is meeting expectations concerning corporate compliance to promote capacity and resource management

(Continued)

Table 9.1 Organizational Management Interconnect Table (Continued)

ACTIVE FEATURE	AREA OF SECURITY FOCUS	PRIMARY FEATURE INTERLOCK (BENEFICIARY)	INTENT AND EXPECTATIONS	FEATURE INPUT	FEATURE PRIMARY PROCESS	SECONDARY FEATURE INTERACTION	TARGETED AREAS OF THE PROCESS	FEATURE OUTPUT	BENEFICIARIES OF OUTPUT	SUMMARY DESCRIPTION
	Performance Improvement and Management	Capability Maturity Management	Gain awareness on the state of effectiveness and efficiency in the realization of policies and standards, and resource capability in delivery and management across the program	All the results from capability maturity management assessments, findings, improvement activities, and innovative approaches	A review of capability maturity management's activities, processes, and improvements to processes, standards, tools, methods, and resources	Compliance Management	Focus on specific improvement and innovation activities and how these relate to measuring their impact on how security is applied and achieving stated program goals and objectives	A report on capability maturity's effectiveness in promoting improvements and innovation within the security organization and in how services are defined, deployed, applied, tracked, and measured within the business	Governance, Risk Management, Compliance Management	In close collaboration with governance on the establishment of measurements and reporting concerning program performance and organizational integrity

Policy and Standards Management	Compliance Management				Governance			Governance, Risk Management, Capability Maturity Management	
		Ensure tight collaboration on the regulatory demands, internally established expectations (policy), and program compliance	All compliance management's activities across all the features in determining adherence to management practices and processes for standards and policy support and enforcement	An evaluation of compliance management's role in assuring overall compliance to program standards and polices within the security program and how these resonate in service delivery and feature activities		Compliance management's reports on organizational compliance, process compliance, risk and service management compliance and regulatory compliance, including processes for measurement, tracking, and monitoring	A report on the overall management of compliance activities and interactions with all the other features of the security program and the interpreted effectiveness in compliance activities in managing the posture of the organization and business		Ensure the alignment to program expectations and overall policy compliance and enforcement by working with services management and governance

(Continued)

Table 9.1 Organizational Management Interconnect Table (Continued)

ACTIVE FEATURE	AREA OF SECURITY FOCUS	PRIMARY FEATURE INTERLOCK (BENEFICIARY)	INTENT AND EXPECTATIONS	FEATURE INPUT	FEATURE PRIMARY PROCESS	SECONDARY FEATURE INTERACTION	TARGETED AREAS OF THE PROCESS	FEATURE OUTPUT	BENEFICIARIES OF OUTPUT	SUMMARY DESCRIPTION
	Services Management and Orchestration	Services Management	Work with services management in the identification of gaps and opportunities in the development and management of the service catalog and the necessary capabilities—skills, partners, etc.—in the delivery of services	Results from all the other feature interactions concerning a review and analysis of service catalog and orchestration of service models and types	An overall analysis of service structure and effectiveness in making necessary overall adjustments to the service catalog based on information from the other features	Risk Management	Working closely with governance, risk management, and capability maturity management, organizational management performs a customer-based review of service models drawing from performance, quality, risk, and capability, and capacity reporting	A report on the overall ability, effectiveness, and efficiency in incorporating demands from customers and inputs from other features in assuring the adaptation of service delivery methods to meet the goals and objectives of the security organization and the business	Governance, Services Management, Capability Maturity Management	Oversee and manage the service catalog, customer interactions, and quality management. Working closely with governance and services management to ensure expectations are met and performance is monitored

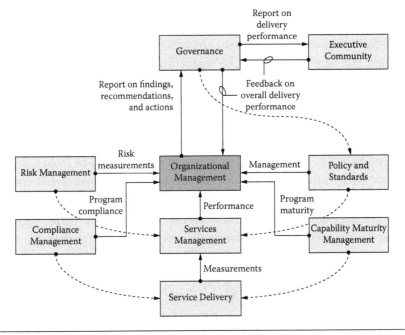

Figure 9.1   Organizational management interconnect process map.

- Governance leadership—There needs to be a dotted-line relationship between risk management, compliance management, services management, and capability maturity management with governance leadership. Governance, with the support of the CSO, will act as the source of tactical information from the business to the other groups. Moreover, expectations concerning the delivery of key information from the other areas into governance need to be well formed.
- Governance committee—The CSO needs to form a committee comprising executive representation from the various areas of the business and the leadership team to provide oversight and direction concerning service delivery, management, compliance, and risk. Moreover, interactions in the committee should also focus on adaptability to emerging changes in the business.
- Customer council—The CSO should formalize a method to support regular meetings with the customer community. This is an opportunity to report on quality, activities, and key performance indicators and for customers to learn from their peers.

9.2 Defining the Customer

The term customer may have an obvious definition, but this does not negate the fact that it must be quantified so that those within the security group and beyond have a clear understanding of who or what is the target for services. So far the term customer has been used generally in association with different business units as the recipient of security services. Although this is true, it is helpful to further refine the meaning of customer so that security organizations have a consistent perspective. This is an important exercise because it will show how the security program differentiates activities. For a company comprising many divisions and business units, this may simplify the process, but even in these situations, how do you ensure that you are servicing the company as a whole? The level of granularity that best represents the ASMA in the company must be determined.

Granularity that is too high, such as IT as a customer, may not relate to different and large groups within IT, such as helpdesk, datacenter services, and the like, which may have varying security needs, not to mention different budgeting methods. Too much granularity and the employment of a service will have mixed results because it will have to cross business lines. For example, a sales organization may be broken into several groups focusing on different products and/or markets. If you target these elements too closely, shared services, resources, applications, platforms, and processes will surface, thus expanding the scope of the service. Normally, this is not complicated. Lines are formed in companies that are usually well understood and may act as a good starting point and be refined over time to reflect security's role in the delivery of services more effectively. However, there are cases in which these lines are not well defined or appear completely meaningless for security. This represents a potential challenge when defining the customer.

In situations where there is lack of clarity, arguments will surface that the "company" is the customer and security services the entire company. Interestingly, stating that the "company" is the customer is how many security organizations identify themselves today and provide security in layers, such as network security, application security, perimeter security, and the like, mostly because these are shared services and they are representative of a horizontal security strategy. However, this single approach does not necessarily provide for specific needs that may surface in certain areas of the business. For example, although HR may have no say or interest in the systems it uses provided by IT, it may be very interested in the control of personal information. The sales and marketing group may interface with the application development group for the creation of a specific solution. Is the application group the customer or sales and marketing?

Are partners customers? For example, there may be a service that is employed to evaluate a partner's security prior to establishing a connection with the company. The service may be designed to have varying levels of activities that are relative to the type of partner, and the results of the service may define the level of access and authority provided to the partner. This raises the question: Is the business unit seeking a partner interaction with the customer and all this implies, or is the partner the customer and the service to them is supporting evidence to the business of having been validated and to what level?

Defining the customer as the entity that is paying for a service is not a good foundation because how money flows in and out of the security group may be completely irrelevant to the target of the service. Additionally, stating that the benefactor of a service is the customer may not work either because a service may be employed for one business unit from another, with the results going to the initiator and not the target entity. For example, the auditing group may want to leverage a security service to generate more detailed analysis of a business unit's security. The results are for the audit group and not the division that is being audited.

As demonstrated, defining the customer is not always easy, but it is important. To assist in this endeavor, following are some general points to consider:

- Think in business terms, not security terms—Traditional security naturally gravitates upward to encompass the company. This is obvious due to the fact that security is omnipresent and security groups need to be tied in at the top of the business due to policy, compliance, and risk factors that may equally affect every corner of the company. However, defining the customer as, for example, business units, does not render this point moot. It's not "lowering the bar," but rather providing the opportunity to demonstrate value. Risk, compliance, and governance, all of which are part of the model, along with organizational management are acutely focused on the company as a whole and bringing these elements together. However, these elements are brought together within the service and the way the service is being applied. Therefore, these are not mutually exclusive, and defining customers at a business unit level strengthens the ability to address broader security demands, and does not weaken it.

- Dealing with shared services—There are a vast number of situations in which multiple parts of the business or the entire company use the same corporate IT services, such as Internet access, core applications, systems, storage, and the like. Therefore, is IT as a group a customer, or are these different IT services the target for security services holistically? In these situations it's best to treat the different areas of IT that are responsible for business services as the customer. This helps with ensuring some degree of granularity, which will help with overall management and reporting and lends itself to aligning with other service models that may exist within IT, such as ITSM.

- It's not written in stone—No matter what the initial approach is in defining the customer, it can always be changed. Of course, this is something that should not be changed often, but certainly changing it to reflect lessons learned and to add additional stability in the program is more than acceptable. Security organizations that have developed a services model approach tend to define the customer and never look back. Although this is understandable, it is not recommended, and evaluating the customer definition and structure is indicative of a healthy and adaptive security organization.

- More may be better—Customers can exist in different forms, and it is very realistic to define them in this way. It is possible to establish a collection of customers based on role, such as business unit customers, IT division customers, corporate customers, and partner customers. Not only does this simplify the process, but some security organizations may also find that this differentiation based on role provides more service delivery and definition options. In other words, it is completely acceptable to have many customers defined within a hierarchy. Therefore, IT may be a customer as much as the helpdesk organization, even though they are part of the IT customer. In virtually all cases this is the most likely direction, but requires good management and definition.

Much of this will rise to the surface and become far more simplified as the program is formalized. Each company is different and will have different definitions based on structure and culture. No matter what comes to fruition, know that while defining the customer is albeit a small point, it will become exceedingly important over time.

9.3 Service Catalog and Life Cycle Management

It is the responsibility of the organizational management team to manage the service life cycle and the service catalog. The service catalog is the collection of services that are offered by the security group and as such must be managed in how services are identified, developed, launched, and retired. It is noteworthy to add that there is a vast amount of information concerning the development, organization, and management of a service catalog. ITSM is an excellent source on the nuances that exist in managing services. Therefore, this section should be considered an introduction and offers points that are important to establishing a basic service catalog within the context of the ASMA, but it is only a starting point.

9.3.1 Service Identification

Over time it will be necessary to add services to the program. How these are identified can come in two forms: a service gap or a service request. Granted, this assumes that a basic collection of services and their delivery options and models have been initially defined. Therefore, these two attributes address post-initial development of starting security services.

- Service gap—Usually identified by the risk, compliance, and/or governance processes. Essentially, this is the security program itself identifying gaps in service options to customers based on demand and therefore will escalate the need for a new service to organizational management via leadership and committee meetings.
- Service request—This is when the customer identifies a need for a service that is not currently available in the service catalog and can't be realized through other service delivery models and methods. The first order of business when receiving a service request is to ensure it is translated effectively. Business units may be unfamiliar with the vernacular being used in the security group and the options that may be available to them. Second, it is important to understand the motivating factors behind the request. In short, what do they need to accomplish and for what reasons? This is not to interrogate the business, but rather to ensure the security team is positioned to provide the best solution.

There are several activities that are common to both these types of service identification processes. When a service has been identified it must go through a number of initial validation processes.

1. The need of the service must be clear and well understood. Regardless of whether the service was identified internally or by a customer, its purpose and expected outcomes must be clearly defined.
2. The service must be compared to other services in the catalog to determine if the need can be addressed through the enhancement of an existing service. There are some risks in combining (forcing combinations of) existing services in an effort to avoid having to create a new service. Organizations will find that managing more than one service that does not display a meaningful marriage for a single objective will cause more difficulties and costs over time when compared to simply creating a new one. This is not always avoidable, but should not become a common practice.
3. The service must be compared to existing delivery capabilities. Although the role of the security group is clear, the ability to

deliver may not be. Initial gaps in capability, resources, tools, technology, and methodologies need to be identified early in the process. Based on these gaps investments in the development and ultimately the delivery of the service will need to be evaluated. In cases where the service requires capabilities that the security group does not have and there are indications that it will be a short-lived service, it may be prudent to seek third-party, or out-tasking, involvement for a short period of time until capabilities are developed or the service has reached the end of its use and is retired.

4. Compare the proposed service structure to established practices concerning management. Specifically, this involves the ability to track, monitor, and collect measurements that can be readily used within the existing governance framework.

These four basic steps provide the foundation for ensuring that each service introduced into the system has a clear role and value.

9.3.2 Service Launch

Launching services does not have to be complicated, but the ASMA is about exploiting opportunities to demonstrate value, leveraging inherent sophistication, and generating a closer relationship with the business. Therefore, services can simply be published on a Web site with a "click here" to request the services, or it can be taken to the next level using information that exists within the services. There are several stages and opportunities that should be investigated when launching a service. Following is a summary of these:

- Validation and Approval—Of course, service identification and development must ultimately result in final approval. The launch process is an overarching one that ensures all the activities in taking a service to publication are managed.
- Publication—A method to publish the services must exist. The formation of a Web site that provides detailed information concerning the service and details is critical. Additionally, the development of a summary sheet explaining the service, features, benefits, options, and applicability that can be downloaded by customers for future reference is essential. In most

cases, a physical services catalog delivered to key customer representatives is highly recommended.

- Articulation—It is not enough to simply describe the service. Details concerning options; pricing (if applicable); the role of the service relative to risk, compliance, and policy; and the type of information that will be needed to define the scope and details concerning delivery need to be included in the service publication.

- Notification—One cannot assume that customers are going to actively seek service information or be aware of changes. Therefore, a notification process that alerts customers to additions and changes must exist.

9.3.3 Service Retirement

Many organizations will find that services will evolve in definition and delivery over time, but will remain applicable. However, there are a number of scenarios in which a service is used less and less and becomes less germane to the security program and customers alike. Moreover, services do not have to be permanent and can be defined for a specific purpose with the full knowledge and intent that they will expire over time.

Through all the service-tracking mechanisms it is usually possible to determine when a service is reaching the end of its life. However, this should not be associated strictly with its employment. There are situations in which a service is very useful, but is only performed for one customer annually. The goal is to determine the applicability of the service to the customers, security, and the business. For example, assume you have a service specifically directed at security for UNIX systems, but the company has completely migrated to Microsoft platforms. As a result, there is likely no need for a UNIX-focused service. Sometimes the best way to determine if a service is ready for retirement is to discuss common scenarios. Following is a summary of some scenarios that may surface to assist in the decision-making process:

- Quality—If a service is receiving poor quality reports, it is not the basis for service retirement. However, it is the basis for modification of the service to increase its quality.

- Use—Introduced above, the volume of service employment is not always a good indicator concerning applicability. However, it may be possible to accommodate one service that is rarely used by incorporating its purpose into a different, more applicable, and more frequently used service. This is a very common practice in the early stages of service development as initial interpretations give way to reality. Clearly, the service that is to be absorbed must have very close alignment to the intent of the one that it is becoming part of. In virtually all cases, services are developed with too few delivery options and models forcing the organization to create many different services. Over time it is learned that what were assumed to be different services are actually best represented as delivery options of a single service. Therefore, organizations implementing the ASMA and services should expect this eventuality; it is security's nature to create a service for every condition, but the intent is to change this perspective. For example, some companies created a VPN security service and a Remote Access Security service. However, all remote access was provided by a VPN solution. Eventually, the two were combined.
- Execution—As a service is delivered there are conditions in which confusion in scope, depth, methods, and tools begin to surface. In other words, each time the service is performed there is always a high degree of scope creep experienced. It is tempting to retire the service and create more than one service as a replacement, which may be prudent. However, the first step is to determine what attributes of the service are causing this problem prior to removing it because it may be easier to fix than to build new services. Nevertheless, it is common for organizations to try to do too much with one service in the beginning and find that breaking the need across more than one service is more effective.
- Granularity—As services are created very similar services may surface, leading to some confusion by customers as to which service is most applicable to their need. As a result, some organizations will retire services to give way to a more consolidated service offering. If this situation occurs, it is likely

that the service development process did not fully take into account service tuning and delivery models. Prior to retiring and combining like services, it is critical to ensure that (1) it does not result as one mammoth service that is unmanageable, and (2) that the needs being provided for in the other similar services actually lend themselves to tuning and delivery models. In short, it is typically more effective to monitor suspect services over time to evaluate options and not be in a constant state of flux.

The process of retirement can be quite simple and organizations may simply employ the reverse of the launch, such as removing the service from the publication system, notifying customers, and removing supporting materials. However, this begins to raise questions about all the supporting elements of the service. For example, once a service is created it is reflected in a number of ways throughout the services management model, such as materials, management tools, tracking, reporting, delivery methodologies, delivery tools and templates, skills matrices, resource management platforms, and any number of systems that are used to manage or are involved in the services model. The rule of thumb is nothing gets "deleted." Retirement means that while the service is no longer employed, its continued existence within the system offers some value. A great deal of work was put into the development of the service and it should be retained in case a similar need surfaces in the future or so that elements of the service can be used to enhance other services.

9.3.4 Technology and Automation

Everything discussed concerning service catalog management must leverage technology and automation to be effective. In fact, this is not limited to service catalog management and applies to the entire program. Service catalog management should be seen as the primary method for managing the life cycle of services and how it is ultimately controlled at the executive level. This does not necessarily have to include all elements of management from risk to delivery, but certainly could. Having one system that combines all elements of services for every feature of the model has enormous benefits and should be a goal of the security leadership team, but this is not always possible, and investments in developing such a tool may be excessive. Nevertheless, products such as Microsoft's SharePoint and myriad business process management systems are available and can be customized to manage an entire security program.

In any case, following are some initial scenarios in which technology can be leveraged to help the overall services management process:

- Collaboration System—Providing a system that allows for the executive, management, and delivery teams to collaborate and do so with customers organized according to services is extremely beneficial to quality and satisfaction.
- Really Simple Syndication (RSS) feeds—Creating a blog or other method for the security team to share insights is helpful to the customer community. Moreover, this is another method for publishing service additions, changes, and the like.
- Methodologies—Having a central system that provides access to methods, tools, templates, and samples that can be leveraged in the delivery of services is not only helpful, but is essential to smooth operations. Moreover, if this is setup as a Wiki service, each time the service is employed modifications to the information can be made to assist in the next delivery.
- Deliverables—It is helpful to create a space for deliverable templates for each service so the delivery team can access them. Additionally, a project site for each customer can be provided on-line that acts as a repository for deliverables, status reports, and other materials generated in the execution of a service.
- Process Management—Unlike methodologies, which may be adjusted during delivery, processes usually act as core guidance on the necessary steps that must be followed. These can include all the processes employed throughout the program, or just key processes in delivery. Organizing processes in a system relative to the features can greatly increase efficiency across the entire program.
- Training and Education—Tracking and managing skills relative to services and management is an important process in assuring a successful program. Performing this manually can become cumbersome. People who are responsible

for delivering security need to have a simple method for evaluating their skills and finding training and education resources to increase their applicability and productivity. Creating a training curriculum based on services and their supporting features ensures the organization is continually improving and new employees have access to institutional knowledge.

These are simply initial areas that offer value. Of course, there are many, many other things that can be accomplished with minimal development effort, such as project management, skills tracking and management, resource management, knowledge sharing, document management, monitoring of external forces (e.g., threat monitoring), metrics tracking and reporting, and a number of other services. It should be noted that the use of technology and automation, and the ability to manage, support, and monitor the use of the system, are enormously advantageous in increasing capability maturity. In fact, there are some challenges in achieving meaningful maturity without a system that supports management and delivery.

9.4 Security Functions

As with any well-formed security program there are fundamental elements that are necessary and are shared across the entire program. Although the ASMA addresses the majority of requirements that are needed in establishing a comprehensive security program, it does not address them all directly. In fact, this is by design. The ASMA is an amalgamation of commonly understood practices that combine to ensure security is applied effectively. Nevertheless, there are supporting features that need to exist in order to ensure the entire program is on a solid foundation. As with a number of things related to security and the ASMA, the responsibility of managing core features and foundational program elements falls within the remit of the organizational management. Clearly, a number of things may be part of existing security programs that fit neatly within organizational management's domain. However, specifically with regard to the ASMA, there are two important aspects of security that must be maintained and managed by organizational management.

9.4.1 Security Policies

Security policies are a method to articulate the expectations of the business regarding security-related scenarios and to govern the environment. They are fundamental to any organization, are typically required by regulations, and provide the basis for decision-making criteria throughout the company. Policies are the formal representation of security expectations of the company and how security is ultimately guided.

Moreover, considering the broadest definition, policies can manifest themselves as documentation, system configurations, or technical controls. No matter how they appear, they usually all boil down to one core security policy that defines the basis for all the others. It is this root policy that must be managed and maintained by the organizational management team. Policies have to be created, approved, updated, published, and maintained throughout their life cycles. Having the organizational management team be responsible for the policies and all these activities is the most natural and common practice. As such, this ensures that information from the leadership team and executive staff has the opportunity to influence policy or be passed through the policy when conflicts occur in decisions.

It should be added that policy may exist within the services and even as a security service. There is typically a policy hierarchy, especially with global organizations, and these layers can be supported and managed through a service. Of course, like standards, root and supportive policies need to resonate throughout the security program to ensure that activities throughout are in alignment and in a position to accurately enforce stated and applicable policies. For example, when processing input and scope for service delivery to a customer, risk and compliance may step in to influence the attributes of the service that may or may not be in alignment. A large part of that decision-making process, especially within compliance, is driven from policy. Therefore, if gaps in expectations surface, policy can be the first source as a reference to ensure all parties understand the requirements.

There is a very important point to be shared. In many organizations the security policy is not actionable or always enforceable, and it will sit on a shelf to be referenced on a rare occasion. This is not always the case, but is more common than not. The ASMA is vastly different in the employment of a policy. Policy exists within each feature of the model and directly influences how services are delivered. This means that policies are actionable and used as a governing factor in the application of security. Moreover, the services catalog will have references to policy to ensure that customers understand the role of the service in achieving compliance with the policy.

Through this and many other scenarios, the management of policy compliance and enforcement becomes more streamlined, easier to visualize, and manageable. It becomes predictive as opposed to reactive. There are a number of policy management and monitoring platforms that are available in the market, and it is likely that you have these available to you. These can (and must) be leveraged in service delivery and integrated into services to help strengthen the connection between policy and how security is applied.

9.4.2 Security Standards

Security standards are a predominant and common force in the security industry. Security organizations use industry-provided standards and create their own security standards in an effort to establish common definitions, expectations, and processes. Of course, there is a broad set of security standards that is available for use and many organizations leverage these as the basis for their security program and even certification. Some standards are very specific, whereas others may be general. In every case, standards act as the common denominator for security. Although security standards exist in support of the services and the features, organizational management is concerned with defining the overall standards of the organization and those overseeing the ASMA. Of course, compliance management is tasked with ensuring these are followed and applied. In short, the ASMA builds a stronger connective force between security and the business relative to the intent of the demands being placed on the business, such as regulation, or those being placed on the security organization by the business to achieve its goals. Within this context, standards within the scope of organizational management are comprehensive in that they provide the foundation for interpreting and translating intent into actionable and consistent expectations of operation within the security organization. Therefore, standards of this nature not only address operational aspects of security, but will also include specific traditional security standards.

There are two important aspects to this. First, this core intent does not conflict with industry standards and in fact promotes such things as ISO certification. This also comprises the foundation of the overall structure of the security architecture within an organization. Although all the features and their roles have been expressed, each organization will differ in how the ASMA is ultimately realized and managed.

Standards will act as a resource pool for the ASMA. As services are developed, delivered, tracked, measured, and managed—as well as all the supporting features in the model, such as risk, compliance, governance, and capability maturity management—standards will ensure overall alignment within the details of these activities and program elements. It is important to add that a single standard may be used in every feature or in one service. There is no one-to-one or one-to-many rule. Standards enable organizational management to have confidence in the foundation of the program and how security is being applied and maintained.

Following are some initial guidelines when dealing with security standards, especially at the onset of implementing the ASMA:

- Identification—Identify and classify industry security standards that are in use or are seen as potential uses in the program. It should be added that there must be clear justification for the standard. Again, standards come in many forms and can be applied in different ways. Too many standards, or ones that do not have clear applicability, may hinder the process and the overall security program.
- Development—Not all industry standards address the unique demands of the company. As a result, some groups develop their own standards or modify industry standards to meet their needs. As with industry standards, these need to be identified, classified, and justified within the model.
- Mapping—Mapping standards to such things as regulations is a common practice. There are a number of methods to accomplish this using everything from spreadsheets to comprehensive applications. In some cases, organizations have

been known to develop a common criteria framework that is unique to their organization, operational characteristics, and culture. From there, control objectives from standards (and even regulations) are mapped to their framework so they can be accurately applied to their environment. The ASMA, and all that it encompasses, can act as this framework and help to integrate existing and future standards. At some point control objectives from standards need to be mapped, even if at a high level, to program features to establish a meaningful interlock.

- Availability—Simply stated, standards must be made available to those operating in the security program and features. This may seem obvious, but it is not always performed or done effectively. A simple internal Web site that provides an indexed, searchable, and useful rendering of the standards that includes the mapping to the services model is essential to ensure they are used effectively.

- Management and Monitoring—Standards are usually living documents and as such need to be updated. For industry standards, changes must be monitored, and when changes occur they need to be remapped and reintegrated into the system— assuming the changes are deemed valuable to the program. Internally defined standards need to be monitored for effectiveness. Much of this activity will come from compliance and governance. They also need to be monitored for use, which will not only come from compliance, but will resonate with capability maturity management. Lastly, standards have to be managed regularly and investigated for applicability, additions, and effectiveness.

The above are relatively basic and well-understood activities within virtually every security group. Nevertheless, without meaningful standards management the overall program will erode over time.

9.5 Security Personnel Training

The ability to deliver a service demands that resources are trained and educated on processes, tools, standards, policies, and procedures and, of course, security. As such, organizational management must be very focused on developing skills within the security organization. There are several reasons for this:

- Meeting goals and objectives—Measurements throughout the features are to ensure performance of the security organization comprehensively. As discussed, measurements have different levels; there are those for service delivery, management, risk, compliance, and strategy, such as those directed at KGIs and KPIs. Employees have to be trained in a manner that empowers them to achieve business and security goals. Although this may sound obvious, it is far too common to make demands of the security team relative to performance metrics and it does not have the necessary training to do so. Much of this stems from "hiring the right skills" and assuming that people's work history and experience is more than enough. While understandable, it ignores the unique characteristics of the organization and the high potential for change that adaptation represents.

- Professional development—It is one thing to measure an employee's performance against stated goals and objectives in meeting the needs of an organization, but this has to be balanced with a mechanism that helps employees achieve professional goals. Although training—certainly that paid for or provided by the company—must have alignment to the goals of the organization, this does not mean that the criteria for training cannot be expanded. For example, those performing technical processes should have the ability to attend training for project management, if this is in alignment with their professional goals. In short, it provides a path for employees to grow and for the company to find ways of exploiting their potential.

- Flexibility—The more training employees receive, the broader their knowledge. And when combined with experience, knowledge helps to create wisdom. The more knowledgeable people are the better they are at addressing dynamics. The intent is to promote adaptability for better business value and enablement. Knowledgeable resources are far more flexible and can be put in challenging, dynamic situations and be successful. Over time and having to deal with structured change regularly, people within the security group become wise, which helps them to be more predictive and confident. On a more tactical level, more knowledge means greater diversity, allowing resources to be moved from one area or task within security to another with minimal retooling.

Taking these into consideration, training needs to be comprehensive, be targeted at developing skills aligned to the business and security goals, empower employees to meet stated objectives, and provide a means to help them as individuals in meeting professional goals. For many this may appear to be expensive and challenging, and in many ways, it is. However, when implemented in a manner that is emblematic of the intent and mission of the ASMA, a meaningful training program can demonstrate substantial returns to the company.

Training programs can take on a number of different shapes and structures. They can be provided internally, use external resources and providers, or a combination thereof. In many cases it will be a combination, with external training being more industry based and internal training being focused on the unique demands of the business. Nevertheless, there are some things to consider, such as the applicability of training versus the awareness it provides. The applicability of external training comes up on occasion in security. For example, what is the applicability to the company in sending several people to BlackHat? Depending on the culture and focus of security within the business the applicability can be very high. Of course, there are situations where sending people to such events may not be obvious and therefore not funded. However, this must be balanced with awareness, as in visibility into the industry that can help the organization better tune its security program. The important aspect of any externally provided training is that there is a mechanism to bring that information back to the organization so that everyone can gain visibility, truly exploiting the investment.

Secondarily, an organization must look at how the trained individuals help others. Related to the previous point, sending someone to training more than simply satisfies the individual's needs by providing them with the ability and wherewithal to return and train others in the security group on what was learned. This is also important with internal training. It is not always possible to train everyone in the group, and therefore only a few may attend training. Depending on the size and diversity of the security organization, combined with the type of training, the organization should promote further collaboration and downstream training to others in the group. An example is resources from compliance management are trained on a regulation and accompanying standards that will inevitably play a role in service delivery. If the information from this training is not passed to the other features it may result in confusion. Moreover, it is clearly valuable for everyone in security to have some knowledge concerning changes to the environment.

Internal training must have a meaningful support and management capability, and it is the responsibility of organizational management to establish a complete program for the organization. As demonstrated above, and as detailed in Chapter 10, capability maturity management ensures the effectiveness of processes to promote a higher level of maturity. Although this is critical to the overall program and drives the very foundation of the ASMA, it is also essential to ensure a mature and comprehensive training program so that the company, organization, and employees get the most from the investment. Therefore, in the spirit of maturity, there are specific elements, characteristics, and processes of a training capability that should exist. They are as follows: identify training needs, select the training method, ensure training availability, perform training, and assess training effectiveness. These directives are an amalgamation of IA-CMM process area 01 and ISO-21827:2008 practice area 21 adjusted to apply to the ASMA.

9.5.1 Identify Training Needs

As implied by the above, knowing what training is necessary is more than simply publishing a collection of materials and curriculum and involves organizational management in working with the other features, and reviewing security and business goals and objectives, and the methods of service delivery, to ensure that any training provided has meaning to the program. Moreover, this more than suggests a clear perspective of current skills and capabilities and therefore also includes the existence of a skills tracking and assessment mechanism, which is worth elaborating upon.

9.5.1.1 Capability Assessment and Tracking   Clearly related to training and education, and the development of a service capability matrix, it is necessary to assess and track skills as they develop. This practice will help in aligning people with services, identify existing and emerging gaps in capability to target training initiatives and investments, and provide constant awareness on the state of delivery effectiveness. As a result of the service matrix (the combination of delivery options and models), management will have greater visibility into the core skills that are required to deliver the service. Moreover, ancillary skills will surface that provide additional value and increase effectiveness. For example, a core skill required for a service may be a high degree of proficiency with UNIX, say, a level 3 on a scale from 0 to 3. However, it can be demonstrated that skills in programming, such as Pearl scripting, although not identified in the service as a requirement, offers greater confidence and therefore less risk in the delivery of the service. As a result it is necessary to define core and ancillary skills and track the level of proficiency of these skills to produce a weighted score that can be used in the assessment of service delivery risk.

Each service will have a set of defined skills associated with it and a predetermined level of proficiency (e.g., ranking, level) required for each that represents the targeted level of capability to perform the service at an acceptable level. Once defined, each resource will be individually ranked, using the same scale, and then mapped to the services. Moreover, there are additional skills that may not be core to the delivery of the service, but offer value; these are ancillary skills as opposed to core skills.

To get started in developing a service delivery skill capability tracking and management system you must first perform an inventory of existing skills. When this is performed, it is very helpful to collect information concerning industry certifications that people have, which can be used later in calculating capabilities and managing gaps. The value of industry certifications is that they can be used to set a baseline of expected performance. Therefore, you will eventually have a collection of skills and certifications that will act as the foundation for a skills database for later service alignment and management.

Performing an inventory as a first step is a critical activity. Although you can simply start by defining skills that you understand are needed to perform security functions and then begin to map to services.

However, at some point an evaluation of existing skills to the defined skills will have to be performed to connect resources to skills and services. If you do not start by working directly with the resources on defining initial skills, the evaluation process will become cumbersome and you will risk disrupting the process. People may begin to feel inadequate when provided a list of skills they may not have and therefore rank at a 0. Moreover, defining skills you may not have, but need to deliver a service, makes one question the viability of the service itself.

The process should start at a very high level and then build more granularity in the skill's definition over time. For example, start with platforms, tools and applications, technologies, standards and compliance, processes, and certifications that are in use, such as

- Operating Systems
  - Microsoft Windows, such as NT 3.51, NT 4.0, Win95, Win98, XP, Server 2003, Vista, Server 2008, and so on
  - Linux/UNIX versions and distributions and even types, such as RedHat (FC, Enterprise, etc.), Solaris, SLES (Novell, etc.), Debian, Ubuntu (Desktop, Server [LTSP, etc.]), Edubuntu, Xubuntu, and so on

- Tools and Applications
  - Virtual machines (XEN, Microsoft, VMware, etc.)
  - HP Openview, Archsight, Archer, etc.

- Technologies
  - Firewalls (product, version, platform, etc.), IDS, IPS, proxy services, VPN, DLP, PKI, etc.

- Processes
  - Change control, patch testing, threat monitoring, system audit, security assessment, risk assessment, etc.

- Standards and Compliance
  - ISO-27000 series, NIST CSRC Special Publications, HIPAA, CoBIT, PCI, FFIEC, GLBA, etc.

- Certifications
  - Security: CISSP, CISA, CISM, GIAC, CCSE
  - Platform: MCSE, CCIE, OCP, CNE
- Process: PMP, ITIL

The information can be organized in any framework you wish. However, it must have a defined structure and support the evolution of the skill, such as version changes to software. Typically, organizations will look to job descriptions and other standard materials to assist in the identification of skills. Of course, connecting with existing people in the security group and organization is necessary to help identify skills that are in use and may not be very obvious.

Also, when developing a skills database, do not forget about soft skills and life skills. For example, soft skills may include proficiencies in writing, speaking, presenting, communicating, comprehension, teaming, and leadership, among others. Myers-Briggs can be a useful source of information and evaluation. Life skills may include multiple languages, culture awareness, working abroad, working in different environments, and overall experiences. Both types of skills may be difficult to define and quantify, yet can represent value as ancillary skills in the delivery of services. However, you will have to check with HR and local laws concerning collecting certain types of information and their use in the evaluation of employees.

Once a list of skills is defined, it is then necessary to define the levels of skills relative to capability. These characteristics of the skill will become the basis of measurement, tracking, and improvement. It will have a dramatic impact on training development and delivery. For example, if a skill is related to the Microsoft Server platform and someone has level 2 characteristics of that skill, what is the specific training material that is appropriate and needed to help this person achieve a level 3? As one would expect, this would include testing and evaluation of skills learned, retention, and the ability to apply those skills.

The following is a general example of defining skill level characteristics, which can be used across all skills. Or it may be elected to define specific skill level characteristics that are unique to the skill. Both of these approaches have pros and cons. Clearly, having one set of characteristics for all skills greatly simplifies the management of levels. However, these may not be detailed enough to truly reflect the expectations related to the levels for a skill. It is recommended to start with a common, general definition and from there add a description or abstract of expectations related to the defined levels that is specific to that skill. If you find that is not enough, then add guidelines and examples to each level that are specific to that skill. In most cases, the general levels with a short description will prevail simply because it is far easier to manage and maintain. In either case, the example levels provided here are from 1 to 3. Of course, any leveling method can be used that aligns best to existing practices and culture. Following is a simple example:

- Level 1
  - Limited knowledge or experience on the subject through training or shadowing
  - Able to engage in a very limited or auxiliary capacity
  - Would need assistance to deliver

- Level 2
  - Reasonable knowledge and experience on the subject
  - Able to deliver on a typical service
  - Might need limited remote assistance, if any

- Level 3
  - Experts who can deliver independently
  - Extensive amount of knowledge and experience on the subject
  - Capable of providing assistance to others
  - Able to engage on any assignment of any complexity
- Multiple certifications on the skill

After the characteristics of each skill level are defined, the process of mapping to proposed security services begins. Unfortunately, this is not always a simple task. You may find that your skills database does not contain all the skills necessary to deliver the service. Depending on the percentage of existing skills compared to the percentage that are needed, it will be necessary to evaluate the service's definition, intent, and structure.

Organizational management should make every effort to perform this evaluation for third parties that may be used for part of the service delivery model for a given service. This process can be as simple as performing interviews with resources from the third party to having its members attend specific training and testing provided by the organization—an aspect of third-party integration that is becoming increasingly common. A number of organizations, especially those in the healthcare and financial industries, provide certification training for security and IT and regularly require professional service partners, providers, and contractors to attend and successfully pass training that the organizations have developed prior to permitting their involvement in security-related activities.

Other scenarios may surface, such as too many or too few skills being assigned to services, which can have an impact on the number of viable resources available to deliver. Nevertheless, it's helpful to understand that this is a living process, and as each service is executed processes such as management and governance will identify areas for improvement in the delivery model.

Of course, assigning skills to the service is only the first step; you have to define the targeted level of capability that is needed to perform the service at the expected level of performance. For example, to execute on a patch management service, what is the meaningful level of capability for a skill related to a Microsoft Server platform versus a UNIX platform, and variances in those platforms? Does this person really need to have a detailed understanding of every aspect of the platform—such as a level 3—or will a level 1 suffice? There are several things to consider when evaluating the target level of a skill when mapping it to a service:

- Should a skill be added to the database specifically for the actions to be taken? This is typically a rare occurrence and is ill advised. If skills are created for a specific task, then the database of skills will become difficult to manage and skills will be mapped only to one specific service, undermining the intent.
- Does the level of skill impact the duration of delivery? If a lower level is feasibly possible, but would take that resource twice as long to complete than a higher-level resource, then one has to evaluate the projected reasonable timeline of a service. This applies directly to cost of the resource compared to meeting expectations of the business.
- What impact does the change in targeted level of skill to the service have on the available number of resources? If the level is defined as 3 and you only have people with a level 2, are you setting the bar too high? If this is desired, then you have to evaluate training and education options.

- What is the impact of setting the level too low? If you set the level required to 1 and you have all level 3s for that skill, are you not exploiting your resources effectively, or have you identified that the skill you have a lot of is not meaningful to the business? This can have a number of positive and negative impacts. In one sense you have better visibility into your resource pool's capability and the applicability of those skills, but you also run the risk of putting an overqualified resource on a project.

The above considerations are important in defining the targeted skill level for a service. However, as more and more skills are added and a target level is defined, these can be used as weights to perform an initial evaluation of one or more services to your available resource pool. Weighting a skill based on targeted level is founded on the philosophy that as the skill capability increases, it becomes more important and valuable when compared to others that may have fewer capability requirements. Using one service as an example, you have 10 skills defined (note: this is for demonstration purposes and you will likely find your experiences very different and have far more skills per service) for the service, each with a targeted level of capability between 1 and 3. We'll weight these using the following:

- Level 3 has a weight of 75.
- Level 2 has a weight of 30.
- Level 1 has a weight of 15.

To calculate the score of the resource's overall capacity to deliver the service based on alignment to skills and levels, we perform some basic calculations. We first divide the resource's skill ranking (or level that has been determined) by the targeted level of the skill. For example, Frank rates his skill as level 2 for a skill with a targeted level of 3, $2/3 = 0.66$. We multiply this with the weight of the skill as defined by the targeted level, in this case 75. Therefore, $0.66 \times 75 = 50$. To get a score we divide the total values from the resource by total targeted weighted values for the skills, in this case $50/75 = 66\%$. We apply this across all the weighted skills and the rankings from the resources to determine an overall score.

As demonstrated in Figure 9.2, we have three resources that have been ranked against 10 skills defined for a service with targeted levels.

	Skill #	Targeted Skill Level (1-3)	Weight (Skill Importance)	Resource Skill Rank	Calculated Resource Weight	Summary
Alice (Overacheiver)	1	3	75	3	75	
	2	3	75	3	75	
	3	3	75	3	75	
	4	2	30	3	45	
	5	2	30	3	45	
	6	2	30	3	45	
	8	1	15	3	45	
	9	1	15	3	45	
	10	1	15	3	45	Score
			360		495	138%

	Skill #	Targeted Skill Level (1-3)	Weight (Skill Importance)	Resource Skill Rank	Calculated Resource Weight	Summary
Bob (right on the mark)	1	3	75	3	75	
	2	3	75	3	75	
	3	3	75	3	75	
	4	2	30	2	30	
	5	2	30	2	30	
	6	2	30	2	30	
	8	1	15	1	15	
	9	1	15	1	15	
	10	1	15	1	15	Score
			360		360	100%

	Skill #	Targeted Skill Level (1-3)	Weight (Skill Importance)	Resource Skill Rank	Calculated Resource Weight	Summary
Frank (different levels)	1	3	75	3	75	
	2	3	75	2	50	
	3	3	75	1	25	
	4	2	30	2	30	
	5	2	30	3	45	
	6	2	30	1	15	
	8	1	15	3	45	
	9	1	15	1	15	
	10	1	15	1	15	Score
			360		315	88%

Figure 9.2 Skills capability matrix.

Alice is a level 3 for all the skills, which exceeds the targeted levels for the majority of identified required skills, resulting in a score of a 138%. Bob has met the level required for each skill, resulting in a score of a 100%, meaning he meets the targeted requirements for delivery. Frank has a mix of capabilities that once weighted demonstrates that he's slightly below target at 88%.

Based on having three levels and the weighting, the maximum score possible is 300%, meaning a ranking of 3 for all skills with a target level of 1. Therefore, given the range, setting windows of applicability is desirable. For example, a score between 90% and 110% may be optimal. Scores above that level indicate you may be underutilizing a resource's skills, but will get the service completed sooner. Below that level this resource may be a good candidate for on-the-job training or additional training. This approach to evaluating skills to determine their relevance to service delivery has been employed in a number of scenarios. Nevertheless, this is only one possible approach. Regardless of approach, focus on weights, targeted versus measured (e.g., ranked) skills, and generating a value that can be used to determine overall applicability of the resource to deliver a service is required in the model.

The important underlying point of performing a service capability matrix and creating a tracking system is about managing service delivery risk and operational integrity risk throughout the program. So far the ASMA has been about excellence and the sophistication of the application of security. However, this is an opportunity to demonstrate that if the people performing services are not empowered with knowledge there is very little hope in achieving the intent of the ASMA. In short, people are everything to security providing value to the business. Secondarily, all the information provided concerning the features and their roles, responsibilities, and activities does not address the fact that there are people behind this architecture. Just as it is important to the security organization to have skilled people in applying security and all that implies, the same holds true for those in all features.

There are a number of products that should come from identifying training needs and taking into consideration the above. Clearly, training needs assessment processes and resulting documentation. As offered above, a process for determining training needs must exist and as with virtually all processes, there are outputs. In this example, an output is the capabilities matrix and service delivery risk. From this a gap analysis is performed resulting in a final report on gaps between skills and what is needed or expected in the delivery of security services. Based on identified gaps and understanding delivery risk, a training plan is the final result. A training plan is simply an agreed upon approach to closing the gaps and minimizing risk. Within the plan is the association of internal or external training that can be used to address the identified gaps. Although this sounds relatively simplistic, it can become challenging and in many cases results in the development of a new curriculum. Do not assume that "gap" implies size or complexity. Gaps in skills could be broad and encompass the entire organization or represent a slight difference in processes or technology.

9.5.2 Select Training Method

Internal groups, external training organizations, or a combination of the two may provide training. In fact, it is not unreasonable to have internal and external training combined into one session or workshop. Once the training plan is formalized, it is necessary to determine the mechanism for delivering the training in order to effectively close the identified gaps. It is also important to understand the method and structure of training, for example, computer-based training, lab-based training, hands-on, on-the-job training, workshop-based training, books and exercises, or mentoring—or some combination thereof. In many cases the topic will help define the method and structure, for instance, technical training is predominately hands-on and may include a lab, whereas management or introductory training may be a combination of books, exercises, and workgroup sessions. However, it is helpful to take into account the audience. Some people learn best through demonstration, whereas others need to have hands-on or direct experiences, or they learn most effectively through reading, discussion, and testing. It is necessary to determine the best overall structure and then understand the audience to either emphasize or deemphasize certain delivery techniques.

From this selective process the organization should have an overall profile of the training and how it will materialize, which may include relationships with external parties and/or internal training groups. More importantly, the outcome will also be training and development plans of the individuals identified for the training. By creating a skills tracking mechanism and using it to evaluate skills capability to service delivery requirements, and from that understand risk to quantify gaps, we also inherently know who needs the training.

However, as introduced in the beginning of the chapter, not taking into consideration employees' goals and performance along with their professional development objectives as individuals can make for poor training results. To put the importance of this into perspective, if someone is trained on a topic that organizational management had determined is needed to reduce delivery risk based on an impersonal, distant measurement of that person, it is likely the person either slept through the training or will have little or no retention simply because it had no meaning to the person—just more corporate policy and politics. Conversely, when an individual is involved and interacted with directly, both the organization and the individual can gain meaningful value from the training. This does not imply that the person will enjoy the training, be engaged, or not fall asleep anyway, but it does provide tangibility to the training for the employee. For example, knowing the professional development objectives of an individual helps to align the training to those objectives. Granted, this is not always possible, but with a well-orchestrated training and skills tracking program—one that is interconnected with overall employee development corporate programs—can be well within reason. Basically, knowing the person as much as understanding the gaps that are driving training is important to ensure meaningful training.

9.5.3 Ensure Training Availability

This is one of those oddities in which the process is exceedingly simple, but when poorly performed or inadequately applied it can have broad negative impacts. Therefore, it is helpful to state that training must be made available. Computer-based training is likely the easiest to provide because it is mainly associated with on-demand, self-service activities. On the other hand, comprehensive training that includes labs, technical manuals, and a trainer/educator requires more planning and scheduling of resources. In such broad scenarios there is a tendency to have the training performed on a specific day or week and that is all. Those who could not attend due to other commitments simply miss out. Effort should be made to understand the scope of attendees and the importance of the training. If for reasons that are not addressable all the proposed students cannot be included, having the materials from the training available to them is important.

Nevertheless, there are some basic things that need to be performed:

- Announcement—When training is planned an announcement should be made to the organization about the training. In fact, several announcements are warranted.
- Schedule—Make certain that a schedule of the training is published and made available to the community.
- Logistics—The training location, facilities, and special requirements, such as access permissions to the room or building, are provided.
- Requirements—The prerequisites for training so that those who may not have been identified as targets for the training can evaluate the value that the training may represent to them and their own development.

9.5.4 Perform Training

Although on the surface this may seem simplistic, it acknowledges the fact that performing training includes responsibilities and management that go well beyond the classroom. Organizations must have a meaningful mechanism for the development of training materials. This can include such things as

- Establishing material templates for presentations, work materials, case studies, and exercises. This also includes version control and material/document management.
- Ensuring the lab architecture and design is aligned to the purpose of the training and is tested against the training plan and activities for students prior to performing training.
- Student activity, attendance, and work product management, maintenance, and tracking. Records must be kept for all students attending training including everything from attendance to performance, qualifications, and work products.
- Validation and vetting (i.e., approval) of training content. This more than implies that management must ensure that the content of the training materials are accurate; applicable to the topic; in alignment with security and business

expectations, goals, and objectives; is meeting quality expectations; and that the overall process of content approval is managed effectively.

- Establishments of quality expectations and methods to determine quality. This involves management setting requirements for quality, such as the use of templates, execution of key processes in preparing for training, and development mechanisms. Moreover, this ultimately drives quality measurements, which covers everything from student surveys and tests to teacher reviews, material quality, and facility quality. This also means creating a method for determining what measurements are taken and how they are taken to ensure they drive improvement.

Arguably, the most important aspect of performing training is for management to surround the entire process to ensure its effectiveness, alignment, and quality.

9.5.5 Assess Training Effectiveness

The best planned, managed, and delivered training does not readily translate to effectiveness. In the discussion on performing training, quality and overall management were introduced. However, training needs to be effective and this also directly applies to the ability to ensure improvements.

The most obvious aspect of determining training effectiveness is student testing and proficiency evaluation. Any training that is performed without determining whether the material is absorbed effectively by the students is fundamentally out of alignment with the overall intent of performing training in the first place. Additionally, performing surveys, evaluations of materials, and trainer evaluations are the basic features to determine effectiveness and improvements.

However, there are other considerations beyond the domain of training. For example, organizational management will need to establish close ties with services management and understand what measurements can help expose whether the intended training had the intended effect on the delivery of security services. Moreover, organizational management's interaction with governance to gain visibility into the overall results of training relative to business views and goals is very important in determining overall effectiveness.

On a more tactical level, the professional development plans that relate to individuals and the training area of interest will also act as the basis for determining effectiveness. The fact that the plan states objectives and whether these were achieved through the training is a good indicator of effectiveness that can be combined with other forms of measurement to get a broad view.

Although much of what it takes to ensure training effectiveness is typically practiced, what is often less defined is how the information is used to promote and manage improvements. In many cases, improvements are limited to the actual training materials or delivery methods. Although these are clearly important targets for improvements, it is also necessary to look at the other areas in which training is meaningful to the security organization, the business, and people. For example, when viewing the results of a training program one must also ask if different measurements need to be taken. Are the right questions being asked in the student test? Are they difficult enough and do they reflect the material accurately? Are we asking the right questions in the survey? Is the student evaluation of trainers giving an accurate picture? Are the measurements of performance from services management exposing the right areas to evaluate effectiveness, or are we seeing naturally occurring improvements? This line of questioning is mainly associated with training that has initially demonstrated good results and the organization is looking to ensure that the results are accurate and to identify any areas for improvement.

The same can hold true for training that has not produced the desired results. The first step is to ensure that the correct elements are being measured. Therefore, the first question, again, is can you trust the measurements? If it is determined that the measurements are an accurate depiction of the effectiveness and quality of the training, then it is necessary to explore what adjustments can be made. For this reason it is essential that measurements are directly related to what is within your ability to change and provide enough granularities in visibility so that the right modifications can be made to directly influence the results.

10

CAPABILITY MATURITY MANAGEMENT

Given that each feature is reliant on the others it is important to ensure that there is a common approach to managing each of them and the processes they employ. A capability maturity model will act as the core foundation for assuring that all the features are functioning as a whole.

Capability maturity models have a long history. One of the earliest versions in the IT space was to address systems engineering and was called CMU/SEI-95-MM-003, which was published in late 1995 by Carnegie Mellon University. This provided the foundation for other models and promoted the development of a security model called the Systems Security Engineering CMM (SSE-CMM), published in 1999 and managed by the International System Security Engineering Association (ISSEA). In 2002, the SSE-CMM was adopted by the International Organization for Standardization (ISO) and became the ISO Standard ISO/IEC DIS 21827, which was updated in late 2008 as ISO-21827:2008. However, there are many other standards that specify the importance of maturity, such as Control Objectives for Information and related Technology (CoBIT), Total Quality Management (TQM), Six Sigma, Business Process Management (BPM), and Capability Maturity Model Integration (CMMI). In fact, utilizing capability maturity models against a standard program model is commonplace. Although such things as COBIT have control objectives and maturity elements, there are mappings to standards such as ISO-17799, PMBOK, and NIST SP-800-53, among others.

In late 2002, as a result of the attacks of September 11, 2001, the formation of the Department of Homeland Security was created in the United States. Part of its role was to be the federal center for cyber security and to act as a focal point for collaboration between local, state, federal, government, and non-government entities in the protection of national assets. Part of its charter was to establish standards concerning the interpretation of information security within the context of evaluation. During this time, the National Security Agency (NSA) established the INFOSEC Assurance Training and Rating Program (IATRP) to build capabilities in the assessment of security functions stretching across multiple areas and standards. (Note: The NSA canceled the IATRP of August 26, 2009.) Subsequently, they created the INFOSEC Assessment Capability Maturity Model (IA-CMM). The IA-CMM, which is based on the SSE-CMM, provides a maturity-based framework for assessing security, and focuses on the ability to establish assurance in the management of processes.

The combination of the SSE-CMM and IA-CMM are applied throughout the ASMA to establish expectations of the management of the program and the processes within each feature. Within this context, the capability maturity model, which is the responsibility of capability maturity management, is focused on the consistent execution of the program, building efficiencies, ensuring effectiveness, and driving process improvement and innovation. Although the IA-CMM defines nine practice areas and ISO-21827:2008 defines as many as twenty-two, the ASMA's use of the model focuses on the security features. Nevertheless, both define five levels of maturity, with an added level of 0 within the IA-CMM to identify a rating representing that nothing is being performed in a given practice area.

The higher the capability maturity level, the greater the confidence that a process is well established throughout the organization and the more likely it is that the processes are applied consistently. This attribute of maturity, and the reason it is essential as the underlying framework, is confidence and consistency. Fundamentally, the ASMA challenges the consistency many organizations seek within the application of security controls and practices. By doing so it allows for greater flexibility, resiliency, and adaptability. However, this comes with a potential risk. The ASMA introduces complexities that tie business and security together. Through the use of services, security is applied based on myriad demands, not just traditional security practices and expectations. Although the ASMA provides for compensating measures in the application of security, without a model to ensure confidence and consistency in the processes to make certain that these are meeting the needs of the business and are mature, the ASMA will fail.

The business's confidence in the ASMA is critical. Given the deep interrelations with the business concerning operations and the application of security in a complex framework, the potential for problems is substantial. This potential is founded on a common theme: people are prone to error. Moreover, the potential for human error is infinite if people are not trained and educated on the processes. Therefore, a significant part of ensuring meaningful capability maturity is institutional knowledge and intimacy with the features. For example, there can be little confidence in the consistency of the security program if someone does not know the existence of a tool, procedure, or process within the program. In-depth knowledge of the program elements is paramount to the success of the program and its ability to achieve a meaningful level of maturity. In short, what use is a process or tool if people don't know it exists, or when or how to employ it? You may have the best-defined and documented program, but without people's understanding of it there is little hope for it being consistent and effectual.

Capability maturity is arguably a shared responsibility across all the features and is a result of collaboration. However, the assessment and management of capability maturity and its underlying processes and standards is the responsibility of a dedicated feature: capability maturity management. It could be argued that compliance management or governance can act as the lead on assessing and managing capability maturity within the overall program. However, there is tangible value in not burdening other features with the ongoing complexities of maturity management. Moreover, compliance is concerned with ensuring process execution and not the processes themselves, and governance is interested in the results.

As a result, governance ensures information accuracy, flow, and structure in between the business and security program. Compliance ensures that external and internal forces are being addressed and processes are being executed as defined. Risk management exists to ensure that security services are being applied in a manner that does not expose the organization to risk. And services management, containing processes, management, procedures, resources, methodologies, and other attributes, is used to apply security within the organization. To ensure that each of these elements is performing consistently and meeting the mission and charter for the program, capability maturity management bonds the program and offers visibility into the overall "trustworthiness" and performance of the program itself. Without this form of oversight, there can be little confidence in the program by the business, much less within the various features. The ASMA is broad and deep and requires diverse resources. Additionally, it can become complex. These two attributes can conspire against the overall success of the program and need to be closely managed (Table 10.1 and Figure 10.1).

Capability maturity management falls under the saying, "Anything worth doing is worth doing well." Organizations are nothing if not a massive collection of people and processes organized to achieve a set of objectives. How well people perform processes can be directly correlated to efficiency and effectiveness, which ultimately translates to quality, satisfaction, and the success of an organization, not to mention reduced risk.

As with other things introduced in this book, capability maturity is an enormous topic and therefore cannot be comprehensively detailed herein. It is assumed that the foundation of capability maturity is well understood, and only a framework for capability maturity as it relates to security services management is provided. In the ASMA, capability maturity management will be highlighted in several key areas. However, it is important to note that this does not replace or assume the omission of all the other characteristics that comprise capability maturity.

10.1 Expectations and Results

The role of capability maturity is to increase confidence and consistency, as stated, with both resulting in greater predictability and ultimately trust within the business. Trust is a key factor in that when business owners and executives trust in the process they are more willing to invest due to greater visibility into the risks of said investment. This translates to more value in the information presented to executives in support of decision-making processes. Moreover, the confidence in the security program's ability to execute effectively is greatly increased. Anyone can see the advantages of this visibility and trust in the program from the business's perspective. Organizations spend vast amounts of money to perform detailed analyses of information to support a decision process concerning an investment. The more valuable, detailed, and comprehensive the information is resulting from

Table 10.1 Capability Maturity Management Interconnect Table

ACTIVE FEATURE	AREA OF SECURITY FOCUS	PRIMARY FEATURE INTERLOCK (BENEFICIARY)	INTENT AND EXPECTATIONS	FEATURE INPUT	FEATURE PRIMARY PROCESS	SECONDARY FEATURE INTERACTION	TARGETED AREAS OF THE PROCESS	FEATURE OUTPUT	BENEFICIARIES OF OUTPUT	SUMMARY DESCRIPTION
Compliance Management	Risk Posture Management	Risk Management	Gain visibility into risk management's interpretation of the application of security relative to maintaining and improving compliance	Results from all forms of rapid risk assessments against service management, organizational capability maturity management	An analysis of risk management findings, changes, and recommendations concerning the overall risk posture to determine implications to program, corporate, or external compliance requirements	Services Management	Risk management's analysis containing interpretations, recommendations, and actions and how these have materialized in delivery standards, processes, and scope of how security is applied to the environment	Identification of areas of risk management modifications that are determined to be misaligned with compliance efforts relative to the application of security services or areas where risk management's modifications have supported compliance efforts	Governance, Organizational Management, Services Management	The goal is to ensure that compliance activities and results are having a positive effect on managing risk and ensuring meaningful security. Compliance alone does not equate directly to security that may be of great interest to the organization

(Continued)

Table 10.1 Capability Maturity Management Interconnect Table (Continued)

ACTIVE FEATURE	AREA OF SECURITY FOCUS	PRIMARY FEATURE INTERLOCK (BENEFICIARY)	INTENT AND EXPECTATIONS	FEATURE INPUT	FEATURE PRIMARY PROCESS	SECONDARY FEATURE INTERACTION	TARGETED AREAS OF THE PROCESS	FEATURE OUTPUT	BENEFICIARIES OF OUTPUT	SUMMARY DESCRIPTION
	Compliance Posture Management	Services Management	Ensure services management and service delivery are being performed in accordance with compliance demands	Results from service delivery and the application of security services throughout the environment, including deliverables, processes, and standards	An analysis of services management's oversight of the delivery of security services to determine adherence to established expectations of compliance demands	Risk Management	Services management's overall management of service delivery specifically focusing on customer interactions, materials and deliverables, application of resources, and role concerning the enforcement of standards and policies in how security is applied	Identified areas of non-compliance, areas for improvement of execution against compliance expectations, and specific areas where services management is exceeding or ensuring compliance through innovative activities	Governance and Organizational Management	Compliance management is tasked with ensuring that overall compliance is achieved and a large part of this responsibility involves ensuring that security is applied—via services management—in a manner that is supportive and promotes compliance demands

Performance Improvement and Management	Capability Maturity Management			Services Management			Governance and Organizational Management	Compliance
	Ensure that services management is operating in a manner that promotes the improvement of compliance-related activities	Results from capability maturity assessments and related document-ation concerning findings, recommend-ations, and specific areas of improvement	An analysis of capability maturity manage-ment's findings and how these have resonated with governance in communi-cating activities to the executive community		Capability maturity manage-ment's compliance with established standards and processes for performing maturity assessments and reviewing results, document-ation, tools, methods, and resources	Documented findings concerning how capability maturity management is performing against expectations, how these are related to changes in services management, and assurance that capability maturity management is providing ongoing monitoring of capability and modifications to delivery		Compliance management wants to ensure that process improvements and changes do not disrupt compliance expectations in the application of security as well as working with capability maturity management to identify opportunities for more efficient and effective compliance efforts

(Continued)

Table 10.1 Capability Maturity Management Interconnect Table (Continued)

ACTIVE FEATURE	AREA OF SECURITY FOCUS	PRIMARY FEATURE INTERLOCK (BENEFICIARY)	INTENT AND EXPECTATIONS	FEATURE INPUT	FEATURE PRIMARY PROCESS	SECONDARY FEATURE INTERACTION	TARGETED AREAS OF THE PROCESS	FEATURE OUTPUT	BENEFICIARIES OF OUTPUT	SUMMARY DESCRIPTION
	Policy and Standards Management	Organizational Management	Ensure that the entire security program is compliant with established policies and standards	Industry standards that are employed, standards that have been defined by organizational management, and standards defining the program	A review of organizational management's oversight and governance of the policies and standards relative to the program and corporate compliance, and the management of the security organization	Governance	Organizational management's processes, deliverables, communications, documentation of changes, program monitoring and reporting, organizational integrity management, performance management, and change management	A report on the integrity of overall program alignment to established standards, interactions, reporting, and management practices and how they relate to program and corporate compliance	Governance, Services Management, Risk Management	Compliance management is responsible for the security program's compliance to self-imposed policies and standards, and as such will work closely with organizational management and all the other features to ensure this is a reality

	Organizational Management			Services Management		Governance, Risk Management, Services Management
Services Management and Orchestration	Ensure that the overall management and oversight of service definition, structure, models, and communication are in alignment with established expectations	Service catalog, service model descriptions, service catalog management processes, change processes, and documentation concerning feature input	An analysis of organizational management's management of the service models, types, and catalog, supporting materials, and processes	Service catalog management practices; evidence of how other feature interactions are performed, managed, tracked, employed, and monitored; team management; customer management; quality and performance management and reporting	Identification of gaps in organizational management's adherence to established practices and standards concerning feature input management, change control of service models and types, and customer feedback and quality control relative to service catalog	As services are defined, managed, and modified to meet the needs of the business, compliance management will perform regular reviews of service models and definition and monitor how and when they are applied to the business through services management

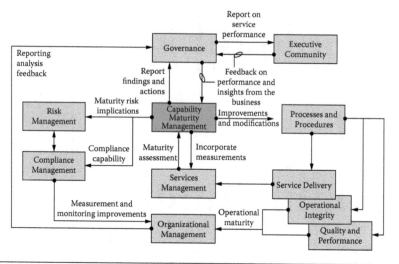

Figure 10.1   Capability maturity management interconnect process map.

an analysis the less the initial interpretation of risk in the decision-making process. Of course, as business leaders gain greater confidence in the ability to execute against the investment to achieve the goal, they are more likely to move forward.

This summarizes the overall intent of program maturity in light of meeting business needs on multiple levels. The first goal is to ensure the effectiveness in security practices of reducing risk and enabling the business to succeed. The second goal is for the program to demonstrate operational integrity and efficiency in the employment of resources. These two goals promote agility and business alignment. Last is the maturity of the program to demonstrate the "potential" for the program overall. In other words, moving forward it is simply not enough to report on activities and results, but to also report on the capability of the program itself and how it is improving.

10.1.1 Process Improvement

A process is a sequence of steps performed for a given purpose. It is a system comprising actions, tools, technology, procedures, and people involved in the production or continual development of a product or service. Clearly, a process system represents a cost to the business and as such is of great importance concerning profitability and quality. Process capability ultimately refers to an organization's or group's potential as a range of performance expectations. Measuring process performance allows the ability to determine if these are falling within or out of this range. The lower the maturity in the program the greater the likelihood that the same process will have varying results. As maturity increases so does the predictability of the outcome. However, this becomes exponentially more difficult simply because there is no such thing as a perfect process or one that can be perfectly executed consistently, if for no other reason than that the environment changes over time. A capability maturity model provides for a control framework for processes in order to establish needs and expectations to identify where process improvements can be made. As this implies, a capability maturity model is a constant oversight to ensure improvement.

It is helpful at this point to introduce the idea that a broad range of business objectives governs the level of maturity targeted for the ASMA and program. In short, the greater the maturity level attained the greater the initial and ongoing investment in resources within the program and outside the program to ensure capability maturity. It will be important for each organization to determine what level of program maturity best resonates with the business and find a balance between "trust" and investment. Unless there are non-security-program-related dynamics in the business, such as reductions in workforce, a decline in capability is an indicator of a breakdown somewhere in the program.

10.1.2 Improving Predictability

As the ASMA moves from development to operations, increasing focus on capability maturity will be realized. Although there are elements within governance, compliance, risk, and services management that promote visibility into effectiveness and efficiency in the management, application, and oversight of security, it will become exceedingly obvious that understanding "how" the program is performing and the predictable nature of its performance is needed and valuable.

As capability increases, the delta between targeted results and actual outcomes from processes diminishes significantly. Although the ASMA is complex and can potentially contain thousands of interrelated processes, this only translates to the ability to increase maturity, not the outcome of maturity. The only risk that can surface is when interconnected processes from different features have gross differences in maturity. As a result, some will find that the "lowest common denominator" takes precedence in certain conditions. However, this can be used to the advantage of the program to focus efforts in a direction that will have the greatest impact, which is the core of meaningful adaptation.

10.1.3 Improving Control

As the maturity of the program increases so does control of the program. For example, with the increase of maturity, and therefore predictability, greater accuracy in establishing and meeting targets can be realized. This falls under the concept that even perfectly defined, managed, and consistently executed processes within the program do not directly equate to desired outcomes. Moreover, control provides a method for applying corrective actions and the ability to evaluate those actions against a high degree of target accuracy from other areas of the program. Control ultimately means that organizations will be far more effective in controlling the performance of processes within the program to ensure they are falling within the desired spectrum.

10.1.4 Improving Effectiveness

Effectiveness has been discussed and its various meanings to security and business have been covered. Within capability maturity, effectiveness applies directly to operational integrity and cost. As maturity increases, target accuracy and control increase exponentially. Therefore, costs associated with process decrease due to a reduction in waste, better efficiencies in execution, and, most importantly, not having to execute a process again after the first process failed to achieve its directive. Another attribute of savings and cost reduction as a result of effectiveness is the ability to create and modify processes rapidly. Basically, when the program operates better—as in maturity—there is a broader and deeper understanding of what does and doesn't work. As new challenges, services, and needs surface within the program the time required for planning, development, and implementation of new processes and controls is reduced significantly, while ensuring accuracy and quality.

10.2 Assessing Capability Maturity

Fundamentally, capability maturity is about how well people execute processes and how well processes are defined and managed. Of course, this introduces how people are trained and educated, how well they perform the processes, and how well defined processes are. People cannot be separated from processes; the relationship between them is at the core of maturity. To continually monitor and manage capability maturity it must be assessed. How often it is assessed is directly related to the level of maturity realized. This is based on the fact that a more mature program is less likely to change over time than a less mature one. (Note: It is important not to confuse maturity assessments with improving process effectiveness, which is covered later in this chapter.)

Assessing maturity does not have to be a long, drawn-out process. In fact, one could argue that it is quite simple, and it should be because maturity is reflective of the existing state. In other words, there is little preparation because either you know it and do it, or you don't—in both cases, it is simple to determine. Of course, the same cannot be said of the results of the assessment. Closing gaps to increase maturity to the desired state can be very complex. However, what will become clear is that all the characteristics of risk, compliance, governance, and services management will converge to make the process far easier.

At this point it is helpful to note that there is a relationship between the level of maturity and the costs associated with attaining and maintaining that level. The process of defining the desired level of maturity can be complicated. Understanding that higher levels increase effectiveness, efficiency, and quality, and play an essential role in demonstrating value and promoting adaptability, one has to relate these advantages to cost. Nevertheless, most organizations will find that there are tangible returns on investments made in increasing maturity. Moreover, the ASMA is founded on and has maturity integrated into features and feature interactions.

As introduced above, the assessment process does not have to be complicated and in most cases it shouldn't be. It is a process that should be able to be performed rapidly, for example, within a week or two for an entire program assessment and not more than a couple of days—or less—for a targeted assessment. There are three major elements to assessing capability maturity: scope and timing, process and standards evaluation, and interviews.

10.2.1 Scope and Timing of Assessment

There are a few considerations to take into account when scoping an assessment and some of these will have to do with timing. In traditional assessments of maturity—as with many things in security—the scope defines the boundaries of what is considered applicable. This is seen in many areas of security, from compliance efforts to ISO-27001 certification. You must define the domain, environment, or feature that falls within the intended outcome.

This applies to the ASMA in a few different ways. First, the entire security program should be included in the assessment. For example, this would encompass compliance management, risk management, governance, services management, and organizational management. In fact, it would include capability maturity management as well. The advantage of assessing the entire program is gaining visibility into the processes and people's understanding of them. In most cases, as the program is becoming normalized, an assessment of the entire program is warranted to establish a baseline and to identify gaps that can be prioritized in the overall project plan. For example, when implementing services management you want to know not only what tasks are completed and need to be completed, but also how well what you have accomplished so far is working. It can help greatly in readjusting future activities to reduce gaps as you move into an operational state.

In most cases, organizations are going to want to perform a program-wide assessment several times during implementation and at least once a year. Nevertheless, this does raise the point of timing. Putting aside initial development time frames and assuming the program is running and developing as expected, an assessment will identify the level of maturity that has been attained. That level basically reveals how well the program is defined and how well people understand and execute those processes. This implies that the greater the maturity level the greater the confidence in the resilience of the program to change, and therefore the longer the program will at least maintain that level.

For example, a program or a feature achieves a level 3 of maturity (e.g., well defined); this implies that processes, standards, practices, and the people that employ them have reached a level of sophistication that is not easily disrupted. Well defined implies that standards and processes are well defined, performance is well defined, and coordination from development to execution are also well defined. This means that it can be expected that new standards and processes will be created more effectively, with fewer errors, and that established processes in everything from publication to training will be used, and proper employment will be assured. As a result, there is greater stability and consistency in the program, and therefore it does not need to be assessed as often when compared to lower levels of maturity that do not offer as much stability. In short, if an assessment is performed that results in a level 3, it is likely that an assessment of the same scope within a year will probably produce similar results.

Of course, this is potentially impacted by the state of the program and its evolution. Early in the implementation process assessments may change dramatically over time. The first may result in a 0.5 level, 1.2 for the next one, and 2.2 for the next. The more dynamic the environment is, the more unpredictability there is in the assessment results. However, this applies only to early stages of implementation. As core features are defined and become practiced more regularly, the results will normalize. Once normalization in the core features is established, then assessments—especially program-wide assessments—can be timed based on level achieved, with lower levels having shorter durations and higher levels representing more time between assessments.

This may lead some to question that if the assessment may only happen once a year or more, why the focus on ensuring it can be performed rapidly? There are two important reasons to make the assessment process very efficient:

1. There are times when an assessment may be performed against a certain part of the program, such as when a new service is launched, three months later, then again in six months to obtain visibility into effectiveness and improvements. If the assessment is an arduous task, this becomes far less attractive and the difficulty of the process outweighs the benefits. It is important to know that governance, compliance, and risk

management are going to be constantly seeking improvements and changes to how security is applied, which will keep compliance management, in a word, busy. Moreover, as changes to processes and standards are made and employed it is necessary to ensure that they are having the desired impact on efficiency and effectiveness. While governance is focused on goals, compliance on integrity, and risk on posture, capability maturity is focused on the effectiveness of the supporting processes and therefore needs to assess maturity quickly.

2. Although an organization does not have to perform assessments often, especially when a high level is obtained, this should not be seen as a limitation to performing an assessment more regularly. In short, just because you do not have to perform an assessment in two years, doesn't mean that you cannot benefit from doing one sooner. Related to the first point, if the process is too complicated and expensive, it won't be performed until it has to be. However, the entire architecture is founded on efficiency, effectiveness, and adaptability. Performing regular assessments can help greatly in ensuring these characteristics. Therefore, organizations should be encouraged to perform assessments, not discouraged by a painful and expensive process. Finally, there are characteristics in high maturity levels that require assessments of this nature.

As previously alluded to, there are degrees of scope. Again, the entire program can be assessed on occasion, or portions of the program, such as features and services. This is where the modularity of the ASMA's features also works to the organization's advantage. If the scope of the assessment is limited to a specific service to determine the capability maturity, it will naturally be focused on how the service is managed and delivered. However, as we've learned, there are interlocks with other features in the program, such as governance, risk, and compliance. From the assessment perspective these represent demarcation points. The assessment of a service is not concerned about what risk management is doing with regard to the service, but simply that people know the interlock exists, what processes are related to it in which they must participate, and that those processes are well defined and executed.

This may not appear all that important on the surface, but it is a huge advantage to the organization. There is a great deal of inter-action and interconnections within the ASMA. As such, each area relies in some way on other areas of the model. This is an advantage and is fully exploited in providing adaptability. However, it is also quite valuable to have clarity on how each element of a feature is func-tioning correctly or poorly. Without the ability to rationalize perfor-mance of each feature independently, there is far more complexity in determining root causes for errors, or more importantly, root causes for positive outcomes, such as an increase in quality, compliance, and the like. If a service has achieved a high level of maturity, but there are indicators that it is not effective, it may be the result of another feature, for example, compliance management is not assisting security management as designed. Until you have a clear perspective of the individual feature or service capabilities, there is far more confusion in focusing remediation efforts.

In this case, the ASMA can be compared to an engine: it is a col-lection of parts working together for a common goal. However, if one of the parts is failing and you do not have a method for uniquely identifying it, you are left to troubleshoot based only on how the problem is ultimately being presented. Capability maturity manage-ment assessments combined with the natural demarcation points within the model used in scoping is analogous to having a sensor on each part of the engine, which allows you to rapidly identify the exact root cause without having to interpret the problem from afar and work inward. This is similar to using inductive reasoning as opposed to deductive. Everything in the ASMA is about interaction and interconnectivity, yet capability maturity assessments represent the one tool that is the antithesis of this, because without it the abil-ity to improve processes with a focus on scope would be virtually insurmountable. As all this implies, the minimal boundaries for an assessment are services. From there the features of the model can represent assessment scopes. After that the next level of scope is the entire security organization.

Of course, not all long-standing programs increase effectiveness or maturity over time. It is very easy to have a program several years old that never gets above a level 1. Nevertheless, if implementing the model as described herein, a level 3 should be considered baseline and anything less would imply that key features are not implemented. Additionally, once governance is in place and measurements are flowing and managed, a level 4 is implied. Finally, when governance, compliance, risk, and organizational management are functioning as designed and improving processes, that is essentially level 5 or slightly below.

Therefore, the ASMA is a mechanism to incorporate capability maturity into the fabric of how security is applied within the business. The value from this characteristic will resonate across the business in the form of savings, cost-effectiveness, meaningful risk and compliance management, efficiency, and the ability to rapidly adjust to business dynamics.

10.2.1.1 The Assessment Team   To perform an assessment, one must have assessors. For small companies this may become difficult if there are not enough resources. For example, the assessing team should not be from the group that is being assessed, which is very different from the other features, which may share resources. The first question is, when the entire program is being assessed, who performs the assessment? The answer is simply whoever owns the capability maturity management feature. There may be situations in which this may represent a conflict, especially if that person also manages other areas of the business. The reality is you can't always ensure separation to avoid conflicts of interests in these cases. Companies can always seek third-party support, but it is unlikely that the third party will be intimate enough with the model to do so. Again, there are no hard rules here. If there is a mechanism to ensure assessor autonomy, use it. If not, then do your best to ensure the process is performed professionally and ethically.

This is where the number of assessors comes into play. In a perfect scenario (having enough people) a minimum is two assessors, but not more than three should perform the assessment together. This does not mean two or three people perform different aspects of the assessment separately to save time. These people must be together at all times to collaborate, interpret findings, and to provide a check and balance, especially in interviews. Interviews should never be performed in a one-on-one session. Having more than one assessor is important to ensure there is diversity of perspective, opinion, and objectivity. Of course, having three assessors is optimal so there is a "tie breaker" in interpreting capability. Assessing capability is not strictly a mathematical or checkbox process. It is as much interpretation as it is science in some cases. Therefore, personalities come into play and there are moments of disagreement. A third person will ensure these are resolved democratically.

Of course, three people may be a lot in an organization comprised of five security resources. As with everything discussed so far, the volume of resources does not govern the ASMA. It is possible to employ the entire model with just a few people. Admittedly, the model scales up far better than down and assessments are a good example of this. In very small organizations it may be easier to simply perform a self-assessment with all the resources in a room and review the entire program in one sitting. The number of resources should not be seen as a constraint when it comes to the program or the assessment of the program. Although fewer resources may not permit a perfect "textbook" execution, the intent of the program and assessment should be the focus.

10.2.2 Preparing for the Assessment

Once the scope is defined the target must prepare for the assessment. As discussed, the assessment is focused on people, processes, and standards. The first step in preparation is collecting materials and evidence demonstrating that processes have been employed as designed. Additionally, the target group must identify people for the interviews.

10.2.2.1 Materials Given the fact that the best method for managing processes, standards, procedures, policies, and other tools used in the program, feature, or service is to place them on an internal Web site or document management tool, the process of collecting materials should be rather moot. What is important is that there is an obvious flow to the information system. For example, a Web page with links to documents is not very "mature" and does not express how the documents are related to one another. An active process map on a page, with content for each process that explains all that is needed with supporting documentation, such as templates, examples, access to knowledge management systems, tools, and the like, demonstrates a high degree of maturity and ease of use. In this case, the assessor simply needs access to the site or tool. If the materials are a combination of documents that are not necessarily interconnected and have obvious relationships, it is typically best to print them out. By doing so, assessors can organize the information that best meets their needs in interpreting the completeness of the materials.

10.2.2.2 People People provide the bulk of information concerning the maturity of a program. As such, people from the targeted scope, such as the manager and delivery personnel from a service, will have to be identified for interviews. Of course, not everyone has to be included, but those who are should represent a meaningful cross-section of the community. For small organizations, this may be one person if there is only one person doing everything. However, if there are five people, you should interview all five. Although there are no hard rules, a general rule of thumb is that more than 12 people is unnecessary regardless of the size of the target group. Finally, at least one person must be identified as the primary point of contact for the team being assessed.

10.2.3 Processes and Standards Evaluation

With the materials from the targeted environment in hand, along with the process frameworks provided in other chapters and the details on the model provided in Section 10.4, Adaptive Architecture Capability Maturity Model, later in this chapter, the assessor will ensure that the processes and standards meet the specifications for each level: maturity requirements and specific requirements. As the materials are reviewed for completeness, the assessor will mark the maturity requirement level as being attained when all the required characteristics are met.

The assessment of processes and standards takes far less time than the interview process, but it is no less important. Even the best people can be rendered ineffective by poor processes, and much of the interview process will come from the assessor's evaluation of materials and evidence. The evaluation of processes and standards doesn't take long for two basic reasons: either the process exists or it doesn't, and processes are documented and therefore only require a one-time review. Clearly the intent is to determine maturity, but this cannot necessarily be determined by the complexity of a process or how "big" it is, but rather its comprehensiveness and focus. A one-page process may be all that is needed, as long as it addresses the purpose of the process's intent. Ultimately, it will be the people's knowledge and employment of the process that will define overall maturity.

However, the difficulty in evaluating processes and standards can be directly contributed to their organization. If the processes are not documented very well, are poorly organized, and there is no clear connection between sets of processes, this alone will have an impact on the maturity score, especially in higher levels, such as level 3 and level 4.

10.2.4 Interviews

Interviews consume the majority of the assessment time and effort. It is important that the people responsible for the management and execution of processes understand every detail concerning the process and all that is implied without the process in front of them as a reference. In other words, the resources have to at least know that the process exists and provide a perspective of how they employ it. The interview is not complicated, but each organization will have to formulate an approach that works best for the organization. Nevertheless, the following provides some guidance.

Each feature, feature element, or service has one or more areas that need to be assessed. For example, services management has several elements, such as initiation, planning, engagement management, and several other processes and process groups that are needed to facilitate the mission of the feature. Each of these elements needs to be assessed for maturity. Therefore, the questioning of interviewees will occur across all the areas in the scope of the assessment against each level of maturity in a hierarchical structure.

Once an answer satisfies a level (or, more accurately, the specific requirement) the next question is about the next specific requirement, continually moving up the stack of maturity. This continues until an unsatisfactory answer appears. However, the question for the specific requirement that received an unsatisfactory answer should be asked again in at least three different ways to ensure there is no misinterpretation. If a satisfactory answer is received through additional questioning, then the process moves to the next requirement, and so on. Interestingly, the same holds true when after several forms of questions are not satisfied, the assessor asks at least one question about the next level requirement. This is important to ensure that additional capabilities are understood, even if the previous requirement was not satisfied. Whether the interviewee answers the question of the next requirement satisfactorily or not, the interview stops. The goal is not to skip the failed requirement, but to gain better visibility into gaps, confirm them, and highlight them in the assessment report for improvement.

10.2.4.1 Interview Example Following is a basic example of how an interview may progress. Assume for a moment that the interviewee is involved in security training.

> Assessor (A): "Is training performed?" [This question is to identify level 0.]
> Interviewee (I): "Yes."
> A: "Please provide examples of what training was performed, when, and the number of attendees." [Although the assessor may have evidence of this in hand, this is to determine the interviewee's awareness of training activities. Since this is focused on level 1, the assessor is simply trying to ascertain whether it is happening.]
> I: "We performed router ACL training to roughly 13 people in the IT department two months ago."
> A: "How is training planned and tracked? For example, have you identified training resources and documented training processes, have you identified training tools, what are the processes for ensuring the trainers are trained, and finally, is there a schedule for training?" [This is an oversimplified example, but the assessor is attempting to see if training is at least reaching the first set of five requirements for level 2.]
> I: "Yes, we've documented roles and responsibilities and assigned resources; we have a documented process for training, including training materials; we have a set of presentation tools and supporting documents for the students, along with a small lab; all our

trainers must be Cisco-certified to a minimal level before providing training and have attended the course as a student; and there is a schedule provided on line." [At this point, the maturity level is a 2.1 out of a possible 2.4.]

A: "Can you provide me with examples of how this is performed? For example, do you have examples of training materials?" [The question is targeted as disciplined performance and use cases.]

I: "Yes and ..." [The interviewee is expected to do more than just show the materials and explain how they are used.]

A: "Are these materials updated and is there some form of version control?" [This question is targeted to the version control of materials for training and the training process. A follow-up question may be: Are roles and responsibilities version controlled or how are tools version controlled?]

I: "Not really. We haven't used the existing materials enough so far." [This answer is not entirely satisfactory, so the assessor tries to determine if version control exists, but may not have been used for training materials.]

A: "Do you have a repository for training materials?"

I: "Yes."

A: "If someone changes a document, is that tracked?"

I: "Yes, the system will show you the date of the last changes to the file." [Not good enough; try some more questions.]

A: "Is there anything in the file that expresses what version it is when changes are made?"

I: "I'm not sure. But we use the date to see that it has been updated." [This implies that there are older versions.]

A: "Does this mean there are older versions in the document management system?"

I: "In some cases yes, but they are typically deleted once people start using the updated file." [In short, there is no version control, but the assessor must confirm this in a straightforward manner to ensure that the interviewee has every opportunity to get back on track.]

A: "Is it true that there is no version control that is identified in the training materials?"

I: "Well ..."

It is likely that the interviewee will attempt to reconcile when he or she realizes there is a gap based on the line of questioning. At this point, unless there is hard evidence that the interviewee is aware of version control, the interview is nearing the end. An interesting attribute to add to this example is when the assessor knows for a fact there is a version control mechanism and there are several version numbers in the training materials that were provided as part of the assessment preparation. Therefore, in this case, the interviewee is unaware this process exists.

Having received an unsatisfactory answer, the assessor must at least move to the next specific requirement. This is especially important if the assessor knows that the current requirement is being met, but the interviewee does not know this. Therefore, the assessor asks another question concerning performance verification, the next level.

A: "Can you discuss examples that demonstrate that training activities are in alignment with the training process? For example, if a training session is scheduled for eight hours, is there anything that you can provide that ensures that training was performed for eight hours, such as a sign-in and sign-out sheet?"

I: "Absolutely. That is part of the employee approval process for managers. As trainers, we have to supply proof that the employee was in training the entire allotted time. Here is an example." [This is a good sign and the assessor decides to ask one more question to round out the last specific control in performance verification, and that is auditing. Normally, it would stop here, but it may be more worth another few minutes of investigation.]

A: "Good. How are these sign-in sheets confirmed by management? In other words, who manages these sign-in sheets and confirms that they are completed and provided to management?"

I: "The trainers collect the sign-in and sign-out sheets at the end of each day and put them in a folder for the managers if they want to see them."

At this point the interview is over. There was a gap concerning version control and the assessor went to the next maturity requirement to see what may surface. Although the interview would have normally stopped after the sign-in sheet discussion, it was an opportunity for the assessor to see how those sheets were managed. Unfortunately, there was no audit process. The sign-in sheets were simply filed and it would be an exception process for a manager to go retrieve them. Moreover, it was not obvious that there was a template, or that someone other than the trainer collecting the sign-in sheets is validating that they were in fact completed, completed correctly, and filed correctly. This is a simple example used to demonstrate the basic interaction between the assessor and the interviewee. Moreover, from this we can see that how well someone knows the process is critical. In the example, there was a versioning control mechanism, but the employee didn't know this. One could argue that if the employee did, the interview would have found a slightly higher rating. But, this is why several people are interviewed.

Given that the interviewee satisfied all requirements up to level 2.1 (all the five specific controls of performance planning, the first of the four maturity requirements (see Table 10.2); see the section Capability Levels below for more information on the specific controls areas of each level of maturity), but only addressed use evidence and failed to meet the second requirement of version control in disciplined performance, the score is 2.1. Of course, the first recommendation for improvement is to ensure that people are being trained on the version control process. Although this may seem to be a basic example, it is an accurate depiction of how an interview typically plays out. The assessor simply asks a question about the target area being assessed seeking to expose if a process is meeting the defined level of maturity. As you can see, it can move rather quickly, but if the maturity is very high, it could take several hours. This is why interviewing more than twelve people is not reasonable.

As an added note, some may expect this to take longer than a few hours, especially if the entire program is being assessed. While there is some truth to this, each specific requirement can be determined by asking questions from different areas. For example, "What are your version controls for documented processes?" This will help determine if this requirement exists in the program. Understandably, effort needs to be applied to home in on specific gaps, but as long as the interviewee knows there is version control, the intent is, for the most part, met. Keep in mind that the assessor, by the time the interviews are performed, already has a good perspective on what exists and what doesn't from reviewing materials and evidence. The goal of the interview is to see if employees involved in the processes know what exists and how it is employed.

Table 10.2 Capability Model Requirements

LEVEL	MATURITY REQUIREMENTS	SPECIFIC REQUIREMENTS
Level 0—Not Performed	NA	NA
Level 1—Performed Informally	1.1—Processes and Practices Are Being Performed	1.1.1—Perform Processes and Practices
Level 2—Planned and Tracked	2.1—Performance Planning	2.1.1—Assign Resources and Responsibilities
		2.1.2—Document Processes
		2.1.3—Tools
		2.1.4—Training
		2.1.5—Plan the Process Execution
	2.2—Disciplined Performance	2.2.1—Use Evidence
		2.2.2—Product Management and Control
	2.3—Performance Verification	2.3.1—Verify Process Compliance
		2.3.2—Audit Products
	2.4—Tracking Performance	2.4.1—Track with Measurement
		2.4.2—Corrective Action
Level 3—Well Defined	3.1—Defining Standard Processes	3.1.1—Standardize the Processes
		3.1.2—Tailor the Standard Process
	3.2—Performing Defined Processes	3.2.1—Use a Well-Defined Process
		3.2.2—Perform Defect Reviews
		3.2.3—Use Well-Defined Data
	3.3—Coordination Practices	3.2.1—Perform Feature Coordination
		3.2.2—Perform Inter-feature Coordination
		3.2.3—Perform External Coordination
Level 4—Quantitatively Controlled	4.1—Establishing Measurable Quality Objectives	4.1.1—Establish Quality Goals
	4.2—Objectively Managing Performance	4.2.1—Determine Process Capability
		4.2.2—Use Process Capability
Level 5—Continuously Improving	5.1—Improving Organizational Capability	5.1.1—Establish Process Effectiveness Goals
		5.1.2—Continuously Improve the Standard Process
	5.2—Improving Processes' Effectiveness	5.2.1—Perform Causal Analysis

10.3 Management

Capability maturity management requires structure, of course, but this also includes clear definitions concerning activities, such as assessments, the definition of levels, and actions to be performed in remediation. Additionally, the scope of these responsibilities and actions must be defined.

An example is that regular meetings need to be performed within the capability maturity management team to discuss all the activities that are in process, with some needing to be performed at certain points in time. The minutes and action items from the meeting and how these are tracked must be documented. What should be become obvious is that the management of capability maturity management is itself a target of maturity. This is very important because the credibility of capability maturity management to the security program and beyond is in many ways tied to its ability to perform against expectations.

Capability maturity management will define maturity requirements and specific requirements to articulate attributes of maturity. Capability maturity is not concerned with complexity, just effectiveness. So, if something can be accomplished easily and in a manner that ensures effectiveness, capability maturity management is satisfied.

10.3.1 Reporting

All activities performed by capability maturity management must result in some form of report. In short, a report will quantify the level of maturity measured and offer recommendations for improvement. As one might expect, recommendations are provided in the form of changes or enhancements to people and processes and are organized with the intent to improve one or both. It is up to organizational management and governance to determine if the recommendations should be implemented, to determine the costs associated with the changes, and to evaluate the short- and long-term value of those changes.

In virtually every situation, governance will provide information in the form of goals, strategic goals and tactical goals, along with interpretations of the effectiveness and quality into capability maturity management. As capability maturity management assesses maturity, it is empowered with this executive-level information to help classify the criticality of gaps. The importance of this interlock cannot be overstated. By having governance intimately attached to capability maturity management, there is greater visibility at the business level of identified gaps, which can be used for justifying improvements. This is how the ASMA begins to move into a predictive position. If certain goals are not being met, capability maturity management, through assessment processes and management of the feature, will have a detailed view into exactly what might be causing the problem. More importantly, as demands from the business emerge and are processed by governance, one of the first activities is going to be to connect with capability maturity management to determine if there are any known gaps that would hinder the security program's ability to meet the business need.

Equally important to the interlock between governance and capability maturity management is the interlock that capability maturity management has with risk management. Governance is concerned about maturity as it relates to improving performance against stated business goals and objectives, and the ability to understand implications—as well as opportunities—relative to efficiencies and effectiveness concerning operational integrity of the security group. Risk management, in collaboration with capability maturity management, will be acutely focused on the state of maturity relative to risk. As discussed, maturity can be directly associated with the comprehensiveness and effectiveness of the overall activity, meaning the more mature a process or service is the greater confidence there is that all aspects of the service are functioning as intended and, more importantly, the potential for error is reduced. Assume for a moment that the level of maturity for the service Vulnerability Management drops in maturity or demonstrates a negative trend. In fact, the level of maturity experiencing a decline may be a specific aspect of the service, such as network scanning, application testing, or code review. Regardless of scope or aspect, the change in maturity represents an increased risk due to the potential for error and reduction in effectiveness. For example, if network scanning is shown as declining in maturity, risk can rightly conclude that the results from the scan, which are directly related to managing risk as an input, are less "trustworthy." The results may include errors, false positives, false negatives, or any representation of misalignment between the act of scanning and the true state of the environment being tested.

The ability for risk management to be truly effective depends on having accurate and complete information from which to draw to establish a meaningful perspective of risk posture. Any flaw in the supporting information will translate through the risk management process, potentially undermining the results and conclusions. Risk management must trust in the results of applied security services and therefore must have clear visibility into the comprehensiveness and effectiveness of how that service is being performed. The role of capability maturity management is to provide that visibility in the form of expressing and reporting on the maturity of services and service elements. The maturity of visibility provided by capability maturity management does not testify for the content of information as a result of security services, but rather for the underlying state of capability of the service delivery team, management team, process quality, and process execution that express effectiveness and thereby more or less trust in the results.

To elaborate, a security service is directed at performing a basic network scan using Nessus as a tool, and the results are provided to risk management. The question becomes, "How accurate are the results from the scan?" The scanner could have been configured or deployed incorrectly. The person performing the scan may not have been fully trained. The deliverables may not have been reviewed or the findings verified. These nuances of delivery capability do not appear in service delivery audits or assessments, which is a more traditional means of conveying completeness of a process. In both cases—audit or assessment—these do not expose the underlying capability of the people, processes, technology, and management interactions that ensure overall effectiveness, repeatability, and quality. Regardless of whether you audit or assess the service delivery team's processes, it is representative of a point in time. Therefore, it is not possible to determine the state of specific processes relative to the scan because they may change in an uncontrolled fashion. Of course, risk management has the option of running the scan again using its own resources, but this is simply transference of "trust" from the interpretations of completeness and capability of the service delivery team relative to the known team performing the scan as part of risk management. This is all too common and is a wasted effort. A more effective method is to integrate maturity into the management and delivery of services and closely monitor them to ensure that expectations concerning performance—and ultimately quality—are well understood over time.

A second aspect of the relationship between risk and maturity, besides trusting in the results, is trusting in the completeness of security services. Albeit somewhat related to deliverables and results, risk management is also concerned with ensuring that stated processes concerning how risk is managed and posture is maintained throughout the environment are being followed and managed effectively. As expressed, poor maturity can introduce the potential for error. Therefore, any lack or reduction in maturity of services can be construed as not having effective security measures, which translates to a potential increase in overall risk posture.

Therefore, within the context of the interconnection between risk management and capability maturity management, risk management will be greatly influenced by the level of maturity realized and any decline in maturity. It must be noted that a decline in maturity can represent a potential increase in risk and undermine the ability for risk management to trust the results and outcomes of services, but what if the maturity increases? Does this mean the company is at less risk or has a better risk posture? Unfortunately, no ... not really. The relation between risk and maturity is founded on the fact that a more mature capability means that there is greater confidence in the intended outcome of applied security. In other words, you are reducing the potential for error and ensuring greater alignment to intent. Therefore, technically speaking, you are not improving your risk posture by simply increasing maturity, but rather you are improving your ability to manage risk more effectively and with a higher degree of confidence that what was applied is an accurate representation of intent relative to the desired risk posture.

10.3.2 Improvement

When it is decided to implement the recommendations, it is the responsibility of capability maturity management to oversee process improvement. It is necessary to put this role into context relative to other features of the program related to improvements. Compliance management is focused on influencing changes so that compliance is achieved; risk management is concerned with ensuring that changes or gaps in execution do not unduly expose the company to increased risks; services management is concerned with the execution of the service relative to customer demands; and governance is focused on making changes to ensure KPIs are being facilitated to meet expected goals and to incorporate feedback from the executive and customer communities. None of these are necessarily directly focused on the idiosyncrasies in the relationship between processes and people. That is the role of capability maturity management. When changes to the program materialize, it is up to capability maturity management to ensure that the processes are well defined and that people understand them and execute against them as designed. This means that improvements to processes, standards, and people are the responsibility of all the features, but the bulk of this activity will appear in capability maturity management.

Within the ASMA and the capability maturity model defined in this chapter, process improvement begins to be represented in the latter part of level 3 and part of level 4. However, in most capability maturity models, process improvement is not identified until level 5. The distinction is that correction to processes is not equivalent to the improvement of processes. As explained in more detail later, improvement is analogous to innovation. Although correcting errors, reducing failures, and removing process defects are improvements, within the vernacular of traditional models, these are not level 5 activities. Basically, the existence of capability maturity management can be equated with corrective activities (level 3) and in some cases with improvement (levels 4 and 5). Nevertheless, like other features, corrective actions begin in level 3. The only material difference in the security model is that improvements are introduced in level 4 and are further defined as real-time improvements in level 5. The role of capability maturity management in the improvement of processes covers upper requirements in level 3 and all of level 4 in the model defined herein. However, in level 5 process improvement scenarios will be performed predominantly by resources within the feature and monitored by capability maturity management due to the real-time nature of the improvement.

One of the more interesting aspects of process improvement by capability maturity management is that this activity is program-wide. For example, risk management is mostly directed at making key changes in the processes, procedures, standards, and methods concerning the delivery of services. Although quite comprehensive, this is a highly targeted role. Conversely, capability maturity management is focused on improving all processes throughout the program including all features. This is very similar to compliance management's role in assuring internal processes are being performed as designed, and this begins to emerge in maturity level 2.3.

10.3.3 Monitoring

Although assessments occur at distinct points in time, this does not mean that the capability maturity management process is only used at these intervals. Based on input from governance, risk, and compliance, and how these resonate in standards, processes, and procedures in the delivery of services controlled by services management, capability maturity management has the ability to monitor these changes and report on positive and negative impacts.

To demonstrate, if compliance introduces a new process that requires certain actions to be performed (e.g., procedures) in order to achieve compliance through service delivery, it must be understood that (1) the process is well defined, and (2) people know how and when to execute the process. This is analogous to how governance is concerned with performance and measurements, or how risk management is concerned with controls relative to threats, vulnerabilities, and impact. Capability maturity management must be very aware of changes that could impact overall maturity.

10.4 Adaptive Architecture Capability Maturity Model

The ASMA capability maturity model draws from the IA-CMM and ISO-21827:2008 models to formulate a structure that works for the ASMA and its features. Each of these standards defines practice areas, and in some cases supporting base practices, that define the scope of activities and processes that are to be compared against the general practices, or the common attributes among all practice and base practice areas that define maturity. The

IA-CMM takes this one more critical step and introduces methodologies that are mapped to the model. These are the INFOSEC Assessment Methodology (IAM) and the INFOSEC Evaluation Methodology (IEM). These are core to the intended purpose of the NSA in formalizing security assessment methods and execution of assessments.

The capability maturity model leverages these attributes specifically for defining the features of the model, which are very similar to the domains, practice areas, categories, and general practices that define common expectations concerning maturity and methods as seen in other models. Those familiar with IA-CMM and ISO-21827:2008 will see a number of similarities within this model. However, additions, changes, and omissions have been made concerning relevance to the ASMA.

In short, many capability maturity models will define one or more of the following:

- The definition of level of maturity,
- The practice areas, domains, categories, or controls that are supported by the levels of maturity and define the attributes for each level for process areas, and
- The methodologies that organize processes within the practice areas.

For example, CoBIT defines a set of IT controls in process areas such as plan and organize, acquire and implement, deliver and support, and monitor and evaluate. Each of these process areas defines controls and those controls are supported by maturity attributes. The similarities with the ASMA exist where process areas are analogous to the features defined in the model with supporting processes. However, there is a closer relationship between the features and the practice areas of IA-CMM and the concept of NSA methodologies with regard to the management of services. Moreover, the definition of general practices in ISO-21827:2008 provides the foundation for the definition of maturity levels for the ASMA.

The only significant shift of the ASMA capability maturity model from the others mentioned is the role of the features in the maturity program. For example, in IA-CMM there is a dedicated process area (specifically Process Area Nine) that is responsible for the program management. Moreover, there is Process Area One in IA-CMM that addresses training and education across the model. These act as bookend process areas for the management of resources and overall program alignment. Comparatively speaking, the six features collectively are responsible for overall program capability maturity, and only organizational management has cross-feature responsibilities that have a direct impact on maturity, such as training and education. In other words, each feature is responsible for the maturity of its respective areas of responsibility. The addition of capability maturity management as a feature ensures that the assessment of maturity and process improvements are identified and supported based on information and insights from governance, as well as the other features.

Therefore, all the features work together to ensure maturity, as opposed to one practice area or feature. The processes in each feature and feature element are directly tied to the maturity requirements and specific requirements provided in this section. The important characteristic to note is that the definition of the features—and the processes defined within them—is structured to ensure meaningful levels of maturity inherently. In other words, maturity is not only foundational; it is intimately integrated into the features and processes within the ASMA. Therefore, one could rightly assume that level 3 and likely level 4 are achievable simply by the existence of the ASMA.

10.4.1 Capability Levels

Capability levels are practices that are applied to each of the features in order to determine the capability of the program. There are several maturity requirements within each practice level. To be assigned any given level—as expressed in the process frameworks—all the practices and maturity requirements for that level must be achieved. Moreover, the maturity requirements for each level are hierarchical, meaning that the maximum maturity level attained is the lowest maturity requirement that is fully implemented.

Following is the list of capability levels:

- Capability Level 0—Not Performed
- Capability Level 1—Performed Informally

- Capability Level 2—Planned and Tracked
- Capability Level 3—Well Defined
- Capability Level 4—Quantitatively Controlled
- Capability Level 5—Continuously Improving

The practices within each level are used as a form of measurement on how well feature processes are being conducted throughout the program. The higher the level and achievement of practices within that level, the more standardized a process has been implemented and understood by those responsible for acting on those processes. This implies that there is greater awareness and the ability to effectively enforce activities in the model's features and overall security program.

The structure of the maturity levels and the relationships with maturity requirements and specific requirements are supported by comments on the applicability of the ASMA and its features. As discussed, the existence of the ASMA will help to ensure that organizations inherently achieve a meaningful level of maturity. What organizations must do first is ensure that these are documented. Following is the structure of maturity elements used throughout the model definition:

#.#.# Level—The overall description of the level of maturity
#.#.#.# Maturity Requirements (MR)—A hierarchical collection of requirements

- Specific Requirements (SR)—A hierarchical list of specific details concerning what must be achieved for the overall maturity requirement
- A short description of how the service model applies to the requirement as guidance

10.4.2 Level 0—Not Performed

Some of the models referenced above do not have a level 0. Starting with level 1 assumes that a process in fact exists and is being performed in some manner, which is not always entirely accurate. Processes may have been identified as a need, but have not been created. Level 0 is used within the ASMA capability maturity model to demonstrate areas that must exist but do not, in order to assist organizations in having a clear understanding of process status and focus, especially during the implementation of the program. In short, knowing a process is not being performed is half the battle.

10.4.3 Level 1—Performed Informally

Performed informally identifies that processes within the features are implemented at a minimum level, but all the processes are being performed in some way; otherwise it would be level 0. The usual reasons for not progressing past level 1 are that processes are not planned or tracked. These are analogous to security groups with resources heavy in institutional knowledge but not supported by documentation, that there is little or no planning in their activities, and that they are not being tracked against defined expectations.

Although things are being accomplished, there is no or limited structure. This does not necessarily imply poor performance, but rather the level of performance is directly related to individual capabilities, experience, and knowledge of the environment. Level 1 is considered an absolute minimum and represents significant risk to an organization because there are single points of failure, an inability to effectively replicate activities, a lack of visibility into activities, an inability to scale, and no documentation to support the program. For example, given the over-reliance on individuals, if a security organization were to lose a resource there are few options to ensure meaningful continuity and the program will suffer greatly.

10.4.3.1 Processes and Practices Are Being Performed

There is only one maturity requirement for level 1, and it is that all processes and practices within the feature, or feature area that is being measured for maturity, are being performed.

- Perform Processes and Practices—There is a fine line between level 0 and level 1. Given that level 1 cannot be supported through documentation, it is necessary to evaluate the individual knowledge of the people performing processes defined with the model's features to ensure they are performed, albeit informally. There are three considerations:

1. All the process and feature elements must be performed,
2. Everyone involved in the delivery of the features must be able to demonstrate that they are in fact performing the processes in some fashion, and
3. The overall performance of the processes must meet the demands and stated goals of the business, security organization, and customers.

In short, although performed informally, processes have to be completed in a manner that meets the objectives of the business. Processes that are being performed that do not achieve business and security goals are not only a level 0, but represent a risk to the organization, are exceedingly wasteful, and, of course, are ineffective.

10.4.4 Level 2—Planned and Tracked

The basis of level 2 is founded on the existence of documented planning and tracking of processes within the feature for feature elements that are being measured. The formality of documentation should be considered, however, as long as there is some form of documentation that expresses that process execution is planned and the activities executed as part of the process are tracked and documented. The key factor is the management of the documentation over time by the resources performing processes and those responsible for managing delivery. One of the aspects of level 2 is that the processes are planned and tracked within a team or group and are not reliant on a single person or various unconnected individuals.

10.4.4.1 Performance Planning Performance planning is predominantly concerned with documentation of the process and resources, and there is clarity on the what, who, and when concerning the employment of a process. Examples of this include services management, rapid risk assessments, governance processes, and service delivery. There are five specific requirements:

1. Assign Resources and Responsibilities—Ensure that resources have been allocated to the process. Organization charts, documented roles and responsibilities, and that there is a clear relationship between the resources and processes are

important. For example, resources responsible for the delivery of a security service must be identified and have proper roles and responsibilities in executing those processes defined.

- Services management predominantly performs this in the delivery of security services. Additionally, organizational management is responsible for the assignment of resources throughout the program and across all model features.

2. Document Processes—Performance planning requires that processes are documented for a given feature or feature elements and that resources have been assigned and responsibilities applied. For example, it is necessary to document the processes concerning services management or the processes used in the execution of the service.

- Each feature will have documented processes.

3. Tools—Tools that are used in the execution of the processes must be identified, classified, and made available to the resources. These tools may be as simple as spreadsheets or comprehensive, such as software or hardware solutions. There is no minimum, just that if the process requires a tool, that tool must be defined and documented.

- There are no tools specifically identified in the ASMA due to the diversity of security programs and existing strategies. However, tools, or more accurately the use of technology, are highlighted herein as a means to increase efficiency—for example, using Web sites to manage the service catalog, methods, storage for processes, document management, and the like. These are important and every effort should be made to employ technology for the management of documents, projects, reporting, and activities.

4. Training—This simply requires that the assigned resources for a process within a feature or feature element are educated on performing the process. For example, resources assigned to a process must understand the documented process, how to execute the process, what tools are required, and how to employ those tools.

- Organizational management is intimately tied to training resources. Therefore, this is a requirement that is the responsibility of organizational management. However, it is noteworthy to add that while organizational management may be responsible for ensuring training, training can be performed and provided in a number of ways and by different groups, features, and third parties. This level of maturity is focused on ensuring it is performed. Later, with higher levels, it is more concerned with how well training is performed.

5. Plan the Process Execution—Once resources are assigned, processes are documented, and tools and training are facilitated, the process execution must be planned. This can materialize as project plans, playbooks, schedules, or the like. Each feature will, by very definition, have process execution plans, especially services management, risk, and compliance.

   • Planning occurs throughout the ASMA and exists in each feature. Much of the material provided in the above chapters is to help organizations design and produce plans.

10.4.4.2 Disciplined Performance   Disciplined performance builds on performance planning by assuring that processes are being applied appropriately. It is noteworthy to add that this is concerned with the fact that the processes are being employed as designed and intended and not focused on the effectiveness, efficiency, or even the improvement of the process employment—just simply that it is being used as planned. There are two specific requirements:

1. Use Evidence—This is the ability to demonstrate through documentation and other evidence that processes have been performed as designed. For example, process outputs, notes, deliverables, reports, communications, and anything that provides evidence that processes are being used.

   • As demonstrated, each feature has a reporting requirement to some other feature and ultimately to organizational management and governance, and governance acts as the business interface for the exchange of information. When performed as prescribed, there will be ample evidence of use. For programs in early development, services management will be the source of most of the use evidence of processes given that it is responsible for the application of security.

2. Product Management and Control—Management and control requires that processes and other features and feature element supporting materials, such as standards, procedures, and the like, are under some form of version control. Moreover, there must exist evidence of process and supporting materials review. In other words, there must exist a version management system and method and proof that those methods and version control processes are being employed. This is a critical element in the improvement of processes and will become increasingly important in higher capability levels.

- Each feature, especially services management, will inherently have management and control of processes, procedures, and standards. Moreover, version control and management is key to the role of compliance and risk management in the enhancement of these elements in the delivery of services. Most organizations over time will find that capability maturity management will become the owner of process and standard version control and management. It is a natural evolution. However, in the early stages of architecture implementation, compliance management is typically most concerned with version control. Nevertheless, over time this will migrate completely to capability maturity management.

10.4.4.3 Performance Verification Performance verification begins to introduce focus on effectiveness. This is not all that is required to demonstrate effectiveness, but it is an attempt to quantify and validate the fact that fundamental attributes of performance are being captured and acknowledged. In short, this maturity requirement is focused on the ability of the program to produce evidence that processes and plans are being implemented as prescribed. In the previous maturity requirement, we were concerned with evidence of use and verification that processes are under management control. This requirement makes certain that use evidence is in alignment with the intent of the process. For example, a process may result in a deliverable, such as with a security service. However, it is necessary to ensure that the deliverable is representative of the process being employed effectively. There are two specific requirements:

1. Verify Process Compliance—Process compliance is verified through evidence, such as schedules, milestone documentation, communications, meeting notes, and other materials that can be tied back to a specific process. For example, a process in services management is performing a kickoff meeting. During the meeting there is a specific process that must be performed to ensure results from the meeting are incorporated into the service delivery and management. Proof of compliance to the kickoff meeting process is evidence of each element of the process. For example, the kickoff process may define obtaining point of contact details, location of work, and emergency contact information. Therefore, verification would be identifying materials that have documented that management did in fact obtain point of contact details, location of work, and emergency contact information.

   • In short, this is the responsibility of compliance management. As defined, as part of compliance management's role, it is required to ensure compliance of the program itself, not simply security compliance of the organization to internal and external forces. Moreover, services management in the oversight and control of service delivery will have front-line visibility into process compliance and must collaborate with compliance management in reporting on process alignment.

2. Audit Products—Process employment results as a variety of information and are also fed by other materials, such as standards. The specific control of auditing products is to ensure that outputs from processes are in alignment with standards. Using the kickoff process as an example again, the process states to collect contact information. The standard may be a meeting status and reporting template; however, the output from the process, while compliant, did not produce results according to the standard for that process. In verifying compliance we were focused on ensuring the process was performed as prescribed. With audit, we move to the next level and want to ensure that the tools, templates, and standards supporting the process were employed.

- Again, compliance management is responsible for this specific requirement. Although working with services management to ensure process compliance, compliance management will perform auditing.

10.4.4.4 Tracking Performance The maturity control tracking performance introduces the need for measuring the process. This involves maintaining a record of the activities, such as status reports, meeting minutes, an action item register, and other materials that are part of the process, but act as tracking information concerning the process. Measuring involves having an established method to identify deviations from the plan or procedures. Processes define activities and tasks and plans, for example, security service plans, acting as a method to forecast process employment over time, such as a project plan. Based on the plan, processes should be executed at certain points in time, have various inputs, and will produce information (status report, deliverable, application, script, etc.) that can be used to track alignment to the plan and identify divergence. There are two specific requirements:

1. Track with Measurement—The specific control is effectively identifying measurements that relate to the plan in support of the process. For example, the plan calls for weekly status reports, and there is a process for performing weekly status meetings and standards for the report itself. When matched to the plan, there are expectations of status reports that can be measured relative to the processes being employed. If there are changes in how the service is being executed against the original plan, these will surface. Of course, there are a number of potential causes, such as scope creep, changes in the environment, and other traditional project-related risks that can be explained. However, this is mostly concerned with the fact that measurements are being taken—a very important attribute. In many situations managers of projects will know when something is deviating from standard and manage it, typically through project risk management. However, this is sometimes the result of familiarity with the project and not the result of tracking measurements.

Tracking of the plan based on outcomes of the process is a critical feature.

- This is a core characteristic of services management. Security services are the ultimate interface with the business and the application of security. Services management will produce measurements from project plans, delivery schedules, status reports, and deliverables. Of course, these are fed into governance and other features that also have responsibilities in tracking and measuring their own activities. Nevertheless, organizations will find that the majority of information will stem from services management. Finally, as discussed in previous chapters, measurement is critical and a metrics program—developed and managed by governance—must be reflective of the different layers in the system. To ensure maturity and have a foundation for comprehensive and high levels of maturity, measurements will act as a gating factor. Therefore, energy placed on developing measurements and a metrics strategy is an absolute requirement for meaningful business alignment and adaptability.

2. Corrective Action—As with any measurement, there are margins of acceptable variations and thresholds where the measurement is indicative of something off target. Corrective action requires that you identify these thresholds and have a method for initiating change. This is usually the result of an unexpected event, or the process is not able to adjust effectively to the environment. By establishing thresholds of measurements, organizations can identify meaningful deviations and actions can be taken to correct them. Additionally, changes to processes, standards, tools, procedures, or methods as a result of the corrective action must be documented. To meet this specific requirement, organizations must have documented measurement thresholds, evidence that measurements are taken (supported by previous requirements), evidence of corrective actions (if applicable), and results of actions. For organizations that have yet to experience a challenge and therefore have not taken corrective action, the existence of defined thresholds and an action plan are needed to achieve this requirement.

- Every feature in the model is organized to ensure improvement to the overall program. Whether security performance or operational performance is concerned, all the features play a role in taking action. Each feature is responsible for tracking its own activities and some, such as the relationship between services management, governance, and capability maturity management, are constantly interacting, which produces corrective actions. Moreover, compliance and risk management's influence on standards, processes, and procedures in the delivery of services can be directly correlated to making corrective actions. In fact, the role of risk and compliance management is predominantly to take action to ensure that risk is managed and compliance is achieved. Again, just the existence of the ASMA and the responsibilities of each of the features greatly lend themselves to a high "default" level of maturity, and represent another example that at the heart of meaningful security and providing business-enabling value through adaptation is capability maturity.

10.4.5 Level 3—Well Defined

The purpose of level 3 is to build on level 2 by focusing on comprehensive process definition, management, and performance. The key distinction is that level 2, although stringent, was focused on processes as they exist within the features. This implies a degree of informality. Comparably, level 3 is focused on the broader standardization of process as opposed to individual characteristics.

In many security programs, which are typically based on a combination of projects and groups, there are usually only a few people who manage the overall strategy. For example, the security resources performing firewall management and monitoring using their own processes, tools, methods, and management structure may be very independent from those in the security group working access controls or identity management, who are also using their own processes, tools, and so forth. Security's executive management and leadership team will typically act as the center point for aligning projects towards larger goals. This does not imply that individual groups are not performing or doing so effectively. But, it does imply that interoperability and consistency in process execution and management may not exist.

The ASMA is founded on the interaction and collaboration between features of security to ensure overall program effectiveness, efficiency, and adaptability, and the use of a common process model. This is not to imply that existing security programs cannot achieve level 3 because of segmentation. Many organizations will have core standards and processes that are common, allowing level 3 to be attained. However, level 3 is inherent to the ASMA and arguably unavoidable if established correctly. Level 3 is focused on broad standards and practices, formal documentation, formal documentation management practices, the control of work products, and the formal and effective communication of the program—and its capability.

What is critical to understand at this point is that level 2—within the context of the ASMA—can be seen as process, procedures, and standards relative to a security service. A security service represents a specific process group for a specific purpose. Conversely, level 3 should be seen as the management model itself. Security is an organization-wide standardization of processes that ultimately governs the delivery of specific services. These processes are institutionalized and greatly affect how specific processes are modified, controlled, managed, and performed for one or more security services. To demonstrate, assume you implement a security services management capability. At that point in time, you have all the elements to achieve level 3. However, this is only possible once a service is defined—you have to achieve all of one level before moving to the next, and security services are associated with level 2. Of course, defining a service and assuming that service is employed inherently satisfied level 1.

This book is based on the assumption that existing security programs are performing activities that are analogous to services, but lack the overriding model to tie these to business needs. This is also the reason why services are defined herein in the form of a framework and are not necessarily specific prescriptions. Therefore, the ASMA effectively leapfrogs low levels and focuses on level 3 and above because it assumes that levels 1 and 2 are inherent and representative of the sophistication we're looking to exploit. Therefore, the fundamental concept behind the ASMA is to act as the "connective tissue" between what is being performed now and higher levels of maturity that provide for greater business alignment and resiliency of the program.

Finally, although the above can be construed as conflicting with the scope of assessment and the ability to focus in features and even services, this is not the case. Keep in mind that while level 3 and higher maturity model attributes are focused on broader aspects, these materialize within the features and services and are supported through close interactions with other features. Take, for example, the section on the source of service initiation—customer, policy, risk, or compliance. The high-level processes offered in ensuring that the service is executed in a meaningful way is directly associated with services management, but obviously includes detailed interactions with other features and the customer. In this sense, it is "broad" from a maturity perspective, but not within the spectrum of the services management feature. This aspect, along with the movement from level 2 to level 3 within the context of the ASMA and the maturity model, has proven to be difficult for some. There are interpretations of scope and interactions that make defining the specifics of maturity above level 3 challenging. Unfortunately, there is no method for reducing this complexity and if there were it would contradict the core value and intent of the ASMA. Simply put, the ASMA works because of its deep interactions, which in turn make scope of maturity compelling. When it comes to capability maturity management and the use of the model defined herein, it is one of those rare cases where oversimplification or cutting corners will have significant implications to the value and intent. Finally, what will become increasingly evident is, again, the existence of the ASMA as described being a maturity-enabling model as much as it is a business-enabling model. Therefore, as higher levels of maturity and specific requirements are offered, many will be realized based on how the ASMA is fundamentally designed.

10.4.5.1 Defining Standard Processes As discussed above for level 3, the main focus is ensuring the comprehensiveness of processes, standards, and procedures throughout the program based on key interactions between services, or in other words, the institutionalization of the ASMA. Again, given the root purpose for the ASMA and the supporting maturity model, and the fact that common processes are foundational, demonstrates that the use of processes consistently is simplified, albeit difficult to maintain scope. For example, in the delivery of security services, which are unique collections of processes, by definition services management will employ a common set of processes in the management of any given service. Moreover, those processes provide interlocks with other features, which in turn apply consistent processes for different conditions. This demonstrates that the orchestration of the model supports institutionalization. Each feature is intimately tied to the others and functions as parts of a machine pointed at a common goal. There are two specific requirements:

1. Standardize the Process—This requires that organizations document a standard process or family of processes that provide a formal direction in the execution of security activities. The key difference is the scope of the processes, their applicability across the program, and the rigor applied to their management. Again, processes defined for specific and discrete activities do not apply here, but rather the processes that are used widely, across and in between multiple features and services.
   - What should become evident is that the processes used in the definition of services, the processes used by risk and compliance to influence delivery, the processes in governance and the interlocks with services management, and the processes that exist to define organizational management meet this requirement.
2. Tailor the Standard Process—This specific requirement defines the existence of information and evidence that common, standardized processes are modified and managed to address program processes and to address specific needs of specialized processes. Although this may appear to be similar to tracking performance and the specific requirement of taking corrective actions, this is focused on the common, standardized processes within the program as opposed to those that may be specific to certain services or projects.
   - Interestingly, this is addressed through the process and results of processes found in risk and compliance management. Again, risk and compliance management employ various standardized processes (i.e., rapid risk assessment) to ensure that specific service processes, standards, and

procedures are applied in a manner to meet program level demands. This, of course, occurs with governance and services management, among other scenarios in the model.

10.4.5.2 Performing Defined Processes The purpose of this maturity requirement is simply to ensure that the standardized processes are in fact being used. Of course, this is similar to using evidence in disciplined performance in level 2, but is applied to the overall program processes and specifically the interactions between features. On the surface this may seem easier to accomplish than what is truly involved. It's relatively complicated because individual processes, such as those in security services, are typically being employed often, and therefore it is easy to track, manage, and produce ample evidence. In contrast, standardized common practices in traditional programs are used less frequently and can become stagnant. However, given that the intent of the ASMA is to drive balance through feature interactions, it is more than implied that program processes of this nature will occur very frequently and therefore become easier to address. Nevertheless, performing defined processes is a comprehensive evaluation of maturity that stretches feature and inter-feature processes.

Performing defined processes requires the ability to demonstrate, through documentation and evidence, that organizations have institutionalized standard processes, that the processes are being performed, and reviews of process results, measurements, tracking, and performance are identifiable. There are three specific requirements:

1. Use a Well-Defined Process—This specific requirement looks to ensure that organizations can provide evidence that the standardized processes are being implemented as designed. Evidence can materialize as policies, standards, inputs, entry criteria, activities, procedures, specified roles, measurements, validation, templates, outputs, and closeout criteria. This is very similar to use evidence in disciplined performance in level 2 for security service processes.
   - This is achieved through all the features of the program, and organizations will find that services management's interaction with risk management, compliance management, and governance will provide a good source

of some of this information. However, the core information and evidence will be found predominantly in organizational management given its role in tying the program together.

2. Perform Defect Reviews—Related to assurance that processes are implemented as specified, organizations must also demonstrate through documentation and evidence that quality assurance is performed against the products of standard and common processes. This is similar to tracking with measurement in tracking performance for level 2.

   • Although services management will address process reviews concerning specific services, compliance management, governance, and in some ways capability maturity management will provide this function.

3. Use Well-Defined Data—This requirement is analogous to corrective action tracking performance for level 2. Nevertheless, in this case, the organization must demonstrate through documentation and evidence that data associated with standard process execution, that influence specific processes (e.g., security services), and that result from process are verified and validated throughout the activity. This introduces a few noteworthy points. For example, program processes must reflect what was defined for service processes in level 2. You must also demonstrate that standard processes are performing as expected in the influence of specific processes, and the output of both need to be verified and validated for compliance to the standard and specific processes. All this implies that the appropriate data are used to support processes and the data are relevant to the intent of the process and applied across the organization.

   • Again, services management will oversee this for services, but may not play a role in the overall program concerning well-defined data. Compliance management in the review of program compliance with its own processes will act as the primary source of this requirement. Moreover, organizational management and governance will be meaningful providers as well.

10.4.5.3 Coordination Practices This is another example of a maturity requirement that is inherent to the model and therefore is typically straightforward in achieving. The control requires that organizations demonstrate that activities throughout the organization, in this case the interactions between features, is occurring. Obviously, the ASMA wouldn't function very well if interactions weren't occurring and interlocks were not exploited. Therefore, the model is designed to achieve this maturity requirement by default. However, this doesn't downplay the importance of coordination—it's critical. Any lack of meaningful interactions between the features throughout the program will result in delays, errors, and incompatibility, and will greatly reduce the intended purpose of the program, which is to demonstrate value to the business. This differs from the previous requirement in that it is focused on the act and evidence of feature interactions as opposed to the existence of processes. There are three specific requirements:

1. Perform Feature Coordination—Simply stated, this requires that features, which are comprised of a number of processes and resources, are effectively coordinating efforts between them. This translates to evidence and documentation that all the activities within a given security area of the model are interacting according to processes defined within that area. Evidence is typically e-mails, schedules, project plans, meeting minutes, or anything that demonstrates that the feature is coordinated. It is typically the responsibility of the manager/leader of the feature to ensure this occurs and is documented.

   - The processes and concepts provided in each of the chapters describing each feature's responsibilities will act as the foundation for coordination. This book does not delve deeply into the organization of features and processes concerning coordination of activities, because each organization is different, each will have different management models, and each will have different approaches to managing such communications. Again, it is assumed that this level of sophistication exists within today's security programs and practice of common management tasks.

2. Perform Inter-feature Coordination—Once internal feature coordination is understood and proven, the same must be done for coordination between features. This is exceedingly important to ensure that interlocks between features are functioning as designed and are having positive influences between features. Evidence can materialize as e-mails, meeting minutes, and the like. However, inter-feature agreements, service level agreements, memoranda of understanding, quality assurance, change control, and exchange of lessons learned are all important characteristics to ensure interoperability and prove coordination.

   • Inter-feature coordination is defined by the interactions and interlocks presented throughout the ASMA. Some of these are specific, while others are implied. Through the definition of features and expression of responsibilities and relationships, organizations implementing the ASMA are strongly encouraged to customize interactions. The goal is to ensure coordination and interactivity within the program and between features and is less concerned with how these are actually performed.

3. Perform External Coordination—This is one of the more comprehensive aspects of maturity for the program. As with inter-feature coordination and the existence of documents, agreements, communications, and project materials, the same must exist for parties outside of the program. In short, these are the business, customers, other divisions, partners, and vendors. However, how coordination is performed and the materials supporting proof of coordination may look very different and come from different features. For example, customer coordination will come predominantly from services management in the delivery of services, whereas business-level coordination will be sourced from governance, and vendor coordination will likely appear from organizational management.

   • Keep in mind that the ASMA creates a relationship with the business and customers. This relationship is going to have supporting characteristics that range from simple reporting to contractual agreements. Although there are obvious contractual elements and the like for third parties that are standard for any organization, these same philosophies should not be avoided in working with the business and customers. Creating well-defined relationships of this nature can help bring validity to the security program and establish new levels of business rapport.

10.4.6 Level 4—Quantitatively Controlled

Moving to level 4 is an evolutionary step and builds on level 3 so that defined processes are quantitatively understood and controlled. The purpose is to define detailed measures of performance and establish procedures to ensure they are collected and analyzed. This leads to greater prediction, the objective management of performance, and the quantitative understanding of the quality of work. Interestingly, the maturity requirements are quite simple and straightforward and are simply concerned with the existence and management of measurements. There is a lot between the lines, but ultimately, you are either doing it or not; there is very little middle ground.

There are a few key points to make here and to provide a refresher on measurements:

- Measurements have to be defined, documented, and the process of measuring must be included,
- Measurements have to be taken on a regular basis, and how regular depends on the measurement and goal alignment,
- Measurements have to be aligned to stated goals, and
- Measurements have to be actionable to ensure improvement.

The foundation for quantitative control is measurements. This level of maturity has eluded many security organizations simply because there was no program in place that influenced metrics. As introduced in earlier chapters, a number of security organizations that generate metrics are doing so from a system that is not open to influence or is supported by a controls framework. This is analogous to basing the measurement of performance and effectiveness on monitoring sun spots and reporting on them, knowing full well that there are no methods for influencing the number or occurrence of sun spots—your performance is defined by activities that are not within your domain of influence—making it meaningless and detrimental.

Metrics have emerged in security as "scientific observation," which involves accurately measuring changes or events to draw conclusions. Of course, there is nothing wrong with this except for the fact that there is no clear and well-understood connection between the measurements and conclusions to actionable attributes that are accurately targeted in making a difference. This is effectively shooting in the dark. If you do not have a meaningfully structured control framework and are measuring events, there is no certainty that resulting activities formed from conclusions of observation will have the intended effect.

Capability maturity models are very consistent with the introduction of measurements, metrics, and quantitative controls at level 4 for a very good reason, which has not entirely resonated in the security industry. It is at level 4 simply because without a level 3 capability and all this implies (levels 1 and 2 are met and all of level 3 is met), measurements are not actionable. In short, you do not have the means to take control of your own view into performance. It is somewhat unsettling that so many within the security industry have failed to see the importance of this, yet still produce metrics and reports on program activities that are completely impossible to influence. Virtually anything can be measured, but that is only half the battle. Not addressing the other half of the equation is why some security organizations simply cannot connect with the business. Regardless of the measurement or direction, when exposed to executives the executives are going to want it to change. If it's moving in the right direction, they want it to move faster in the right direction. If it's moving in the wrong direction they obviously want it to move in the right direction or at least not get worse. Therefore, observations are meaningless in the eyes of the business unless you can make them move in the direction the business wants.

Nevertheless, it's more than just changing, but rather changing accurately. It is using a scalpel as opposed to an ax. You don't replace the entire wheel and suspension of a car when the tire is flat; you change the tire. Consistent decline in tire pressure is the measurement and the conclusion is the tire is failing. An accurately and efficiently applied change is replacing the tire. This is possible because there are understood methods for removing the wheel and then removing the tire. The interworking, the details of the mechanics of the wheel and tire, are understood so that change can be accurately applied. Without a control framework there is no clarity on the mechanical and detailed nuances of security. As a result, some broad changes may be applied and a wide net cast, when all along all you needed was a small change. What makes this worse is that you'll never truly know that only a small change was needed and you will assume it was the entirety of the net that resulted in success. In reality, you could have saved thousands, even millions, in investment and resources. This embodies the importance of the ASMA and the maturity model, and why measurements are important.

10.4.6.1 Establishing Measureable Quality Objectives The first primary focus for achieving this level of maturity is demonstrating through documentation and evidence of established, measurable targets the quality (i.e., quality goals) for the products that are a result of organizational processes, which includes standard processes and targeted processes, such as those related to services. There is only one specific control:

1. Establish Quality Goals—Quality goals can also include or encompass performance and security goals due to the nature of the services management program and the association between performance and security with business alignment and value. In most cases, quality goals will exist, but these do not have to be the only attribute in the measurement of quality objectives. Quality objectives directly relate to performance and security. In this case, quality can be seen as an overall goal relative to the combined focus of performance and security. Nevertheless, quality goals can be set, especially for services management. More importantly, goals of this nature have to be tied to strategic goals. As introduced in early chapters, there are business goals and security goals and these are met by achieving performance objectives and security quality.

   The bonding of program quality measurements with strategic goals is critical and is directed at the needs and priorities of the end customer as well as the delivery of services. Therefore, setting measureable goals is and should be a comprehensive process, but it doesn't have to be overwhelming. Goals, of course, have to be meaningful and simply not, "Be the best," but rather, "Be the best by achieving ____ number of ____s in area ___ within the year." Also, and importantly, there is no prerequisite as far as the number of measurable quality objectives and metrics or even what is best. As long as the metric has meaning, is supported by measurements, can be directly tied to strategic goals, and is sourced from the program to ensure it can be made actionable, then it qualifies as meeting this specific requirement.

- The overview of measurements, their importance and alignment with the business and security goals, was covered in previous chapters. The purpose of the ASMA is orchestration and allows companies and security groups to define specific characteristics.

10.4.6.2 Objectively Managing Performance The previous control was concerned with establishing measurements and aligning to goals, and all this implies. This control builds on defining measurements by ensuring that there is a defined approach for determining and implementing quantitative measurement processes and making use of them to manage, take corrective action, and improve the process. It may seem obvious that to measure something the intent is to manage against those measurements once they are calibrated. However, as discussed in the section on level 4, this is astonishingly rare in security. This is usually because the wrong things are being measured or there is no established method to influence change and actually improve a process accurately. The ASMA closes this gap.

In regard to objectively managing performance, following is a basic, evolutionary example using training. Of course, level 0 means you're not training, but the existence of the 0 means this is something that is missing. Level 1 means that you have basic training capabilities that are focused on one aspect of the program and are not documented or managed. Level 2 means that the process and related activities are better defined, but are limited in scope, such as training people on Microsoft's encrypting file system. Level 3 means that the processes for training are comprehensive, program wide, and are well defined and understood. A security training program for the organization meets this need.

In level 4 we introduce measurements, perform them, manage them, align them to goals, and ensure that improvements are made relative to the measurements. Therefore, in a training program, measurements may be student satisfaction surveys to measure the training materials and the teacher. It will include testing of students to ensure the training was effective (i.e., they learned the material, which of course is the intent of the process). A goal for security may be to ensure that 90% of the students achieve 90% scoring on the exam, and the survey should have a rating of 8.3 or greater on a scale from 0 to 10. These measurements are aligned to goals, such as a security goal of, "Ensure resources responsible for the planning, design, implementation, and management of the security controls are subject matter experts." And they may be connected to a business goal of, "Maintain expert workforce," which may be tied to a strategic goal of "increase quality of customer experience."

At this point we have a well-defined program, but it's not level 4 until you can prove that you can use those measurements to improve training. As discussed, the ability to have influence in the program and close the gap between the results of measurements and the ability to change the inner workings of the program to directly impact the measurements and ultimately the relation to goals is the fundamental and deeply rooted intent of the ASMA. Without this as a foundation there is little hope for meaningful adaptation.

Therefore, what if the survey is 3.7, or 30% of students get a score of 50%, 40% get 80%, and 30% get 90% on the exam, what do you do? Obviously, you have to improve the training; otherwise, you're just doing something ineffective over and over and hoping that eventually scores will get better, which is wasteful. The controls concerning training materials, how the materials were defined, managed, and updated, and defined methods for delivery act as points in the system to influence change. The process of training, how students are selected, and the prerequisites defined act as points of change. What are the lab components, how are these performing in the learning process?

All these questions have to be answered before a training program is formalized, which is intended in the definition and management of measurements and the ability to take corrective actions. For example, the content of the survey to students should seek to highlight measurements that can be tied to areas of control, just as they are tied to strategic goals. Organizations that seek high levels of maturity in security will typically fail because of the lack of downward alignment and far too much focus on upward alignment. To illustrate, a question in a survey, such as "Did you feel there was appropriate time allocated for the training?", will help to isolate a downward control that governs the time consumed in training. Comparatively, the question, "Did you like the instructor?", may be helpful to some, but is not actionable downstream and may actually be germane to a higher goal.

This, of course, is a gross oversimplification, but the key takeaway is that measurements have to be actionable and this impacts what measurements are taken and how they are taken. You start with understanding the goal and the process. From there, as expressed in the previous requirement, you define the measurements. However, to achieve this control—objectively managing performance—the measurements must be aligned to downward capabilities to ensure that they can be improved based directly on the information obtained from the measurement; otherwise, the goal can never be truly managed effectively and improvements will be best guesses. This maturity requirement has two specific requirements:

1. Determine Process Capability—This simply states that an organization can prove through documentation and evidence from the execution of processes targeted at measurement management that improvement plans and activities exist. This can appear as quality goal assessments, performance studies, progress against stated goals (i.e., metrics), and measurement improvement plans that tie measurements to actionable, corrective activities. This is a good point to reiterate that a measurement is a point in time. Several measurements over time are a metric, and metrics are required at this level of maturity to demonstrate process capability.
   - Within the ASMA, governance and capability maturity management play a key and critical role in this requirement. Clearly, it is up to each feature, through guidance from organizational management and governance, to

create its own measurements and localized goals and to make certain those goals can be aligned to strategic goals and fed into governance. Each feature is responsible for its measurements and all this implies. However, it is governance that will influence these to ensure (1) they align to security and business goals, and (2) they are actionable. Capability maturity management will act as the enabler for governance to support and manage details concerning capability. In short, capability maturity management will be very focused on determining and supporting process capability in all features.

2. Use Process Capability—As highlighted in the introduction of objectively managing performance, measurements have to be actionable. Measurements and the metrics they represent over time must have downward alignment to controls to ensure corrective action is possible and meaningful for improvement. To achieve this specific requirement, organizations have to be able to prove and demonstrate through evidence that corrective actions—as a result of measurements—have been taken, or at a minimum that there are processes and meaningful standards, procedures, and guidance that empower the program to perform corrective action when identified. This may appear complicated, but it doesn't have to be. For example, a simple document of lessons learned and what changes were applied to the process based on those lessons is satisfactory. The goal is to ensure that measurements are collected and actions are taken to increase quality and reduce the potential for future failures, and that a method to aid in the evolution of the program exists.

- Within the context of the ASMA, governance and capability maturity management also work together with other features to ensure that the program is employing measurements for action. However, this is also reflected in the role and responsibility for compliance management concerning its oversight of meeting internally defined processes. Influencing change within a feature or throughout the program in an inter-feature scenario requires processes. As such, compliance management is focused on ensuring that each aspect of the program is employing stated processes. Compliance management will work very closely with governance and capability maturity management to gain insights into potential failures to target investigations (e.g., an audit), and activities will be governed (i.e., managed, approved, etc.) by organizational management.

10.4.7 Level 5—Continuously Improving

Needless to say, level 5 can be extraordinarily difficult to achieve and as such many organizations may elect to not even attempt to meet this level because the costs may outweigh the benefit. However, as with many things explained concerning the model, if an organization achieves level 4 by defining appropriate and actionable measurements aligned to goals, level 5 is well within reach.

In level 4, process improvement was implied as the core driver because not developing measurements that are actionable and support improvement are, in the opinion of the author, utterly worthless in security. However, it must be noted that traditional maturity models, such as the ones referenced herein, do not introduce "improving" until level 5. IA-CMM, ISO/IEC 21827:2008, among others define level 4 as "quantitatively controlled," meaning measured, and level 5 as "continuously improving," meaning improving process based on measurement. Although these attributes of maturity were intermingled in the description of level 4, technically speaking level 4 can be achieved by having measurements and demonstrating that they are managed and used, not necessarily that the use is directly involved in process improvement.

Therefore, the true distinction between level 4 and level 5 in the noted standards is that defined processes consistently undergo continuous refinement and improvement based on quantitative visibility into process activities, and far more importantly, visibility into the impact of changes for the improvements occurring in level 5. This last point is targeted specifically at the downward alignment of measurements, not simply at the upward alignment to goals. Nevertheless, within the context of the ASMA capability maturity model, improvement involves the foundation of measurement and metrics being quantitatively controlled. In other words, the standard of level 5 must be met in level 4 as far as the intent of the ASMA is concerned. However, with this in mind, the importance of level 5 is not diminished, and as far as the ASMA and the models presented herein and in relation to industry standard models for maturity, the differentiating factor is real-time improvements.

Continuous improvement, as defined in level 5, is the underlying intent of the ASMA and can be best reflected in the benefits of the program, such as business alignment and the ability to ensure adaptability. Of course, organizations do not have to be a level 5 to accomplish alignment and adaptability. However, when viewed from the perspective of intent, level 5 is not only the highest maturity level, but it also represents optimization that conveys a strong identity of effectiveness, efficiency, accuracy, quality, and adaptability. When businesses have challenges and security organizations have the capacity and structure to respond in ways that enable the business to meet its goals, this is radically different from traditional security programs. More importantly, having a model that supports capability maturity means that it is repeatable, predictable, manageable, scalable, and well founded, which in business are very valuable attributes of an organization.

10.4.7.1 Improving Organizational Capability Improving capability involves ensuring that the standardized processes throughout the organization in making quantitative comparisons of a process's employment over time exist and are executed, managed, and documented. As processes are employed, quantitative measurements are used to find opportunities for improvements. In level 4, the overall intent—putting aside the introduction of improvement by the author—is predominantly concerned with addressing errors and failures in process execution and therefore the processes themselves. Level 4 states that you have to measure your processes against goals to ensure that goals are being met. If they are not being met, one could rightly assume there is an error or failure that has to be corrected. Again, the perspective of the author is that without including the ability to influence the measurements—as normally defined in level 5—the true value of reaching level 4 is not entirely realized.

Nevertheless, as defined by standards, level 4 is a very different form of improvement. Although the correction of failures is an improvement, the process of improving organizational capability involves actually seeking out opportunities for improvement when there may be no evidence of problems. Level 5 in the context of the ASMA is about innovation. It's about making things better, not simply ensuring things are going as planned. To illustrate using training again, assume that all the metrics and goals are being achieved and the program is running exactly as designed and meaningfully supporting security, performance, and business goals. Level 5 essentially asks, "How can we make it better?" Of course, energy applied into making something better has to demonstrate meaningful returns. For example, will pushing the envelope on training and the costs involved play a role in strategic goals? The answer is, maybe. For example, many elementary and middle schools are introducing contemporary technology in very interesting ways to increase the value of the learning experience. Does this investment have a direct impact on scores? Maybe not when compared to traditional methods. However, strategically, it makes for greater sophistication in the learning process that may offer long-term dividends. Of course, any example is objective, but in business, innovation must be a constant theme and security must participate, especially when one considers the changes in technology and threats. There are two specific requirements:

1. Establish Process Effectiveness Goals—In short, this involves establishing not necessarily security, performance, or business goals, but rather the quantitative goals for improving the effectiveness of standard processes based on the security, performance, and business goals. This is effectively stating that you have to set a goal to innovate—making improvement a goal and defining that goal. For example, an improvement goal may be related to the intended outcome of increasing effectiveness and efficiency, as in greater returns on investment or increased savings, and the like, as a result of the improvement. Using the training example, although things are running smoothly, you feel that innovating and refining and improving processes proactively will allow more students to be effectively trained, which may reduce the number of times the training is given and therefore reduce costs. In other words, once you're doing it well to meet business goals, how can it be improved upon to meet other goals, and more importantly, enable the business? Tying back to level 4, it was mostly concerned with quality

(i.e., errors and failures), whereas with respect to level 5 we are now focused on key, strategic goals that push the proactive and predictive nature of adaptation.

- Within the ASMA, goals are detailed but are implied in the coverage of the various features and inter-feature activities. Goals concerning improvements are unique to each organization, and the ability to ensure they are actionable against strategic goals is comprehensive. Nevertheless, readers are encouraged to look beyond the basics of process definition, management, and measurements defined within the model and seek out opportunities to express innovation and how these can be tied to business goals. It is likely that the program will have to be in place and function for some time before this level can be approached. However, setting goals is an exercise that can be performed at any stage and is encouraged.

2. Continuously Improve the Standard Process—As stated in the previous specific maturity requirement, organizations are measured for maturity in setting process effectiveness goals. This requirement completes the circle by ensuring that established goals for improvements and innovation are acted upon in the form of continuous improvement goals.

- This is the crux of level 5, which is acting on measurements for the improvement related to strategic goals that were set in the previous specific requirement. Information gained from service delivery through service management and communicated to governance is the core enabler of performing analyses on where improvements and refinement can be had and the potential outcome related to goals. Although the predominant characteristics will come from the relationships between governance and services management, this level of innovation against established performance improvement goals will occur in risk and compliance management supported by capability maturity management and governance. Governance will act as the ultimate purveyor of improvement. This is due to the direct and intimate interaction with the business and the visibility it is afforded from those activities. It's helpful to add that all aspects of the model—every feature, governance included—are expected to set improvement goals for their respective areas and collaborate via organizational management on inter-feature goal identification and setting. In short, improvement is the intent of the ASMA and is expected in the interaction between features and their role and responsibilities to the program, customers, and the business.

10.4.7.2 Improving Processes' Effectiveness   Setting goals and seeking to improve processes is half of the equation. Having the ability to make those changes, monitor the changes, and ensure that the changes were not disruptive is an entire process area unto itself. Organizations should be able to identify and demonstrate areas where standard processes are in a continual state of controlled innovation. In other words, setting a goal and improving a process to meet that goal is simply not enough. Frankly, that isn't difficult to do. What is difficult is demonstrating that innovation is an ongoing, managed, and controlled process.

It is analogous to having one or more resources dedicated to investigating well-defined and quantitatively controlled processes for opportunities to improve them, and doing so continually. In fact, once a process is improved and validated against projected goals, it must go back into a process implement strategy to look for more opportunities for refinement.

The significant difference from level 4, which is more about correction after the fact, to level 5 is that level 5 is the act of continuous improvement performed in real time. At this level of maturity, organizations have a very comprehensive and sophisticated platform of processes and management. Constant vigilance over execution is the natural next step. There are two specific requirements that combine to make this a reality:

1. Perform Causal Analysis—Causal analysis is a process that looks to identify basic problems that prevent the process from achieving its goals more effectively. Also, this should be seen as an opportunity for innovation. This is analogous to having an

expert observer in a training session monitoring the execution of training processes. This is the real-time aspect of improving process effectiveness—observations and high-level investigations. The reason for this is quite elegant. There are conditions where process execution is meeting goals, but goals are not refined and the overall program, while effective, may become static. This is a significant issue with security and companies will seek outside experience to ensure that program activities—which may be very effective and mature—are reflective of evolving best practices and changing industry expectations. Causal analysis states that no matter how well things are performing, companies need to be looking forward and evolving with the environment. In other words, what you are doing well today may simply not be meaningful tomorrow, or although you are performing very well there is opportunity to enable the business. Analysis such as this is important to ensure that organizations evolve and become proactive.

- Within the ASMA, it is the responsibility of all features to take part in reviewing processes while in progress. However, many organizations will find that capability maturity management represents the optimal focal point for this activity. Nevertheless, this is highly dependent on resources and expertise, and may at times require external third parties. In many ways, in the design of the ASMA, capability maturity management was seen as the focal point for virtually all maturity expectations for levels 4 and 5. However, it is also understandable that not all security organizations have enough resources to dedicate to such an effort and many aspects of the model were adjusted so that this would not be required to be effective. Nevertheless, the advantages of such activities can become very significant in demonstrating value as well as ensuring that the program has strategic sustainability. In short, even minimal investments in this area have the potential to provide tangible returns.

2. Continuously Improve the Defined Process—Of course, all this planning, measuring, goal setting, and observation must eventually come down to making improvements

and promoting innovation—it's just that simple. To achieve this level of maturity, organizations have to produce a revised process and show how that revision came to pass. Demonstrating what was observed, what goal was to be met, the level of quality measured, and how these translated into specific changes are all expectations. Moreover, the critical characteristic is that the corrections, modifications, improvements, and innovations are made in real time, meaning they were identified and acted upon within the scope of the process execution. This is not an example where improvements are passed to the next phase, project, or service delivery. It is the accurate and effective modification of processes as they are being employed. As one might conclude, this is representative of an extraordinarily refined system with all parts fully meshed and pointed in the same direction. It is also the reason that level 5 is rarely achieved.

- Ultimately, the ability to change processes in motion are the responsibility of each feature and its area of control. Although assistance can be gained from other features, the task will fall on the shoulders of those working the process. For example, management from services management overseeing the delivery of a security service may be the first to recognize an opportunity. If the modified process came from risk or compliance management from their original influences, they will have to be consulted. Nevertheless, the change will have to be implemented by the management within the feature and the resources performing the process.

11
CONCLUSION

Security is reaching a critical turning point because businesses are changing, technology is changing, and people are changing. The economic turmoil forced companies to take a hard look at their business model and in doing so they set new perspectives of value, focus, and goals. Granted, at the time of this writing the economy is demonstrating signs of recovery with the Dow Jones Industrial Average in the United States breaking the 11,000 mark for the first time in over 18 months, Europe FTSE 100 nearing 6,000 in nearly two years, and the HIS and NIKKEI in Asia showing progression against massive declines in late 2008. Nevertheless, even as markets express revitalization, unemployment remains high and the threat of inflation looms. The effect of this on businesses runs deep. Although companies have generally stabilized and are now looking to grow and expand, they are doing so carefully and methodically. Unproven practices will be weeded out as the burden of proof for future investments becomes a dominating tone in the boardroom. Effectiveness and efficiency will come second only to adaptability and flexibility as organizations seek to do more with less.

Part of this trend has implications concerning how corporations view their technological infrastructures. Once viewed as a differentiating factor, the burden of IT seems excessive when compared to cloud computing models that offer elasticity and greater simplicity in an increasingly global and diverse operating environment. Add to this the ability to reduce the costs and overhead of supplying employees with phones and laptops by allowing them to use their own systems, given the rapid conversion to Web-enabled applications promoting ubiquitous access. Businesses are beginning to see opportunity in technical efficiencies to drive down costs while creating an environment that promotes flexibility and rapid expansion. Nevertheless, companies are also very aware of the value of their information relative to their products and services and competitive advantages. This represents conflicting forces. There is a need to be more agile and efficient by taking advantage of abstracting the business from traditional technical architecture, but doing so in a manner that does not undermine the confidentiality, integrity, and availability of vastly expanding information assets. The pressure on businesses to be competitive, cost conscious, and demonstrate growth is enormous, forcing them to explore innovative solutions despite legacy interpretations of risk.

Security is in the proverbial hot seat and is faced with moving in two very clear and frankly opposing directions. On one hand, security can remain focused on working to create a predictable environment through the comprehensive standardization of practices focused on managing risk despite the increasing fluidity of business dynamics and the moving target of risk appetite. Although this is a meaningful direction for security and is a proven strategy, it is likely that the business will continue to evolve, broadening the divide between business and security, with security ultimately becoming simply an underlying, commoditized feature shouldered with compliance and audit. In many scenarios, security will eventually be seen as a barrier to the business being able to realize opportunities or meet strategic objectives. For most, security will materialize as having the primary role of risk management, but not having the means to fully articulate risk much less address it in a manner that aligns to company objectives. The gap that has already formed between business and security will further manifest, leaving security as a protector bearing all accountability with little or no authority. The lack of authority is based on the inability of security to demonstrate a proactive, business-enabling capability. The tenuous balance that is being realized today will become more and more difficult to maintain. From a traditional security perspective the day-to-day activities of managing vulnerabilities, implementing controls, monitoring events, and the like will remain unchanged. Nevertheless, the relationship with the business will become strained and the identity of security will decay.

On the other hand is an opportunity to radically change how security is applied and doing so in a manner that takes advantage of the naturally occurring underlying security capabilities. By shifting the fundamental philosophies of security towards intent and permitting the security community to explore possibilities that promote business objectives as opposed to simply interpretations of risk and limitations, the business will see security in a completely new light. Of course, the ability to address dynamics quickly and effectively requires a different mindset. It becomes less about security in a traditional sense and more about the system that produces meaningful security. It's not about the firewall; it is about the mechanisms that ensure the firewall is meaningful relative to the business and the integrity of the security operations responsible for the firewalls. It's not about ensuring that people are trained, but rather how well they understand the intent of the training as much as the content. Security can become more intertwined with the business, not simply integrated. A common understanding of mission and goals with an intense focus on enablement is needed. By embracing change and approaching each dynamic from a perspective of opportunity as opposed to being seen as a disruptive force seeking to undermine security's stability, security organizations will find themselves in a position of trust. However, this isn't achieved through simple modifications or thinly veiled strategy adjustments. It requires commitment to detail, tenacity, and the willingness to challenge one's own convictions.

The adaptive security management architecture creates an environment that has checks and balances, ensuring that security is not simply for security's sake. It forces security groups and the businesses they serve to ask the difficult questions, confirm expectations, and be accountable. It demands partnerships and collaboration between entities that are typically at odds. The ASMA is about the business and meeting business objectives in a concerted manner that respects inherent security challenges. A goal-oriented structure is needed that is acutely focused on performance and quality results that enable the business to move forward in a compliant and meaningful way by taking a comprehensive view of risk. The ASMA is not about dismissing threats, risk, or compliance, but about embracing these challenges supported by a model that ensures flexibility and adaptability from a position of visibility and sophistication.

The ASMA comprises many features that are well established and are not new to the industry or businesses. However, how these features are defined and how they interact is new. The goal is to take proven practices and bond them together in a compelling way that is supported by exploiting the rich and untapped sophisticated security capabilities and applying them to a broader scope. There is real value in the core capabilities in security that need to be unleashed, but in a framework that ensures a degree of control, measurement, and management. To accomplish this the ASMA is not simply a collection of processes that could result in mounds of red tape, but rather processes that are specifically organized to draw out the best security can offer to the business. Far too many organizations create processes and standards that have little to do with an end product or function, or simply pile up and lose their purpose for being created in the first place, but people continue to employ them without question. The ASMA forces organizations to inspect what they expect. How security is applied should be about intent, purpose, mission, and goals, not simply what the procedure specifies or the standard demands. Processes, procedures, standards, policies and all the other elements that comprise today's security are valuable, but they have simultaneously become an anchor, and, in some cases, an excuse, again contributing to the divide between business and security.

Businesses will continue to evolve, take on new risks, explore opportunities, and demand agility, and if security organizations do not prepare themselves for an increasingly dynamic business environment they will be marginalized. Security has naturally reached critical mass and is rapidly entering into a time of renaissance. Whether you want security to change or not is irrelevant; it is inevitable and must happen because the fragile relationship between security and business is becoming strained. The paths of business and security have become misaligned and it is security that will have to course correct, not business. How security answers the call for change will define its identity for the next decade. The only question that remains is, will security become a business-enabling force or fall into obscurity?

Index

Milton Keynes UK
Ingram Content Group UK Ltd.
UKHW021904071024
449327UK00021B/1619